WOMEN'S HEALTH, POLITICS, AND POWER: ESSAYS ON SEX/GENDER, MEDICINE, AND PUBLIC HEALTH

Editors

Elizabeth Fee

Johns Hopkins School of Hygiene and Public Health

and

Nancy Krieger

Kaiser Foundation Research Institute

POLICY,
POLITICS,
HEALTH AND
MEDICINE
Series
Vicente Navarro, Series Editor

BAYWOOD PUBLISHING COMPANY, Inc.
Amityville, New York 11701

Library of Congress Catalog Card Number: 94-42
ISBN: 0-89503-121-3 (paper)
ISBN: 0-89503-120-5 (cloth)

Library of Congress Cataloging-in Publication Data

Women's health, politics, and power : essays on sex/gender, medicine,
    and public health / Nancy Krieger and Elizabeth Fee, editors.
        p. cm. - - (Policy, politics, health, and medicine series)
    Includes bibliographical references and index.
    ISBN 0-89503-120-5 : - - ISBN 0-89503-121-3 (pbk.)
    1. Women's health services- -Political aspects. 2. Women's health
services- -Social aspects. 3. Women- -Health and hygiene- -Social
aspects. 4. Women- -Health and hygiene- -Political aspects.
I. Krieger, Nancy. II. Fee, Elizabeth. III. Series : Policy,
politics, health, and medicine series (Unnumbered)
RA564.85.W683 1994
362.1'082- -dc20   94-42
                                                                        CIP

TABLE OF CONTENTS

Section VII: Gender, Social Policy, and Women's Lives 285

Introduction

This collection of essays addresses the broadening array of issues on the agenda of the women's health movements of the 1980s and 1990s, just as a previous collection, *Women and Health: The Politics of Sex in Medicine* (1), gathered contributions from the earlier wave of the women's health movement in the 1970s. The essays in both volumes are selected from the *International Journal of Health Services,* a journal that has nurtured political analyses of health and medicine from a variety of critical perspectives.

Some 25 years ago, the women's health movement began energetically and irreverently to expose the multiple aspects of sexism in medicine that permeated scientific and popular views of women's bodies and women's health. Inspired by the new analyses of feminism and the insights gained through shared knowledge and shared experience, activists of the 1960s and 1970s set about questioning everything thought to be known about women's health. They challenged the fundamental view of biology as destiny, refuted the depiction of women as mentally and physically fragile, and raised questions about hazards to women's health at home and in the paid labor force. They rejected the notion that women's health needs were limited to obstetrics and gynecology; sought to demedicalize pregnancy, menopause, and other aspects of women's reproductive lives; promoted access to birth control and sex education; contested restrictions on abortion; denounced population control and sterilization abuse directed against women of color; and began to make international ties with women in other countries concerned about women's health and women's social status. Taking on issues of sexuality and power as related to women's health, these activists vividly made clear the distinction between sex and gender, fought for more liberated, less restricted views of women's sexuality, supported lesbian rights, and broke the silence surrounding rape and domestic violence.

The women's health movement both criticized health and medical institutions and began to build alternative ones. Examining the health workforce, women's health advocates noted that men dominated and controlled the health professions and took for granted women's provision of health care at home. While seeking to change existing medical institutions and practices, activists established feminist health centers and abortion clinics, fought for the training and licensing of midwives, encouraged women to enroll in medical schools, challenged the sexism of traditional medical curricula, and expanded women's knowledge of their bodies through self-help groups. Embodying the spirit of this movement, *Our Bodies, Ourselves* (2) quickly grew from a small, informal publication produced by a women's health collective to become a worldwide best seller, read by millions of women in more than 12 languages.

Reflecting a belief in the fundamental unity among women, some of those active in the early women's health movement wrote and spoke as though all women faced the same issues and had the same interests. From the start, however, activists were confronted by questions of race and class in relation to women's health. Critical differences were most clearly articulated in the struggles around women's reproductive rights. Many women of color felt that women's health movement activists were insufficiently sensitive to issues of sterilization abuse and to the need for financial—not simply legal—access to abortion. The unsuccessful fight in 1977 against the Hyde amendment, which forbade the use of Medicaid funds for abortion, illustrated how conservative forces could exploit race and class divisions among women to restrict reproductive rights.

The Hyde amendment was to set the stage for the battles of the 1980s. With the election of Ronald Reagan, the women's health movement was transformed from a hopeful, expansive movement into a beleaguered set of organizations trying to defend women's basic reproductive rights. Working on a state-by-state basis, conservatives attempted to whittle away the right to abortion by imposing a succession of restrictions such as waiting periods and parental consent; anti-abortionists blockaded and firebombed abortion clinics and were able to prevent the import of RU-486, the "morning after" pill. In the 1980s, the AIDS epidemic provided another target for groups such as the Moral Majority in their efforts to reverse the liberalizing trends of the 1970s.

Even as traditional conservatives and the New Right were mounting their assaults against the feminist and other progressive movements, however, more and more women were entering the health professions, enrolling in medical schools, training for research careers, rising to positions of influence in federal and state agencies, and running for—and increasingly winning—political office. New organizations—such as the National Black Women's Health Project and the National Latina Health Organization—began to advance more inclusive women's health agendas. Other activists built on the experience of successful grassroots organizing around AIDS and began to address the specific issues of women and AIDS, women and breast cancer, breast implants, and treatment for menopause.

In the 1990s, we are witnessing a resurgence of interest in women's health as the result of the intersection of two trends in the women's health movement. One is the growing impact of women as health professionals, as elected politicians, and as policy makers. The other is the continuing tradition of feminist grassroots organizing around women's health. The influence of these two trends can be seen in the recent creation of the Office of Research on Women's Health, established in September 1990, in the National Institutes of Health. The mandate of this office is to identify the gaps in knowledge about women's health, formulate a comprehensive research agenda for women's health, and ensure that women are included in clinical studies (3). Its formation would not have been feasible without leadership from Congresswomen and influential women researchers and physicians in the biomedical establishment on the one hand, and from feminist activists and organizations on the other. This office simultaneously represents a major accomplishment and an arena of contest. The central question is whether women's health issues can best be addressed by following the usual practices of biomedical research and health policy—now applied equally to female bodies—or whether the questions and methods of health research must themselves be changed if the health of all women is to be understood and improved across the social divisions of race/ethnicity and class.

REFLECTING ON WOMEN'S HEALTH: ESSAYS AND THEMES

The essays in this volume were originally published in the 1980s and early 1990s. Together, they present a framework for understanding the struggles over women's health that have occurred in this time period, and provide specific analyses of women's health in relation to race/ethnicity and class, the work of health care, the health of women workers, international reproductive health, sexuality, AIDS, and public health policy.

SECTION I: WOMEN AND HEALTH: FRAMEWORKS

The first section begins with an essay by Nancy Krieger and Elizabeth Fee on "Man-Made Medicine and Women's Health: The Biopolitics of Sex/Gender and Race/Ethnicity." This chapter examines the categories that public health professionals in the United States normally use in generating health data, epidemiological explanations of disease, and health policies. The authors examine the historical reasons why race and sex—typically treated as biological variables—came to be perceived as essential categories for the analysis of health and disease and discuss the need for alternative approaches that recognize the long-ignored social categories of class, ethnicity, and gender. The second chapter, "Latina and African American Women: Continuing Disparities in Health" by Marsha Lillie-Blanton, Rose Martinez, Andrea Taylor, and Betty Robinson, examines racial/ethnic differences in women's social conditions, health status, exposure to environmental and occupational risks, and use of health services. It argues that most of these racial/ethnic differences in women's health stem not from differences in "lifestyle choices" but from inequities in social conditions that need to be addressed by appropriate social policies and community-based interventions.

The third chapter, "Women, Health, and the Sexual Division of Labor," takes us to Britain where Lesley Doyal examines the historical development of the women's health movement. In an analysis that is also relevant to North America, she describes how the contemporary women's health movement began in the 1960s with a critique of sexism in medical care. Then, during a period of Thatcher's cutbacks, it moved to a more systematic analysis of the provision of health services, including the role of women as health workers. Most recently, women have been questioning traditional biomedical conceptions of women's health and have been developing socialist feminist approaches to epidemiology. Together, these first three chapters point to the importance of the social determinants of health and make it clear that if we are to speak of women's health in an inclusive manner, we must address similarities and differences among women within and across social classes, within and across racial/ethnic groups, and within and across nations.

SECTION II:
WOMEN AND THE WORK OF HEALTH CARE

The first chapter in this section, "Gender Hierarchies in the Health Labor Force," by Irene Butter, Eugenia Carpenter, Bonnie Kay, and Ruth Simmons demonstrates that, despite the fact that women constitute 75 percent of the health labor force, men still monopolize the most powerful and prestigious occupations. Intersecting with racial and class hierarchies, these gender divisions lead to a particularly rigid set of occupational categories. The authors point out that "female" functions—primarily caring, psychosocial, and supportive—are poorly paid whereas "male" functions—primarily instrumental and technical—are more highly rewarded. These patterns have changed little, despite the recent increase in the numbers of women physicians. In "Community Care Policies and Gender Justice," Suzanne Osterbusch, Sharon Keigher, Baila Miller, and Nathan Linsk describe how gender inequities are even more obvious in the informal (unpaid) health labor force. Stated simply, when a family member is sick, women are usually the care-givers. It is still tacitly assumed that women will quit their jobs to provide health care at home; the authors of this chapter argue that a more equitable health policy would both recognize and compensate this labor.

SECTION III:
THE HEALTH OF WOMEN WORKERS

Exploring the realities of "Double Exposure," Ellen Hall discusses the strain caused by women's dual labor at home and at work. She presents the results of her study of Swedish women and men, which found that, even in this relatively egalitarian culture, women experience more psychosomatic strain than do men from the interaction of home and job demands. Ruth Zambrana and Marsha Hurst also emphasize the interaction of home and work demands in their discussion of the health of urban Puerto Rican women. They point out that low-income urban women in the United States are often kept out of regular employment by health-related home and family demands. The women in their study, for example, were fired or forced to leave their jobs if they were ill, pregnant, or had a sick child. In "Sugar and Spice and Everything Nice," Karen Messing, Ghislaine Doniol-Shaw, and Chantal Haëntjens vividly describe the job demands and sexual division of labor among French train cleaners—a set of jobs in which women, contrary to stereotype, are given the most noxious and filthy, physically tiring, and technically demanding work. The point of all these essays is that women, at home and on the job, are likely, in all countries, to be subject to far more strain and pressure than their male counterparts in the same socioeconomic strata.

SECTION IV:
WOMEN'S REPRODUCTIVE HEALTH:
ASIA, AFRICA, AND LATIN AMERICA

In "The Untold Story," T. K. Sundari first looks at how the health care systems and economic problems of developing countries contribute to high maternal mortality rates. She highlights two aspects of this complex problem: the economic and social constraints that prevent women from obtaining health care, and the many failures and inadequacies of the available services. Proposing an activist agenda, Sundari recommends reallocation of health resources, reorganization of health services, and mobilization of the powerless to demand change. In "Abortion Policy and Women's Health in Developing Countries," Ruth Dixon-Mueller reviews the international prevalence of clandestine abortions and discusses the legal, medical, and social forces responsible for making abortion illegal and thus causing the deaths of hundreds of thousands of women each year. One of her recommendations—restoring the family planning budgets cut by the Reagan administration—has recently been implemented by the Clinton administration.

SECTION V:
SEXUALITY, WOMEN'S BODIES, AND WOMEN'S HEALTH

In "Medical Metaphors of Women's Bodies," Emily Martin shows how medical images of women's bodies have, for the past two centuries, been based on metaphors of industrial production and hierarchical organization. Menstruation, in this set of metaphors, is an example of failed production, while menopause is a complete breakdown of the productive system; ultimately, the purpose of woman is reproduction. The medical profession's preoccupation with—and distortions of—female sexuality is also the theme of Patricia Stevens and Joanne Hall's chapter "A Critical Historical Analysis of the Medical Construction of

Lesbianism." They show how moral condemnation of homosexuality has fed the medical construction of lesbianism as pathology and in turn has structured the discriminatory treatment of lesbians by contemporary health care providers.

SECTION VI:
WOMEN AND AIDS

Issues of women and AIDS are likewise inextricably entangled with social and medical assumptions about women as sexual beings. In "More than Mothers and Whores," Kathryn Carovano documents how these narrow constructions of women's roles have affected the design and delivery of AIDS prevention services around the world. Existing programs for women are either targeted at sex workers, to prevent transmission of the disease to heterosexual men, or at mothers, to prevent maternal-fetal transmission—ignoring the AIDS prevention needs of women themselves. In "Women and AIDS in Zimbabwe," Mary Bassett and Marvellous Mhloyi explain the social context of the spread of AIDS in one African country. Here, the colonial expropriation of land, breakdown of family structure, and forced migration of labor led to a situation in which many women's social and economic survival was dependent on their sexual relations with men; sexually transmitted diseases became rampant. Any serious effort to reduce HIV transmission must therefore go beyond simple barrier methods and seek to expand women's limited social and economic choices.

SECTION VII:
GENDER, SOCIAL POLICY, AND WOMEN'S LIVES

The chapters in the final section present different perspectives on gender, social policy, and women's lives. Here, Martha Gimenez questions recent formulations of the "feminization of poverty" and their emphasis on the rising rates of poverty among divorced and single mothers. She argues that the concept of "feminization" obscures the persistent and increasing levels of poverty across communities of color and the declining economic well-being of the postwar generation. She sees increasing poverty as a consequence of policies that have deliberately undermined the welfare state and lowered overall standards of living. In the next chapter on "Women and Children at Risk," Evan Stark and Anne Flitcraft analyze the phenomena of family violence, battering, and child abuse from a feminist perspective. They explain that whereas men are responsible for most serious child abuse—often in the context of wife battering—women are typically the ones blamed and punished. As an alternative, the authors argue that child health workers, backed by appropriate social policies, should help women gain the independence they need to break free from the cycle of battering and abuse.

In the final chapter, "Older Women in the Post-Reagan Era," Terry Arendell and Carroll Estes draw together many of the themes elaborated by other authors in this volume. Tracing the problems of older women to longstanding gender inequities in the treatment of women as workers, as caregivers, and as beneficiaries of public policy, the authors show how the policies of the 1980s shifted resources from women to men and from minorities to whites, leaving women to undertake an ever larger burden of unpaid service and caring work. They argue the need not only for adequate income, health, and long-term care, but also for an end to the gendered division of labor and the lifelong discrimination that women experience.

CONCLUSION: TOWARD A NEW SYNTHESIS

The essays in this volume are contributions to a fast-growing literature on women, gender, and health. They represent efforts to analyze women's health issues within a political and social context, rather than simply as technical, biological, or clinical concerns. As such, they form part of an interdisciplinary and collective project that draws upon social history, anthropology, history of science, women's studies, and political economy (4–10).

As this burgeoning literature suggests, as the essays in this book argue, and as the more critical segments of the women's health movement urge, the answers to women's health concerns will not be found simply in an expansion of biomedical research along traditional lines. The current demand for more research is necessary, but not sufficient. Activists lobbying for increased funding for women's health research must ask for the appropriation of new money; otherwise, the budgets for other health programs will be raided. Even more critical, however, is the need to support new kinds of research. The biomedical research enterprise has long worked to unravel the specific mechanisms of disease processes by tracing the biochemical pathways and pathological mechanisms of the body; in addition to this narrowly focused research effort, we need socially-oriented research that seeks to understand the social production and construction of health and ill-health. This will require delineating the reasons for differences and similarities in health between women and men, and also—and just as important—the reasons for social inequalities in health among women. We hope that the essays in this volume will contribute to an emerging synthesis on the social analysis of gender and health, help frame some of the issues that still need to be addressed, provide useful suggestions for future work, and thus eventually lead to more appropriate public health policies.

REFERENCES

1. Fee, E. (ed.). *Women and Health: The Politics of Sex in Medicine.* Baywood, Amityville, N.Y., 1983.

2. Boston Women's Health Book Collective. *Our Bodies, Ourselves.* New England Free Press, Boston, 1971 [Simon & Schuster, New York, 1973].
3. National Institutes of Health. *Opportunities for Research on Women's Health.* Bethesda, Md., 1992.
4. Roberts, H. (ed.). *Women's Health Counts.* Routledge, London, 1990.
5. Apple, R. D. (ed.), *Women, Health, and Medicine in America: A Historical Handbook.* Rutgers University Press, New Brunswick, N.J., 1990.
6. Martin, E. *The Woman in the Body: A Cultural Analysis of Reproduction.* Beacon Press, Boston, 1987.
7. Hubbard, R. *The Politics of Women's Biology.* Rutgers University Press, New Brunswick, N.J., 1990.
8. Muller C. F. *Health Care and Gender.* Russell Sage Foundation, New York, 1990.
9. Haraway, D. *Simians, Cyborgs and Women: The Reinvention of Nature.* Routledge, New York, 1991.
10. Gordon, L. *Woman's Body, Woman's Right: A Social History of Birth Control in America.* Grossman, New York, 1976 [rev. ed., Penguin, New York, 1990].

Section I
Women and Health: Frameworks

Man-Made Medicine and Women's Health: The Biopolitics of Sex/Gender and Race/Ethnicity

Nancy Krieger and Elizabeth Fee

Glance at any collection of national health data for the United States, whether pertaining to health, disease, or the health care system, and several obvious features stand out (1–5). First, we notice that most reports present data in terms of race, sex, and age. Some races are clearly of more interest than others. National reports most frequently use racial groups called "white" and "black," and increasingly, they use a group called "Hispanic." Occasionally, we find data on Native Americans, and on Asians and Pacific Islanders. Whatever the specific categories chosen, the reports agree that white men and women, for the most part, have the best health, at all ages. They also show that men and women, across all racial groups, have different patterns of disease: obviously, men and women differ for conditions related to reproduction (women, for example, do not get testicular cancer), but they differ for many other conditions as well (for example, men on average have higher blood pressure and develop cardiovascular disease at an earlier age). And, in the health care sector, occupations, just like diseases, are differentially distributed by race and sex.

All this seems obvious. But it isn't. We know about race and sex divisions because this is what our society considers important. This is how we classify people and collect data. This is how we organize our social life as a nation. This is therefore how we structure our knowledge about health and disease. And this is what we find important as a subject of research (6–9).

It seems so routine, so normal, to view the health of women and men as fundamentally different, to consider the root of this difference to be biological sex, and to think about race as an inherent, inherited characteristic that also affects health (10). The work of looking after sick people follows the same categories.

Originally published in the *International Journal of Health Services* 24(2): 265-283, 1994.

Simply walk into a hospital and observe that most of the doctors are white men, most of the registered nurses are white women, most of the kitchen and laundry workers are black and Hispanic women, and most of the janitorial staff are black and Hispanic men. Among the patients, notice who has appointments with private clinicians and who is getting care in the emergency room; the color line is obvious. Notice who provides health care at home: wives, mothers, and daughters. The gender line at home and in medical institutions is equally obvious (11–15).

These contrasting patterns, by race and sex, are longstanding. How do we explain them? What kinds of explanations satisfy us? Some are comfortable with explanations that accept these patterns as natural, as the result of natural law, as part of the natural order of things. Of course, if patterns are that way by nature, they cannot be changed. Others aim to understand these patterns precisely in order to change them. They look for explanations suggesting that these patterns are structured by convention, by discrimination, by the politics of power, and by unreasonable law. These patterns, in other words, reflect the social order of people.

In this chapter, we discuss how race and sex became such all-important, self-evident categories in 19th and 20th century biomedical thought and practice. We examine the consequences of these categories for our knowledge about health and for the provision of health care. We then consider alternative approaches to studying race/ethnicity, gender, and health. And we address these issues with reference to a typically suppressed and repressed category: that of social class.

THE SOCIAL CONSTRUCTION OF "RACE" AND "SEX" AS KEY BIOMEDICAL TERMS AND THEIR EFFECT ON KNOWLEDGE ABOUT HEALTH

In the 19th century, the construction of "race" and "sex" as key biomedical categories was driven by social struggles over human inequality. Before the Civil War, the dominant understanding of race was as a natural/theological category—black–white differences were innate and reflected God's will (16–19). These differences were believed to be manifest in every aspect of the body, in sickness and in health. But when abolitionists began to get the upper hand in moral and theological arguments, proponents of slavery appealed to science as the new arbiter of racial distinction.

In this period, medical men were beginning to claim the mantle of scientific knowledge and assert their right to decide controversial social issues (20–22). Recognizing the need for scientific authority, the state of Louisiana, for example, commissioned one prolific proponent of slavery, Dr. Samuel Cartwright, to prove the natural inferiority of blacks, a task that led him to detail every racial difference imaginable—in texture of hair, length of bones, vulnerability to disease, and even color of the internal organs (23–25). As the Civil War changed the status of blacks from legal chattel to bona fide citizens, however, medical journals began to question old verities about racial differences and, as importantly, to publish new views of racial similarities (26, 27). Some authors even attributed black–white differences in health to differences in socioeconomic position. But by the 1870s, with the destruction of reconstruction, the doctrine of innate racial distinction again triumphed. The scientific community once again deemed "race" a fundamental biological category (28–32).

Theories of women's inequality followed a similar pattern (33–36). In the early 19th century, traditionalists cited scripture to prove women's inferiority. These authorities agreed that Eve had been formed out of Adam's rib and that all women had to pay the price of her sin—disobeying God's order, seeking illicit knowledge from the serpent, and tempting man with the forbidden apple. Women's pain in childbirth was clear proof of God's displeasure.

When these views were challenged in the mid-19th century by advocates of women's rights and proponents of liberal political theory, conservatives likewise turned to the new arbiters of knowledge and sought to buttress their position with scientific facts and medical authority (37, 38). Biologists busied themselves with measuring the size of women's skulls, the length of their bones, the rate of their breathing, and the number of their blood cells. And considering all the evidence, the biologists concluded that women were indeed the weaker sex (39–41).

Agreeing with this stance, medical men energetically took up the issue of women's health and equality (42–45). They were convinced that the true woman was by nature sickly, her physiological systems at the mercy of her ovaries and uterus. Because all bodily organs were interconnected, they argued, a woman's monthly cycle irritated her delicate nervous system and her sensitive, small, weak brain. Physicians considered women especially vulnerable to nervous ailments such as neurasthenia and hysteria. This talk of women's delicate constitutions did not, of course, apply to slave women or to working-class women—but it was handy to refute the demands of middle-class women whenever they sought to vote or gain access to education and professional careers. At such moments, many medical men declared the doctrine of separate spheres to be the ineluctable consequence of biology.

At the same time, 19th century medical authorities began to conceptualize class as a natural, biological distinction. Traditional, pre-scientific views held class hierarchies to be divinely ordained; according to the more scientific view that emerged in the early 19th century, class position was determined by innate, inherited ability. In both cases, class was perceived as an essentially stable, hierarchical ranking. These discussions of class usually assumed white or Western European populations and often applied only to males within those populations.

With the impact of the industrial revolution, classes took on a clearly dynamic character. As landowners invested in canals and railroads, as merchants became capitalist entrepreneurs, and as agricultural workers were transformed into an industrial proletariat, the turbulent transformation of the social order provoked new understandings of class relationships (46). The most developed of these theories was that of Karl Marx, who emphasized the system of classes as a social and economic formation and stressed the contradictions between different class interests (47). From this point onward, the very idea of social class in many people's minds implied a revolutionary threat to the social order.

In opposition to Marxist analyses of class, the theory of Social Darwinism was formulated to suggest that the new social inequalities of industrial society reflected natural law (48–51). This theory was developed in the midst of the economic depression of the 1870s, at a time when labor struggles, trade union organizing, and early socialist movements were challenging the political and economic order. Many scientists and medical men drew upon Darwin's idea of "the struggle for survival," first expressed in the *Origin of the Species* in 1859 (52), to justify social inequality. They argued that those on top, the social elite, must by definition be the "most fit" because they had survived so well. Social hierarchies were therefore built on and reflected real biological differences. Poor health status simultaneously was sign and proof of biological inferiority.

By the late 19th century, theories of race, gender, and class inequality were linked together by the theory of Social Darwinism, which promised to provide a scientific basis for social policy (48–51). In the realm of race, for example, proponents of Social Darwinism blithely predicted that the "Negro question" would soon resolve itself—the "Negro" would naturally become extinct, eliminated by the inevitable workings of "natural selection" (29, 53). Many public health officers—particularly in the southern states—agreed that "Negroes" were an inherently degenerate, syphilitic, and tubercular race, for whom public health interventions could do little (54–57). Social Darwinists also argued that natural and sexual selection would lead to increasing differentiation between the sexes (34, 48, 58). With further evolution, men would become ever more masculine and women ever more feminine. As proof, they looked to the upper classes, whose masculine and feminine behavior represented the forefront of evolutionary progress.

Over time, the Social Darwinist view of class gradually merged into general American ideals of progress, meritocracy, and success through individual effort. According to the dominant American ideology, individuals were so mobile that fixed measures of social class were irrelevant. Such measures were also un-American. Since the Paris Commune, and especially since the Bolshevik revolution, discussions of social class in the United States were perceived as politically threatening. Although fierce debates about inequality continued to revolve around the axis of nature versus nurture, the notion of class as a social relationship was effectively banished from respectable discourse and policy debate (48, 59). Social position was once again equated only with rank, now understood as socioeconomic status.

In the early 20th century, Social Darwinists had considerable influence in shaping public views and public policy (48, 59–64). They perceived two new threats to American superiority: the massive tide of immigration from eastern and southern Europe, and the declining birth rate—or "race suicide"—among American white women of Anglo-Saxon and Germanic descent. Looking to the fast-developing field of genetics, now bolstered by the rediscovery of Gregor Mendel's laws and T. H. Morgan's fruit fly experiments (65–68), biological determinists regrouped under the banner of eugenics. Invoking morbidity and mortality data that showed a high rate of tuberculosis and infectious disease among the immigrant poor (69–71), they declared "ethnic" Europeans a naturally inferior and sickly stock and thus helped win passage of the Immigration Restriction Act in 1924 (72–74). This legislation required the national mix of immigrants to match that entering the United States in the early 1870s, thereby severely curtailing immigration of racial and ethnic groups deemed inferior. "Race/ethnicity," construed as a biological reality, became ever more entrenched as the *explanation* of racial/ethnic differences in disease; social explanations were seen as the province of scientifically illiterate and naive liberals, or worse, socialist and Bolshevik provocateurs.

Other developments in the early 20th century encouraged biological explanations of sex differences in disease and in social roles. The discovery of the sex chromosomes in 1905 (75–77) reinforced the idea that gender was a fundamental biological trait, built into the genetic constitution of the body. That same year, Ernest Starling coined the term "hormone" (78) to denote the newly characterized chemical messengers that permitted one organ to control—at a distance—the activities of another. By the mid-1920s, researchers had isolated several hormones integral to reproductive physiology and popularized the notion of "sex hormones" (79–83). The combination of sex chromosomes and sex hormones was imbued with almost magical powers to shape human behavior in gendered terms; women were now at the mercy of their genetic limitations and a changing brew of hormonal imperatives (84, 85). In the realm of medicine, researchers turned to sex chromosomes and hormones to understand cancers of the uterus and breast and a host of other sex-linked diseases (86–90); they no longer saw the need to worry about environmental influences. In the workplace, of course, employers said that sex chromosomes and hormones dictated which jobs women could—and could not—perform (45, 91, 92). This in turn determined the occupational hazards to which women would be exposed—once again, women's health and ill-health were really a matter of their biology.

Within the first few decades of the 20th century, these views were institutionalized within scientific medicine and the new public health. At this time, the training of physicians and public health practitioners was being recast in modern, scientific terms (93–95). Not surprisingly, biological determinist views of racial/ethnic and sex/gender differences became a natural and integral part of the curriculum, the research agenda, and medical and public health practice. Over time, ethnic differences in disease among white European groups were downplayed and instead, the differences between whites and blacks, whites and

Mexicans, and whites and Asians were emphasized. Color was now believed to define distinct biological groups.

Similarly, the sex divide marked a gulf between two completely disparate groups. Within medicine, women's health was relegated to obstetrics and gynecology; within public health, women's health needs were seen as being met by maternal and child health programs (8, 45, 96). Women were perceived as wives and mothers; they were important for childbirth, childcare, and domestic nutrition. Although no one denied that some women worked, women's occupational health was essentially ignored because women were, after all, only temporary workers. Outside the specialized realm of reproduction, all other health research concerned men's bodies and men's diseases. Reproduction was so central to women's biological existence that women's non-reproductive health was rendered virtually invisible.

Currently, it is popular to argue that the lack of research on white women and on men and women in nonwhite racial/ethnic groups resulted from a perception of white men as the norm (97–99). This interpretation, however, is inaccurate. In fact, by the time that researchers began to standardize methods for clinical and epidemiologic research, notions of difference were so firmly embedded that whites and nonwhites, women and men, were rarely studied together. Moreover, most researchers and physicians were interested only in the health status of whites and, in the case of women, only in their reproductive health. They therefore used white men as the research subjects of choice for all health conditions other than women's reproductive health and paid attention to the health status of nonwhites only to measure degrees of racial difference. For the most part, the health of women and men of color and the nonreproductive health of white women were simply ignored. It is critical to read these omissions as evidence of a logic of difference rather than as an assumption of similarity.

This framework has shaped knowledge and practice to the present. In the United States, vital statistics present health information in terms of race and sex and age, conceptualized only as biological variables—ignoring the social dimensions of gender and ethnicity. Data on social class are not collected. At the same time, public health professionals are unable adequately to explain or to change inequalities in health between men and women and between diverse racial/ethnic groups. We now face the question: Is there any alternative way of understanding these population patterns of health and disease?

ALTERNATIVE WAYS OF STUDYING RACE, GENDER, AND HEALTH: SOCIAL MEASURES FOR SOCIAL CATEGORIES

The first step in creating an alternative understanding is to recognize that the categories we traditionally treat as simply biological are in fact largely social. The second step is to realize we need social concepts to understand these social categories. The third step is to develop social measures and appropriate strategies for a new kind of health research (10).

With regard to race/ethnicity, we need to be clear that "race" is a spurious biological concept (100–102). Although historical patterns of geographic isolation and migration account for differences in the distribution of certain genes, genetic variation within so-called racial groups far exceeds that across groups. All humans share approximately 95 percent of their genetic makeup (100, p. 155). Racial/ethnic differences in disease thus require something other than a genetic explanation.

Recognizing this problem, some people have tried to substitute the term "ethnicity" for "race" (103, 104). In the public health literature, however, "ethnicity" is rarely defined. For some, it apparently serves as a polite way of referring to what are still conceptualized as "racial"/biological differences. For others, it expresses a new form of "cultural" determinism, in which ethnic differences in ways of living are seen as autonomous "givens" unrelated to the social status of particular ethnic groups within our society (105, 106). This cultural determinism makes discrimination invisible and can feed into explanations of health status as reductionist and individualistic as those of biological determinism.

For a different starting point, consider the diverse ways in which racism operates, at both an institutional and interpersonal level (107–109). Racism is a matter of economics, and it is also more than economics. It structures living and working conditions, affects daily interactions, and takes its toll on people's dignity and pride. All of this must be considered when we examine the connection between race/ethnicity and health.

To address the economic aspects of racism, we need to include economic data in all studies of health status (110, 111). Currently, our national health data do not include economic information—instead, racial differences are often used as indicators of economic differences. To the extent that economics are taken into account, the standard approach assumes that differences are either economic or "genetic." So, for those conditions where racial/ethnic differences persist even within economic strata—hypertension and preterm delivery, for example—the assumption is that something biological, something genetic, is at play. Researchers rarely consider the noneconomic aspects of racism or the ways in which racism continues to work within economic levels.

Some investigators, however, are beginning to consider how racism shapes people's environments. Several studies, for example, document the fact that toxic dumps are most likely to be located in poor neighborhoods and are disproportionately located in poor neighborhoods of color (112–114). Other researchers are starting to ask how people's experience of and response to discrimination may influence their health (115–118). A recent study of hypertension, for example, found that black women who responded actively to unfair treatment were less likely to report high blood pressure than women who internalized their responses

(115). Interestingly, the black women at highest risk were those who reported *no* experiences of racial discrimination.

Countering the traditional practice of always taking whites as the standard of comparison, some researchers are beginning to focus on other racial/ethnic groups to better understand why, within each of the groups, some are at higher risk than others for particular disease outcomes (119–121). They are considering whether people of color may be exposed to specific conditions that whites are not. In addition to living and working conditions, these include cultural practices that may be positive as well as negative in their effects on health. Some studies, for example, point to the importance of black churches in providing social support (122–124). These new approaches break with monolithic assumptions about what it means to belong to a given racial/ethnic group and consider diversity *within* each group. To know the color of a person's skin is to know very little.

It is equally true that to know a person's sex is to know very little. Women are often discussed as a single group defined chiefly by biological sex, members of an abstract, universal (and implicitly white) category. In reality, we are a mixed lot, our gender roles and options shaped by history, culture, and deep divisions across class and color lines. Of course, it is true that women, in general, have the capacity to become pregnant, at least at some stages of our lives. Traditionally, women as a group are defined by this reproductive potential. Usually ignored are the many ways that gender as a social reality gets into the body and transforms our biology—differences in childhood expectations about exercise, for example, affect our subsequent body build (38, 125).

From a health point of view, women's reproductive potential does carry the possibility of specific reproductive ills ranging from infertility to preterm delivery to cervical and breast cancer. These reproductive ills are not simply associated with the biological category "female," but are differentially experienced according to social class and race/ethnicity. Poor women, for example, are much more likely to suffer from cervical cancer (119, 126). By contrast, at least among older women, breast cancer is more common among the affluent (126, 127). These patterns, which at times can become quite complex, illustrate the general point that, even in the case of reproductive health, more than biological sex is at issue. Explanations of women's reproductive health that ignore the social patterning of disease and focus only on endogenous factors are thus inadequate.

If we turn to those conditions that afflict both men and women—the majority of all diseases and health problems—we must keep two things simultaneously in mind. First are the differences and similarities among diverse groups of women; second are the differences and similarities between women and men.

For a glimpse at the complexity of disease patterns, consider the example of hypertension (128, 129). As we mentioned, working-class and poor women are at greater risk than affluent women; black women, within each income level, are more likely to be hypertensive than white women (5). The risks of Hispanic women vary by national origin: Mexican women are at lowest risk, Central

American women at higher risk, and Puerto Rican and Cuban women at the highest risk (130, 131). In what is called the "Hispanic paradox," Mexican-American women have a higher risk profile than Anglo-American women, yet experience lower rates of hypertension (132). To further complicate the picture, the handful of studies of Japanese and Chinese women in the United States show them to have low rates, while Filipina women have high rates, almost equal to those of African Americans (130, 133, 134). Rates vary across different groups of Native American women; those who live in the Northern plains have higher rates than those in the Southwest (130, 135). From all this, we can conclude that there is enormous variation in hypertension rates among women.

If we look at the differences between women and men, we find that men in each racial/ethnic group have higher rates of hypertension than women (129). Even so, the variation among women is sufficiently great that women in some racial/ethnic groups have higher rates than men in other groups. Filipina women, for example, have higher rates of hypertension than white men (5, 133). Obviously, the standard biomedical categories of race and sex cannot explain these patterns. If we want to understand hypertension, we will have to understand the complex distribution of disease among real women and men; these patterns are not merely distracting details but the proper test of the plausibility of our hypotheses.

As a second example, consider the well-known phenomenon of women's longer life expectancy. This difference is common to all industrialized countries, and amounts to about seven years in the United States (136, 137). The higher mortality of men at younger ages is largely due to higher accident rates, and at older ages, to heart disease.

The higher accident rates of younger men are not accidental. They are due to more hazardous occupations, higher rates of illicit drug and alcohol use, firearms injuries, and motor vehicle crashes—hazards related to gender roles and expectations (136, 137). The fact that men die earlier of heart disease—the single most common cause of death in both sexes—may also be related to gender roles. Men have higher rates of cigarette smoking and fewer sources of social support, suggesting that the masculine ideal of the Marlboro man is not a healthy one. Some contend that women's cardiovascular advantage is mainly biological, due to the protective effect of their hormone levels (138). Interestingly, however, a study carried out in a kibbutz in Israel, where men and women were engaged in comparable activities, found that the life expectancy gap was only four and a half years—just over half the national average (139). While biological differences between men and women now receive much of the research attention, it is important to remember that men are gendered beings too.

Clearly, our patterns of health and disease have everything to do with how we live in the world. Nowhere is this more evident than in the strong social class gradients apparent in almost every form of morbidity and mortality (110, 140–143). Yet here the lack of information and the conceptual confusion about the relationship between social class and women's health is a major obstacle. As previously noted, in this country, we have no regular method of collecting data on socioeconomic position and health. Even if we had such data, measures of social class generally assume male heads of households and male patterns of employment (111, 144). This, indeed, is one of the failures of class analyses—that they do not deal adequately with women (144–147).

Perhaps the easiest way to understand the problems of class measurements and women's health is briefly to mention the current debates in Britain, a country that has long collected social class data (148, 149). Men and unmarried women are assigned a social class position according to their employment; married women, however, are assigned a class position according to the employment of their husbands. As British feminist researchers have argued, this traditional approach obscures the magnitude of class differences in women's health (149). Instead, they are proposing measures of household class that take into account the occupations of both women and their husbands, and their ownership of household assets.

Here in the United States, we have hardly any research on the diverse measures of social class in relation to women's health. Preliminary studies suggest we also would do well to distinguish between individual and household class (150, 151). Other research shows that we can partly overcome the absence of social class information in U.S. medical records by using census data (126, 152). This method allows us to describe people in terms of the socioeconomic profile of their immediate neighborhood. When coupled with individual measures of social class, this approach reveals, for example, that working-class women who live in working-class neighborhoods are somewhat more likely to have high blood pressure than working-class women who live in more affluent neighborhoods (152). We thus need conceptually to separate three distinct levels at which class operates: individual, household, and neighborhood.

As a final example of why women's health cannot be understood without reference to issues of sex/gender, race/ethnicity, and social class, consider the case of AIDS (153–155). The definition of disease, the understanding of risk, and the approach to prevention are shaped by our failure fully to grasp the social context of disease. For the first decade, women's unique experiences of AIDS were rendered essentially invisible. The first definition of AIDS was linked to men, because it was perceived to be a disease of gay men and those with a male sex-linked disorder, hemophilia. The very listing of HIV-related diseases taken to characterize AIDS was a listing based on the male experience of infection. Only much later, after considerable protest by women activists, were female disorders—such as invasive cervical cancer—made part of the definition of the disease (156, 157).

Our understanding of risk is still constrained by the standard approaches. AIDS data are still reported only in terms of race, sex, and mode of transmission; there are no data on social class (158). We know, however, that the women who have AIDS are overwhelmingly women of color. As of July 1993, of the nearly 37,000 women diagnosed with AIDS, over one half were

African American, another 20 percent were Hispanic, 25 percent were white, and about 1 percent were Asian, Pacific Islander, or Native American (158). What puts these women at risk? It seems clear that one determinant is the missing variable, social class. Notably, the women at highest risk are injection drug users, the sexual partners of injection drug users, and sex workers (154). The usual listing of behavioral and demographic risk factors, however, fails to capture the social context in which the AIDS epidemic has unfolded. Most of the epidemiological accounts are silent about the blight of inner cities, the decay of urban infrastructure under the Reagan–Bush administrations, unemployment, the drug trade, prostitution, and the harsh realities of everyday racism (159, 160). We cannot gain an adequate understanding of risk absent a real understanding of people's lives.

Knowledge of what puts women at risk is of course critical for prevention. Yet, just as the initial definitions of AIDS reflected a male-gendered perspective, so did initial approaches to prevention (161). The emphasis on condoms assumed that the central issue was knowledge, not male–female power relations. For women to use condoms in heterosexual sex, however, they need more than bits of latex; they need male assent. The initial educational materials were created without addressing issues of power; they were male-oriented and obviously white—in both the mode and language of presentation. AIDS programs and services, for the most part, still do not address women's needs, whether heterosexual, bisexual, or lesbian. Pregnant women and women with children continue to be excluded from most drug treatment programs. And when women become sick and die, we have no remotely adequate social policies for taking care of the families left behind.

In short, our society's approach to AIDS reflects the larger refusal to deal with the ways in which sex/gender, race/ethnicity, and class are inescapably inter-twined with health. This refusal affects not only what we know and what we do about AIDS, but also the other issues we have mentioned—hypertension, cancer, life expectancy—and many we have not (162). As we have tried to argue, the issues of women's health cannot be understood only in biological terms, as simply the ills of the female of the species. Women and men are different, but we are also similar—and we both are divided by the social relations of class and race/ethnicity. To begin to understand how our social constitution affects our health, we must ask, repeatedly, what is different and what is similar across the social divides of gender, color, and class. We cannot assume that biology alone will provide the answers we need; instead, we must reframe the issues in the context of the social shaping of our human lives—as both biological creatures and historical actors. Otherwise, we will continue to mistake—as many before us have done—what is for what must be, and leave unchallenged the social forces that continue to create vast inequalities in health.

REFERENCES

1. National Center for Health Statistics. *Health, United States, 1991.* DHHS Pub. No. (PHS) 92-1232. U.S. Public Health Service, Hyattsville, Md., 1992.
2. National Center for Health Statistics. *Vital Statistics of the United States—1988. Vol. I, Natality.* DHHS Pub. No. (PHS) 90-1100. U.S. Government Printing Office, Washington, D.C., 1990.
3. National Center for Health Statistics. *Vital Statistics of the United States—1987. Vol. II, Mortality, Part A.* DHHS Pub. No. (PHS) 90-1101. U.S. Government Printing Office, Washington, D.C., 1990.
4. National Center for Health Statistics. *Vital Statistics of the United States—1988. Vol. II, Mortality, Part B.* DHHS Pub. No. (PHS) 90-1102. U.S. Government Printing Office, Washington, D.C., 1990.
5. U.S. Department of Health and Human Services. *Health Status of Minorities and Low-Income Groups,* Ed. 3. U.S. Government Printing Office, Washington, D.C., 1991.
6. Krieger, N. The making of public health data: Paradigms, politics, and policy. *J. Public Health Policy* 13: 412–427, 1992.
7. Navarro, V. Work, ideology, and science: The case of medicine. In *Crisis, Health, and Medicine: A Social Critique,* edited by V. Navarro, pp. 142–182. Tavistock, New York, 1986.
8. Fee, E. (ed.). *Women and Health: The Politics of Sex in Medicine.* Baywood, Amityville, N.Y., 1983.
9. Tesh, S. *Hidden Arguments: Political Ideology and Disease Prevention Policy.* Rutgers University Press, New Brunswick, N.J., 1988.
10. Krieger, N., et al. Racism, sexism, and social class: Implications for studies of health, disease, and well-being. *Am. J. Prev. Med.,* 9(suppl 2): 82–122, 1993.
11. Butter, I., et al. *Sex and Status: Hierarchies in the Health Workforce.* American Public Health Association, Washington, D.C., 1985.
12. Sexton, P. C. *The New Nightingales: Hospital Workers, Unions, New Women's Issues.* Enquiry Press, New York, 1982.
13. Melosh, B. *The Physician's Hand: Work, Culture and Conflict in American Nursing.* Temple University Press, Philadelphia, 1982.
14. Wolfe, S. (ed.). *Organization of Health Workers and Labor Conflict.* Baywood, Amityville, N.Y., 1978.
15. Feldman, P. H., Sapienza, A. M., and Kane, N. M. *Who Cares for Them? Workers in the Home Care Industry.* Greenwood Press, New York, 1990.
16. Krieger, N. Shades of difference: Theoretical underpinnings of the medical controversy on black/white differences in the United States, 1830–1870. *Int. J. Health Serv.* 17: 256–278, 1987.
17. Stanton, W. *The Leopard's Spots: Scientific Attitudes Towards Race in America, 1815–59.* University of Chicago Press, Chicago, 1960.
18. Stepan, N. *The Idea of Race in Science, Great Britain, 1800–1860.* Archon Books, Hamden, Conn., 1982.
19. Jordan, W. D. *White Over Black: American Attitudes toward the Negro, 1550–1812.* University of North Carolina Press, Chapel Hill, 1968.
20. Rosenberg, C. E. *No Other Gods: On Science and American Social Thought.* Johns Hopkins University Press, Baltimore, Md., 1976.

21. Daniels, G. H. The process of professionalization in American science: The emergent period, 1820–1860. *Isis* 58: 151–166, 1967.
22. Rothstein, W. G. *American Physicians in the 19th Century: From Sects to Science.* Johns Hopkins University Press, Baltimore, Md., 1972.
23. Cartwright, S. A. Report on the diseases and physical peculiarities of the Negro race. *New Orleans Med. Surg. J.* 7: 691–715, 1850.
24. Cartwright, S. A. Alcohol and the Ethiopian: Or, the moral and physical effects of ardent spirits on the Negro race, and some accounts of the peculiarities of that people. *New Orleans Med. Surg. J.* 15: 149–163, 1858.
25. Cartwright, S. A. Ethnology of the Negro or prognathous race—A lecture delivered November 30, 1857, before the New Orleans Academy of Science. *New Orleans Med. Surg. J.* 15: 149–163, 1858.
26. Reyburn, R. Remarks concerning some of the diseases prevailing among the Freed-people in the District of Columbia (Bureau of Refugees, Freedmen and Abandoned Lands). *Am. J. Med. Sci.* (n.s.) 51: 364–369, 1866.
27. Byron, J. Negro regiments—Department of Tennessee. *Boston Med. Surg. J.* 69: 43–44, 1863.
28. Foner, E. *Reconstruction: America's Unfinished Revolution, 1863–1877.* Harper & Row, New York City, 1988.
29. Haller, J. S. Jr. *Outcasts from Evolution: Scientific Attitudes of Racial Inferiority, 1859–1900.* University of Illinois Press, Urbana, 1971.
30. Stocking, G. W. *Race, Culture, and Evolution: Essays in the History of Anthropology.* Free Press, New York, 1968.
31. Lorimer, D. *Colour, Class and the Victorians.* Holmes & Meier, New York, 1978.
32. Gamble, V. N. (ed.). *Germs Have No Color Line: Blacks and American Medicine, 1900–1940.* Garland, New York, 1989.
33. Barker-Benfield, G. J. *The Horrors of the Half-Known Life: Male Attitudes toward Women and Sexuality in Nineteenth-Century America.* Harper & Row, New York, 1976.
34. Fee, E. Science and the woman problem: Historical perspectives. In *Sex Differences: Social and Biological Perspectives,* edited by M. S. Teitelbaum, pp. 175–223. Anchor/Doubleday, New York, 1976.
35. Jordanova, L. *Sexual Visions: Images of Gender in Science and Medicine between the Eighteenth and Twentieth Centuries.* University of Wisconsin Press, Madison, 1989.
36. Ehrenreich, B., and English, D. *Complaints and Disorders: The Sexual Politics of Sickness.* The Feminist Press, Old Westbury, N.Y., 1973.
37. Russett, C. E. *Sexual Science: The Victorian Construction of Womanhood.* Harvard University Press, Cambridge, Mass., 1989.
38. Hubbard, R. *The Politics of Women's Biology.* Rutgers University Press, New Brunswick, N.J., 1990.
39. Fee, E. Nineteenth-century craniology: The study of the female skull. *Bull. Hist. Med.* 53: 415–433, 1979.
40. Smith-Rosenberg, C., and Rosenberg, C. E. The female animal: Medical and biological views of woman and her role in 19th century America. *J. Am. Hist.* 60: 332–356, 1979.
41. Gould, S. J. *The Mismeasure of Man.* W. W. Norton, New York, 1981.

42. Smith-Rosenberg, C. Puberty to menopause: The cycle of femininity in nineteenth-century America. *Feminist Stud.* 1: 58–72, 1973.
43. Smith-Rosenberg, C. *Disorderly Conduct: Visions of Gender in Victorian America.* Knopf, New York, 1985.
44. Haller, J. S., and Haller, R. M. *The Physician and Sexuality in Victorian America.* University of Illinois Press, Urbana, 1974.
45. Apple, R. D. (ed.). *Women, Health, and Medicine in America: A Historical Handbook.* Rutgers University Press, New Brunswick, N.J., 1990.
46. Williams, R. *Culture & Society: 1780–1950,* revised edition. Columbia University Press, New York, 1983 [1958].
47. Marx, K. *Capital,* vol. I. International Publishers, New York, 1967 [1867].
48. Hofstadter, R. *Social Darwinism in American Thought.* Beacon Press, Boston, 1955.
49. Young, R. M. *Darwin's Metaphor: Nature's Place in Victorian Culture.* Cambridge University Press, Cambridge, U.K., 1985.
50. Kevles, D. J. *In the Name of Eugenics: Genetics and the Uses of Human Heredity.* Knopf, New York, 1985.
51. Chase, A. *The Legacy of Malthus: The Social Costs of the New Scientific Racism.* Knopf, New York, 1977.
52. Darwin, C. *On the Origin of Species by Means of Natural Selection, or the Preservation of Favoured Races in the Struggle for Life.* Murray, London, 1859.
53. Anderson, M. J. *The American Census: A Social History.* Yale University Press, New Haven, Conn., 1988.
54. Hoffman, F. L. *Race Traits and Tendencies of the American Negro.* American Economic Association, New York, 1896.
55. Harris, D. Tuberculosis in the Negro. *JAMA* 41: 827, 1903.
56. Allen, L. C. The Negro health problem. *Am. J. Public Health* 5: 194, 1915.
57. Beardsley, E. H. *A History of Neglect: Health Care for Blacks and Mill Workers in the Twentieth-Century South.* University of Tennessee Press, Knoxville, 1987.
58. Geddes, P., and Thompson, J. A. *The Evolution of Sex.* Walter Scott, London, 1889.
59. Ludmerer, K. M. *Genetics and American Society: A Historical Appraisal.* Johns Hopkins University Press, Baltimore, Md., 1972.
60. Higham, J. *Strangers in the Land: Patterns of American Nativism, 1860–1925.* Rutgers University Press, New Brunswick, N.J., 1955.
61. Haller, M. H. *Eugenics: Hereditarian Attitudes in American Thought.* Rutgers University Press, New Brunswick, N.J., 1963.
62. Pickens, D. K. *Eugenics and the Progressives.* Vanderbilt University Press, Nashville, Tenn., 1968.
63. King, M., and Ruggles, S. American immigration, fertility, and race suicide at the turn of the century. *J. Interdisciplinary Hist.* 20: 347–369, 1990.
64. Degler, C. N. *In Search of Human Nature: The Decline and Revival of Darwinism in American Social Thought.* Oxford University Press, Oxford, 1991.
65. Allen, G. E. *Life Science in the Twentieth Century.* Cambridge University Press, Cambridge, U.K., 1978.
66. Castle, W. E. The beginnings of Mendelism in America. In *Genetics in the Twentieth Century,* edited by L. C. Dunn, pp. 59–76. Macmillan, New York, 1951.

67. Wilkie, J. S. Some reasons for the rediscovery and appreciation of Mendel's work in the first years of the present century. *Br. J. Hist. Sci.* 1: 5–18, 1962.
68. Morgan, T. H. *The Theory of the Gene.* Yale University Press, New Haven, 1926.
69. Kraut, A. M. *The Huddled Masses: The Immigrant in American Society, 1800–1921.* Harlan Davison, Arlington Heights, Ill., 1982.
70. Stoner, G. W. Insane and mentally defective aliens arriving at the Port of New York. *N. Y. Med. J.* 97: 957–960, 1913.
71. Solis-Cohen, S. T. The exclusion of aliens from the United States for physical defects. *Bull. Hist. Med.* 21: 33–50, 1947.
72. Ludmerer, K. Genetics, eugenics, and the Immigration Restriction Act of 1924. *Bull. Hist. Med.* 46: 59–81, 1972.
73. Barkan, E. Reevaluating progressive eugenics: Herbert Spencer Jennings and the 1924 immigration legislation. *J. Hist. Biol.* .24: 91–112, 1991.
74. Kraut, A. M. Silent travelers: Germs, genes, and American efficiency, 1890–1924. *Soc. Sci. Hist.* 12: 377–393, 1988.
75. Farley, J. *Gametes & Spores: Ideas About Sexual Reproduction, 1750–1914.* Johns Hopkins University Press, Baltimore, Md., 1982.
76. Allen, G. Thomas Hunt Morgan and the problem of sex determination. *Proc. Am. Philos. Soc.* 110: 48–57, 1966.
77. Brush, S. Nettie M. Stevens and the discovery of sex determination by chromosomes. *Isis* 69: 163–172, 1978.
78. Starling, E. The Croonian lectures on the chemical correlation of the functions of the body. *Lancet* 2: 339–341, 423–425, 501–503, 579–583, 1905.
79. Lane-Claypon, J. E., and Starling, E. H. An experimental enquiry into the factors which determine the growth and activity of the mammary glands. *Proc. R. Soc. London [Biol.]* 77: 505–522, 1906.
80. Marshall, F. A. *The Physiology of Reproduction.* Longmans, Green and Co., New York, 1910.
81. Oudshoorn, N. Endocrinologists and the conceptualization of sex. *J. Hist. Biol.* 23: 163–187, 1990.
82. Oudshoorn, N. On measuring sex hormones: The role of biological assays in sexualizing chemical substances. *Bull. Hist. Med.* 64: 243–261, 1990.
83. Borrell, M. Organotherapy and the emergence of reproductive endocrinology. *J. Hist. Biol.* 18: 1–30, 1985.
84. Long, D. L. Biology, sex hormones and sexism in the 1920s. *Philos. Forum* 5: 81–96, 1974.
85. Cobb, I. G. *The Glands of Destiny (A Study of the Personality).* Macmillan, New York, 1928.
86. Allen, E. (ed.). *Sex and Internal Secretions: A Survey of Recent Research.* Williams & Wilkins, Baltimore, Md., 1939.
87. Frank, R. *The Female Sex Hormone.* Charles C Thomas, Springfield, Ill., 1929.
88. Lathrop, A. E. C., and Loeb, L. Further investigations of the origin of tumors in mice. III. On the part played by internal secretions in the spontaneous development of tumors. *J. Cancer Res.* 1: 1–19, 1916.
89. Lane-Claypon, J. E. *A Further Report on Cancer of the Breast, With Special Reference to its Associated Antecedent Conditions,* Reports on Public Health and Medical Subjects, No. 32. Her Majesty's Stationery Office, London, 1926.

90. Wainwright, J. M. A comparison of conditions associated with breast cancer in Great Britain and America. *Am. J. Cancer* 15: 2610–2645, 1931.
91. Chavkin, W. (ed.). *Double Exposure: Women's Health Hazards on the Job and at Home.* Monthly Review Press, New York, 1984.
92. Ehrenreich, B., and English, D. *For Her Own Good: 150 Years of the Experts Advice to Women.* Anchor Books, Garden City, N.Y., 1979.
93. Starr, P. *The Social Transformation of American Medicine.* Basic Books, New York, 1982.
94. Fee, E. *Disease and Discovery: A History of the Johns Hopkins School of Hygiene and Public Health, 1916–1939.* Johns Hopkins University Press, Baltimore, Md., 1987.
95. Fee, E., and Acheson, R. M. (eds.). *A History of Education in Public Health: Health that Mocks the Doctors' Rules.* Oxford University Press, Oxford, 1991.
96. Meckel, R. *Save the Babies: American Public Health Reform and the Prevention of Infant Mortality, 1850–1920.* Johns Hopkins University Press, Baltimore, Md., 1990.
97. Rodin, J., and Ickovics, J. R. Women's health: Review and research agenda as we approach the 21st century. *Am. Psychol.* 45: 1018–1034, 1990.
98. Healy, B. Women's health, public welfare. *JAMA* 266: 566–568, 1991.
99. Kirchstein, R. L. Research on women's health. *Am. J. Public Health* 81: 291–293, 1991.
100. Lewontin, R. *Human Diversity.* Scientific American Books, New York, 1982.
101. King, J. C. *The Biology of Race.* University of California Press, Berkeley, 1981.
102. Cooper, R., and David, R. The biological concept of race and its application to epidemiology. *J. Health Polit. Policy Law* 11: 97–116, 1986.
103. Cooper, R. Celebrate diversity—or should we? *Ethnicity Dis.* 1: 3–7, 1991.
104. Crews, D. E., and Bindon, J. R. Ethnicity as a taxonomic tool in biomedical and biosocial research. *Ethnicity Dis.* 1: 42–49, 1991.
105. Mullings, L. Ethnicity and stratification in the urban United States. *Ann. N. Y. Acad. Sci.* 318: 10–22, 1978.
106. Feagin, J. R. *Racial and Ethnic Relations,* Ed. 3. Prentice-Hall, Englewood Cliffs, N.J., 1989.
107. Feagin, J. R. The continuing significance of race: Anti-black discrimination in public places. *Am. Sociol. Rev.* 56: 101–116, 1991.
108. Essed, P. *Understanding Everyday Racism: An Interdisciplinary Theory.* Sage Publications, Newbury Park, Calif., 1991.
109. Krieger, N., and Bassett, M. The health of black folk: Disease, class and ideology in science. *Monthly Rev.* 38: 74–85, 1986.
110. Navarro, V. Race or class versus race and class: Mortality differentials in the United States. *Lancet* 2: 1238–1240, 1990.
111. Krieger, N., and Fee, E. What's class got to do with it? The state of health data in the United States today. *Socialist Rev.* 23: 59–82, 1993.
112. Polack, S., and Grozuczak, J. *Reagan, Toxics and Minorities: A Policy Report.* Urban Environment Conference, Washington, D.C., 1984.
113. Commission for Racial Justice, United Church of Christ. *Toxic Wastes and Race in the United States: A National Report on the Racial and Socioeconomic Characteristics of Communities with Hazardous Waste Sites.* United Church of Christ, New York, 1987.

114. Mann, E. *L.A.'s Lethal Air: New Strategies for Policy, Organizing, and Action.* Labor/Community Strategy Center, Los Angeles, 1991.
115. Krieger, N. Racial and gender discrimination: Risk factors for high blood pressure? *Soc. Sci. Med.* 30: 1273–1281, 1990.
116. Armstead, C. A., et al. Relationship of racial stressors to blood pressure and anger expression in black college students. *Health Psychol.* 8: 541–556, 1989.
117. James, S. E., et al. John Henryism and blood pressure differences among black men. II. The role of occupational stressors. *J. Behav. Med.* 7: 259–275, 1984.
118. Dressler, W. W. Social class, skin color, and arterial blood pressure in two societies. *Ethnicity Dis.* 1: 60–77, 1991.
119. Fruchter, R. G., et al. Cervix and breast cancer incidence in immigrant Caribbean women. *Am. J. Public Health* 80: 722–724, 1990.
120. Kleinman, J. C., Fingerhut, L. A., and Prager, K. Differences in infant mortality by race, nativity, and other maternal characteristics. *Am. J. Dis. Child.* 145: 194–199, 1991.
121. Cabral, H., et al. Foreign-born and US-born black women: Differences in health behaviors and birth outcomes. *Am. J. Public Health* 80: 70–72, 1990.
122. Taylor, R. J., and Chatters, L. M. Religious life. In *Life in Black America,* edited by J. S. Jackson, pp. 105–123. Sage, Newbury Park, Calif., 1991.
123. Livingston, I. L., Levine, D. M., and Moore, R. D. Social integration and black intraracial variation in blood pressure. *Ethnicity Dis.* 1: 135–149, 1991.
124. Eng, E., Hatch, J., and Callan, A. Institutionalizing social support through the church and into the community. *Health Ed. Q.* 12: 81–92, 1985.
125. Lowe, M. Social bodies: The interaction of culture and women's biology. In *Biological Woman—The Convenient Myth,* edited by R. Hubbard, M. S. Henefin, and B. Fried, pp. 91–116. Schenkman, Cambridge, Mass., 1982.
126. Devesa, S. S., and Diamond, E. L. Association of breast cancer and cervical cancer incidence with income and education among whites and blacks. *J. Natl. Cancer Inst.* 65: 515–528, 1980.
127. Krieger, N. Social class and the black/white crossover in the age-specific incidence of breast cancer: A study linking census-derived data to population-based registry records. *Am. J. Epidemiol.* 131: 804–814, 1990.
128. Krieger, N. The influence of social class, race and gender on the etiology of hypertension among women in the United States. In *Women, Behavior, and Cardiovascular Disease,* proceedings of a conference sponsored by the National Heart, Lung, and Blood Institute, Chevy Chase, Md., September 25–27, 1991. U.S. Government Printing Office, Washington, D.C., 1994, in press.
129. U.S. Department of Health and Human Services. *Report of the Secretary's Task Force on Black & Minority Health, Volume IV: Cardiovascular and Cerebrovascular Disease, Part 2.* Washington, D.C., 1986.
130. Martinez-Maldonado, M. Hypertension in Hispanics, Asians and Pacific Islanders, and Native Americans. *Circulation* 83: 1467–1469, 1991.
131. Caralis, P. U. Hypertension in the Hispanic-American population. *Am. J. Med.* 88(Suppl. 3b): 9s–16s, 1990.
132. Haffner, S. M., et al. Decreased prevalence of hypertension in Mexican-Americans. *Hypertension* 16: 255–232, 1990.
133. Stavig, G. R., Igra, A., and Leonard, A. R. Hypertension and related health issues among Asians and Pacific Islanders in California. *Public Health Rep.* 103: 28–37, 1988.

134. Angel, A., Armstrong, M. A., and Klatsky, A. L. Blood pressure among Asian Americans living in Northern California. *Am. J. Cardiol.* 54: 237–240, 1987.
135. Alpert, J. S., et al. Heart disease in Native Americans. *Cardiology* 78: 3–12, 1991.
136. Waldron, I. Sex differences in illness, incidence, prognosis and mortality: Issues and evidence. *Soc. Sci. Med.* 17: 1107–1123, 1983.
137. Wingard, D. L. The sex differential in morbidity, mortality, and lifestyle. *Annu. Rev. Public Health* 5: 433–458, 1984.
138. Gold, E. (ed.). *Changing Risk of Disease in Women: An Epidemiological Approach.* Colbamore Press, Lexington, Mass., 1984.
139. Leviatan, V., and Cohen, J. Gender differences in life expectancy among kibbutz members. *Soc. Sci. Med.* 21: 545–551, 1985.
140. Syme, S. L., and Berkman, L. Social class: Susceptibility and sickness. *Am. J. Epidemiol.* 104: 1–8, 1976.
141. Antonovsky, A. Social class, life expectancy and overall mortality. *Milbank Mem. Fund Q.* 45: 31–73, 1967.
142. Townsend, P., Davidson, N., and Whitehead, M. *Inequalities in Health: The Black Report and The Health Divide.* Penguin, Harmondsworth, U.K., 1988.
143. Marmot, M. G., Kogevinas, M., and Elston, M. A. Social/economic status and disease. *Annu. Rev. Public Health* 8: 111–135, 1987.
144. Roberts, H. (ed.). *Women's Health Counts.* Routledge, London, 1990.
145. Dale, A., Gilbert, G. N., and Arber, S. Integrating women into class theory. *Sociology* 19: 384–409, 1985.
146. Duke, V., and Edgell, S., The operationalisation of class in British sociology: Theoretical and empirical considerations. *Br. J. Sociol.* 8: 445–463, 1987.
147. Charles, N. Women and class—A problematic relationship. *Sociol. Rev.* 38: 43–89, 1990.
148. Morgan, M. Measuring social inequality: Occupational classifications and their alternatives. *Community Med.* 5: 116–124, 1983.
149. Moser, K. A., Pugh, H., and Goldblatt, P. Mortality and the social classification of women. In *Longitudinal Study: Mortality and Social Organization, Series LS, No. 6,* edited by P. Goldblatt, pp. 146–162. Her Majesty's Stationery Office, London, 1990.
150. Krieger, N. Women and social class: A methodological study comparing individual, household, and census measures as predictors of black/white differences in reproductive history. *J. Epidemiol. Community Health* 45: 35–42, 1991.
151. Ries, P. Health characteristics according to family and personal income, United States. *Vital Health Stat.* 10(147). DHHS Pub. No. (PHS) 85-1575. National Center for Health Statistics. U.S. Government Printing Office, Washington, D.C., 1985.
152. Krieger, N. Overcoming the absence of socioeconomic data in medical records: Validation and application of a census-based methodology. *Am. J. Public Health* 82: 703–710, 1992.
153. Carovano, K. More than mothers and whores: Redefining the AIDS prevention needs of women. *Int. J. Health Serv.* 21: 131–142, 1991.
154. PANOS Institute. *Triple Jeopardy: Women & AIDS.* Panos Publications, London, 1990.
155. Anastos, K., and Marte, C. Women—The missing persons in the AIDS epidemic. *HealthPAC,* Winter 1989, pp. 6–13.

156. Centers for Disease Control. 1993 Revised classification system for HIV infection and expanded surveillance case definition for AIDS among adolescents and adults. *MMWR* 41: 961–962, 1992.

157. Kanigel, R. U.S. broadens AIDS definition: Activists spur change by Centers for Disease Control. *Oakland Tribune,* January 1, 1993, p. A1.

158. Centers for Disease Control and Prevention. *HIV/AIDS Surveillance Rep.* 5: 1–19, July 1993.

159. Drucker, E. Epidemic in the war zone: AIDS and community survival in New York City. *Int. J. Health Serv.* 20: 601–616, 1990.

160. Freudenberg, N. AIDS prevention in the United States: Lessons from the first decade. *Int. J. Health Serv.* 20: 589–600, 1990.

161. Fee, E., and Krieger, N. Thinking and rethinking AIDS: Implications for health policy. *Int. J. Health Serv.* 23: 323–346, 1993.

162. Fee, E., and Krieger, N. Understanding AIDS: Historical interpretations and the limits of biomedical individualism. *Am. J. Public Health* 83: 1477–1486, 1993.

Latina and African American Women: Continuing Disparities in Health

Marsha Lillie-Blanton, Rose Marie Martinez,
Andrea Kidd Taylor, and Betty Garman Robinson

Race and gender are powerful determinants of life experiences in the United States. A legacy of racial discrimination and segregation continues to affect the quality of life of U.S. racial and ethnic minority populations. Similarly, discrimination based on gender has affected the life experiences of women. As members of both population subgroups, Latina and African American women have encountered discrimination based on their gender and race. Blatant and subtle barriers have affected minority women's access to educational and employment opportunities. Moreover, racism affects where individuals live and the quality of resources available within those neighborhoods. Both gender and race have historically triggered social relations (i.e., in the family and work environment) that are risk factors for diminished health.

Social class stratification in the United States also shapes the life experiences of women of color. Social class status, sometimes referred to as socioeconomic status (SES), is generally measured by an individual's family resources and/or the occupation and educational attainment of the head of household (1). These indices, however, are affected by discriminatory policies and practices that persist despite legislation and judicial decisions prohibiting discrimination based on race and gender. Thus, social class status is socially determined and inseparably linked to this nation's history of social inequities. As such, the burden of illness and injury facing minority women reflects the common life experiences they share as a consequence of their race, gender, and social class.

Women represent about half of the 30.8 million African Americans and 21.4 million Latino Americans identified in the 1990 Census. Although stereotypically

Originally published in the *International Journal of Health Services* 23(3): 555–584, 1993.

portrayed by contrasting profiles, Latina and African American women represent a diversity of socioeconomic and psychosocial backgrounds. For example, African American women often are described as disproportionately poor, single heads of household who are dependent on public welfare programs such as AFDC (Aid to Families with Dependent Children). The profile is one of women who are irresponsible and a financial burden on society. In contrast, there is an abundance of research—some disputed—on the "black matriarchy" (2). Sociologists have portrayed African American women as the "rocks of Gibraltar" who provide the stabilizing and nurturing foundation for the black family (3, 4). Latina women are often characterized as submissive, self-denying, and self-sacrificing (5). Within the family environment, the profile is one of women who place the needs of children and husband first and ask little for themselves in return. Their submissiveness and self-denial are said to contribute to their general lack of power and influence within American society.

As with most women, Latina and African American women have had what paradoxically could be considered both the good fortune and ill-fortune of being the primary caretaker of the family's children and elderly. While caretaking roles expand the depth of compassion women feel for others, they also compromise women's ability to compete in a rapidly evolving market economy. While there is substantial evidence for their portrayal as pillars of strength, the health consequences of being a primary caretaker in a frequently hostile social environment deserve investigation.

The meaning of racial/ethnic classifications is a subject of intense debate and controversy. In U.S. census and survey data, respondents are generally asked to report their racial group as: white; black; Asian or Pacific Islander; Aleut, Eskimo, American Indian; or other. In another question, information about Hispanic national origin is asked and persons of Hispanic origin may be of any of the racial categories. When individuals have an opportunity to self-define their race, a small but sizable percentage report their race as "other" rather than one of the four major racial groups. We recognize that these categories oversimplify race/ethnic origin, but they are the social designations used for U.S. census and survey purposes.

Racial/ethnic classifications denote group membership in which there is some assumed commonality of inheritance and contemporary life experiences. Nonetheless, women classified by U.S. census or survey data as of Hispanic origin are a tremendously heterogeneous group ethnically, consisting primarily of individuals with Mexican, Puerto Rican, Cuban, and South and Central American ancestry. These ethnic groups share a common bond of language and culture, but there are major subgroup differences in terms of their inclusion in society and access to resources. African American women are a more homogeneous group but are also ethnically diverse, including individuals with African, Caribbean, Indian, and European ancestry. Latina and African American women, as evidenced by their varying shades of color, have experienced considerable cross-generational mixing of racial/ethnic groups. As a consequence, racial/ ethnic classifications are more a measure of the sociocultural experience of being a member of a particular racial/ethnic group than a marker of biological inheritance. Although a number of biological explanations for racial differences in health have been advanced, there is little scientific evidence to support these theories (6, 7).

SCOPE OF THE INVESTIGATION

In an effort to assess the quality of life experienced by Latina and African American women, this chapter provides descriptive information on racial/ethnic differences in women's social conditions, health status, exposure to occupational and environmental risks, and use of health services. We examine indices of the quality of life using a framework that considers life experiences associated with being female, a racial/ethnic minority, and a member of a particular social class. This assessment attempts to address some of the limitations of past research but, at most, represents an initial exploration into an issue that deserves more in-depth review.

Framework for the Study of Minority Women's Health

Several articles assisted us in establishing a framework for examining the health of minority women (8–10). Zambrana (8) provides a thoughtful and poignant critique of the research on the health of minority women, noting that even authors sensitive to women's issues have failed to address social class and racial/ethnic differences among women. She proposes a conceptual model for studying the health of minority women that considers health status as an interactive relationship among socioeconomic, behavioral, and environmental factors. Focusing on reproductive health issues, Zambrana applies this conceptual model while illustrating the limitations of existing research. Asserting that adolescent sexuality and childbearing are influenced by sociocultural background and SES, Zambrana also sees their consequences for the mother's education and employment opportunities and the child's health. In reviewing data on pregnancy outcomes, she notes that Mexican American women have high childbirth mortality rates and African American women have high rates of low birthweight infants. Zambrana advances the premise that poorer outcomes are due to differences in use of prenatal care, social class, and psychosocial factors such as chronic stress and social support.

Bennett (9) and Bassett and Krieger (10) have examined minority women's health from a perspective that acknowledges the impact of social class on health. Bennett explores the premise that life stressors associated with poverty are risk factors for emotional distress and even mental illness. The relation between social class and mental health has been well documented (11); research, however, is limited regarding the impact of race, gender, and SES on mental health (12, 13). Bennett asserts that social strata are not necessarily comparable across racial/ethnic groups because who is considered poor is relative, depending on the wealth among one's peers. Using clinical case studies, Bennett describes some of the economic circumstances of African American single women that potentially exacerbate life stressors associated with loneliness or parenting. The author argues that, depending on a woman's problem-solving skills, poor resolution of problems could lead to diagnosable emotional distress. Bassett and Krieger (10) examine the impact of race and social class on breast cancer survival in a population-based sample. After adjusting for social class, in addition to age and other medical predictors of survival, the authors found that black-white differences in breast cancer survival rates diminished greatly. The results provide strong evidence that racial differences in today's breast cancer survival rates are largely attributable to the poorer social class standing of black women.

Data Sources and Key Measures

Data on health indices of minority women are presented from a number of sources, including the 1990 U.S Census, the National Health and Nutrition Examination Survey II (NHANES; 1976–1980), and the Hispanic Health and Nutrition Examination Study (HHANES; 1982–1984). We also analyze and present original data on women aged 18 to 64 from the 1988 Health Interview Survey (HIS).

When possible, this chapter presents data on mutually exclusive racial/ethnic categories. In most of the analyses, women are classified as: white American, not of Hispanic origin; African American, not of Hispanic origin; or Latina.[1] Although these categories inadequately capture the racial/ethnic diversity within a population subgroup, they are used to yield a more accurate comparison of the indices of racial/ethnic minority women with those of nonminority women. Since most Latinos are classified racially as white (in the 1990 census, 96 percent of the 21.4 million persons of Hispanic origin are identified as white), analyses in which they are not examined as a distinct population group could diminish the magnitude of the race/ethnicity differentials.

Additionally, health and access indices from the HIS are stratified by family income categories of: below $10,000; $10,000 to $19,999; $20,000 to $34,999; and $35,000 and above. Stratifying by income is intended to limit the confounding effects of social class on the comparison of racial differences and also to gain some insight into the impact of income differences on the health indices of racial/ethnic minority women. When racial differences in health are presented, questions inevitably arise about the extent to which disparities can be attributed to racial differences in poverty, or more broadly, to differences in social class. Despite the imprecision of family income as a measure of social class, we considered it the best of the readily available indicators.

---

[1] Women of other racial groups (i.e., Asian and Pacific Islanders, Native Americans, etc.) were excluded from the analysis of the HIS data.

SOCIAL CONDITIONS OF LATINA AND
AFRICAN AMERICAN WOMEN

Social environmental conditions are recognized as one of several determinants of a population's health. The term "social condition" is used to refer to socio-demographic factors (e.g., employment) and to physical surroundings (e.g., neighborhood of residence). Factors such as these, individually and in combination with more personal factors, are determinants of health status. Employment, for example, is not only a source of income, it is often important to an individual's sense of self-worth and is a potential source of life stress. Additionally, it is the means by which most Americans obtain health insurance. Social conditions also affect other determinants of health such as physiological factors, lifestyle behaviors, and access to and use of health services.

For racial/ethnic minority women, the social environment has undergone tremendous change during the last three decades (1960s through 1980s). Progress has been achieved in legally and socially challenging traditional male-female gender roles. Minority women have benefited from policies that foster greater inclusion of women in all sectors of society. Enforcement of antidiscrimination laws helped to assure minority women greater equity in access to educational and employment opportunities. Nonetheless, data on indicators of life conditions continue to suggest that minority women encounter barriers that prevent full participation in the opportunities available in society.

Income, Poverty, and Family Structure

A disproportionate share of racial/ethnic minority women face circumstances of low-wage jobs and/or poverty. After a sharp decline in poverty rates between 1960 and 1970, the percentage of the population with incomes below the federal poverty level has remained relatively unchanged in the last two decades (Figure 1).[2] In 1990, about three times as many African Americans (32 percent) and Latino Americans (28 percent) as white Americans (11 percent, including whites of Hispanic origin), had family incomes below poverty (14). (The rate for whites not of Hispanic origin was 8.8 percent). While the poverty rate is similar for Latino and African Americans, families headed by women represent 75 percent of all poor African American families, as compared with 46 percent of all poor Latino families.

Family composition has major implications for the economic resources and social support available to a family. Nearly one-third (31 percent) of African

---

[2] The average poverty threshold for a family of four was $13,359 in 1990.

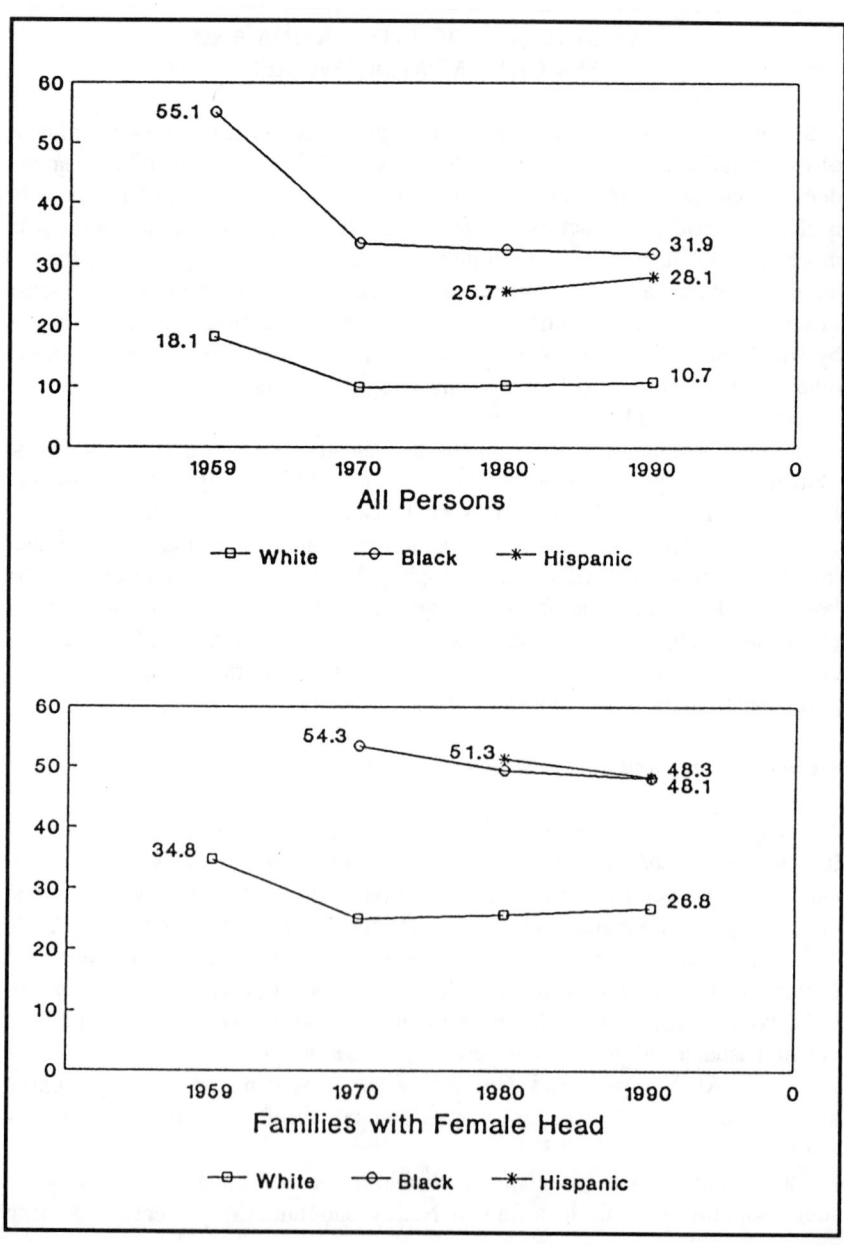

Figure 1. Poverty rates in the United States, by race/ethnicity, for all persons and for families with a female head of household, 1959–1990. Persons of Hispanic origin may be of any race. Source: reference 14.

American and 19 percent of Latino American families were headed by women in 1990. In contrast, only 9 percent of white American families were headed by women. As shown in Figure 1, about half of Latino and African American families headed by women had incomes below poverty. High rates of poverty among minority populations have been attributed to the shift in the number of families with a female head of household.[3] However, the National Research Council's report on the Status of Black Americans (16) found that if family structure in 1984 were the same as in 1973, the percentage of children and/or persons in poverty would have changed only modestly. The report concluded that the decline in wages, not an increase in female-headed households, accounts for persistently high poverty rates.

Median income, another measure of a person's economic condition, shows continuing disparity between men and women, as well as racial/ethnic differences among women. Table 1 shows that despite greater opportunities, the 1988 median income for households headed by women barely approached two-thirds of the median income for households headed by men. For Latina and African American families headed by women, the median income was slightly more than half that reported for white American families headed by women. Findings are somewhat better for single women (i.e., nonfamily households headed by women), with median incomes for African American and Latina American women being about three-quarters of the income for white American women. Thus, even with considerable growth in employment opportunities, the earnings of women of color are still lower than those of whites.

The increasing number of African American families headed by women is a recurring subject of policy debate. A number of factors, such as increasing rates of divorce and separation among all racial/ethnic groups, contribute to the rise in families headed by women; however, the small and declining pool of marriageable black males is one factor that cannot be overlooked. In 1989, the ratio of males to females aged 25 to 44 years was 87 per 100 for blacks, compared with 101 and 107 per 100 for whites and Latinos, respectively (17). These statistics reflect, in part, the high rates of incarceration and premature mortality among young African American males.[4] The difficulties facing minority males are directly linked to the options and resources of minority families.

---

[3] The percentage of Latino and African American families headed by women increased by about 40 percent between 1970 and 1990, from 21.8 to 31.2 percent among African American families and from 13.3 to 18.8 percent among Latino American families (15).

[4] There was a twofold increase in the prison population during the 1980s, with young black males comprising almost half of that population in 1986 (15). Moreover, African American males aged 25 to 44 years have the highest mortality rates, 2.5 times the rate for white males in 1988 (10).

Table 1

Sociodemographic characteristics of the U.S. population
by race and ethnicity, 1990[a]

Characteristic	White	Black	Hispanic[b]	Ratio B:W	Ratio H:W
Household composition (1990), %					
Married couple	58.6	35.8	57.2	0.61	0.98
Male householder	2.9	4.3	5.5	0.48	1.90
Female householder	9.1	31.2	18.8	3.43	2.07
Nonfamily households	29.4	28.8	18.4	0.98	0.63
Years of school completed (1989), %					
<12 yrs	21.7	35.0	49.3	1.60	2.27
12 yrs	42.3	36.7	29.6	0.87	0.70
12+ yrs	35.9	28.4	21.2	0.79	0.59
Median income (1988), thousands of dollars					
Family					
Male householder	$30.7	$19.5	$23.7	0.64	0.77
Female householder	18.7	11.0	11.3	0.59	0.60
Nonfamily					
Male householder	19.6	10.9	12.7	0.56	0.65
Female householder	12.1	7.1	7.5	0.59	0.62
Occupation of employed females (1989), %[c]					
Managerial/professional	30.1	20.0		0.66	
Technical/sales administrative	43.4	35.5		0.82	
Service	14.6	28.0		1.92	
Precision production	2.4	2.6		1.08	
Operators/fabricators	8.4	13.6		1.62	
Farming/forestry	1.2	0.4		0.33	

[a]Source: reference 17, Tables 58, 224, 725, and 656, respectively, for the listed characteristics.
[b]Persons of Hispanic origin may be of either race.
[c]Data not available for Hispanic women.

Demographic and Housing Patterns

Racial and ethnic minority populations are primarily concentrated in densely populated large urban areas. In 1988, over half (57 percent) of African Americans resided in central cities of metropolitan areas, compared with 27 percent of whites. Similarly, 90 percent of Latinos reside in urban areas, with the largest concentration living in four cities: New York, Los Angeles, Chicago, and San Antonio. African Americans and white Americans live primarily in racially segregated neighborhoods. Using an index in which 100 means a racially homogeneous neighborhood, Jaynes and Williams (16) found that although residential segregation declined during the 1970s, the average index for black-white neighborhoods in 1980 was about 80 points. Indices for Latino and Asian American neighborhoods, however, averaged about 45 points. It is likely that the impact of residential segregation varies depending on the quality of life in a particular neighborhood. However, the life experiences of minority women living in urban ghettos and barrios or in rural slums differ considerably from those of minority women living in more affluent, although segregated, neighborhoods.

Education and Employment

Educational achievement, as measured by years of completed school, provides some of the explanation for income differentials by race/ethnicity. Table 1 shows that in 1989, twice as many Latina American as white American women aged 25 and older had not completed high school (49 versus 22 percent). For African American women, the percentage not completing high school (35 percent) was somewhat less than the percentage for Latina American women but was still about 60 percent more than that for white American women. Women without a high school degree, or its equivalent, are more likely to enter the work force in low-wage, dead-end positions.

Employment patterns also help to explain the lower income of minority women. Over half of African American (58.7 percent), Latina American (53.5 percent), and white American (57.2 percent) women were in the labor force in 1989. Government enforcement of antidiscriminatory policies, however, has occurred in an era when there are fewer employment and business opportunities for those with less technically sophisticated skills. Data from the Bureau of Labor Statistics presented in Table 1 show that in 1989, African American women were less likely than white American women to work in managerial, professional, and technical positions and more likely to be employed in service occupations (17). Almost twice as many African American as white American women were employed in service positions such as food service, health service, and private household work (28 versus 15 percent). Additionally, 60 percent more African American women than nonminority women were employed in positions classified by the U.S. census as operators or fabricators (e.g., machine operators and assemblers). Current statistics are not stratified by gender for Latino Americans, although statistics similar to those of African American women probably hold true.

Due to long-standing inequities in education and training, minority women face difficulty taking advantage of new opportunities. As a consequence, the economic benefits of the transitions occurring in society have been shared unevenly across racial/ethnic groups.

Linking Health and Social Conditions

Latina and African American women have lower median incomes than white American women, and nearly half of Latino and American families headed by women have faced conditions of poverty for the last two decades. Also, minority populations live primarily in inner cities that lack the economic resources to address the varied problems associated with high rates of poverty. Many factors contribute to disparities in health; however, inadequate financial resources, limited education, and the stress of life in densely populated inner cities are important contributing factors that cannot be discounted. Furthermore, when illness or injury occurs, it not only raises a family's health care costs but can compromise an income earner's ability to work. Our society recognizes airline pilots, combat soldiers, and police officers, for example, as individuals who face life circumstances that place them at risk for stress-related illnesses and premature mortality. Yet we fail to recognize the similar impact of having inadequate resources to live, being perceived as inferior, or being part of a marginal, expendable workforce. Many racial/ethnic minority women, irrespective of their status as parents, experience life conditions that place them at risk for ill-health and injury. Measurement tools for the impact of these factors are not yet well developed, but statistics capturing the social environments of minority women are objective indications of the risks.

MINORITY HEALTH: A DEARTH OF RESEARCH

In our review of the literature, we found that most reports addressing the health status of racial/ethnic minority population groups did not provide data by gender and race or were limited in the ethnic groups included (18–24). Also, research involving the health of women in general, and of minority women in particular, is limited (15, 25), and few studies have explored the effects of race and social class on health (24, 26–29). The Secretary's Task Force on Black and Minority Health (18), reporting in 1985, was a first attempt at providing a national perspective on the health of racial/ethnic minority groups. In many cases, data were disaggregated by gender. However, information on the health of Latinos was not included in this report due to the lack of data specifically identifying ethnic origin.

Since 1960, U.S. racial/ethnic minority population groups have experienced considerable gains in health status (18–21). The magnitude of racial disparities, however, has changed little in the last two decades. In some cases, the gap has widened. Mortality statistics, one of the most dramatic and reliable indicators of a population's health, are evidence of continuing racial disparities.

The Secretary's Task Force contributed significantly to our understanding of the differences in mortality between African Americans and white Americans. As an indicator of the severity of racial disparities in health, the Task Force computed the number of "excess deaths" that occur among racial/ethnic minority women and men. Excess deaths reflect the number of deaths that would not have occurred if racial/ethnic minority populations experienced the same death rates, by age and sex, as whites. The measure reflects a standard of health that presumably could be achieved given the current state of knowledge and use of comparable resources. Using this approach, six health problems were identified as accounting for most of the excess deaths among African Americans of both genders.[5] The health problems that contributed most to the average annual excess deaths among female African Americans under the age of 70 were: cardiovascular disease (41 percent), infant mortality (12 percent), cancer (10 percent), homicide (6 percent), diabetes (5 percent), cirrhosis (3 percent), and accidents (1 percent). All other deaths continued to account for the remaining 22 percent of excess deaths for females in this age group.

More current information on the mortality experience of African American and Latino Americans as compared to white Americans is presented in Table 2 (22). Although the data are not gender specific, they provide an indication of the causes of death experienced more frequently among racial/ethnic minority groups than among white Americans. In 1990, African Americans of all age groups showed higher rates of mortality than white Americans for almost all causes of death examined. However, death rates for homicide, cerebrovascular disease (ages 45 to 64), HIV infection, and diseases of the heart (ages 25 to 44) were substantially higher for African Americans than for white Americans.

The mortality experience of Latino Americans differs greatly from that of African Americans. For the majority of causes, Latino American mortality rates are similar to or lower than those of white Americans. Two exceptions are the higher death rates for homicide and HIV infection. It should also be noted that death rates for malignant neoplasms, diseases of the heart, and cerebrovascular disease were lower for Latinos than for white Americans.

Several recent articles have examined the effects of race and social class on health (26–29). Navarro (26) estimated mortality rates for heart disease using data from the 1986 National Mortality Followback Survey and the 1986 U.S. Occupational Census. Blue-collar workers such as operators, fabricators, and laborers had mortality rates for heart disease that were 2.3 times higher than those of managers and professionals. Navarro found that class differentials in mortality were larger than race differentials. Lerner and Henderson (27, 28), using Baltimore, Maryland, census tract data on neighborhood characteristics, found that both race and income were significant factors in mortality due to cerebrovascular disease and cancer, but race was not independently associated with mortality due to heart disease. Since both of these studies analyzed aggregate population-based

---

[5] These health problems were heart disease and stroke, cancer, cirrhosis and other liver disease, diabetes, homicide and unintentional injuries, and infant mortality.

Table 2

Ratio of African American and Latino American to white American
death rates for selected causes and age groups, 1988[a]

Age group/selected causes	African Americans	Latino Americans
Age group 1–14		
Total	1.6	1.0
Injuries	1.5	0.9
Homicide	5.0	2.0
Malignant tumors	1.0	1.0
Other	1.6	1.1
Age group 15–24		
Total	1.5	1.2
Injuries	0.7	0.9
Homicide	7.4	3.5
Suicide	0.6	0.7
Other	2.0	1.2
Age group 25–44		
Total	2.5	1.2
Injuries	1.4	1.2
Homicide	7.0	3.1
Diseases of the heart	2.6	0.7
HIV infection	3.6	2.3
Other	2.3	1.1
Age group 45–64		
Total	1.7	0.8
Injuries	1.7	1.2
Diseases of the heart	1.7	0.7
Malignant neoplasms	1.4	0.5
Cerebrovascular disease	3.0	1.1
Other	2.1	1.1
Age group 65+		
Total	1.1	0.7
Diseases of the heart	1.1	0.6
Malignant neoplasms	1.2	0.6
Cerebrovascular disease	1.2	0.6
Other	1.1	0.8

[a]Source: reference 22.

indicators (e.g., occupational group and census tract median income) rather than person-specific data, relations among variables must be interpreted with caution. Using multivariate analytic techniques and person-specific data, Otten and associates (29) found that about one-third (31 percent) of the mortality differential by race could be explained by six well-established risk factors and that 38 percent could be accounted for by family income. This left 31 percent of the mortality differential by race unexplained.

HEALTH INDICES OF LATINA AND
AFRICAN AMERICAN WOMEN

It is generally known that women have a longer life expectancy, report more symptoms of acute illness, and are more likely to make a physician visit than men; very little is known, however, about the extent to which women vary by race/ ethnicity in patterns of illness and risk factors for ill-health. In this section, we provide descriptive information on several health indicators and risk factors for ill-health. The health measures (perceived health status, percentage with activity limitations due to chronic conditions, and percentage unable to work due to activity limitations) are indicators of the quality of life experienced by Latina and African American as compared with white American women. Data on risk factors (e.g., smoking, being overweight) reflect lifestyle behaviors that, while generally described as personal choices, also reflect sociocultural patterns, historic dietary practices, and financial resources.

Perceived Health Status

Self-assessment of health status has been found to correlate reasonably well with objective measures of health, including mortality and physician ratings of health (30). As such, it is a good indicator of the extent of health problems in a population. About one in ten women assess their health as fair or poor. As expected this finding varies by race and by income (Table 3). Twice as many African American (17.2 percent) as white American women (8.5 percent) reported their health as fair or poor in the 1988 HIS, and 1.5 times as many Latina American (13.0 percent) as white American women reported their health as fair or poor.

The proportion reporting their health as fair or poor is inversely related to income, with nearly one in four women with incomes under $10,000 feeling that their health was fair or poor, compared with one in 25 women with incomes of $35,000 or more. When examining self-reports of health by race and income, some racial differences persist but they are modest. For example, among women with incomes under $10,000, there are small differences by race/ethnicity in the percentage reporting fair or poor health (21 percent of white Americans, 24 percent of Latina Americans, 30 percent of African Americans). Similarly, among women with incomes of $35,000 or more, the percentage in fair or poor health is less than 10 percent irrespective of race/ethnicity, even though there is an almost twofold difference in the percentage of African Americans and white Americans reporting their health as fair or poor. In each income category, a larger percentage of Latina and African American women than white American women reported their health as fair or poor. Differences across racial groups, however, are smaller than the differences by income within a racial group.

Limitation of Activity

One frequently used indicator of a population's health is the percentage with limitation of major activity due to a chronic condition. The prevalence of reported chronic conditions is higher among older (aged 45 to 64) than younger (under age 45) women; however, heart disease, high blood pressure, orthopedic impairments, arthritis, sinusitis, and migraine headaches ranked among the leading chronic conditions for women of both age groups (31). Table 3 includes information on the percentage of women that reported limitation of the major activity associated with their age group in the 1988 HIS. For persons aged 18 to 64, the major activity is considered working or keeping house. As noted earlier, over half of women in each racial/ethnic group work outside the home.

Table 3

Health status measures by race/ethnicity and family incomes, women aged 18 to 64 (weighted), 1988[a]

Health status measure/ family income	African Americans	Latina Americans	White Americans	Ratio	
				AA:WA	LA:WA
Fair or poor health, %					
All income groups	17.2	13.0	8.5	2.02	1.53
Under $10,000	29.5	24.4	21.0	1.40	1.16
$10,000–19,999	18.0	16.7	12.7	1.42	1.31
$20,000–34,999	9.2	9.6	7.5	1.23	1.28
$35,000+	7.8	5.0	4.2	1.86	1.19
Any activity limitation, %					
All income groups	15.6	10.3	12.9	1.21	0.80
Under $10,000	24.6	20.2	27.6	0.89	0.73
$10,000–19,999	17.8	9.7	18.0	0.99	0.54
$20,000–34,999	8.4	7.7	12.1	0.69	0.64
$35,000+	8.9	5.0	8.2	1.09	0.61
Unable to work due to activity limitations, %					
All income groups	8.2	5.3	4.8	1.71	1.10
Under $10,000	14.4	12.1	14.5	0.99	0.83
$10,000–19,999	9.3	4.9	7.1	1.31	0.69
$20,000–34,999	3.4	3.6	3.8	0.89	0.95
$35,000+	3.6	1.1	2.2	1.64	0.50

[a]Source: Analysis of data from the 1988 HIS.

Of women aged 18 to 64, 13 percent reported limitation of activity due to chronic conditions. This estimate includes individuals reporting they were (*a*) unable to perform the major activity, (*b*) able to perform the major activity but limited in the kind or amount of this activity, or (*c*) not limited in the major activity but limited in the kind or amount or other activities. Small differences by race/ethnicity are observed, with about 20 percent more African Americans (15.6 percent) and about 20 percent fewer Latinas (10.3 percent) than white Americans (12.9 percent) reporting limitation of activity. Differences by income are striking. Three times as many low-income women (25.7 percent) as upper-income women (7.9 percent) reported limitation of activity. When stratified by income and race, the effects of race observed among all women persist only for women in the highest income category. Data suggest that lower-income and middle-income racial minority women are as likely as or less likely than their white counterparts to report activity limitations. For example, in the $20,000 to $34,999 income group, about 30 percent fewer Latinas (7.7 percent) and African Americans (8.4 percent) reported limitation of activity than did white Americans (12.1 percent).

Inability to Work Due to Activity Limitations

Another measure used to assess health status is the degree to which health problems limit one's ability to work. Table 3 shows the percentage of women who reported they were unable to work due to activity limitations, a subset of those reporting any activity limitation. Health problems limited the working capacity of more African American women than Latinas or white Americans. The percentage of African Americans who were unable to work is 1.7 times greater than that for white Americans and 1.5 times greater than that for Latinas. The proportion of women unable to work is inversely related to income levels, with nearly one of every seven women (13.9 percent) with incomes below $10,000 unable to work because of their health problems. At the higher spectrum of the income level (more than $35,000), one of every 45 women was unable to work (2.2 percent) due to health problems.

When income and race/ethnic group are considered, there are some differences across racial groups within each income level, but these are modest compared with the differences within a racial/ethnic group by income. For example, among women with incomes below $10,000, a similar percentage of African Americans and white Americans were unable to work (14.4 and 14.5 percent, respectively). When considering African American women by income, those with incomes under $10,000 were four times more likely to be unable to work than those with incomes above $35,000. Among white American women, those in the lowest income group were close to seven times more likely to be unable to work due to health problems than women in the highest income group. In general, a lower percentage of Latina women than both African American and white American women were unable to work. However, differences by income are more striking. Latinas in the lowest income level were 11 times more likely to be unable to work than were those in the highest income level.

Lifestyle Behaviors

The health profiles of racial/ethnic minority women often include characteristics of risk factors that are known to be associated with specific states of ill-health and are modifiable. Four common risk factors—overweight, hypertension, high cholesterol, and smoking—are noted in Table 4 for racial/ethnic minority women, with Latina women grouped according to their country of origin.

Being overweight is one of the most common nutritional problems among racial/ethnic minority women. It is an indicator of dietary practices and often signals a diet poor in quality and variety. In the NHANES, almost twice as many African American (44.4 percent) as white American women (23.9 percent) were overweight. A sizable percentage of Latina women in the HHANES were also overweight. The rate varies, however, by ethnic group. Cuban Americans had the lowest percentage of overweight women, and Mexican Americans the highest. The disproportionate number of overweight racial/ethnic minority women is disturbing given the strong associations between obesity and such diseases as diabetes, hypertension, and breast and uterine cancer.

The prevalence of hypertension, an important risk factor for cardiovascular disease, differs considerably among the various racial/ethnic minority groups. Cuban American women, for example, had the lowest rate of hypertension (14.4 percent), compared with 25.1 percent for white women. African American women had the highest rate, 1.7 times that of white American women. Hypertension rates for Latina women of Puerto Rican and Mexican ancestry were about 20 percent lower than that of white women. Higher rates of hypertension among

Table 4

Age-adjusted prevalence rates for specific health risk factors for women, by race/ethnic group, percentages[a]

Health risk factor	Mexican American	Puerto Rican	Cuban	Non-Hispanic black	Non-Hispanic white
Overweight	41.6	40.2	31.6	44.4	23.9
Hypertension	20.3	19.2	14.4	43.8	25.1
High cholesterol	20.0	22.7	16.9	25.0	28.3
Smoking	15.5	23.4	20.2	29.1	28.6

[a]Sources: For all factors except smoking, data for Hispanics are from the 1982–84 Hispanic HANES; data for non-Hispanic blacks and whites from the 1976–80 National HANES. For smoking, data are from the 1988 HIS.

African Americans are believed to be related to environmental factors (e.g., diet and stress) and genetic predisposition (21, 32).

High serum cholesterol level and cigarette smoking are important risk factors for several chronic diseases including heart disease, stroke, and lung cancer. Data from the HIS (Table 4) show Latinas as having a lower prevalence of high serum cholesterol levels and fewer smokers than white American women. Data from the HHANES provide estimates of smoking rates among subgroups of Latinas that are higher than the HIS estimates but are still lower than the rates for white American women. Prevalence rates for high serum cholesterol level and cigarette smoking do not differ substantially for African American and white American women. This finding suggests that these risk factors, although very important to healthy living, are unlikely to be major contributors to the excess heart disease and lung cancer mortality of African American women when compared with white American women.

Another behavior pattern that affects the health of racial/ethnic minority women is drug abuse. In addition to the adverse physiological effects of the drugs used, users today are at higher risk of ill-health due to behaviors related to drug acquisition and use. For example, women who engage in sexual activity in exchange for cocaine are at a higher risk of exposure to sexually transmitted diseases, including HIV infection. Data from the Centers for Disease Control (33) indicate that African American and Latina women represent 86 percent of the AIDS cases among women (13 years and older) reported in 1991. Annual AIDS case rates were 14.5 times higher among African American women and 7.4 times higher among Latinas than among white American women. The high risk of AIDS among minority women is also reflected in the rising number of pediatric AIDS cases among minority children. Children born to minority women make up 81 percent of the cumulative pediatric AIDS cases reported through December 1991.

The risks of HIV infection are enormous for racial/ethnic minority populations because drug use, which can compromise one's judgment, is one of the major modes of transmission. Intravenous drug use was the mode of transmission in 48 percent of the AIDS cases among women in 1991, and having sex with an intravenous drug user exposed another 22 percent of the women to the virus. The high rates of transmission related to intravenous drugs could be an indicator of the prevalence of such drug use in minority communities or reflect racial/ethnic differences in the use of clean needles. For either case, changing the behavior of persons addicted to drugs is one of the greatest challenges facing society. Efforts to reduce HIV infection in racial/ethnic minority women will depend, in part, on the effectiveness of drug abuse prevention and treatment programs.

OCCUPATIONAL AND ENVIRONMENTAL RISKS

The work and home environments, where individuals spend most of their waking hours, often contribute to the experience of ill-health. Hazards in the work place such as exposures to noxious agents, the pace of work, and general safety concerns, among others, have been found to be associated with higher rates of injury, disease, and death. Additionally, some ill-health experiences are localized within a geographic area. In such cases, surrounding environmental conditions may be suspect in contributing to ill-health. Combining information on occupational and environmental hazards with information on health indicators helps us to construct a profile of the health of Latina and African American women.

Occupational Safety and Health

One legacy of discrimination in the United States has been the percentage of Latino Americans and African Americans employed in the lowest paid and least desirable jobs. When racial minorities gained entrance into many industries and skilled trades, they often were assigned the most dangerous jobs (34). Even after controlling for racial differences in years of education and work experience, the disproportionate representation of African American workers in more hazardous jobs and occupations remains strong (35).

The devastating fire that occurred in 1991 in a Hamlet, North Carolina, poultry plant is one example of the dangerous working conditions of minority women. Twenty-five workers (men and women) were killed in the fire because locked safety doors kept them from escaping. Although the majority of the persons fatally injured were white, two-thirds of the plant workforce were African Americans. This tragedy increased the public's awareness of the magnitude of the problems in the workplace and the lax enforcement of Occupational Safety and Health Act (OSHA) guidelines. Over 240 such poultry plants exist today, employing 150,000 workers, the majority of whom are women. Nearly 75 percent of these industries are located in the south, in predominantly poor and African American neighborhoods. The health and safety conditions within these plants are abhorrent. Each year, almost 28,000 workers in poultry plants lose their jobs or become disabled due to work-related accidents or injuries. Icy temperatures, dull knives and scissors, fat and grease build-up, line speed-up, and hand and wrist injuries are only a few of the health and safety problems (36). The majority of these plants are nonunionized, pay minimum wages, and offer no health care benefits to their employees.

A large proportion of Latina American women are employed in the semiconductor and agricultural industries. Studies show that workers in the semiconductor industry experience occupational illness at three times the rate of workers in the general manufacturing industries (37). Farmworkers and their families are exposed to dangerous pesticides, and occupational injuries occur at an alarming rate as the result of using faulty equipment.

The garment industry is another industry in which women of color constitute the majority of workers. Although conditions have improved somewhat with the passage of the OSHA standards regulating exposure to cotton dust, many hazards, similar to the sweatshop conditions of the 19th century, remain. Many garment shops are poorly lit working areas with inadequate ventilation. These conditions are similar to those that existed in New York's Triangle Shirtwaist Factory, where in 1911, a tragic fire killed 146 immigrant women (36). Workers suffer from formaldehyde exposure, carpal tunnel syndrome, and other ergonomic problems.

The majority of office employees are women. For minority women, many of whom are employed in lower level clerical positions, the health risks are substantial (38). The occupational hazards of office work are well known; however, current OSHA standards apply poorly to these hazards. The production line pace of most office settings and the modernization of offices with video display terminals, along with poor office design and inadequate ventilation, have increased employees' risk of developing job-related health problems. Ergonomic problems related to the hands and back (i.e., carpal tunnel syndrome, tendinitis, and back strain), vision problems, headaches, fatigue, colds and allergies due to poor indoor air quality, and job stress are among the most frequently reported health problems of office workers (39).

Environmental Exposures

Three of every five Latino Americans and African Americans live in areas with uncontrolled toxic waste sites (40). The most infamous dumping groups are to be found in rural areas in the South. "Cancer Alley" located in Louisiana, along the Mississippi River between Baton Rouge and New Orleans, is among the worst. The area is lined with oil refineries and petrochemical plants, and its residents are predominantly African American and poor. The abnormally high cancer rates of the alley's residents have prompted one health official to call the alley a "massive human experiment" (41).

From the landfills of rural America to the "fly dumpsites" and toxic incinerators of urban America, the lives and health of racial minority populations are threatened. For example, excess cancer rates, respiratory problems, and birth deformities have been identified in Altgeld Gardens of Chicago, Illinois, and in East Los Angeles, California. These predominantly African American and Latino American communities have toxic dumpsites and incinerators located literally in residents' backyards (42). In Warren County, North Carolina, residents of a predominantly African American community protested against the proposed site of a polychlorinated biphenyl (PCB) landfill (43). In spite of their protest, however, the community became a dumping site for these cancer-causing agents. PCBs not only cause cancer, but also can affect the reproductive system of adults and may pass to a child through the mother's breast milk. Repeated and high exposure to PCBs can also cause liver and nervous system damage.

In a study conducted by the Commission for Racial Justice (40), investigators analyzed a cross section of U.S. commercial hazardous waste facilities and uncontrolled toxic waste sites, and correlated them with the ethnicity of the communities in which they were located. The study found that race/ethnicity is the most significant variable associated with the location of hazardous waste facilities and that African Americans are overrepresented in the populations of metropolitan areas with the largest number of uncontrolled toxic waste sites. The study also found that even though socioeconomic status plays an important role in the location of hazardous waste sites, race is more significant. Bullard and Wright (44) explain that because of housing patterns and limited mobility, middle-income and lower-income blacks, unlike whites, often cannot "vote with their feet" and move when a polluting facility arrives.

ACCESS TO HEALTH SERVICES

Dramatic changes have occurred in the U.S. system of financing and delivery of health services during the last three decades. New initiatives improved the availability of health resources (providers and facilities) within inner city and rural communities. Additionally, with enactment of Medicaid and Medicare in 1965 and federal enforcement of antidiscrimination laws, health care services have become more financially accessible for low-income, elderly, and ethnic minority populations. Yet inequities in access to health care persist, and there are indications that barriers to care have increased for some populations (45, 46). In the last decade, access to care has been threatened by rising uncompensated care (i.e., bad debt and charity care) as well as the increasing costs of medical care.

Blendon (45) and Freeman (46) and their colleagues, analyzing data from a 1986 national survey on access, provide evidence of continuing disparities for racial/ethnic minority populations. Blendon and associates (45) found that the proportion making a physician visit and the average number of visits are significantly lower for African Americans than white Americans. The gap is experienced by all income levels. Racial differences persisted even after using multiple regression analysis to take into account respondent differences in age, gender, health status, and income. In addition to lower rates of use, African Americans reported greater dissatisfaction than white Americans with the care received. Freeman and associates (46) compared access indicators of Latino Americans with those of African Americans and white Americans. This study found that Latino Americans, on average, saw physicians at about the same rate as white Americans, but were less likely to receive hospital care, despite a larger proportion reporting poorer health.

With approximately 38 million people uninsured for their medical costs (47), access to care is problematic for many Americans. Problems are particularly acute for racial/ethnic minority populations. Barriers of language, cultural insensitivity, and the lack of health providers in minority communities compound problems in financial access for the uninsured and underinsured. Moreover, national policy emphasis during the 1980s shifted from expanding access to containing costs.

Table 5 presents information on racial/ethnic differences in indicators of women's access to ambulatory and hospital care (i.e., percentage without a physician visit, average number of physician visits, and hospital discharges per 100 persons), derived from HIS data. Health services utilization is an indicator of a population's health status as well as its access to health services. In general, individuals in poorer health may require more medical care and use services at higher levels than those who are healthier. However, financial and physical barriers to care could reduce utilization. Since many factors determine use of services, the most important of which is health status, measures of utilization, at most, provide suggestive evidence of barriers to care.

Table 5

Utilization measures by race/ethnicity and family incomes,
women aged 18 to 64 (weighted), 1988[a]

Utilization measure/ family income	African Americans	Latina Americans	White Americans	Ratio	
				AA:WA	LA:WA
No physician visit in last year, %					
All income groups	19.8	24.8	19.2	1.03	1.29
Under $10,000	19.0	23.3	18.4	1.03	1.27
$10,000–19,999	21.3	27.8	21.0	1.01	1.32
$20,000–34,999	19.9	23.7	19.3	1.03	1.23
$35,000+	14.6	22.4	17.2	0.85	1.30
Physician contacts, per person per year					
All income groups	4.8	4.1	4.8	1.00	0.85
Under $10,000	6.0	5.3	6.9	0.87	0.77
$10,000–19,999	5.1	4.3	5.2	0.98	0.83
$20,000–34,999	4.3	3.8	4.7	0.91	0.81
$35,000+	4.0	3.7	4.6	0.87	0.80
Short-stay hospital discharges, per 100 persons per year[b]					
All income groups	10.7	7.2	9.6	1.11	0.75
Under $10,000	14.9	11.4	17.9	0.83	0.64
$10,000–19,999	12.4	8.3	10.8	1.15	0.77
$20,000–34,999	7.5	5.3	9.3	0.81	0.57
$35,000+	7.4	4.4	7.1	1.04	0.62

[a]Source: Analysis of data from the 1988 HIS.
[b]Excluding childbirth.

Ambulatory Care

The percentages of African American and white American women not visiting a physician in the last year do not differ (Table 5), with about one in five reporting no contact with a physician. Among Latina women, on the other hand, a larger percentage were without a physician visit (24.8 percent). When income is considered, women with incomes between $10,000 and $19,999 were the least likely to visit a physician among all racial/ethnic groups. This finding could reflect gaps in health coverage that are particularly severe for the working poor. Regardless of the reason, it is a disturbing finding that the population group with the largest percentage in fair or poor health has the smallest percentage making contact with our health care system.

Latina American women in all income groups were less likely than either white American or African American women to report contact with a physician. For example, 23.3 percent of Latinas were without a physician visit in 1988, compared with 19 percent of African American and 18.4 percent of white American women with incomes under $10,000. At the higher end of the income spectrum, more Latina American (22.4 percent) than African American (14.6 percent) or white American (17.2 percent) women were without a physician visit. The data suggest that factors other than income may be important determinants of whether Latina women obtain health care services.

The average number of physician visits per person per year also varies by race/ethnicity and income (Table 5). Low-income women in each racial/ethnic group reported more physician contacts than women in higher income groups. This is likely a consequence of their poorer health status. However, when comparing women of similar income, Latina and African American women made fewer physician visits than white American women. Racial/ethnic differences are greatest between Latinas and white American women. The finding provides some evidence that minority women use health services less frequently than non-minority women of comparable income.

Hospital Care

Short-stay hospital discharge rates, unadjusted for health status, show higher annual rates of hospitalization for African American women (10.7 per 100 persons) and lower rates for Latinas (7.2 per 100) than for white American women (9.6 per 100) (Table 5). When hospital discharges are examined by family income, an inverse relation is observed for all racial/ethnic groups. Women in the lowest income groups had close to double the number of hospital discharges compared with women in the highest income category. Given the larger percentage of African American and low-income women in fair or poor health, higher rates may reflect their greater need for care.

Hospitalization rates also were found to vary by race and income. Among women with incomes below $10,000, fewer Latinas (11.4 per 100 persons) and African Americans (14.9 per 100) than white Americans (17.9 per 100) were hospitalized, even though a larger percentage of minority women reported being in poorer health. Also, fewer African American than white American women with incomes of $20,000 to $34,999 received hospital care. Latina women, on the other hand, had lower overall hospitalization rates than white American women and lower rates of hospital care in each income group. The data suggest that racial/ ethnic barriers to hospital care exist for Latina women regardless of income; whereas for African American women, possible racial barriers are evident in only two of the four income groups.

DISCUSSION

Latina and African American women, when compared with nonminority women, are more likely to face social environments (e.g., poverty and hazardous work conditions) that place them at risk for illness and injury. Although persistent racial disparities in health are often attributed to the lifestyle behaviors of racial minority populations, they are also a consequence of poorer social conditions as well as barriers in access to quality health services. The complex interplay of racial, economic, and gender-specific barriers has resulted in many minority and poor women experiencing social conditions that adversely affect their health. The health effects of these barriers may be cumulative across generations, with cause and effect difficult to disentangle.

This chapter provides evidence that low-income women, regardless of race/ ethnicity, have poorer health indices than their higher income racial/ethnic peers. Moreover, racial disparities in health are reduced when considering a measure of social class such as family income. Nonetheless, within most income categories, African American women have poorer health indices than whites. The unexpected finding, however, is that Latina and African American women experience similar social environments, yet Latinas have health indicators that more closely resemble those of white American women. Many studies have documented a positive relation between socioeconomic conditions and health status, an association that generally holds true for U.S. racial groups. White Americans and Asian Americans, as a group, complete more years of school and have higher incomes and better health indices. In contrast, African Americans and Native Americans, as a group, complete fewer years of school and have lower incomes and poorer health indices. Latinas, for some reason, may be the exception.

Health indicators of Latina women must be considered with caution given the difficulties in accurately identifying ethnic origin. Mortality ratios showing lower or modest differences in death rates between Latinos and whites, for example, may reflect a problem of misclassification of ethnicity. As late as 1988, only 30 states included a Hispanic identifier on their death certificate. Misclassification has been found to be a significant problem plaguing infant mortality statistics. A recent study showed that 30 percent of infants assigned a specific Hispanic origin at birth were assigned a different origin at death (48). Another hypothesis is that the indicators we analyzed do not truly capture the health experiences of Latinas. It is also possible that the indicators are not sufficiently sensitive to detect racial/ ethnic health differences for Latinas in aggregate. The inability to disaggregate Latinas into subgroups based on their country of origin or ancestry (due to the small number of cases) is one of the limitations of the HIS data and thus a limitation of this effort. For example, HHANES health indicators for Cuban-American women differed from those for Puerto Rican women. One must consider whether these differences are related to culture or to the social histories of the population subgroups. Cuban women living in the United States may disproportionately represent white Cubans (of Spanish origin), while Puerto Ricans and Mexican Americans may disproportionately represent black Puerto Ricans (of African descent) and Mexican Indians, respectively. Thus, efforts to understand Latina health will require sample populations of sufficient size and clarity of definition to examine differences in population subgroups.

Utilization indicators suggest that racial/ethnic barriers to care persist, particularly for low-income women. The finding that Latinas are less likely to visit a physician, make fewer visits per person, and receive less hospital care than white women across income groups is an indication of possible barriers in access to care. Latinas who are primarily Spanish-speaking, for example, may prefer to use alternative healers than face the language barriers encountered in the general health care system. For African American women, data suggest that while entry into the health care system may be approaching levels that are somewhat comparable to those for nonminority women, some differences persist in the amount of care women receive. However, an assessment of whether levels of use are appropriate cannot be made without considering health needs. This analysis shows that low-income (under $10,000) and middle-income ($20,000 to $34,999) African American women receive less hospital care than nonminority women, but overall racial differences in receipt of hospital care as reported by Blendon and associates (45) are not evident from this analysis. One possible explanation for the varying findings is the effect of gender on insurance coverage and thus access to care. Since a larger percentage of minority women than men have health coverage (because of their eligibility for Medicaid through AFDC), they may experience fewer barriers to care than minority men even if problems persist in the quality of care received.

Gaps in Knowledge Hinder Policy and Interventions

Knowledge about the relative impact of race/ethnicity and social class on women's health and use of services is limited. Given the interrelated nature of economic, racial/ethnic, and gender-specific barriers, debate on the primary nature of one factor over the other is, to some extent, an academic exercise. Future research, however, should strive to improve our knowledge about the health effects of all three factors so as to develop interventions that will more precisely target causal factors. Disentangling the interrelated factors is complicated methodologically, but the limited progress to date is more a function of the lack of effort than the complexity of the task.

Much of the published research on the health of minority populations has been descriptive, with few studies exploring causal or contributing factors for ill-health. There are many reasons that could account for the lack of etiologic research, including a dearth of researchers interested in exploring such issues. Also, many epidemiologic studies exclude nonwhites from study populations because of concern about the confounding effects of race, even though there is little scientific evidence to support biological differences among racial/ethnic groups (6, 49). However, the lack of data by race/ethnicity is undoubtedly one major factor accounting for the lack of research. Although vital statistics and national surveys now routinely collect and report data by race/ethnicity, a paucity of national data persists for Latino, Asian, and Native Americans. Vital statistics are collected by state agencies, which vary considerably in definition and data quality. Several national surveys have oversampled racial/ethnic minority populations in the last decade, but the number of observations is generally too small for analyses of specific ethnic groups (e.g., Mexican Americans, Puerto Ricans) or for analyses of nonwhite/nonblack racial groups (e.g., Native Americans and Asian Pacific Islanders) with any confidence.[6]

Moreover, health and safety hazards that largely affect women on the job, including women of color, have not been thoroughly investigated even by the Occupational Safety and Health Administration. Since OSHA's passage in 1970, considerable improvements have been made in occupational safety and health. However, regulating exposures to occupational hazards in jobs traditionally held by women has been slow. As a result of a recent Congressional mandate, in 1991 the Occupational Safety and Health Administration issued a standard covering occupational exposure to bloodborne pathogens. The issuance of this standard is a major step forward and should improve protections available to health care employees, the majority of whom are women.

Limited knowledge about the factors associated with racial disparities in health has hindered the development of policies and programs that could seek to reduce these disparities. In the absence of more precise knowledge, public health interventions can only vaguely address rather than specifically target factors

---

[6] Two notable exceptions are the Hispanic Health and Nutrition Examination Study (HHANES) and the Survey of American Indians and Alaskan Natives (SAIN).

contributing to the greater burden of illness and injury among racial minority women. Future research must move beyond descriptive analyses and investigate causal and contributing factors to ill-health, particularly those associated with modifiable social environmental conditions. Such investigations are critical for identifying risk factors and developing more effective preventive interventions.

The recent National Institutes of Health policy (50) requiring inclusion of "women and minorities in study populations for clinical research, unless compelling scientific or other justification for not including them is provided" is important if this nation is to advance its knowledge of the nature of health problems and the most effective interventions for reducing the health problems of racial/ethnic minority populations. Navarro's (26) urging federal research agencies to collect and analyze information on indicators of social class, such as occupation and income, is also critically important. In order to help us in moving toward a more egalitarian society, our data collection systems and analytic methods should have the capability of monitoring progress in reducing differentials by race/ethnicity and by social class.

Improving Minority Women's Health Provides Challenge and Opportunity

Further gains in the health of minority women will require a recognition of the role of the socioeconomic environment in facilitating or hindering improvements in health. From generation to generation, minority women's worth has been devalued because of their race/ethnicity and their gender. This has resulted in conditions of poverty and powerlessness. With limited financial resources and minimal political influence, minority women have faced conditions of life defined by others. As is apparent from this study, poorer health indices of minority women are due in part to the disproportionate share of minority women living in poverty, but a disproportionate share live in poverty because of racial and gender-specific barriers that persist in this country.

The major health problems facing minority and nonminority women (e.g., lung cancer, breast cancer, heart disease, AIDS, substance abuse, violence) have behavioral and psychosocial etiologic components that affect their prevention and treatment. Having an impact on these conditions will require multidisciplinary, community-based programmatic efforts. This perspective may result in fewer expenditures on health or shared funding for health and social programs. The challenge confronting public health researchers and practitioners is to deepen the level of understanding of the link between health and social conditions. Social factors theoretically are recognized as important determinants of health, but they are generally considered outside the domain of public health practice. One consequence of our failure to make practical linkages between health and social conditions has been a fragmentation of related interventions, with programmatic efforts addressing different dimensions of the same problem viewed as competing rather than complimentary. In some cases, barriers to improved linkages are organizational as well as conceptual. For example, human service delivery systems that address poverty are organizationally independent of those that seek to prevent injury and illness. Also, service efforts are often organized by bureaucracies that are only modestly informed about the population groups they serve.

To achieve further gains in the health of minority women, public policies must reduce social inequalities and assure greater equity in access to resources that facilitate healthier environments and lifestyles. Minority communities in general, and minority women in particular, must be active participants in efforts that seek to improve their health and well-being. Public health initiatives should be community-based, that is, they should reflect a shared partnership that actively engages minority women in decision-making about their lives and is responsive to the *health* and *social* needs of minority women. Efforts that improve social conditions objectively provide opportunities for healthier lives and lifestyles. However, the need to continue to improve the quality of life of minority women should not overshadow the successes that have been made. The vast majority of Latina and African American women have survived the degrading experiences of second-class citizenship and are productive members of society. The gains achieved by minority women were, in large part, a consequence of public policies that reduced racial and gender-specific barriers to the economic opportunities available in this society. If we seek further progress, we should work to implement public policies that help overcome continuing discrimination and thus serve the goal of social equity and improved health status for all.

REFERENCES

1. Hollingshead, A., and Redlich, F. *Social Class and Mental Illness*. John Wiley and Sons, New York, 1958.
2. Jackson, J. J. Black women in a racist society. In *Racism and Mental Health*. University of Pittsburgh, Pittsburgh, 1973.
3. Frazier, F. E. *The Negro Family in the United States*. University of Chicago Press, Chicago, 1939.
4. Clark, K. *Dark Ghetto*. Harper & Row, New York, 1965.
5. Texidor del Portillo, C. Poverty, self-concept, and health: Experience of Latinas. *Women Health* 12(3/4): 229–242, 1987.
6. Cooper, R., and David, R. The biological concept of race and its application to public health and epidemiology. *J. Health Polit. Policy Law* 11: 97–115, 1986.
7. Krieger, N. Shades of difference: Theoretical underpinnings of the medical controversy on black/white differences in the United States, 1830–1870. *Int. J. Health Serv.* 17: 259–278, 1987.
8. Zambrana, R. E. A research agenda on issues affecting poor and minority women: A model for understanding their health needs. *Women Health* 12(3/4): 137–160, 1987.
9. Bennett, M. B. Afro-American women, poverty and mental health: A social essay. *Women Health* 12(3/4): 213–228, 1987.

10. Bassett, M. T., and Krieger, N. Social class and black-white differences in breast cancer survival. *Am. J. Public Health* 76: 1400–1403, 1986.
11. Dohrenwend, B. P., and Dohrenwend, B. S. *Social Status and Psychological Disorder: A Casual Inquiry.* Wiley Interscience, New York, 1969.
12. Neighbors, H. The distribution of psychiatric morbidity in black Americans: A review and suggestions for research. *Community Mental Health J.* 20(3): 5–18, 1984.
13. Neff, J. Race differences in psychological distress: The effect of SES, urbanicity, and management strategy. *Am. J. Community Psychol.* 12(3): 337–351, 1985.
14. U.S. Bureau of the Census. *Poverty in the United States: 1990.* Series P-60, No. 175. Washington, D.C., 1991.
15. U.S. Department of Health and Human Services. *Women's Health.* Report of the Public Health Service Task Force on Women's Health Issues, Vol. II. Washington, D.C., 1985.
16. Jaynes, G. D., and Williams, R. M., Jr. (eds.). *A Common Destiny: Blacks and American Society.* National Academy Press, Washington, D.C., 1989.
17. U.S. Bureau of the Census. *Statistical Abstract of the United States: 1991*, Ed. II. Washington, D.C., 1991.
18. U.S. Department of Health and Human Services. *Report of the Secretary's Task Force on Black and Minority Health*, 1: Executive Summary. Washington, D.C., 1985.
19. Trevino, F. M., and Moss, A. J. *Health Indicators for Hispanic, Black, and White Americans.* Vital and Health Statistics, Series 10, No. 148. DHHS Publication No. (PHS) 84-1576. National Center for Health Statistics, Washington, D.C., 1984.
20. Davis, K., et al. Health care for black Americans: The public sector role. In *Health Policies and Black Americans*, pp. 213–247. Transaction Publishers, New Jersey, 1989.
21. U.S. Department of Health and Human Services. *Health Status of Minorities and Low-Income Groups: Third Edition.* GPO:1991 271-848/40085. Washington, D.C., 1991.
22. U.S. Department of Health and Human Services. *Health, United States, 1990.* DHHS Publication No. (PHS) 91-1232. Washington, D.C., 1991.
23. Trevino, F. M., Falcon, A. P., and Stroup-Benham, C. A. (eds.). Hispanic Health and Nutrition Examination Survey, 1982–84: Findings on health status and health care needs. *Am. J. Public Health* 80 (Suppl.): 1–72, 1990.
24. Miller, W. J., and Cooper, R. Rising lung cancer death rates among black men: The importance of occupation and social class. *J. Natl. Med. Assoc.* 74: 253–258, 1982.
25. Muller, C. F. *Health Care and Gender.* Russell Sage Foundation, New York, 1990.
26. Navarro, V. Race or class or race and class? Growing mortality differentials in the United States. *Lancet* 336: 1238–1240, 1990.
27. Lerner, M., and Henderson, L. A. Income and race differentials in heart disease mortality in Baltimore City, 1979–81 to 1984–86. In *Health Status of Minorities and Low-Income Groups: Third Edition.* GPO:1991 271-848/40085. U.S. DHHS, Washington, D.C., 1991.
28. Lerner, M., and Henderson, L. A. Cancer mortality among the disadvantaged in Baltimore City by income and race: Update from 1979–81 to 1984–86. In *Health Status of Minorities and Low-Income Groups: Third Edition.* GPO:1991 271-848/40085. U.S. DHHS, Washington, D.C., 1991.
29. Otten, M. W., Jr., et al. The effect of known risk factors on the excess mortality of black adults in the United States. *JAMA* 263: 848–850, 1990.

30. Yergan, J., et al. Health status as a measure of need for medical care: A critique. *Med. Care* 19(Suppl. 12): 57–68, 1981.
31. U.S. Department of Health and Human Services. *Current Estimates from the National Health Interview Survey, 1988.* Vital and Health Statistics, Series 10, No. 173, DHHS Publication No. (PHS)89-1501. Washington, D.C., 1989.
32. Klag, M. J., et al. The association of skin color with blood pressure in US blacks with low socioeconomic status. *JAMA* 265: 599–602, 1991.
33. Centers for Disease Control (National Center for Infectious Diseases, Division of HIV/AIDS). *HIV/AIDS Surveillance.* Atlanta, 1992.
34. Michaels, D. Occupational cancer in the black population: The health effects of job discrimination. *J. Natl. Med. Assoc.* 75: 1014–1017, 1983.
35. Robinson, J. Racial inequality and occupational health in the United States: The effects on white workers. *Int. J. Health Serv.* 15: 23–34, 1985.
36. Cromer, L. Plucking Cargill: The RWDSU in Georgia. *Labor Res. Rev.* 16: 15–23, 1991.
37. Lee, P. T. An overview: Workers of color and the occupational health crisis. Labor Occupational Health Program. U.C. Berkeley, California. In *The First National People of Color Environmental Leadership Summit,* pp. 76–79. Washington, D.C., October 1991.
38. Haynes, S. G., and Feinlieb, M. Women, work, and coronary heart disease. *Am. J. Public Health* 70: 133–141, 1980.
39. Rabinowitz, R. *Is Your Job Making You Sick?* Coalition of Labor Union Women, New York, 1991.
40. Commission for Racial Justice, United Church of Christ. *Toxic Wastes and Race in the United States.* Public Data Access, Inc., 1987.
41. Elson, J. Dumping on the poor. *Time Magazine,* August 1990, pp. 46–47.
42. Grossman, K. Environmental racism. *Crisis* 98(4): 14–17, 31–32, 1991.
43. Lee, C. The integrity of justice: Evidence of environmental racism. *Sojourners,* 1990, pp. 23–25.
44. Bullard, R., and Wright, B. H. Environmentalism and the politics of equity: Emergent trends in the black community. *Mid-Am. Rev. Sociol.* 12: 21–38, 1987.
45. Blendon, R. J., et al. Access to medical care for black and white Americans: A matter of continuing concern. *JAMA* 261: 278–281, 1989.
46. Freeman, H. E., et al. Americans report on their access to health care. *Health Aff.* 6(1): 6–18, 1987.
47. Short, P. F., Cornelius, L. J., and Goldstone, D. E. Health insurance of minorities in the United States. *J. Health Care Poor Underserved* 1(1): 9–24, 1990.
48. Hahn, R., Mulinare, J., and Teutsch, S. Inconsistencies in coding of race and ethnicity between birth and death in U.S. infants: A new look at infant mortality, 1983 through 1985. *JAMA* 267(2): 259–263, 1992.
49. Jones, C. P., LaVeist, T. A., and Lillie-Blanton, M. Race in the epidemiologic literature: An examination of the *American Journal of Epidemiology,* 1921–1990. *Am. J. Epidemiol.* 134: 1079–1084, 1991.
50. National Institute on Drug Abuse. *Research Grants Program Catalog of Federal Domestic Assistance,* No. 93.279: Announcements and Guidelines. U.S. DHHS, Rockville, Md., 1990.

CHAPTER 3

Women, Health, and the Sexual Division of Labor: A Case Study of the Women's Health Movement in Britain

Lesley Doyal

The feminist critique of medicine emerged in the late 1960s and early 1970s, forming one of the earliest areas of struggle for the women's liberation movement (1, 2). The reasons behind this are not difficult to determine. Women use medical services more than men—both in sickness and in health—and they also comprise the majority of health workers (3, 4). Yet medicine in general, and reproductive technology in particular, has remained firmly in the hands of men, providing a powerful tool in the creation and reinforcement of women's oppression (5–7). Not surprisingly, then, health and medicine have continued to be areas of major concern for feminists.

This chapter provides a brief history of the women's health movement in Britain, and focuses on two main themes. First, it shows how the priorities of feminist health activists have changed in response to wider social and economic developments, particularly monetarist economic policies and attempts to dismantle the welfare state. At the same time, it describes the emergence of a socialist feminist analysis of women's health issues, illustrating the value of this approach in both theoretical and also more immediate political terms. Before proceeding, however, two provisos are in order

First, this chapter divides the history of the women's health movement into distinct periods and treats the movement itself as though it were a homogeneous whole. Naturally, reality is rather more complex than this. Health activists hold a wide range of views within a broadly feminist perspective, and the different

Originally published in the *International Journal of Health Services* 13(3): 373–387, 1983.

historical periods overlap each other to a very considerable degree. However, this simplification is essential if the main features of the women's health movement are to be identified. Second, it is important to stress that while the chapter discusses only the contemporary women's health movement, women have always been involved in struggles around health—often in ways that have gone unrecognized and entirely unrecorded (8, 9).

THE WOMEN'S HEALTH MOVEMENT:
THE EARLY STAGES

The early phase of feminist struggles around health consisted of several interconnected strands. First, there was a concern to redefine women as healthy, i.e., to replace the medical view of women as inferior and "sickly" creatures with a recognition of their status as normal, healthy human beings (10, 11). This entailed exposing and struggling against sexist beliefs and practices in medical care. At the same time, there was a growing awareness that certain areas of knowledge which previously had been monopolized by doctors were potentially of immense value to women—knowledge about how our bodies work, for example. Systematic efforts were therefore made to demystify medical knowledge and to make it more widely available.

Feminists were also concerned to remove the control exercised by doctors over reproductive technology. It is clear that the safer and more effective methods of birth control, abortion, and sterilization developed during the 20th century have been of major importance in the achievement of greater emancipation for women. However, the potential for women to control their own fertility is still limited by the power of the medical profession to make decisions on behalf of their patients or to withhold the information essential for an informed choice. As a result, much of the early activity of the women's health movement was directed toward "the seizure of the means of reproduction"—toward the appropriation by women of the means to control their own fertility.

If we look at the political practices of feminist health activists in these early stages, we can see that their goals were translated into action in a variety of ways. The most basic was probably the creation of small self-help groups, which have continued to flourish in Britain and the United States in particular (12). These groups can be seen as the health equivalent of the more general consciousness-raising groups that formed the basis of the women's liberation movement itself. They have been concerned primarily with self-examination, and with the bolstering of women's confidence and capacities for action through the sharing of knowledge. An important element in this process has been the attempt to validate women's own experiences of their bodies and their own observations of the physiological processes taking place within them. That is to say, women began to challenge the so-called "objective" clinical knowledge for which most doctors claim inevitable superiority and argued instead that "subjective" knowledge of women themselves can often be just as relevant to any understanding of their health problems.[1]

The development of these new skills and new areas of knowledge formed the basis for another important form of political practice: what might be called feminist health education. This was the process of spreading new ideas to as many women as possible, through channels that reflected the nonauthoritarian and nonelitist values that were such a central part of the women's movement itself. The best-known work of this kind was, of course, the publication of *Our Bodies, Ourselves* (14) by a collective of Boston women in 1971. This book was not just a political but also a commercial success, and has since been translated into several languages and sold millions of copies. However, in Britain, as in other countries, the women's health movement has also produced a large amount of more informal material, often written by health groups for local circulation, and has built up a network of speakers and other resources to provide health education in small group settings.

Feminist health politics have also involved more traditional pressure group activities and single-issue campaigns. In Britain, as elsewhere, abortion has provided the major focus for campaigns of this kind. However, it is important to note that the 1967 Abortion Act, which liberalized abortion provision in Britain, was in fact passed before the emergence of the contemporary women's health movement (15). As a result, feminist participation in recent abortion campaigns has mainly been directed toward the defense of earlier gains. Since the early 1970s, several attempts have been made to restrict the laws on abortion, and only massive opposition from many thousands of feminists and their supporters has prevented their implementation.

In all these ways, then, the early development of the women's health movement in Britain was very similar to that in other Western countries, particularly the United States. However, there are also marked differences between the two countries, one of the most important being the varying degrees of importance attached to the provision of alternative services. Given the sexism inherent in most medical practice, and the demeaning experiences so many women have to suffer, it is not surprising that feminists quickly began to think about providing their own services: health care by and for women. Feminist services of this kind have been extremely important in the United States where a network of feminist clinics has now been set up, many of them challenging some of the most basic assumptions about how medical care should be provided (12). Indeed, there has sometimes been a tendency to judge the vitality of feminist health politics in a particular country by the quantity and quality of "alternative" services of this kind.

---

[1]For a good illustration of the belief of some doctors in their own omniscience, see Oakley and Graham (13). They recount an incident in which a woman receiving prenatal care was asked by the doctor about her existing children. When the woman stated that she had a boy and a girl, the doctor asked whether she was "sure" because the medical notes suggested something different!

In countries like Britain, however, such strategies have proved neither economically nor politically viable, mainly because of the existence of a nationalized medical care system providing treatment free at source. Under such conditions, alternative services always run the risk of appearing to promote private medicine, while at the same time they are likely to attract an entirely middle-class clientele. Those most in need are then left either to brave the rigors of the National Health Service (NHS) or to get no care at all. For most feminists, these consequences have been unacceptable— increasingly so, as the drive toward the privatization of the NHS increases—and no attempts to set up feminist alternatives outside the health service have so far been successful.[2] The only real exception to this is the Women's Therapy Center in London, which provides a referral and treatment service for women seeking feminist psychotherapy (16, 17). The success of this center can be explained not only by the high level of need that undoubtedly exists for nonsexist psychotherapy, but also by the fact that psychotherapy of any kind is extremely difficult to obtain through the NHS; thus, those women who can afford it will have to pay anyway, and will therefore be more likely to turn to a feminist alternative.

So how can we summarize the early stages of the women's health movement? Basically the emphasis was on the problems faced by women as "patients"—as consumers of medical care—with particular attention on reproductive health. Feminist health activists were concerned primarily with facilitating the rights of women to get information about their own bodies, to obtain nonsexist medical care, and to control their own fertility. Although, as we have seen, few attempts were made to set up alternative services on a formal basis, most of these activities took place outside the NHS. Thus the emphasis was on women taking care of themselves and each other; challenging the policies and practices of the NHS was not seen as a major political priority.[3]

There can be no doubt that these developments have been of fundamental importance. The exposure of medical sexism and its confrontation have been of inestimable value and need to continue, while the fight for female control of reproductive technology is just beginning. Moreover, it is worth pointing out that action on health issues has provided a unifying link between different groups of feminists, as well as politically engaging many women who might not otherwise have seen the relevance of feminism to their own lives. However, wider economic and political developments have now shown that strategies of this kind, pursued in isolation, can provide only a partial solution to the health problems currently facing British women. This has prompted both a new way of thinking about

---

[2]This excludes the more limited services such as pregnancy testing sometimes offered by local groups.

[3]It is worth noting that British feminists have generally been less likely than their sisters in some other countries to become involved in struggles that directly confront the state. For an interesting discussion of this point, see Barrett (18).

women's health needs and a reorientation of political practice. We go on to look at the reasons for this in the next section.

WOMEN AND THE CRISIS IN THE NATIONAL HEALTH SERVICE

The factor most immediately responsible for recent developments in the women's health movement in Britain has been the attacks on welfare begun under Labour and pursued with such vigor by the Conservative government elected in 1979.[4] The fact that a reasonably effective health service could no longer be taken for granted served to highlight the undoubted value of the service in meeting some of women's most basic health needs. Thus the NHS could no longer be pushed into the background, and its defense became an important priority for feminist health activists. Cutbacks in the NHS have affected women even more seriously than they have men, for several reasons. First, women are the major consumers of medical care and therefore suffer most when services are reduced or withdrawn. Moreover, in Britain it has often been the community services, which are used primarily by women and children, that have been defined as "nonessential" and easily removable. Women are also the major producers of health care. They constitute over 70 percent of all NHS workers, so reductions in staffing and a deterioration in working conditions affect them most acutely. This is made worse by the fact that most staffing cuts are taking place at the lowest levels of the work force where the majority of women are concentrated. Finally, women have always been responsible for the care of the people whom the NHS will not look after. Thus their hidden work in the home is now increasing to make up for services no longer provided by the state—a particularly "neat" solution at a time when the rate of female unemployment is so high (21, 22). Even more ironically, some of these women are unemployed health workers, so they are now doing for nothing, or for "love," work for which they previously received wages.

For all these reasons, women have been profoundly affected by the continuing attacks on the NHS and this has had an obvious impact on the practical politics of the women's health movement. The most important change has been the broadening of the basis of political activity to include a concern with the defense of the NHS. Thus women have become increasingly involved with campaigns to save hospitals, jobs, and services and to oppose the increasing privatization of medical care. One of the most significant aspects of this shift is that it has forged a much stronger link between women as providers and women as users of health care. In recent years women working in the NHS have increasingly joined trade unions, and women's health groups have been joined by new groups of feminist health workers, e.g., radical nurses' groups, a radical midwives' group, radical health visitors, and a group representing feminist doctors and medical students. In 1981,

---

[4]For informative discussion of these developments, see recent issues of *Marxism Today* and *Critical Social Policy*. For an analysis of the NHS, see references 19 and 20.

a particularly important step was taken when the Association of Carers was formed as a support network and pressure group for unpaid health workers at home. All these organizations have been involved in one way or another with women's health groups and with health trade unions in resisting the cuts and closures now being implemented in the NHS.

The involvement of women in these struggles in defense of the NHS illustrates the basic paradox facing all socialist and feminist campaigns to defend what are essentially capitalist welfare services. This paradox arises from the contradictory nature of the services themselves. On the one hand, state services can be a source of oppression, as the feminist critique has shown; but on the other hand, they do contain elements of considerable value that need to be defended. This is an obvious dilemma: in criticizing services, we can be accused of giving support to those who wish to cut them, and our defense of these services can seem contradictory and even hypocritical. The answer, of course, lies in a more sophisticated strategy that involves both the defense of services in order to maintain those aspects we really need, as well as a campaign for qualitative changes in those services to meet the real needs of both users and workers (23).

Feminists have been at the forefront of such campaigns in Britain, as illustrated by the following practical examples of their activities. One of the most important was a four-year struggle to keep open the Elizabeth Garrett Anderson Hospital in London. Founded by Anderson, this hospital for women had been staffed by women for over a century. In 1974 it was scheduled for closure, providing one of the first targets for reductions in public expenditure. Women's groups campaigned with trade unionists to keep the hospital not just open but also providing new services in which women would have a real say in the care they were receiving. The campaign met with only partial success, but some of the hospital's services have been retained. In another case, some groups of general practitioners have been trying to use the relative freedom offered by their contract with the NHS to set up services organized along feminist lines *within* the health service. Thus they are setting up practices with nonhierarchical working relationships and the active involvement of users in the running of the organization. Within this context, they have concentrated particularly on the provision of "well women clinics" to avoid the identification of healthy women as sick patients (24). A final example is provided by the campaign to influence the way in which women are allowed to give birth. Here women concerned with their rights as patients have joined with male supporters, and with groups of radical nurses and midwives, to campaign for both greater freedom of parental choice in how and where births should be conducted and also the protection of nursing and midwifery skills that are often ignored or eroded in the pursuit of what is defined as "technical excellence" in obstetrics (25, 26).

It should be clear, then, that feminists in the women's health movement are now active participants in the defense of the NHS, although it must be said that their approach has sometimes brought them into conflict with the more orthodox defensive strategies of male-dominated trade unions. Indeed, the experience of health struggles over the past few years has shown that the presence of feminists is essential if these campaigns are to go beyond mere defense of the status quo toward a critical reevaluation of the beliefs and practices of Western scientific medicine.

This shift in the political priorities of the women's health movement has been accompanied by a growing sophistication in the understanding of women's experiences of the NHS. These new developments in theoretical analysis have been informed by the continuing debate within the women's movement about the relationship between patriarchy and capitalism (18, 27). While this debate has usually been conducted in fairly general terms, it is, as we shall see, of obvious relevance for any discussion of the relationship between women and medicine. Put at its simplest, radical feminists argue that the oppression experienced by women can be explained simply in terms of patriarchy—the universal tendency for male domination—though they would see the form of patriarchy as changing with historical circumstances. They therefore view the major division in society as that between the sexes, and claim that the situation of women has to be understood in that light. Socialist feminists, on the other hand, argue that the position of women is also directly affected by the mode of production, understood in the Marxist sense. Thus, in a society such as Britain, women's oppression is said to be explicable not just in terms of the existence of a patriarchal and male-dominated culture, but also in the light of the *capitalist* nature of British society, making both gender and class divisions of analytic and strategic significance.

This debate is very important for feminist health politics. It will be argued here that patriarchy alone cannot provide an adequate explanation of the complex and multifaceted nature of medical sexism. Furthermore, it will be shown that socialist feminists are right to raise serious doubts about how far the women's health movement can succeed while remaining largely outside the wider political arena. Socialist feminism has provided the potential for a more coherent understanding of medical sexism—of the ways in which medicine oppresses women. This makes it possible to move beyond the simple explanations of "nasty" doctors sometimes found in early feminist writings, or the belief in the ahistorical universality of male domination suggested by some radical feminists. In this way, we can achieve a more structural understanding of why women are treated as they are by most orthodox medicine, as well as formulate more effective strategies for change.

The concept of "reproduction" has been central in many areas of the socialist feminist analysis of women's oppression, and it is particularly useful when looking at the relationship between women and medicine. However, we need to begin by distinguishing between two very different uses of the term: the ideological and the biological. At the ideological level, it is clear that medical knowledge and medical practice are part of the means by which gender divisions in society are maintained (3). In other words, although sexism is mediated through the actions of individual health workers who have particular beliefs about the nature and duties of women, the behavior of these workers also contributes to the overall process of maintaining the sexual division of labor which has come to be characteristic of advanced capitalism. Indeed, it seems clear that the institution of scientific medicine does not merely *reflect* the discriminatory views of women held in the wider society, but plays a particularly strategic role in actively creating these stereotypes and in controlling women who may deviate from them (28–30). In this sense, then, medicine is involved in the reproduction of a particular view of the nature of women, and with the socialization of women in accordance with that ideology. Thus, in Marxist terms, medicine plays a part in the overall reproduction of the relations of production. This is an important point for socialist feminists, both theoretically and strategically.

There is also a more commonplace use of the term "reproduction" which applies to the biological reproduction of the species. Radical feminists have paid particular attention to the question of biological reproduction, since for them it is the capacity of women to give birth that is *in itself* the source of much of their oppression (31). However, these arguments have been criticized for being biologically reductionist and leaving little possibility for change (18). Socialist feminists, on the other hand, would argue that male attempts to control biological reproduction—often carried out by means of organized medicine—not only have to be set against the background of a patriarchal culture, as radical feminists rightly assert, but also have to be seen in the context of a capitalist mode of social and economic organization. Thus, while much sexual repression is directly related to an ideology of male domination, it is also clear that if social relations are to remain basically unchanged and capital accumulation is to be maximally facilitated, then some degree of social control has to be exercised over women's sexuality, over who gives birth, and under what conditions (32). The size of the population, for instance, or the maintenance of a particular family structure, have both been deemed matters of general social concern at different historical periods. Under these circumstances, the medical care system functions as a mechanism by which state policies are translated into practice. Moreover, it is important to recognize that women's access to fertility control will have profound implications not just in an immediate biological sense, but also in terms of women's other social and economic roles. Thus governments can significantly affect the degree of freedom women have in their own lives and the part they are able to play in the wider society by controlling their access to abortion or birth control. While the concept of patriarchy gives us some lever for explaining these processes, it cannot *in itself* account for the historical changes that have taken place in society's attitude toward women, sexuality, and reproduction; nor can a simplistic Marxist view that sees all such changes as attributable to the economic base.

So far, we have examined different ways of analyzing women's experiences as consumers of medical services. However, socialist feminists in particular have also emphasized the fact that women are not only patients and consumers. As we have seen, they are also the major producers of health care. Yet women are not evenly distributed within the health labor force, and recent research has emphasized the ways in which women's work in the health sector reflects the sexual division of labor in the wider society. In Britain, only about 25 percent of doctors are female (33), and most women health workers are to be found lower down the hierarchy, especially in nursing and ancillary work, which involve both the traditionally "female" skills of caring for the intimate needs of the sick and the domestic duties of cooking, cleaning, and laundering. Most health work is therefore "women's work"; indeed, in the NHS much of it is also "black women's work" (34, 35). This sexual and sometimes racial stereotyping is reflected in the low pay, low status, and unpleasant conditions that characterize many women's jobs in the health sector, mirroring women's jobs elsewhere in the economy. Finally, and very importantly, there has been a growing awareness of women's unwaged and often unrecognized work in both caring for the sick and disabled at home and also in maintaining the health of their families through their daily domestic labor (21, 22, 36, 37). In both theoretical and practical terms, there has been an important shift away from a concentration on the role of women as consumers toward an understanding of their role as producers of health care. In particular, it has become clear that the use of women who have been socialized into seeing themselves as care givers and who have a weaker position in the labor market has played an important part over the years in maintaining a low-cost health sector in Britain.

We have discussed above the more immediate political developments in the women's health movement and also the growth of new ideas about women and health. We have emphasized the importance of linking feminist health issues to wider political struggle while at the same time we have stressed the need to maintain an autonomous women's health movement. However, only issues directly concerned with the organization and context of medical care have been discussed. The final section examines what has in many ways been the most exciting contemporary development in health politics: the beginnings of a socialist feminist understanding of how society makes women sick.

TOWARD A SOCIALIST FEMINIST EPIDEMIOLOGY

As we have seen, in its early stages the feminist health movement tended to take women's health problems for granted, concentrating instead on the treatment women receive at the hands of doctors. In the last few years there has been a growing recognition of the need to go further and to try to understand the causes of ill-health in women.[5] Thus feminists have begun to examine more carefully the nature of the sicknesses and disabilities that bring women into the orbit of the health care system. In particular, they have attempted to discover how far these

---

[5]For a general account of the social causes of ill-health, see Doyal (10); for an outline of women's health problems in the United States and a detailed bibliography, see Marieskind (38).

patterns of morbidity and mortality can be explained by the nature of women's lives. At the theoretical level, this has entailed the beginnings of a socialist feminist epidemiology: the understanding of women's sickness and health in the context of the patriarchal and capitalist nature of society. In more practical terms, it has involved campaigns to improve the living and working conditions of women, and a greater degree of cooperation between sections of the women's health movement and other groups with similar goals.

We can begin to understand the importance of these new developments by examining the impact of women's labor on their health. Traditional accounts of women's health problems usually focus on the reproductive role, emphasizing the health needs engendered by women's capacity for biological reproduction. While this aspect of women's lives is obviously of major importance, it is by no means the only factor influencing their health. Feminists have therefore begun to stress the social and economic—as opposed to biological—dimensions of women's role by examining the impact of both domestic labor and waged labor on female patterns of morbidity and mortality.

The major problem with any assessment of the health hazards of domestic labor is the invisibility of these hazards. Very little attention is paid to the work of women at home, which is usually carried out by individual women in isolation (39). Evidence about the health effects of working conditions in the home is therefore difficult to obtain, but preliminary research has suggested four major areas of concern. First there are immediate physical hazards: the general condition of the house itself will affect women more than other members of the family since they tend to spend more of their time there. Dampness, for instance (a growing problem in Britain as the housing stock deteriorates), has been shown to damage the health of women and young children in particular (40). Women also suffer frequent accidents from unsafe electrical wiring and other hazards connected to the physical structure of the building, a fact which is borne out by their over-representation in the statistics for domestic accidents (38, 41). In addition, women are increasingly at risk from the use of toxic or even carcinogenic chemicals in the home. The recent discovery that many garden sprays commonly used in Britain contain the notorious 2,4,5-T or dioxin serves to illustrate this point with particular clarity (42).

The second type of domestic hazard women face comes from the work of their husband or partner. Many men unwittingly transport dangerous substances home from work. There is evidence, for instance, of asbestosis among the wives of asbestos workers (43), as well as a growing recognition that the very high rates of cervical cancer found among the wives of some groups of unskilled workers may not result from their "greater promiscuity" as the orthodox epidemiological explanation suggests. Rather, it appears to be due, at least in part, to the fact that sexual intercourse brings them into contact with carcinogenic substances such as mineral oils, to which their husbands have been exposed at work (44, 45).

In looking at the hazards women face at home, we also need to consider the impact of male violence on women's health. Although men also suffer on occasions from the effects of violence, domestic violence against women has its own particular characteristics. Most importantly, it tends to be sustained over a considerable period of time, since the structure of marriage as a social and economic institution makes it difficult for women either to get help or to leave. Furthermore, the violence often involves children, making it an even more devastating experience. The result is likely to be both physical and psychological damage, usually of a deep and long-lasting nature (46).

Finally we need to look at what could be called the major occupational illness associated with being a "housewife": depression. Recent research in South London has borne out more impressionistic studies conducted elsewhere in showing that working-class mothers who stay at home to look after small children are considerably more likely to suffer from depression than other groups in the population (47). Obviously the reasons for this are complex, but they seem to relate to lack of adult relationships, shortage of free time, and the low social status awarded to housework or mothering. Interestingly, it would appear that female socialization tends to predispose women to express their problems in the form of depression, and those who conform most closely to the socially expected female role are most likely to suffer in this way. Thus we need to consider the relationship between health and "femininity" in the broadest possible terms. Indeed, feminists are now suggesting that the female role, as it is constructed in our society, is itself conducive to certain forms of psychological ill-health (48–52).

If we turn to the hazards women face in their work outside the home, lack of information again presents a serious problem. Since the 1974 Health and Safety at Work Act, there has been increasing political activity in Britain over the issue of the dangers to health found in the workplace. However, very little of this activity has been directed toward the occupational hazards faced by women, apparently because it is still assumed that women rarely work outside the home and that, if they do, they are employed in safe jobs. Neither of these assumptions is true, of course. Despite the recession, women are still in paid employment in unprecedented numbers; and although they are not generally employed in traditionally dangerous industries such as mining, there is growing evidence that they do face occupational health hazards of their own.

Women in the labor force tend to be concentrated in specific industries with their own particular health risks. Secretaries and clerical workers, for instance, are at risk from toxic chemicals such as trichloroethylene, the stress produced by noise and bad lighting, and the physical damage that can be caused by badly designed seating (53, 54). In addition, many women face the health risks generated by the new technology, e.g., headaches and eyestrain from the use of computer terminals (55). Hotel and catering workers are often injured because of the dangerous conditions prevailing in kitchens and laundries (56), while hairdressers may be at risk from the hazardous properties of sprays, dyes, and detergents (38). Ironically, female hospital workers also have been found to be a high risk group: these workers may be exposed to hazards such as infection, radiation, or anesthetic gases, and to toxic chemicals such as formaldehyde or the cytotoxic drugs used to treat cancer. Nurses also suffer frequently from accidents while moving patients, often without the necessary help or equipment. In Britain these dangers are exacerbated by the fact that most hospitals are Crown Property and thereby exempt from prosecution under the Health and Safety at Work Act; thus many women workers are denied even the most minimal degree of protection (57).

The hazards described above tend to affect women in particular because of their concentration in the relevant jobs, but they can also of course affect men who happen to be exposed to these situations. In conclusion, we need to look briefly at those hazards that affect women alone. The first of these is sexual harrassment at work. Women have recently begun to draw attention to the problems they face in dealing with the sexual attentions of fellow workers, particularly their male superiors, and research (58) has shown that this can be a cause of considerable psychological distress. However, the major occupational hazards unique to women are those associated with reproduction. While there is strong evidence that some forms of occupational exposure may damage a man's chances of fathering a healthy child, e.g., exposure to lead or radiation (59), it is the reproductive capacities of women that are potentially most affected by such hazards (60). These can damage the growing fetus, produce a miscarriage or even lead to permanent sterility. When reproductive hazards of this kind were recognized in the past, the response was usually to introduce "protective" legislation—to exclude pregnant or even fertile women from the relevant jobs. However, activists in the women's health movement are now arguing that this is an inadequate response which usually ends up being discriminatory to women (61). They are therefore campaigning, first, for workplaces to be made safer for everyone—men and women—and, second, for more attention to the nonreproductive hazards facing women, both inside the workplace and outside it (62, 63).

Thus the third stage of the women's health movement has focused attention on the identification and removal of threats to women's health and well-being. This has involved the slow but sure beginnings of feminist epidemiological research and the production of a growing volume of literature, as well as more direct campaigns on a wide range of issues. Representative of this trend was the first national conference on the social causes of ill-health among women, which was held in London in 1981 and was attended by a large number of individuals and groups. As we have seen, feminists have increasingly been involved in health and safety issues (a women and work hazards group was set up in 1978), and have campaigned on wider environmental and community health issues as well (see Appendix for contact list). However, again, cooperation with trade unions and health and safety groups has not always been easy. British trade unions, with a few honorable exceptions, have tended to give health and safety issues a distinctly low priority and their campaigns have usually centered on hazards faced by male workers. As a result, research and struggles with a specifically feminist orientation continue to be essential, and will need to be conducted from both within and outside the traditional trade union structure.

CONCLUSION

We have seen that waged work and domestic labor can each be hazardous to women's health, and of course many women do both. Hence, the psychological stress and physical exhaustion of trying to do two jobs—often with very little reward—may be a basic cause of ill-health (64). This point is important because it provides some explanation of what could be called the "diseases of liberation." The most striking feature of the patterns of health and illness now found among women in the developed countries is that not only are female rates of the supposedly "male" diseases such as lung cancer and heart disease actually rising, but the incidence of psychiatric illness among women also remains high. It seems, therefore, that the gains of "liberation" have in many ways been illusory: women have gained the right to work in the world outside, but often on very unhealthy terms. That is to say, women are now exposed to new stresses and hazards outside the home but have not been relieved of their traditional role obligations, and this "double burden" is reflected in their changing patterns of morbidity and mortality. If this situation is to be changed, feminist health activists in Britain and elsewhere must continue the struggle not only for nonsexist and appropriate medical care, but also for a broader social and economic transformation leading to healthier living and working conditions for both women and men.

REFERENCES

1. MacKeith, N. *The New Women's Self-Health Handbook.* Virago, London, 1978.
2. Elston, M. A. Medicine as "old husbands' tales": The impact of feminism. In *Men 's Studies Modified,* edited by D. Spender. Pergamon, Oxford, 1981.
3. Doyal, L., and Elston, M. A. Health and medicine: Unit 14 Course U221. *The Changing Experience of Women.* Open University, Milton Keynes, 1983.
4. Macfarlane, A. Women and Health: Official Statistics on Women and Aspects of Health and Illness. Paper presented at the Social Science Research Council/Equal Opportunities Commission Seminar on Women in Government Statistics, London, June 5, 1980.
5. Roberts, H. *Women, Health and Reproduction.* Routledge and Kegan Paul, London, 1982.
6. Brighton Women and Science Group. *Alice Under the Microscope.* Virago, London, 1980.
7. Cambridge Women's Studies Group. *Women in Society.* Cambridge University Press, Cambridge, 1981.

8. Ehrenreich, B., and English, D. *Witches, Midwives and Nurses: A History of Women Healers.* Writers and Readers Publishing Cooperative, London, 1976.
9. Chamberlain, M. *Old Wives' Tales: Their History, Remedies and Spells.* Virago, London, 1981.
10. Doyal, L., with Pennell, I. *The Political Economy of Health.* Pluto Press, London, 1979.
11. Ehrenreich, B., and English, D. *The Sexual Politics of Sickness.* Writers and Readers Publishing Cooperative, London, 1976.
12. Ruzek, S. B. *The Women's Health Movement: Feminist Alternatives to Medical Control.* Praeger, New York, 1979.
13. Oakley, A., and Graham, H. Competing ideologies of reproduction. In *Women Health and Reproduction,* edited by H. Roberts, pp. 50–71. Routledge and Kegan Paul, London, 1982.
14. Boston Women's Health Book Collective. *Our Bodies, Ourselves: A Health Book by and for Women.* Penguin, Harmondsworth, 1978.
15. Greenwood, V., and Young, J. *Abortion in Demand.* Pluto Press, London, 1976.
16. Ernst, S., and Goodison, L. *In Our Own Hands.* Women's Press, London, 1981.
17. Eichenbaum, L., and Orbach, S. *Inside Out, Outside In.* Penguin, Harmondsworth, 1982.
18. Barrett, M. *Women's Oppression Today: Problems in Marxist Feminist Analysis.* Verso, London, 1980.
19. Politics of Health Group. *Cuts in the NHS.* London, 1980. (Available from 9 Poland Street, London W1 3DG, England)
20. Politics of Health Group. *Going Private.* London, 1982. (Available from 9 Poland Street, London Wl 3DG, England.)
21. Taylor, J. Hidden labour and the NHS. In *Health and the Division of Labor,* edited by M. Stacey et al. Croom Helm, London, 1977.
22. Stacey, M. Who Are the Health Workers? Patients and Other Unpaid Workers in Health Care. Paper presented at the World Congress of Sociology, Mexico, 1982.
23. Carpenter, M. Left orthodoxy and the politics of health. *Capital and Class,* Summer 1979.
24. Gardner, K. Well woman clinics: A positive approach to women's health. In *Women, Health and Reproduction,* edited by H. Roberts, pp. 129–144. Routledge and Kegan Paul, London, 1982.
25. Chard, T., and Richards, M. *Benefits and Hazards of the New Obstetrics.* Heinemann, London, 1977.
26. Rakusen, J., and Davidson, N. *Out of Our Hands: What Technology Does to Pregnancy.* Pan, London, 1982.
27. Fee, E. Women and health care: A comparison of theories. *Int. J. Health Serv.* 5(3): 397–415, 1975.
28. Hutter, B., and Williams, G. *Controlling Women: The Normal and the Deviant.* Croom Helm, London, 1981.
29. Smart, B., and Smart, C. *Women, Sexuality and Social Control.* Routledge and Kegan Paul, London, 1978.
30. Ehrenreich, B., and Ehrenreich, J. Medicine and social control. In *The Cultural Crisis of Modern Medicine,* edited by J. Ehrenreich. Monthly Review Press, London, 1978.
31. Firestone, S. *The Dialectic of Sex.* The Woman's Press, London, 1979.
32. Gordon, L. *Woman's Body, Woman's Right: A Social History of Birth Control in America.* Penguin, Harmondsworth, 1977.
33. Elston, M. A. Women doctors, whose problem? In *Health and the Division of Labour,* edited by M. Stacey. Croom Helm, London, 1977.

34. Brent Community Health Council. *Black People and the NHS.* 1981. (Available from Rear Block, 16 High Street, London NW10, England.)
35. Doyal, L., Hunt, G., and Mellor, J. Your life in their hands. *Critical Social Policy* 1(2): 54–71, 1981.
36. Molyneux, M Beyond the domestic labour debate. *New Left Review* 16, 1979.
37. Himmelweit, S., and Mohun, S. Domestic labour and capital. *Cambridge Journal of Economics* 1: 15–31, 1977.
38. Marieskind, H. *Women in the Health System.* C.V. Mosby, St. Louis, 1980.
39. Oakley, A. *The Sociology of Housework.* Martin Robertson, London, 1974.
40. Bedale, C., and Fletcher, T. A damp site worse. *Times Health Supplement,* Feb. 12, 1982.
41. Eddy, T. P. Deaths from domestic falls and fractures. *Br. J. Prev. Soc. Med.* 26: 173–179, 1972.
42. Cooke, J., and Kaufman, C. *Dioxin, the Deadly Poison.* Pluto Press, London, 1982.
43. Women and Work Hazards Group. Health and Safety Information Packet. 1979. (Available from BSSRS, 9 Poland Street, London W1 3DG, England.)
44. Robinson, J. Cancer of the cervix: Occupational risks of husbands and wives and possible preventive strategies. Proceedings of the Ninth Study Group of the Royal College of Obstetricians and Gynaecologists, R.C.O.G., London, 1982.
45. Robinson, J. A feminist critique of cervical cancer. *Times Health Supplement,* Nov. 27, 1981.
46. Dobash, R. E., and Dobash, R. P. *Violence Against Wives: A Case Against the Patriarchy.* Free Press, New York, 1980.
47. Brown, G. W., and Harris, T. *Social Origins of Depression: A Study of Psychiatric Disorder in Women.* Tavistock, London, 1978.
48. Gove, W. R, and Tudor, J. F. Adult sex roles and mental illness. *Am. J. Sociol.* 78: 812–835, 1973.
49. Fox, J. W. Gove's specific sex-role theory of mental illness. *J. Health Soc. Behav.* 21: 260–267, 1980.
50. Jordanova, L. J. Mental illness, mental health: Changing norms and expectations. In *Women in Society,* edited by the Cambridge Women's Studies Group. Cambridge University Press, Cambridge, 1981.
51. Nathanson, C. Illness and the feminine role: A theoretical review. *Soc. Sci. Med.* 9: 57–62, 1975.
52. Weissman, M., and Klerman, G. L. Sex differences and the epidemiology of depression. *Arch. Gen. Psychiatry* 34: 98–111, 1977.
53. Craig, M. *The Office Workers' Survival Handbook.* British Society for Social Responsibility in Science, London, 1981.
54. Working Women's Educational Fund. *Health Hazards for Office Workers.* Cleveland, 1981.
55. Huws, U. *Your Job in the Eighties: A Woman's Guide to New Technology.* Pluto Press, London, 1982.
56. Counter Information Services. *Hardship Hotel.* London, 1981. (Available from CIS, 9 Poland Street, London W1, England.)
57. Lunn, J. A. *The Health of Staff in Hospitals.* Heinemann London, 1976.
58. Farley, L. *Sexual Shakedown.* McGraw-Hill, New York, 1979.
59. Lancranjan, I. Reproductive ability of workmen occupationally exposed to lead. *Arch. Environ. Health* 30: 396–401, 1975.
60. Sullivan, F. M., and Barlow, S. M. *Reproductive Hazards of Industrial Chemicals.* Academic Press, London, 1982.

61. Lehmann, P. Protecting women out of jobs. *Science for the People* 9, 1977.
62. Stellman, J. *Women's Work, Women's Health.* Pantheon, New York, 1977.
63. Hricko, A., and Brunt, M. *Working for Your Life—A Woman's Guide to Job Health Hazards.* LOHP, California, 1976.
64. Waldron, I. Employment and women's health: An analysis of causal relationship. *Int. J. Health Serv.* 10(3): 435–454, 1980.

APPENDIX

Contact List of British Groups Concerned with Women's Health Issues

ACTIVE BIRTH MOVEMENT, 32 Cholmely Crescent, London N6

ASSOCIATION FOR IMPROVEMENT IN THE MATERNITY SERVICES, Elisabeth Cockerell, 21 Franklin Gardens, Hitchin, Herts SG4 OBE

ASSOCIATION OF RADICAL MIDWIVES, 8A The Drive, Wimbledon, London SW20

DOCTORS FOR A WOMAN'S RIGHT TO CHOOSE, 23 Hazelbank Terrace, Edinburgh EH11 1SN

ENDOMETRIOSIS SELF-HELP GROUP, c/o Ailsa Irving, 65 Holmdene Avenue, Herne Hill, London SE24 9LD

HYSTERECTOMY SELF-HELP SUPPORT GROUP, c/o Judy Vaughan, Rivendell, Warren Way, Lower Heswall, Wirral Merseyside

MISCARRIAGE ASSOCIATION, 2 West Vale, Thornhill Road, Dewshury, West Yorks WF12 9 QH

NATIONAL CHILDBIRTH TRUST, 9 Queensborough Terrace, London W2

PELVIC INFLAMMATORY DISEASE SELF-HELP GROUP, c/o Jessica Pickard, 32 Parkholme Road, London E8

POLITICS OF HEALTH GROUP, c/o British Society for Social Responsibility in Science, 9 Poland Street, London W1

RADICAL HEALTH VISITORS, c/o British Society for Social Responsibility in Science, 9 Poland Street, London W1

RADICAL NURSES GROUP, 20 Melrose Road, Sheffield 3

SISTERS AGAINST DISABLEMENT, 54 Whitby Court, Parkhurst Road, London N7 0SU

WOMEN AND WORK HAZARDS GROUP, c/o British Society for Social Responsibility in Science, 9 Poland Street, London W1

WOMEN IN MEDICINE (for feminist doctors and medical students), 10 Sotheby Road, London N5

WOMEN'S HEALTH INFORMATION CENTRE (a resource center unable to deal with individual problems, but has information on literature and relevant organizations and can put women in touch with local women's health groups), Ufton Community Centre, 12 Ufton Road, London N1

WOMEN'S THERAPY CENTRE (for feminist psychotherapy), 6 Manor Gardens, London N7

Section II
Women and the
Work of Health Care

CHAPTER 4

Gender Hierarchies in the Health Labor Force

Irene H. Butter, Eugenia S. Carpenter,
Bonnie J. Kay, and Ruth S. Simmons

Patterns of sex segregation in the health labor force are evident to the most casual observer, but understanding of the interaction between gender and other characteristics of the occupational hierarchy is less accessible. A gender-based division of labor has remained one of the constants in the health industry, where women constitute at least 75 percent of the total work force. Separate spheres of activity, distinct institutional settings, differing degrees of autonomy, and varying educational requirements and incomes are key dimensions along which men and women, who have sought employment in the health field, are set apart from each other. Closely mirroring traditional roles and domains of influence in society, patterns of gender-based segregation in the health work force assign secondary status to women. Valued work functions, prestigious positions, and scarce resources are controlled by men.

Despite the prevalence of gender-based segregation in the health work force, accurate data by gender on occupational distributions, income, education, and job functions are difficult to obtain. Data are available only in fragmented form, often from occupation-specific sources. Invariably there are inconsistencies among these diverse sources. This chapter represents a major effort to draw together the available information within a framework that compares men and women in the health labor force in terms of job function, work setting, autonomy, education, and income. In documenting patterns of segregation along these dimensions, we seek to demonstrate that structural characteristics of the health care industry help to perpetuate these patterns .

Originally published in the *International Journal of Health Services* 17(1): 133–149, 1987.

PATTERNS OF SEGREGATION

Employment in the health field has been growing rapidly in recent decades. During the 1970s, health sector jobs grew by 55 percent, compared to 23 percent for the total U.S. work force, and by 1979 they constituted over 4 percent of total civilian employment (1). Although the ratio of men to women is not necessarily affected by such growth, a large influx of new workers is one condition that may facilitate changes in job structure. In fact, we find that patterns of gender segregation persist in the health work force.

The existence and persistence of sex stereotyping in health occupations has received considerable attention from social scientists and health care practitioners over the past decade or so. Researchers have pointed to (a) the social and economic role of the family in society as a determinant of the division of labor in the economy (2), (b) the relegation of women (along with blacks and other minorities) to secondary labor markets (3), (c) role socialization and sex role stereotyping that devalue the feminine (4), and (d) the hierarchical organization and rigid barriers between levels of the health occupations (5).

The term segregation is used to describe the process of dividing people by race, gender, age, and other characteristics. Here the term segregation is employed primarily to reflect differentiation by gender. Sometimes analysts have classified occupations as gender segregated when 70 percent or more of the workers are of one gender (6), but the criterion of 70 percent is arbitrary and other researchers have used different cutting points. No matter which of the commonly used cutting points is chosen, most of the health occupations are gender segregated. Occupational segregation usually implies functional segregation, i.e., differential assignment of functions, roles, and tasks. Within the health system, occupational segregation also implies stratification within a notably hierarchical structure, differentiation by status, power, and prestige in the work setting, and wide differentials in the distribution of autonomy between the sexes.

Segregation is most evident across health occupations: e.g., nursing is 96 percent female and medicine is 88 percent male. Less obvious is the segregation of men and women in the same health occupation into different types of jobs and organizational units. Examples of this phenomenon are the tendency of male nurses to be promoted to administrative jobs more frequently than female nurses, and the tendency for female health administrators to be assigned to personnel and housekeeping departments more often than their male counterparts.

Specialization is more prevalent in the health field than in many other segments of the labor force, especially in such high-status occupations as medicine and dentistry. There is a pronounced pattern of gender segregation across specialties, exemplified in medicine by the concentration of female physicians in such specialties as pediatrics, psychiatry, and public health and the very high ratio of males in surgical specialties and pathology.

Segregation by gender, both inter- and intra-occupationally, is complex. To help gain an understanding of this complexity, we have developed two analytical constructs to examine different forms of segregation: the Health Occupations Matrix and the Health Occupations Hierarchy. The Matrix presents a taxonomy of health occupations by job functions, work settings, and levels of autonomy; the Hierarchy portrays the distribution of men and women in health occupations arrayed by education and economic rewards. Together, these frameworks demonstrate that women always cluster at the bottom of whatever hierarchy or scale is chosen.

The Health Occupations Matrix categorizes health occupations along three dimensions—job function, work setting, and level of autonomy and allows us to compare the distributions of men and women with respect to these important attributes of their work. Thus, the Matrix indicates where and how people function in their jobs, providing an overview of occupational categories, selected structural characteristics, and their relationship to gender segregation.

The Health Occupations Hierarchy is a second conceptual framework to portray differences in distributions of female and male workers with respect to status, in this case by level of education and income. The Hierarchy reflects structural aspects of a system in which occupational groups are highly stratified and constrained by severe blockages to occupational mobility. The Hierarchy allows us to examine gender segregation along additional dimensions and suggests how the different forms of segregation reinforce one another to produce differential opportunities for attainment of status, prestige, and rewards by men and women.

THE HEALTH OCCUPATIONS MATRIX

Distributions of female and male workers across health occupations are presented in Figure 1, which categorizes occupations according to their primary function, predominant work setting, and level of autonomy. Occupations are grouped in accordance with three primary functions in patient care:

1. the psychosocial healing functions of teaching, caring, counseling, motivating, and supporting of patients by helping them to cope with disease, training them to prevent or overcome illnesses or disabilities, aiding them in functional restoration;
2. somatic-diagnostic curative functions oriented toward the use of procedures and devices in diagnosis and treatment with a primary focus on services that are interventionary and curative in nature;
3. technical functions, which range from the use of equipment, technology, and drugs to the application of computers, records, and management skills to facilitate the functioning of institutions in health care delivery.

HEALTH OCCUPATIONS MATRIX

		PSYCHOSOCIAL HEALING		SOMATIC-DIAGNOSTIC CURING		TECHNICAL	
NON-BUREAUCRATIC/ NON-INSTITUTIONAL	High Autonomy			Chiropractic[a]	11.0	Opticians[h]	40.5
				Medicine[b]	12.0	Pharmacy[i]	19.0
				Osteopathy[c]	6.0		
				Dentistry[d]	3.8		
				Optometry[e]	5.7		
				Podiatry[f]	5.0		
				Veterinary Medicine[g]	12.3		
	Mixed Autonomy	Nurse Practitioner[j]	87.9	Dental Assistant[f]	98.0	Dental Technician[f]	32.9
				Dental Hygienist[f]	99.0		
				Physician Assistant[k]	36.4		
BUREAUCRATIC/ INSTITUTIONAL	High Autonomy	Registered Nurse[l]	96.0			Health Administrator[h]	51.0
		Nurse Midwife[m]	99.2				
		Psychologist[h]	47.0				
		Medical Social Worker[n]	66.4				
	Mixed Autonomy	Speech Therapist[f]	93.2	Physical Therapist[f]	71.5	Medical Record Specialist[f]	91.1
		Occupational Therapist[f]	93.2	Respiratory Therapist[f]	56.4	Medical Librarian[o]	83.4
		Health Educator	NA	Dietitian[f]	92.7	Clinical Lab Technologist[f]	75.6
						Orthotist and Prosthetist	NA
	Low Autonomy	Practical Nurse[f]	96.7	Dietetic Assistant[f]	86.8	Radiologic Technician[f]	72.9
		Home Health Aide[f]	87.9	Physical Therapy Assistant	NA	Anesthesia Assistant	NA
		Nursing Aide & Orderly[f]	87.9	Respiratory Therapy Aide	NA	Medical Secretary[o]	100.0
		Health Aide (Non-nursing)[f]	84.5			Electroencephalogram Technician	NA
		Occupational Therapy Assistant[f]	93.8			Electrocardiogram Technician	NA
						Emergency Medical Technician	NA

82

Figure 1. Health Occupations Matrix: representation of women (as percentage) in selected health occupations classified by job function, autonomy, and work setting.

Sources of data are as follows (NA, data not available):

[a]U.S. Department of Labor, Bureau of Labor Statistics. *Detailed Occupation by Industry Tables: Annual Averages for Year Ending December 1982.* (unpublished).

[b]American Medical Association, Division of Survey and Data Resources. *Physician Characteristics and Distribution in the U.S., 1982 Edition.* AMA, 1983.

[c]U.S. Department of Health and Human Services. *Report to the President and Congress on the Status of Health Personnel in the United States.* DHHS Pub. No. HRS-P-OD 84-4, Government Printing Office, Washington, D.C., May 1984. Percent female as of February 1983.

[d]Estimated by Health Resources and Services Administration, Bureau of Health Professions, Division of Associated and Dental Health Professions; based on data from the American Dental Association, Bureau of Economic and Behavioral Research. Percent female as of December 31, 1982.

[e]Projection of the Health Resources and Services Administration, Bureau of Health Professions, Division of Associated and Dental Health Professions; based on data from the National Center for Health Statistics' 1978 Inventory of Optometrists. Percent female as of December, 1980.

[f]Stancavage, F. B. *An In-Depth Examination of the 1980 Decennial Census Employment Data for Health Occupations.* Contract No. 232-82-0017. Unpublished Final Report sponsored by the Department of Health, Education, and Welfare, Public Health Services, Health Resources and Services Administration, Bureau of Health Professions, Office of Data Analysis and Management. American Institute for Research, September 28, 1982 to February 29, 1984, Palo Alto, California.

[g]Health Resources and Services Administration, Bureau of Health Professions, Division of Associated and Dental Health Professions; based on data tape of the American Veterinary Association. Percent female as of December 31, 1982.

[h]1980 Decennial Census.

[i]*Third Report to the President and Congress on the Status of Health Professions Personnel in the U.S.* DHHS Publication No. (HRA) 82-2. Health Resources Administration, Bureau of Health Professions, Division of Health Professions Analysis, Rockville, Maryland, January 1982; *Supply and Characteristics of Selected Health Personnel.* DHHS Publication No. (HRA) 81-20. Health Resources Administration, Bureau of Health Professions, Division of Health Professions Analysis, June 1981. Reported in F. B. Stancavage,[f] p. E-27. Percent female as of December 1980.

[j]Scheffler, R. M. *The Supply and Demand for New Health Professionals, Physician's Assistants and MEDEX.* Contract No. HRA-1-44184. Bureau of Health Manpower, Health Resources Administration, Hyattsville, MD, 1978; Sultz, R. A. et al. *Longitudinal Study of Nurse Practitioners, Phase III* (to be published). Personal communication from Division of Nursing, Bureau of Health Manpower, reported in *Health United States 1979.* U.S. Department of Health, Education, and Welfare, Public Health Service, Office of Health Research, Statistics, and Technology, DHEW Pub. No. (PHS) 80-1232, p. 46. Percent female as of 1979.

[k]Carter, R. D., with the assistance of Muhlbaier, L., and Stafford, J. *Preliminary Report (Prepublication Draft)—1981 National Physician Assistant Survey,* May 20, 1982; Perry, H. B., and Fisher, D. W. *Present Status of the Physician Assistant Professions: Results of the 1978 Survey of Graduates* (undated). Reported in F. B. Stancavage,[f] p. E-47. Percent female as of 1981.

[l]U.S. Department of Health and Human Services, Public Health Service, Health Resources and Services Administration, Bureau of Health Planning, Office of Data Analysis and Management. *The Registered Nurse Population: An Overview.* DHHS Publication No. HRS-P-OD-83-1, p. 14. From the National Sample of Registered Nurses, November 1980, revised November 1982.

[m]Telephone interview with the American College of Nurse Midwives, June 1984.

[n]U.S. Department of Labor, Bureau of Labor Statistics. *Household Data Annual Averages, January 1983, Employment and Earnings;* Membership survey shows practice shifts. *NASW News,* November 1983.

[o]U.S. Department of Labor, Bureau of Labor Statistics. *Household Data Annual Averages, January 1983, Employment and Earnings* (unpublished).

For example, nurses, social workers, and health educators perform functions that are primarily psychosocial and supportive; physicians, dentists, and podiatrists engage chiefly in curative care of a physical nature; and opticians, pharmacists, and dental technicians focus on application of technical services. In practice, these distinctions become blurred, since few workers function in one modality exclusively. As nursing has become increasingly technical, for example, many nurses perform somatic-diagnostic and technical, as well as psychosocial functions. Pharmacists' services are mainly technical, but pharmacists may also engage in counseling and patient education. Some physicians emphasize curing (surgeons), while others often perform psychosocial functions (pediatricians, psychiatrists), and still others combine somatic-diagnostic and technical procedures with psychosocial support (cardiologists and internists). Nevertheless, most observers would agree that the main thrust of nursing is psychosocial and that of dental technicians is technical. These distinctions are reflected in the Matrix.

The Matrix further classifies health occupations into two major categories of work settings: bureaucratic and nonbureaucratic. As shown in the two upper right-hand cells of the Matrix, there are several occupations for which the dominant work setting is nonbureaucratic—private, independent, self-employed practice—notably medicine, dentistry, and podiatry. Although a growing number of physicians, and to a lesser extent dentists, hold salaried positions in bureaucratic settings, salaried practitioners are still in the minority in nonbureaucratic settings. Some salaried health workers who perform supportive functions in the employ of and under the supervision of self-employed practitioners are found chiefly in nonbureaucratic settings. The most notable example is dentistry, in which dental hygienists and dental assistants usually work in small, office-type settings. The bureaucratic/institutional setting is the dominant work context for most nurses, health aides, therapists, medical laboratory and radiologic technicians, health administrators, and the majority of other health care providers.

The level of autonomy conferred to health workers, the third dimension addressed in the Matrix, is subject to considerable variation within and between occupations. Autonomy is a multifaceted concept that itself has several dimensions. It is used here to mean the ability to control the conditions of one's work. Within nonbureaucratic settings we identify two levels of autonomy: high and mixed. Workers in occupations whose predominant mode of practice takes place in self-employed settings almost invariably enjoy the highest form of autonomy because they are legally authorized to practice independently of the supervision of others. Members of other health occupations are required to practice only under the supervision of autonomous practitioners whom they support and assist, e.g., physician assistants supervised by physicians; dental hygienists supervised by dentists. These dependent workers are limited in their autonomy by the control of their employers in nonbureaucratic settings. However, since most licensing laws do not require either over-the-shoulder or continuous supervision, these so-called dependent practitioners may function at high levels of autonomy in some situations and at lower levels in others. We have classified such occupations as having mixed autonomy.

Within bureaucratic settings there is generally a continuum of levels of autonomy ranging from high to low. Professional nurses, for example, exercise control over many aspects of their work. In the professional sphere they may initiate actions on behalf of patients, even though they frequently require the approval of attending physicians. In complying with physicians' standing orders, nurses generally do not have autonomy with respect to procedures employed, drugs to be prescribed, or the equipment to be used for treatment. Nor do they have bureaucratic autonomy allowing them to control which patients to serve, or the workers with whom they collaborate. Thus the amount of autonomy exercised by professional nurses varies with the aspect of work considered and perhaps with the presence/absence of someone in a position of authority. We have classified professional nursing as a high autonomy occupation, a classification shared by nurse midwives, psychologists, social workers, and health administrators. Physicians, when working in bureaucratic settings, function in a highly autonomous manner, although they are subject to some institutional controls that do not exist in self-employed practice.

We have designated a group of health occupations whose primary employment is in bureaucratic/institutional settings as having mixed autonomy. By this term we mean that their work is controlled to a certain extent by institutional rules and policies as well as by supervisors or department heads under whose direction they function, but at the same time these workers may enjoy a considerable degree of clinical autonomy. Examples of such are physical and occupational therapists, health educators, dietitians, and some technical workers. Workers who perform routine assisting functions under close supervision of their superiors, e.g., health aides and dietetic assistants, have very little opportunity to exercise autonomy or independent judgment.

The Matrix reveals a strong association between gender, type of occupation, work setting, and level of autonomy. If men and women were randomly distributed among occupations one would expect their distributions among occupations and settings to reflect their overall representation: 25 percent male and 75 percent female. As indicated by the two upper right-hand cells of the Matrix we find that men are overrepresented in somatic-diagnostic (88–96 percent male) and technical occupations (60–80 percent male) in self-employed settings with high autonomy. In these same two cells, women are vastly underrepresented. Moreover, while the two right-hand cells of the upper level are male dominated, the upper left-hand cell remains empty, indicating that the combination of non-bureaucratic setting and high autonomy is not an available option for occupations engaged primarily in psychosocial functions. By and large such occupations are female dominated.

In almost all other cells of the Matrix, i.e., psychosocial, somatic-diagnostic, and technical occupations with mixed or low autonomy, women are overrepresented.

While clearly concentrated in psychosocial occupations, female providers also cluster to a somewhat smaller degree in somatic-diagnostic and technical occupations in bureaucratic settings with limited autonomy. These female workers have little or no control over activities and types of services they perform, nor do they control activities and types of services performed by male health workers.

There are many reasons for women's numerically prominent representation in the health work force. A partial explanation is that health care jobs are perceived to be overwhelmingly "women's" jobs, characterized by Wilensky to encompass the following: (a) traditional housewives' tasks—cooking, cleaning, sewing and caring; (b) few or no strenuous physical activities and hazards; (c) patience, waiting, routine activities (receptionists, salesworkers, telephone operators); (d) rapid use of hands and fingers, such as office-machine operating and electrical assembling; (e) distinctive welfare or cultural orientation; (f) contact with young children; and (g) sex appeal (7). Based on these perceptions, jobs have become gender typed and selectively offered to either male or female job seekers. The concentration of women in female-typed jobs occurs in other labor markets as well as the health care industry. The concentrations come about because employers may demand exclusively male or female workers—they associate jobs with traits that are percieved to be attributes of either men or women and they attempt to avoid hiring gender-mixed work groups (8).

The traditional division of labor between men and women in the family is mirrored in the health labor force. The functions usually performed by women in the family— such as cooking, cleaning, and educating, as well as caring, consoling, counseling, nursing, and nurturing—become institutionalized in the health care system in the form of female-typed jobs. The traditional division of work between men and women in the family is generally found to be complementary rather than competitive. This tends to be reflected in labor markets in the form of noncompeting gender groups. The Matrix sets forth a family of health occupations that is gender-divided along the lines of work in the family: women are concentrated in so called "feminine" occupations, which are predominantly psychosocial and supportive. Complementarity rather than competition governs the placement of men and women in different fields of work and shapes the occupational sphere of the health sector into predominantly male or predominantly female occupations.

THE HEALTH OCCUPATIONS HIERARCHY

Irrespective of gender, the health labor force is notorious for its hierarchy of status and power. Certain structural characteristics differentiate health care from other industries in that the work force is heavily populated in the lower ranks and relatively well represented in upper ranks with an underrepresentation of a so-called "middle class" of workers. Fuchs and associates (9) found that the income distribution of the health labor force showed a greater degree of inequality than that of other industries. Mick's analysis of the health professions hierarchy also drew attention to wide disparities of wealth and power (10). Still other researchers have made reference to the "vertical gap" of the health occupational hierarchy, which they consider to be a result of blockages to interoccupational mobility (11). Mechanisms that constrain movement across occupations in health are rigidly enforced by interest groups, thereby maintaining the occupational hierarchy regardless of its gender distribution.

Superimposed on the occupational hierarchy is a gender hierarchy based on differential opportunity structures for male and female entrants into health occupations. Workers are selectively channeled according to gender into particular health occupations and specific career tracks pointing to differential entry paths and promotion tracks within the status hierarchy. As shown previously, male workers are heavily concentrated in high autonomy, elite occupations whose status often entitles them to control subordinates in usually preponderantly female occupations. If entry barriers and mobility blockages have unequal effects on men and women, these mechanisms would serve not only to reinforce and perpetuate the health occupations hierarchy itself but also the gender divisions within the hierarchy.[1]

Education and income are two dimensions selected here for analysis of gender status within the hierarchy, and both suggest systematic gender imbalance. Figure 2 shows that women are concentrated in occupations associated with the five lowest educational levels, as measured by years of post-high school education; 87 percent of all female workers are in these groups in contrast to 31 percent of all males. Male workers dominate occupations ranked in the four highest educational levels: 69 percent of all male workers are at the top four levels in comparison to 13 percent of all females. The disparity in educational attainment of male and female health workers stems from the fact that most female-dominated health occupations do not require a professional degree involving six or more years of higher education as do most male-dominated occupations. Why more women than men enter occupations requiring fewer years of education is an important question that lies beyond the scope of this chapter.

Income is the second dimension of the Health Occupations Hierarchy, as shown in Figure 3. Its distribution across health occupations mirrors the phenomenon described by Fuchs: extreme income inequality. The six highest income occupations, with median annual incomes ranging from $40,000 to $94,500, represent a relatively small segment of the total health work force—approximately 12 percent. In contrast, 53 percent of health workers have median incomes below $20,000. Approximately 35 percent of the health work force earns between $20,000 and $26,500. Notable is the absence of health occupations with median incomes between $26,500 and $40,000, a reflection of the vertical gap mentioned earlier.

---

[1] See reference 12 for a discussion of credentialing as a factor that reinforces hierarchy in the health occupations.

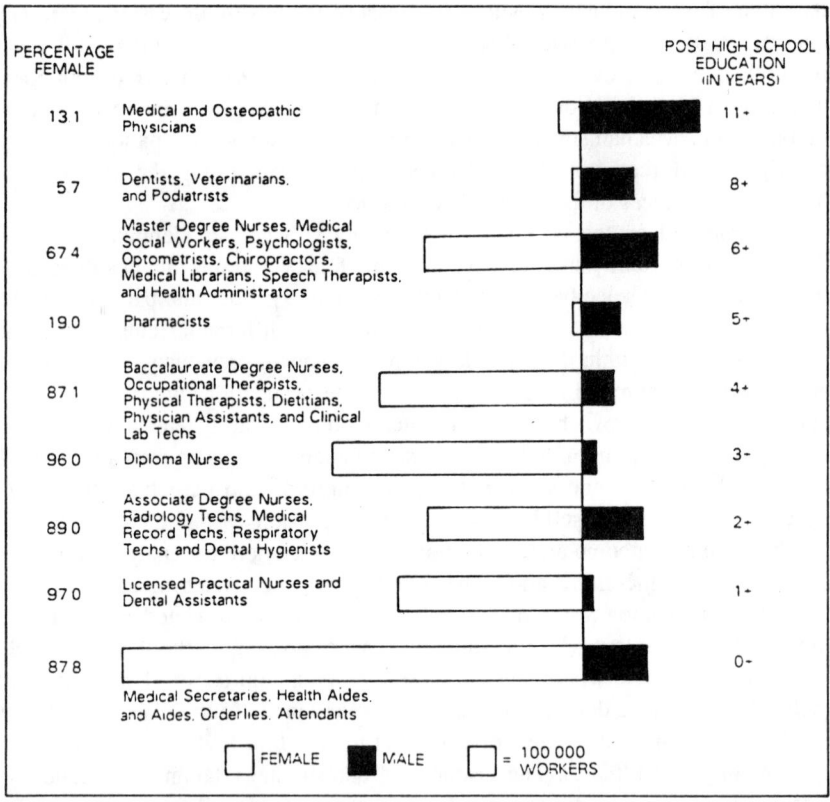

Figure 2. Health Occupations Hierarchy: education by gender. Sources of data: U.S. Department of Labor. *Health Careers Guidebook.* U.S. Government Printing Office, Washington, D.C., 1979; U.S. Department of Health and Human Services. *Report to the President and Congress on the Status of Health Personnel in the United States, May 1984.* DHHS Pub. No. HRS-P-OD 84-4, U.S. Government Printing Office, Washington, D.C., 1984; telephone interview with the Council on Chiropractic Education, October 1984. For further sources and information see Butter, I. et al. *Sex and Status: Hierarchies in the Health Workforce,* Chapter 4, end notes. American Public Health Association, Washington, D.C., 1985.

Inequalities in the distributions of men and women among income levels are consistent with those shown in Figure 2: women are severely underrepresented in the six highest income occupations (11 percent female) in contrast to their overrepresentation in occupations with incomes below $20,000 (87 percent female). Even though there are three times as many female as male health workers in the total work force, men outnumber women by a factor exceeding eight to one in the six highest-income health occupations, and only 2 percent of all female health workers earn the higher levels of income realized by 46 percent of all male health workers. Female representation in these highest-income occupations ranges

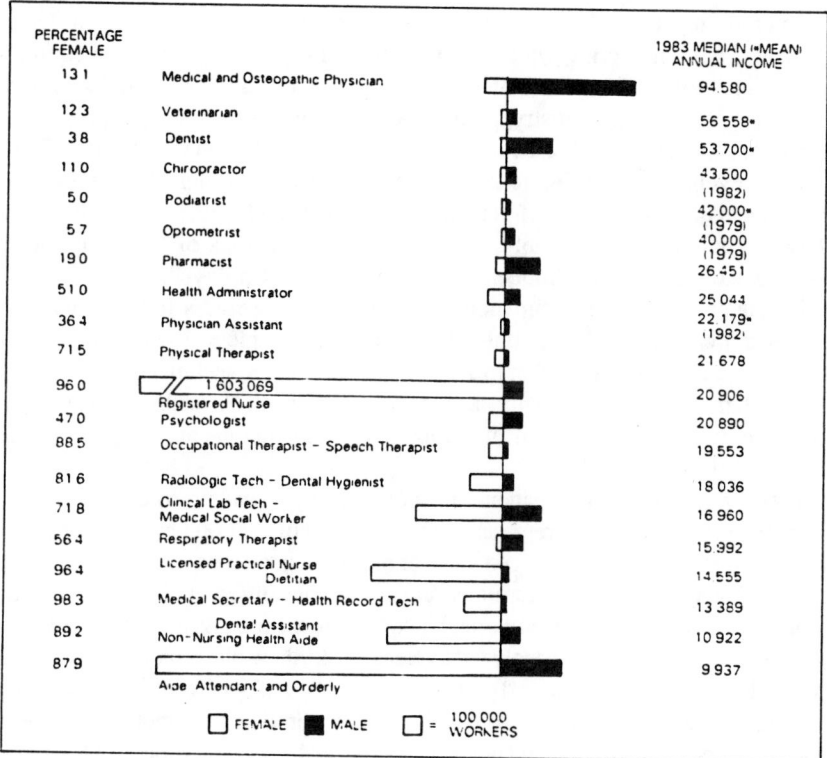

Figure 3. Health Occupations Hierarchy: income by gender. Sources of data: U.S. Department of Labor, Bureau of Labor Statistics. *The Current Population Survey.* 1983 Annual Income Averages (unpublished); Stancavage, F. B. An in-depth examination of the 1980 Decennial Census employment data for health occupations. *Medical Economics*, September 17, 1984, pp. 180–190; U.S. Department of Health and Human Services. *Report to the President and Congress on the Status of Health Personnel in the United States, May 1984.* DHHS Pub. No. HRS-P-OD-84-4. U.S. Government Printing Office, Washington, D.C., 1984; telephone interviews with the American Optometric Association, American Podiatry Association, American Chiropractic Association, and American Osteopathic Association, October 1984.

from about 4 to 13 percent, in contrast to 56 to 98 percent in occupations found in the lower ranges of the income distribution.

Again the question must be raised why female-dominated occupations rank consistently in the lower levels of the income distribution. Is it due to educational and occupational segregation that results in "crowding" of feminine fields, or is the work that women do valued differently from work done by men?

The gender gap in earnings exists within as well as between occupations. Table 1 ranks occupations according to the size of the earnings gap and shows that the largest differential is found when women work in elite, male-dominated professions in which they earn 42 to 64 percent of men's incomes. An important caveat in interpreting these data is that they are derived from the Bureau of Labor Statistics' earnings series, which excludes the self-employed. Thus, the earnings shown in Table 1 for practitioners in the predominantly male professions of medicine, osteopathy, dentistry, podiatry, optometry, chiropractic, pharmacy, and veterinary medicine are biased downward. This is evident in comparing overall income levels shown in Figure 2 with the sex-specific earnings data in Table 1. Nevertheless, the earnings differentials between men and women as employees in these occupations are probably reasonable approximations of the male-female earnings ratios for all practitioners, employed and self-employed.

In female-dominated occupations, in which most workers are employed in bureaucratic settings, the earnings data are more complete. Even among these occupations, e.g., physical therapist, dietitian, radiologic technician, and speech therapist, men's earnings usually exceed those of women. Nevertheless, the higher the representation of women in an occupation, the smaller the male pay advantage in that occupation.

There are two health occupations shown in Table 1—health record specialist and practical nurse, both with a representation of women of over 90 percent—for which women's earnings actually exceed those of men by a small amount. Further investigation of factors responsible for male-female earnings differentials in bureaucratic health settings could provide important insights into the process of wage determination. Earnings data for 1978 analyzed by Sekscenski show that women employed as health therapists and registered nurses earned about 85 percent of the weekly earnings of men in these occupations, and the same earnings ratio applied to licensed practical nurses, nurse aides, and nonprofessional health service workers (1).

Although the data are fragmented and incomplete, they strongly suggest that relative to men, women health workers almost always earn lower incomes. Reasons behind the gender wage gap in the health system are not fully understood and therefore it is important that differences in educational attainment, skill levels, and other job characteristics pertaining to income differentials of male and female health workers be further investigated.

The combined evidence presented in the Health Occupations Matrix and the Health Occupations Hierarchy underscores the observation that gender imbalance is pervasive in the health work force. Different forms of segregation are interconnected and reinforcing to the effect that women are systematically situated in occupations and positions that are female typed and have lower educational requirements, lower status, less autonomy, and lower pay.

In the last two decades a series of legislative changes and policy initiatives have been enacted to bar employment discrimination and occupational segregation by gender. Among these are Title VII of the 1964 Civil Rights Act, and Executive Orders 11246 and 11375. Title VII of the Act, as amended by the Equal Opportunity Act of 1972, forbids employment discrimination on the basis of race, color, national origin, religion, or sex by any employer of 15 or more persons, public or private, whether or not that employer receives federal funds. The civil rights

Table 1

Income differentials between men and women in selected health occupations[a]

	1983 median annual incomes (dollars)		Women's income as percentage of men's income	Percentage of women in occupation
Occupation[b]	Men	Women		
Optometry	44,194	18,480	41.7	5.7
Veterinary medicine (1980)	38,808	21,622	55.7	12.3
Medicine (1979)	67,450	39,820	59.0	12.0
Physician assistant	20,789	12,993	62.5	36.4
Dentistry	32,646	20,987	64.3	3.8
Physical therapist	31,327	21,128	67.4	71.5
Health administrator	31,216	22,638	72.4	51.0
Medical social worker	20,688	16,020	77.4	66.4
Respiratory therapist	20,011	15,586	77.9	56.4
Aide, attendant, orderly	12,018	9,664	80.4	87.9
Dietitian	18,228	15,036	82.5	92.7
Radiologic technician	19,860	16,485	83.0	72.9
Health aides (non-nursing)	12,730	10,775	84.6	84.5
Pharmacist	27,494	23,613	85.9	19.0
Clinical lab technician	19,288	16,733	86.7	75.6
Dental assistant	12,260	10,749	87.7	98.0
Occupational therapist	20,948	18,393	87.8	93.2
Speech therapist	20,840	19,152	91.9	89.4
Medical librarian	20,912	19,322	92.4	83.0
Psychologist	21,715	21,052	96.9	47.0
Registered Nurse	20,962	20,901	99.7	96.0
Health records specialist	13,844	13,955	101.0	91.1
Practical nurse	14,205	14,527	102.0	96.7

[a]Sources: U.S. Department of Labor, Bureau of Labor Statistics (BLS). Unpublished tabulations from the Current Population Survey, 1983 Annual Averages; *Medical Economics*, February 18, 1980, pp. 98–110; telephone interview with the American Veterinary Medicine Association, November 1984.

[b]The main source of data, the BLS earnings series, excludes self-employed workers and would therefore exclude the majority of workers in medicine, osteopathy, dentistry, chiropractic, podiatry, optometry and veterinary medicine. We therefore explored other sources, but succeeded in only two cases: medicine and veterinary medicine. Annual averages from the BLS were added to the Table for optometry and dentistry, though these data are probably biased because of exclusion of the self-employed. For podiatry, chiropractic, and osteopathic medicine we were not able to obtain any data.

movement also penetrated the education sector. Title IX of the 1972 Education Amendments, the 1976 amendment to the Vocational Education Act, and the 1978 reauthorization of CETA required affirmative action efforts to eliminate gender barriers in federally funded educational programs (13, 14).

The effectiveness of federal antidiscrimination policies can be examined using data displayed in Tables 2 and 3. Table 2 shows trends in enrollment, by gender, of health professional training programs in 1970 and in the early 1980s, and reflects a rising trend of female entry into preponderantly male occupations, notably pharmacy, health administration, and veterinary medicine.

In medicine—the most prestigious and closely watched health profession— women constituted almost one-third of first year enrollment in 1982. This is a sizable increase from the 9.6 percent female enrollment twelve years earlier. There is also a growing representation of women as practitioners; however, with the exception of health administration, numbers lag behind those of first year enrollment. This lag reflects the lengthy training period for several of these occupations—an average of seven years for medicine. Female practitioners in medicine increased from 9.0 to 12.0 percent, those in pharmacy almost doubled

Table 2

Representation of women in first year enrollment and among total practitioners of preponderantly male health occupations[a]

	1970		Early 1980s	
	Percentage of women in first year enrollment	Percentage of women practitioners	Percentage of women in first year enrollment	Percentage of women practitioners
Allopathic medicine	9.6	9.0[b]	31.7 (1982–83)	12.2 (1981)
Osteopathic medicine	2.7	7.1	23.9 (1981–82)	6.0 (1983)
Chiropractic	–	8.0	–	11.0 (1982)
Dentistry	2.1	3.0	22.2 (1982–83)	3.8 (1982)
Optometry	2.9	4.1	27.0 (1981–82)	6.0 (1982)
Pharmacy	21.6	12.0	47.3 (1980–81)	21.4 (1982)
Podiatry	1.4	9.5	13.0 (1980–81)	5.0 (1980)
Veterinary medicine	10.1	5.7	48.0 (1981–82)	12.3 (1982)
Health administration	14.0	44.7	51.9 (1980–81)	50.8 (1982)

[a]Sources: U.S. Department of Health and Human Services, Bureau of Health Professions. Report to the President and Congress on the Status of Health Personnel in the United States. DHHS Publication No. HRS-P-OD-4, U.S. Government Printing Office, Washington, D.C., May 1984; Sommers, D. Occupational rankings for men and women by earnings. *Monthly Labor Rev.* August 1974, pp. 34–51.
[b]Physicians, medical and osteopathic, 9% female in 1970.

Table 3

Representation of men as percentage of total
practitioners in preponderantly female
health occupations[a]

	Percentage of men in occupation	
	1970	1982
Registered nurses	2.7	4.0
Practical nurses	3.6	3.3
Aide, orderly, attendant	15.2	12.1
Health aide (non-nursing)	15.4	15.5
Clinical lab technician	28.0	24.4
Radiologic technician	32.1	27.1
Dental hygienist	6.0	1.0
Dental assistant	2.1	2.0
Dietitian	8.0	7.3
Health therapists[b]	39.9	23.9[c]
Occupational	NA	6.8
Respiratory	NA	43.6
Physical	NA	28.5
Speech	NA	10.6
Medical record specialist	7.9	8.9
Medical librarian	11.5[d]	16.6
Medical secretary	1.1[e]	0
Medical social worker	34.3[f]	33.6

[a]Sources (unless otherwise noted): For 1970, U.S. Department of Health Education and Welfare. *Minorities and Women in the Health Fields.* DHEW Publication No. (HRA) 76-22. U.S. Government Printing Office, Washington, D.C., pp. 57–58; for 1982, matrix sources, as given in Figure 1.

[b]In the 1970 census, occupation, speech, respiratory, and physical therapists were aggregated into one category–therapist. The individual therapy occupations data are therefore unavailable (NA).

[c]U.S. Department of Labor, Bureau of Labor Statistics. Annual Average Industry and Occupation Tables for year ending December 1983 (unpublished).

[d]U.S. Department of Labor, Bureau of Labor Statistics. Annual Average Industry and Occupation Tables for year ending December 1970 (unpublished).

[e]Sommers, D. Occupational rankings for men and women by earnings. *Monthly Labor Rev.* August 1974, pp. 34–51.

[f]U.S. Department of Labor, Bureau of Labor Statistics. Annual Average Industry and Occupational Tables for year ending December 1971 (unpublished).

from 12.0 to 21.0 percent, and in veterinary medicine they more than doubled from 5.7 to 12.3 percent. Note that women's representation in these occupations should be viewed against an overall female representation of 75 percent in the total health work force. However, a slightly more balanced situation is emerging only in a small number of elite health occupations found in the two upper right-hand cells of Figure 1.

Table 3 presents data on the representation of men in preponderantly female health occupations in 1970 and 1982, showing no progress toward gender balance in occupations that have traditionally been female dominated, i.e., the psychosocial and supporting occupations or somatic-diagnostic and technical occupations with little or no autonomy. Only registered nurses, medical record specialists, and medical librarians have seen small increases in male practitioners. Nursing aides and orderlies, clinical laboratory technicians, radiologic technicians, dietitians, therapists, and others have shown a decline. Thus the move toward greater balance is occurring only at the top of the Health Occupations Hierarchy.

It is clear that, so far, antidiscrimination and affirmative action legislation and policies have addressed only a small part of the problem of gender segregation in the health work force. Progress occurs at a slow pace, and most of the changes have been confined to integration of preponderantly male occupations. Traditionally female fields of employment remain in a status quo of gender imbalance. These occupations comprise by far the numerical majority of female health workers. At the same time, they are the less prestigious jobs in the middle and lower levels of the Health Occupations Hierarchy.

DISCUSSION

Only modest change has occurred in the gender distribution of the health work force. While women have made visible progress in entering a small number of preponderantly male occupations, segregational patterns in the vast majority of female-dominated jobs have persisted. Why has there been so little progress toward balancing the representation of men and women across health occupations in both bureaucratic and nonbureaucratic sectors? Why have the gender disparities in income and educational attainment been reduced so little? One might observe that educational differentials play a causal role in the representational imbalance, with the earnings disparities flowing from the skewed representation of the sexes within and across occupations. But this observation merely raises another set of questions. Do women choose their occupations because they are either attracted to or pushed into female-typed work roles? And why are the educational requirements of female-typed occupations lower than those of male-typed fields?

One could objectively argue that nursing and pharmacy require comparable levels of knowledge, skill, and judgment. Yet pharmacy education has traditionally been a professional program in an academic setting, while the majority of nursing training has occurred in technical/vocational settings, until recently largely in hospitals.

The status and income differential we see between male- and female-dominated occupations are mirrored within male-dominated professions such as medicine. When men choose what we have termed psychosocial specialties, they too tend to be penalized by lower earnings and less status. On a system-wide scale, similar biases are evident in the far greater resources allocated to curative and interventionist strategies relative to prevention and health promotion. Does this imply a set of masculine values so deeply entrenched in the health care system that it is rarely acknowledged or challenged in a male-dominated hierarchy?

Based on this notion, some have expressed the hope that the growing influx of women into medicine and other prestigious health professions will bring a shift in values and beliefs toward a new emphasis on psychosocial healing, prevention, and rehabilitation (15, 16). From a different perspective, the influence of female physicians has been seen as a welcome impetus toward cost containment, on the supposition that women would be more willing to accept subordinate roles and lower pay. "They may be the salvation of the health-care system," according to Dr. Richard Restak (17).

It is not unreasonable to expect that the health care system will place greater emphasis on prevention, rehabilitation, health promotion, and social support systems in response to changing patterns of morbidity and to the growing numbers of the elderly in the population. The rate of this response to demographic and other system-wide change will be hastened to the extent that female health workers, both those in traditional female-typed occupations and the increasing numbers in high status male-dominated professions, actively seek to affirm and advocate the intrinsic value of what we have called the psychosocial healing functions in health care.

REFERENCES

1. Sekscenski, E. S. The health services industry: A decade of expansion. *Monthly Labor Rev.* 104(5): 9–16, 1981.
2. Navarro, V. Women in health care. *N. Engl. J. Med.* 292(8): 398–402, 1975.
3. Weaver, J. L., and Garrett, S. D. Sexism and racism in the American health care industry: A comparative analysis. *Int. J. Health Serv.* 8(4): 677–703, 1978.
4. Bullough, B., and Bullough, V. L. Sex discrimination in health care. *Nursing Outlook* 23(1): 40–45, 1975.
5. Brown, C. A. Women workers in the health service industry. *Int. J. Health Serv.* 5(2): 173–183, 1975.
6. Epstein, C. I . *Woman's Place*, p. 152. University of California Press, Berkeley, 1970.
7. Wilensky, H. L. Women's work: Economic growth, ideology, structure. *Industrial Relations* 7(3): 235–247, 1968.
8. Oppenheimer, V. K. The sex-labeling of jobs. *Industrial Relations* 7(3): 219–234, 1968.
9. Fuchs, V. et al. The distribution of earnings in health and other industries. *J. Hum. Resources* 5(3): 382–389, 1970.

10. Mick, S. S. Understanding the persistence of human resource problems in health. *Milbank Mem. Fund Q.* 56(4): 463–499, 1978.
11. Kissick, W. L. Health manpower in transition. *Milbank Mem. Fund Q.* 46(1) (Part 2): 53–90, 1968.
12. Butter, I. et al. *Sex and Status: Hierarchies in the Health Workforce.* American Public Health Association, Washington, D.C., 1985.
13. Strelnick, H. and Younge, R. Double Indemnity: The Poverty and Mythology of Affirmative Action in the Health Professional Schools. A Health/PAC Special Report. Health Policy Advisory Center, New York, 1980.
14. Reskin, B. F. Sex segregation in the workplace. In *Gender at Work: Perspectives on Occupational Segregation and Comparable Worth,* pp. 6–7. A Publication of Women's Research and Education Institute, Washington, D.C., 1984.
15. Howell, M. Can we be feminist physicians? Mirages, dilemmas and traps. *J. Health Politics Policy Law* 2(2): 168–172, 1977.
16. Bluestone, N. R. The future impact of women physicians on American medicine. *Am. J. Public Health* 68(8): 760–763, 1978.
17. Restak, R. We need doctors we can pay less and boss more—namely women. *Washington Post National Weekly Edition,* May 26, 1986, p. 23.

CHAPTER 5

Community Care Policies and Gender Justice

Suzanne E. England*, Sharon M. Keigher,
Baila Miller, and Nathan L. Linsk

> *When men and women are given the opportunity and the capacity to choose, then justice is possible.*
>
> D. Kirp, M. Yudof, and M. Franks, *Gender Justice*, 1986

What is the proper role of government in family care for the ill and disabled elderly? The question raises the thorny policy conflict between the public's concern with the needs of a dependent population and the presumed right of families to decide most matters privately, without interference by the State. Family-provided and other "informal" (i.e., unpaid) care of the dependent elderly is largely structured along gender lines, with women providing most of the personal and health-related care for elderly relatives. The feminized structure of family caregiving raises issues of equity because, in order to fulfill what can be viewed as both a private and a public responsibility, women must often forego other opportunities and the freedom to make choices that may be critical to their well-being.

In the United States, the debate about policies to support or encourage family and informal caregiving has largely ignored the issue of gender. The issues are most often framed in terms of the need to reduce or control public expenditures and to design policies that achieve a "proper balance" between incentives and disincentives to families to provide care [see, for example, Burwell (1)] . With a few notable exceptions (2–4), discussion of these policies, which fall under the general rubric of community care policy, tends to assume that the processes and outcomes of these policies are gender neutral.

*Formerly Suzanne E. Osterbusch

Originally published in the *International Journal of Health Services* 17(2): 217–232, 1987.

The conceptualization of community care policy options must extend to include the gender structure of family caregiving and the effect of these policies on women who are the spouses, daughters, and other relatives of ill and disabled elderly persons. The social dynamics underlying present community care policies are rooted in traditional concepts about the family, women, and the responsibility of the State. These concepts have generally supported a laissez-faire approach to family caregiving, including an appropriate concern for preserving the liberty of the family to make its own decisions about allocating carer tasks. However, the privacy of these decisions is largely illusory. The capacity of women to freely choose caring is severely limited by the paucity of caregiving alternatives and the constriction of their choices elsewhere.

The assumptions underlying present policies arise from a social system in which, despite much-heralded change, women as a class remain at an economic disadvantage. Socialized to accept the caregiver role, and finding fewer opportunities in the workplace, their choices are further limited by services that are fragmented and difficult to obtain. Policies that accept this constriction of choice are supported by a political climate that regards the marketplace as an efficient and sufficient mechanism for distributing services to families. The result is that nothing is being done to protect carers from the undue risks to which they are exposed, and many women are left with no choice but to provide care.

The design and implementation of policies that affect family care of the elderly must take into account how policies foster inequities. Because family caregiving is feminized, government policies should be organized in such a way as to assure "gender justice" (5) by providing support that promotes the capacity of both sexes to make life choices unhampered by limitations rooted in sexual stereotypes.

Most analyses of community care policy options assume that the policies have been developed and implemented without gender bias. In this chapter, we challenge those assumptions by analyzing the relationship between community care policy and the gender structure of caregiving, and by explicating two major dynamics:

1. The interaction of community care policy provisions with the gender structure of family caregiving, which results in heavy dependence on the unpaid labor of female family members.
2. The inequities for women, which result from the current emphasis on controlling costs by restricting supportive services and benefits.

The intent of our analysis is threefold: to examine community care policies from a perspective of gender justice; to direct attention to the needs of carers and to the social costs of neglecting these needs; and to suggest a direction for future policy development.

DYNAMICS OF COMMUNITY CARE POLICY AND GENDER

Assumptions Underlying Present Policies

Our perspective is similar to that of the symbolic interactionists, who view social policy as "constructed" from social negotiations and based on cultural assumptions (6). Present community care policies are derived from a general acceptance of an interrelated set of assumptions, as outlined in the left-hand column of Table 1. The basic policy model is the welfare safety net in which government-supported care is the "last resort" for families.

The safety net approach has meant that elders (not their carers) qualify for benefits according to need as defined by lack of income or resources. By excluding as many persons as possible, and limiting benefits to the minimum needed for survival outside a nursing home, costs are "saved." Underlying the present community care model is the fear—so far unsubstantiated by research—that people will cease or reduce their own efforts and let the government take over. Apparently, this so-called "substitution effect" is of central concern to those who develop the Medicaid regulations at the U.S. Department of Health and Human Services (HHS) and at the Office of Management and Budget. According to a report in the *Washington Post,* officials from both agencies based their restrictions on Medicaid coverage of home care on the belief that new or extended benefits would just substitute government money for the home care now being provided "free" by relatives and friends (7).

Also underlying present policies is the concern that even programs designed to help only those who would otherwise have to live in a nursing home would bring numbers of people "out of the woodwork" to apply for them (7). In fear of the "woodwork effect," Congress imposed two major restrictions on Medicaid. First, a state cannot provide Medicaid-funded home care benefits unless HHS agrees to waive normal Medicaid rules—hence the term Medicaid waivers; and second, to prevent the states from making home care an entitlement program, a ceiling was imposed so that per capita costs can be no higher than if the waiver were not granted.

By supporting home-based care only as a lower-cost substitute for institutional care, the Medicaid waiver-related policies shape programs to limit payment for home support solely to those who are so ill or disabled as to be eligible for nursing home care. A key concept of these community care policies is that the target for benefits should meet the "but for" criterion, as in "this person would be in a nursing home 'but for' the services provided by the community care program" (8). The "but for" approach discounts the unpaid caregiving of friends and relatives from the total amount of benefits to be paid. Thus, an elderly person without friends and family available to provide care will receive a higher benefit than an equally disabled person who is receiving care from family members. This family

Table 1

Comparison of assumptions of present community care policies with policies to maximize gender justice

Policy dimensions	Assumptions	
	Present policies	Policies to maximize gender justice
Basic policy model	Community care is welfare e.g., a safety net	Community care must be a social utility, like public education
	It must be rationed and means-tested	It should be available according to a broadened definition of need
	Only the minimum benefits should be given	Equal access should be provided through income support, availability of goods and services, and, when appropriate, compensated family care
	Government-supported care should be the "last resort"	Public provision should be the foundation for care
Locus of responsibility	Care of the elderly is a family responsibility	Care of dependent individuals is a responsibility shared by family and government
	Government's only responsibility is to fill the gap	Most families provide as much care as they can
	Families should exhaust their own resources before turning to the government for help	Many families need government help to carry on
	Government-assisted care should not substitute for unpaid family care	Government help is an add-on rather than a substitute for family care
Values	Women are the primary caregivers in the family	Women are not obliged to be the primary caregivers in the family
	Women are responsible for the direct care of dependent members of the family, even if they have to give up other roles	Men and women family members should be equally free to choose between caregiving and other roles
	It is more important for men to realize their full economic potential than it is for women	Women are entitled to realize their full economic potential

	Family care is a "private good"	Family care is a "social good"
	The State's primary responsibility to the family is to assure freedom from State intrusion	In addition to freedom *from* intrusion, the State should assure the freedom *to* provide care, by making the necessary resources available
	Families, not society, benefit from family care	Families contribute to society by providing care
	Most family care is not compensable	Family care is compensable
Target of benefits	The impaired individual at highest risk is the sole target	Those too ill or disabled to be helped effectively by the health care system alone and those who care for them are the targets
	Those with available family carers need fewer services	Over-burdened caregivers need service and support
	Those without available family qualify for government help	Those with family qualify for government help
Objectives	Avoid or delay institutionalization as a way to curtail costs to the government	Provide support for family care and protection to family carers
	Encourage families to provide care	Integrate family care into a continuum of services and programs
	Maintain the "balance" between family and government care, that is, let families "pay the first dollar"	Provide cash transfers to elders and/or their carers
Cost-benefit concerns	Benefits are measured by savings to taxpayers first and the welfare of caregivers last	Benefits are measured by family and community welfare
	Benefits or incentives to caregivers would bring caregivers "out of the woodwork" and drive up costs	There is no evidence of the "woodwork effect"; initial increase in cost may be due to pent-up demand but costs will probably level off
	Family-provided care saves government money because it does not cost anything	Family stress from unsupported caregiving burden can result in costs to the community
	The costs borne by families are not accounted for, even if they become public costs in the future	Women presently bear an inequitable share of the social and economic costs of caregiving

care is not calculated as a direct contribution to the program, nor are the family caregivers accorded any recognition or provided any compensation for their services.

The assumption underlying present policies is that the costs incurred by families in providing care are not a critical factor in the decision to place a relative in a nursing home and therefore are of no concern to government. One estimate of the total cost to individual carers was $18 billion dollars in 1979 (9). A pilot project in Maryland found that families were making a significant monetary contribution toward providing care and that subsidized families reported an increased capacity to cope and higher levels of life satisfaction (10).

Interaction of Policies with the Feminized Structure of Family Care

Policies designed to avoid the costs of institutionalization by providing for home-based services to those elderly who are at risk of placement in nursing homes affect mainly those areas of caregiving associated with health problems, difficulties with self-care, and relatively severe limitations in mobility and activities of daily living. These are the areas of family caregiving that are the most sex-segregated (3, 11). Because functionally impaired elderly men are much more likely than functionally impaired women to be married (12), the burden on wives is especially great. In addition to the greater likelihood that they will be less well off financially, they tend to provide care for the more disabled elderly (13), over longer periods of time (14), with fewer outside sources of assistance (15), and at a greater risk to their own health and well-being (16, 17).

It has been demonstrated that the relative involvement of adult sons and daughters in the care of an elderly parent is influenced by the nature of the caregiving tasks performed and certain characteristics of the parent's situation. In a study by Coward and Rathbone-McCuan (11), adult daughters were eight times more likely to be helping with indoor household chores and personal health care than were adult sons. Adult sons were more likely to be named as helpers with routine household maintenance and repairs. In addition, daughters were more likely to be identified as the caregiver when the parent perceived that his or her health represented a major obstacle to performing the daily tasks of living—the circumstances in which government-supported services come into play for elderly persons with no available family members. This means that many female relatives are providing care that might otherwise be assisted by the government. In policy terms, the presence of an unpaid female carer results in reduced eligibility for services and benefits. Not only are the contributions of these women minimized and unacknowledged by society, but when family caregiving is taken into account in determining eligibility, they and their families are also being indirectly penalized.

Present community care policies ignore the very cornerstone of their construction: the interaction between the economic structural conditions of women's lives and a set of social expectations that devalues and underestimates the care they provide. Indeed, some critics have suggested that "community care" is a euphemism for female members of families (18). Policies based on the assumption that women are and should be available as unpaid caregivers do not legitimize family carers as targets for services or benefits. The inequity of the situation aside, this arrangement is unlikely to survive in the future, when the costs of caregiving will become too great for women who must also work outside the home.

Impact of the Carer Role on Women

The shift to more egalitarian attitudes toward family roles notwithstanding, the care of dependent family members is still largely the responsibility of women (3, 19, 20). Preliminary data from the 1982 National Long Term Care Study indicate that 72 percent of the estimated 2.3 million persons providing unpaid care to the 1.2 million noninstitutionalized frail elderly were wives or adult daughters (21).

There is some evidence that economic position may influence the caregiving role, with lower income and less attachment to the paid labor force being associated with greater likelihood of being the provider of care. Archbold's (22) phenomenological study of adult daughter carers found that the more affluent "career woman" daughters were more likely to be involved with a dependent parent as a "care manager," while less economically well-off daughters were more likely to be providing direct care. In a micro-analysis of caregiver selection, Ikels (23) concluded that all other things being equal, if two candidates for carer are employed, the one with the least-paying job or the most marginal participation in the labor force is selected. This suggests that families may use a form of cost-benefit analysis, assigning caregiving roles to the member whose wages are lower and therefore more "disposable." Given the differential between the incomes of men and women, it is most likely the woman who will be expected to leave the paid work force to stay home with the relative or modify her paid work in ways that compromise her earning power. If the choice is between two women, the woman who is less attached to the labor force is more likely to find herself with the major caregiving responsibilities.

The "division of caring labor" within the family has both social and economic implications for women. The demands on one's time when responsible for the performance of indoor household chores, personal care, health care, and simply "being there" tend to be daily and ongoing, whereas household maintenance, helping with finances, etc., can be scheduled so as not to interfere with other role demands. Women, by being involved in the time-intensive tasks of caring, more frequently report stress and burden in terms of "lack of discretionary or leisure time" and conflicts with other demands at work or from other family members (22). The tasks of caring that are most likely to be performed by women—personal care and body contact tasks—are most strongly associated with perceived burden by caregivers (24). The responsibility that women take on when they carry out these indoor, personal, and health-related care tasks carries with it losses in other important areas of their lives.

Women, who continue to be economically disadvantaged as a class, lose more ground as individuals when they take on caring responsibilities. They lose wages by interrupting their employment or settling for lower paid work that fits into their caregiving schedule. Women who cannot work outside the home because of caregiving responsibilities, or who are simultaneously employed and attempting to care for an elderly relative, are at increased risk of economic dependency. Data from the survey of caregivers that was conducted as part of the 1982 National Long Term Care Study (4) document these risks: 14 percent of the wives and 12 percent of the daughters were forced to leave their jobs because of caregiving responsibilities; and of those who remained employed during their caregiver experience, 22 percent had taken time off from work (without pay) to provide care. Brody's (25) study of families providing care to an elderly relative found that 28 percent of the women who were staying home to care for their mothers said they had quit work for that purpose. A similar percentage of the women who were employed said that they had reduced their working hours or were considering quitting. In her review of the research on family caregiving, Horowitz (26) concluded that the impact of caregiving on the ability to work is substantial for significant numbers of carers.

A survey of workers in a large corporation found that of the employees who reported that they were caring for an elderly relative—some at levels exceeding 30 hours per week—women were much more likely than men to be the primary providers of care (27). The average amount of time per week that the women employees were providing direct care was reported as 16.1 hours, whereas the males reported an average of only 5.3 hours (27, p. 7). Most of these women reported that the combination of work and caregiving interfered with other family responsibilities and social and emotional needs. Despite the conventional wisdom that employment draws women from caregiving roles, it appears that it draws men much more than women. The employee survey found that in addition to the disparity between the overall caregiving responsibilities reported by men and women, men reported relying more heavily on outside help or their spouses to provide the primary care (27, p. 7).

Many women apparently struggle with the dual roles of employee and caregiver. Stoller (20), for example, found that employment significantly decreased the hours of assistance provided by sons, but not by daughters. Others have found that while women who are employed may produce fewer hours of direct care than those who are not, the level of total care received by the elderly person is not affected by the employment status of the primary carer (28, 29). There is even evidence that the parents of employed daughters may be at an advantage in that, in addition to receiving levels of care similar to those with nonworking daughters, they are also more likely to receive financial help (26).

Warshaw and associates (30) report that many female employees are involved in providing care for elderly relatives. For these women, the strain of caregiving on role performance at work can result in excessive absences, lowered productivity, and less job security. What has not been reported, but is an obvious cost to these women, is the reduction in their opportunities to get additional training or education or to take on additional work responsibilities that could result in advancement and/or higher pay.

The interruption and compromising of their work lives by caregiving responsibilities contributes to women's overrepresentation in the "secondary" labor market in which workers receive low wages and few benefits. For many women, the "tri-cycle" of caregiving begins when they have children, is renewed when a parent becomes ill, and again when their aging spouse needs care. As a result of job segregation, discrimination, and role expectations, most women reach retirement age with significantly lower benefits, asset income, and pension protection than men (31).

The research to date strongly supports the proposition that much of family caregiving is structured along gender lines, with women providing more of the caring overall and doing more of the personal and health-related tasks that tend to be daily and ongoing and associated with greater perceived burden. Although research has yet to adequately document the nature and extent of the social and economic costs to families and individual carers, there is sufficient evidence that many family caregivers, most of whom are women, are incurring the costs of lost or reduced opportunities in the workplace and elsewhere. These costs are likely to have a lasting impact on them, their families, and society.

GENDER JUSTICE AND
PRESENT COMMUNITY CARE POLICIES

Medicare/Medicaid

Because the major purpose of present community care policies is to avoid the government expense of providing institutional care, present policies and programs for community care of the elderly, particularly those tied to state Medicaid waivers, depend heavily on the unpaid care provided in the home by relatives. The hidden sexist bias of Medicaid policies, perhaps the most pervasive and far-reaching of the policies that affect care of the elderly, has recently been recognized in the courts and by recent changes in state policies regarding "spend-down" requirements. The bias may be seen by examining both the impact of Medicaid policies and the efforts to provide financial incentives to families.

An example of the problem was described in an article in *The New York Times* about Bertha Hafner, 75, who was left so impoverished by the spend down that

Medicaid required before it would provide payment for nursing-home care for her husband that she was left with no alternative but to sue him for support (32). Because New York law did not allow the inclusion of the spouse's living expenses in the calculation of Medicare spend-down requirements, suing was Mrs. Hafner's only means of securing some income to keep her from being forced to live in poverty. Mrs. Hafner, like most women of her generation who married, was dependent on her husband's pension and social security, yet was considered by law to be financially responsible for her spouse and required to pay for his nursing home costs out of their joint income. For her and others in her position who carried out the traditional responsibilities of homemaker and mother, the economic costs of resorting to institutional care for a husband are potentially devastating. Many have spent months and years taking care of their husbands at home, yet when it becomes necessary to use institutional care, their contribution to saving Medicaid costs is not acknowledged.

The options that Medicaid's present rules leave for women whose spouses need long-term care are: (*a*) spend down to poverty level in order to be eligible, (*b*) divorce or sue for support, (*c*) quit work to provide full time care, or (*d*) pay for care (2). Each option puts these women at risk of poverty and permanent economic dependency. In apparent recognition of this inequity, several states have recently changed or are considering changing their spend-down requirements so that these wives are not left destitute.

Other dilemmas exist for the women who provide most of the informal care for the estimated 5.2 million elderly disabled Americans who remain in the community (19). Many of the same women who are caught in the spend-down problem have spent years taking care of their ill and disabled husbands at home, receiving little or nothing in the way of services or compensation for the care they provided during those years. The small minority [estimated at 15 percent by Macken (12)] who do receive publicly-supported services to help care for their relatives are constrained by Medicare-related community care policies that limit the services to the minimum amount of additional care that is needed to prevent institutionalization.

Such cases highlight a major issue concerning the impact of policies for long-term care of the elderly on female carers. Policies to promote home-based informal care for ill and disabled elderly that are driven by concerns of controlling costs on an individual-by-individual basis actually constrict the choices of the elderly and their carers, and in so doing, have the potential to reduce the capacity of families to provide adequate care. Those provisions that attempt to control costs by limiting eligibility and rationing benefits raise the threshold of access to services and benefits to heights that require many elders and their carers to choose between no support and total support. The feminized structure of caregiving means that women may be reduced to choosing between providing all of the care or none of it.

Compensation for Family Caregiving

One approach to reducing some of the inequities of community care is to provide some form of compensation for family caregiving. At present, there are three types of community care policies that have potential for compensating family carers: the federal Child and Dependent Care Credit that provides a benefit to families through a tax credit; various state community care programs that allow in one way or another for direct payments to family members for some portion of the care they provide; and the Veterans' Administration's Aid and Attendance Allowance.

Child and Dependent Care Credit. The Child and Dependent Care Credit is the least adequate of these mechanisms for compensating family members who provide direct care. At present the credit is not refundable and therefore of no benefit to families who owe no taxes or do not itemize deductions. For example, it has been estimated that in 1981 only 6 percent of the credits—including credits for child care as well as care for elderly family members—went to families with incomes below $10,000 (33). The result is that many low-income families, which are predominantly headed by women, derive no benefit from the program.

In addition to these and other problems that limit the distribution of the benefit, the tax credit[1] does not presently benefit families unless all taxpayers in the household are gainfully employed. Women who are not employed outside the home, or who prefer to leave or reduce their employment to provide some or all of the care themselves, are not eligible for the credit. The credit, which differs from a deduction in that it reduces the taxpayer's total tax liability, is only for expenditures for care, not for direct care provided by a relative. Although it may enable some women and men to continue to work outside the home, the subsidy, which ranges from 20 to 30 percent of the expenditures up to a maximum of $2,400 (1), may not be a sufficient incentive to families who are deciding between the benefits of the subsidy and having a member of the family (usually a woman) leave employment to stay home and provide the needed care. In an analysis of the benefits of current tax provisions for offsetting a family's costs for caregiving, Perlman (34) concluded that, because the provisions take into account only a small part of the family's actual effort and exclude all unpaid work by family members, they are "woefully inadequate."

State Policies. Similar problems exist with state-level policies that allow some family members to receive payment for the care that they provide. In a recent study of state policies on paid family caregiving, Linsk, Keigher, and Osterbusch

---

[1]When signed into law, the recent revision of the tax code will apparently retain the credit, but, because the tax bill as a whole represents a significant shift away from using the tax code as a means of social change, it is now unlikely that the tax credit will be extended beyond its present limits.

(35) found that some provisions for payment to family members were made by at least 34 states and the District of Columbia. Only 13 states clearly prohibited reimbursement or payment to relatives for care.

While state policies vary widely in the amount of benefit and the eligibility of family members to receive payment, most tend to provide a benefit based on the gap between the informal care already provided and the care necessary to keep the elderly person from being institutionalized. Medicaid regulations restrict payment for personal care to those who are not members of the recipient's family, but some states have used other definitions of the family or service, and other sources of funding to circumvent this policy.

Some states take the restriction against paying relatives to mean those related to the recipient while others, such as Illinois, deny eligibility only to those family members who are "financially responsible" for the recipient. When the "financially responsible" definition is used, the regulations usually deny payment to spouses. The denial of eligibility to spouses tends to affect more wives than husbands since impaired elderly males are far more likely to be married than are elderly females (12).

Many states have programs other than Medicaid that place less stringent limits on the payment of relatives (1, 35). All but two states provide supplementation to Supplemental Security Insurance (SSI), which clients can spend at their own discretion. In most cases these payments are not sufficient to benefit caregivers. Of the 25 states that administer their own supplementation program, payment levels vary greatly from state to state, with lows of $10 in Utah and $20 in Wyoming to highs of $294 in Indiana and $248 in North Carolina (36). The study by Linsk and associates (35) reported provisions for payments to relatives ranging from virtually no restrictions on the eligibility of relatives to receive payment, to requirements that carers meet welfare income guidelines. Other restrictions tend to severely limit the eligibility of family carers, including payment only if no other home help is available; payment to family members only if they had to give up employment; licensing of carers; and requirements that the carer must be employed by a provider agency.

Aid and Attendance Allowance for Veterans. The Veterans' Administration's Aid and Attendance Allowance allocates an amount based on need to the elderly person who may use the funds to pay someone for care provided. This can be used to compensate family caregivers. By allowing veterans to employ relatives, the program gives eligible families decision-making power regarding distribution of the benefit. The benefit is set according to the disability level rather than unmet need and allows a measure of freedom to families. The Allowance is discounted by dollar amounts contributed by other sources but not by the in-kind contributions of friends and relatives. Moreover, surviving spouses are also eligible for the benefit. Although the benefit is not tied to the care giving relationship, the allowance is a more equitable approach than those that indirectly penalize families who provide a carer. Of the existing approaches to compensating family carers, the Aid and Attendance Allowance is a relatively unobtrusive method of cash transfer and no doubt does more than other approaches to reduce the caregiving burden on wives and other family carers.

Trends

Profound demographic and social changes threaten the present social contract between families and society. Changes in family roles and expectations, the increasing attachment of women to the labor force, the increase in the ratio of dependent elderly to available family members (2), and the advent of prospective payment for medical care combine to put more strain on the entire long-term care system. Women and their families will experience increasing conflict as women make choices and compromises in their dual roles as caregivers and breadwinners. Many families will rely upon community services or nursing homes, or be forced to "make do," in effect neglecting the needs of their older relatives. Others may suffer from the consequences of women being unable to realize their full economic potential. Many are risking permanent financial dependency due to the demands of providing care in a context of competing family and employment demands. When these social and personal costs are taken into account, traditional models of community care become inadequate.

Among the options currently being considered are policies and programs that are thought to act as incentives for families to continue to provide care. These include (1):

- Expansion and formalization of state policies and programs to allow family members to be paid as Medicare providers.
- Changes in the dependent tax credit that would expand eligibility criteria for the credit, increase the level of the credit to compensate family care costs, and expand the types of care expenses that could be claimed.
- Caregiver leave and dependent-care benefits as employee benefits.
- Requirements that families contribute toward the care of their elderly members.

The latter so-called "family responsibility" policies have ominous implications for women. Policies that attempt to define and prescribe the role of the family in providing care would pressure families, especially low-income women, to take on caring tasks, irrespective of personal resources or needs of either the carer or care recipient. The social and individual costs of policies that coerce families into caregiving would fall most heavily on those least able to bear them.

Policies to provide benefits to caregivers are one way to address the question of how to maintain the family caregiving effort in a changing environment. Although some form of compensation to carers is certainly fairer than no compensation at all, the basic intent of these policies remains reducing government costs. The inequities are still not addressed, because the benefits do nothing to lower the threshold of access to alternative forms of care, or to compensate carers for the opportunities they forego by taking on caregiving responsibilities.

POLICIES TO MAXIMIZE GENDER JUSTICE

Changing the Assumptions

What is necessary is development of policies based on a different set of assumptions about family and community care. The right-hand column of Table 1 summarizes these assumptions. The central model for community care policies that would maximize gender justice is that of the social utility—a universally available array of supports to dependent adults to which families would have access as needed. Direct cash transfers to elders and/or their carers would be an integral part of such a system. Instead of attempting to ensure family responsibility by requiring families to participate in care, government would provide the resources necessary to enable families to respond adequately to the needs of their elderly members. The present approach, which pressures families with the entire caregiving burden until they break down to the point of "eligibility" for government support, is not only mean-spirited; it is inevitably a more costly alternative (37).

The values underlying community care policies are shifting somewhat as sex role expectations change. There is evidence that the needs of the elderly and their families are being increasingly recognized. Public opinion tends to support increased access to community care even if it means tax increases (38). Sheppard and Kosberg (39) report that a majority of their public opinion poll respondents still believed in 1981 that government should assume more responsibility for the elderly. However, family-provided care continues to be regarded as a "private good." Without an acknowledgment that family-provided care is a "social good"—a contribution to society made by women and men who often incur substantial personal, economic, and social costs—benefits to carers will continue to be minimal.

The cost-benefit concerns of community care policies that would maximize gender justice differ from the present concern with avoiding the costs of institutionalization. Policies to maximize gender justice would take into account the needs of the elderly who are disabled and ill but not necessarily at risk of placement in a nursing home. Research indicates that those who are placed in nursing homes are a much smaller and substantially different population than those who are cared for in their communities, suggesting that more effective targeting to meet the "but for" criteria could lead to higher costs for screening and less efficient programs (40). The evidence is that when community care is available, it is used more as an add-on than as a substitute for nursing home care, and it may be cheaper to extend home-care benefits and serve the very sickest and most dependent patients in nursing homes (37, 40).

Although research on the substitution effect is somewhat contradictory because the question is posed differently in different studies, there is little evidence to support concern that community care would substitute for family efforts (26). The results from the Channeling Demonstration, which tested the feasibility and cost-effectiveness of alternative community-based long-term care service delivery, show that formal interventions did not significantly reduce the amount and type of informal care provided to clients (1). There is also evidence that when formal services are used, families continue to provide the major portion of the care (29). They seek support in the form of respite, help with very highly impaired elders, or with selected tasks (26) rather than total relief from caregiving. In her review of the research on the substitution effect, Horowitz concluded that "the provision of formal services does not significantly reduce the previous level of care provided by family caregivers" (26, p. 224).

Contrary to the fears of policymakers (7), there is no evidence to date that carers will come "out of the woodwork" just because a benefit is available. Based on the findings of Montgomery and Hatch (14) who reported a low level of participation by families in a respite care program, the more appropriate metaphor might be "beating the bushes" (35). There is, however, evidence of a relationship between level of carer stress and the use of community services, with higher levels of care need being associated with greater use of community services. Bass and Noelker (41) found that elders whose primary caregivers were experiencing greater burden and stress effects from providing care were using more in-home community services. Even when elder need was controlled, caregiver need explained a significant portion of the variance in the elder's use of services. These results directly contradict the assumptions of present policies which determine need based on the individual recipient, not the recipient's informal helpers.

Several researchers (37, 40) have concluded that, if the definition of need were extended beyond the highly impaired individual in need of nursing home care, an integrated continuum of services based on functional disability could be cost-effective. The Canadian experience as documented by Rosalie and Robert Kane (37) led them to conclude that a very desirable package of services can be offered at about 10 percent of the nursing home budget, and the presence of an alternative system of care makes it both politically and economically feasible to restrict the growth of the institutional sector. Kane and Kane found that "despite the fear . . . that expanded home care benefits might lead to runaway use, the Canadian experience shows a consistent pattern of demand leveling off after about three years" (37, p. 1362).

Other analysts have suggested that home- and community-based care has been oversold as a way of controlling long-term costs (8, 40). Weissert's review of a decade of research on the cost-effectiveness of community care led him to conclude that "few who use home- and community-based services would otherwise have been longstayers in nursing homes" (40, p. 423). He proposes that an alternative to the cost–savings rationale for community care is one which would recognize that those not sick enough to be placed in a nursing home but too sick and otherwise too dependent to be helped by the existing episodic and medically oriented health care system—and their caregivers—are deserving of help.

CONCLUSIONS

Private family decisions about caregiving roles are not within the purview of public policy, nor should they be. Government's role is to assure that those who contribute to society by providing care to dependents have the full opportunity to choose that role free from coercion. Adequate and accessible supports to families, which include, when appropriate, compensation to family carers commensurate with that paid to others who provide comparable care, provides the capacity to choose.

The inequities and hidden personal costs associated with unpaid care cannot be fully rectified by changes in community care policies alone. Related issues of gender justice, including the distribution of social security benefits and the treatment of wives by the tax code [see Kirp and associates (5) for a discussion of these issues], directly affect the equity of remedies. Broader issues related to employment and economic opportunity also affect the ultimate outcome of community care policies designed to be gender-neutral, and even those policies that would maximize gender justice cannot replace necessary government programs for housing, income, health care, and transportation. However, by reexamining these policies from a perspective that acknowledges the fact and impact of the feminized structure of informal care, we can devise alternatives that preserve the freedom of individuals to choose to provide care by providing the support that is essential to that freedom.

REFERENCES

1. Burwell, B. O. *Shared Obligations: Public Policy Influences on Family Care for the Elderly*. Medicaid program evaluation working paper 2.1. U.S. Department of Health and Human Services, Health Care Financing Administration, Office of Research and Demonstration, Washington, D.C., May 1986.
2. Estes, C. L., Gerard, L. E., and Clarke, A. Women and the economics of aging. In *Readings in the Political Economy of Aging,* edited by M. Minkler and C. L. Estes, pp. 75–93. Baywood Publishing, Farmingdale, N.Y., 1984.
3. Brody, E. M. "Women in the middle" and family help to older people. *Gerontologist* 21(5): 471–480, 1981.
4. Stone, R., Cafferata, G. L., and Sangl, J. *Caregivers of the Elderly: A National Profile.* Paper presented at the 32nd Annual Meeting of the American Society on Aging, San Francisco, March 1986.
5. Kirp, D. L., Yudof, M. G., and Franks, M. S. *Gender Justice*. University of Chicago Press, Chicago, 1986.

6. Estes, C. L., and Edmonds, B. C. Symbolic interaction and social policy analysis. *Symbolic Interaction* 4(1): 75–85, 1981.
7. Rich, S. The home-care debate. *The Washington Post National Weekly Edition,* June 10, 1985, p. 84.
8. Doty, P. *Family Care of the Elderly: The Role of Public Policy.* Office of Legislation and Policy, Health Care Financing Administration, Washington, D.C., 1985.
9. Paringer, L. Forgotten costs of informal long term care. *Generations* 9(4): 55–58, 1985.
10. Whitfield, S., and Krumpholz, B. *Report to the General Assembly on the Family Support System Demonstration Program.* State of Maryland Office on Aging, Baltimore, 1981.
11. Coward, R. T., and Rathbone-McCuan, E. Illuminating the Relative Role of Adult Sons and Daughters in the Long-term Care of their Parents. Paper presented at the 1985 Professional Symposium of the National Association of Social Workers, Chicago, November 1985.
12. Macken, C. *A Profile of Functionally Impaired Persons in the Community* (draft report). Health Care Financing Administration, Office of Research and Demonstration, Washington, D.C., 1985.
13. Hess, B. B., and Waring, J. Family relationships of older women: A women's issue. In *Older Women: Issues and Prospects,* edited by E. W. Markson. Lexington Books, Lexington, Mass., 1983.
14. Montgomery, R. J. V., and Hatch, L. R. The feasibility of volunteers and families forming a partnership for caregiving. In *Families and Long Term Care,* edited by T. H. Brubaker. Sage Publications, Beverly Hills, Cal., 1986.
15. Johnson, C., and Catalana, D. A longitudinal study of family supports to impaired elderly. *Gerontologist* 23(2): 612–618, 1983.
16. Cantor, M. H. Strain among caregivers: A study of experience in the United States. *Gerontologist* 23(6): 597–604, 1983.
17. Noelker, L. S., and Wallace, R. W. The organization of family care for impaired elderly. *J. Mar. Fam. Issues* 6: 23–44, 1985.
18. Greater London Council Women's Committee. *Community Care and Women as Carers—Revised Report.* Report submitted to the Greater London Council, London, 1984.
19. Day, A. *Who Cares? Demographic Trends Challenge Family Care for the Elderly.* Population Trends and Public Policy No. 9. Population Reference Bureau, Washington, D.C., 1985.
20. Stoller, E. P. Parental caregiving by adult children. *J. Mar. Fam* 45(4): 851–858, 1983.
21. Stone, R. The Feminization of Poverty and Older Women: An Update. Paper presented at the 113th Annual Meeting of the American Public Health Association, Washington, D.C., November 1985.
22. Archbold, P. G. Impact of parent-caring on women. *Fam. Relations* 32(1): 39–45, 1983.
23. Ikels, C. The process of caretaker selection. *Res. Aging* 5: 491–510, 1983.
24. Hooyman, N., Gonyea, J., and Montgomery, R. The impact of in-home services termination on family caregivers. *Gerontologist* 25(2): 141–145, 1985.
25. Brody, E. M. Parent care as a normative family stress. *Gerontologist* 25: 19–29, 1985.
26. Horowitz, A. Family caregiving to the frail elderly. *Annu. Rev. Gerontol. Geriatrics* 5: 194–246, 1985.
27. Ball, G. T., and Greenberg, B. *The Travelers Employee Caregiver Survey.* The Travelers Companies, Personnel Research, Personnel Services Division, Personnel-Administration Department, Hartford, Conn., 1985.

28. Brody, E. M., and Schoonover, C. B. Patterns of parent-care when adult daughters work and when they do not. *Gerontologist* 26(4): 372–381, 1986.
29. Arling, G., and McCauley, W. J. The feasibility of public payments to family caregiving. *Gerontologist* 23: 300–306, 1983.
30. Warshaw, L. J. et al. Employer Support for Employee Caregivers. Paper presented at the 113th Annual Meeting of the American Public Health Association, Washington, D.C., November 1985.
31. Minkler, M., and Stone, R. The feminization of poverty and older women: An update. *Gerontologist* 25(4): 351–357, 1985.
32. Sullivan, R. Nursing costs force elderly to sue spouses. *The New York Times*, March 6, 1986, pp. 1, 17.
33. U.S. House of Representatives, Select Committee on Children, Youth and Families. *Demographic and Social Trends: Implications for Federal Support of Dependent-Care Services for Children and the Elderly.* U.S. Government Printing Office, Washington, D.C., December 1983.
34. Perlman, R. Use of the tax system in home care: A brief note. *Home Health Care Serv. Q.* 3(34): 280–283, 1982.
35. Linsk, N., Keigher, S., and Osterbusch, S. E. *Paid Family Caregiving: A Policy Option.* Final Report to the Illinois Association of Family Service Agencies. University of Illinois at Chicago, Department of Medical Social Work, Chicago, 1986.
36. Social Security Administration, U.S. Department of Health and Human Services. Current operating statistics. *Soc. Secur. Bull.* 48(8): 72, 1985.
37. Kane, R. L., and Kane, R. A. *A Will and a Way: What the United States can Learn from Canada about Caring for the Elderly.* Columbia University Press, New York, 1985.
38. Harris, L. *Aging in the Eighties.* National Council on Aging, Washington, D.C., 1981.
39. Sheppard, H., and Kosberg, J. I. Public Opinion about the Issues of Public Responsibility for the Aged and Means Testing. Paper presented at the Annual Scientific Meeting of the Gerontology Society of America, New Orleans, November 1985.
40. Weissert, W. G. Seven reasons why it is so difficult to make community care cost-effective. *Health Serv. Res.* 20(4): 421–433, 1985.
41. Bass, D. M., and Noelker, L. The Influence of Family Caregivers on Elder's Use of In-home Services: An Expanded Conceptual Framework. Paper presented at the Annual Scientific Meeting of the Gerontology Society of America, New Orleans, November 1985.

Section III
The Health of
Women Workers

Double Exposure: The Combined Impact of the Home and Work Environments on Psychosomatic Strain in Swedish Women and Men

Ellen M. Hall

The present investigation addresses a simple question: are working women and men experiencing substantially the same episodes and events in daily life? More specifically, are the structurally determined sources of either stress and/or resources largely the same for women ("worker, parent, and spouse") as for men? And of the patterns observed, which are predictive of psychosomatic strain? Although these may appear to be a rather simple set of questions, there is a good deal of debate about the extent to which the life experiences (and therefore exposures to stress) of men and women are equivalent.

Do underlying biological differences, or differences in socialization and in daily life experience, account for differences in morbidity and mortality? Can one generalize from studies of men and occupational stress to women, or should women be studied separately? When evaluating both men and women in existing populations, should the researcher *control* for sex, *analyze* for sex, or simply *ignore* sex? All of these approaches have been taken in contemporary investigations, but we know little about the influence of each approach upon the results or upon the interpretation of findings. Nor do we know whether the assumptions underlying each approach are useful and valid for purposes of future research.

There continues to be considerable discussion concerning the extent to which the role experiences (and therefore the exposures) of men and women may differ. Pearlin (1) in particular has emphasized that being born a man or a woman influences the structures and their stresses that may be encountered in ordinary

Originally published in the *International Journal of Health Services* 22(2): 239–260, 1992.

life. Pearlin's view is part of an emergent perspective, shared by other investigators such as Moen, Dempster-McClain, and Williams (2), and Aneshensel and Pearlin (3), that emphasizes the need to evaluate the context of any given social role in order to grasp its potential impact on stress and illness processes.

The theoretical concerns underlying this study are drawn from two somewhat distinct research literatures that might be characterized broadly as the "work and stress" and the "gender and role" perspectives. The wealth of literature on stress will not be summarized in this chapter; the impact of stress on human (and animal) functioning has been explored over the last decades using a variety of orientations and approaches: laboratory studies and neuroendocrine research (4–9), field investigations (10, 11), studies of stressful life events (12–15), and investigations of personality (16), of particular groups (17) and mediators (18). Of this literature, studies that include female subjects constitute only a modest proportion of both the quantitative and qualitative research on stress and health.

On the other hand, research concerning the effects of other role domains (such as spouse and parent) on stress and health—indeed, most of the work on multiple roles in general (i.e., the gender and role perspective)—has tended to rely heavily on populations that include women. Before suggesting an integration of these two perspectives, we must briefly review some of their more salient findings.

LITERATURE REVIEW

As discussed in an earlier paper (19), comparatively little is known from within the work and stress perspective about how working life affects women (20, 21), although there is increasing interest in the issue of women and work stress (20–27).

Investigations of the health consequences of multiple role occupancy are comparatively recent and address a concern that the increased entry of women into the labor force would be accompanied by increased stress and related health problems in working wives and mothers. Most of the research has tended to show that the reverse is true: multiple roles can be health-enhancing. Although a number of important large-scale epidemiological studies confirm that health has not been adversely affected by the entry of women into the labor market (24, 28, 29), much of the literature has been concerned with the social and psychological impacts of multiple roles, of stressful life events, and of caring work, with the influence of spouse and/or children on affective responses to home and job, and with a variety of related questions (22, 30–50).

By contrast, the work and stress perspective tends to focus on the impact of psychosocial work organization upon physical health and has generally relied on relatively spare theoretical formulations. Studies of work and stress may be said to accentuate the importance of broad independent factors (such as control over the pace of work), to explore objective occupational conditions, and to rely on large-scale prospective studies as the preferred research design. Perhaps because of its largely biomedical origins, work stress research emphasizes medically significant outcomes, such as increased risk of fatal illness. The ability to demonstrate biological plausibility in linking the independent and dependent variables is taken to be of critical importance as well.

Within this perspective, research focuses on the nature and the content of the employment situation as a set of exposure characteristics. A great deal of attention has been paid to delineating the precise set of key variables that can predict adverse health outcomes (23, 51–72).

However, we cannot rely on this wealth of research to determine with a reasonable degree of certainty whether there are strong and consistent parallels that would allow us to extrapolate from the exposures to psychosocial work conditions and related health outcomes observed in men to exposures and responses that might be occurring in women. Furthermore, it is rare to find studies of occupational stress that address factors such as the marital and parental status of respondents as a set of characteristics that might interact with occupational conditions in producing, reducing, or otherwise influencing the relationship between occupational stress and health.

Within the research on multiple roles, debates and developments along theoretical lines are robust. Researchers have used a variety of qualitative and quantitative measures, including self-report and interviews, in addition to objective measures. Biological plausibility is not particularly emphasized as the *sine qua non* for producing research (1). The sociology of gender and health has emerged as a rather distinct literature with an emphasis different from that encountered in the study of occupational stress. While psychological and other health outcomes may be used as dependent variables, the approach taken to the research is more holistic; investigators are permitted a wider approach, so that discussions of the meaning of work and other epistemological matters (rarely encountered in occupational epidemiology) are considered suitable domains for investigation and discussion (73).

Extensive research from this perspective supports the view that the psychological well-being of women is improved as a result of employment (33, 35, 36, 74, 75). Although it appears that intimate relationships are particularly protective against depression in women, employment is also an important factor in life satisfaction and happiness and in reducing depression (19, 30, 47).

The literature supports the view that employed women have fewer sick days and better self-reported health and psychological well-being than do housewives (21, 22, 26, 76–79). Verbrugge (80, 81) has found that for both women and men, those with the multiple roles of worker, spouse, and parent have the best health. On the other hand, women who are neither employed, married, nor parenting have poor health. Employment has a strong and a consistent tie to good health for women; with marriage the tie is smaller and less consistent, while parenthood differentials are typically small and inconsistent. According to Verbrugge (81), the triple roles of employed worker, spouse, and mother are associated with a positive health profile. Thoits' research (48, 49) supports this *role enhancement* perspective. She found that the acquisition or loss of roles over a two-year period affected the psychological distress of both men and women.

There are, however, suggestions that role strain can lead to overload and related declines in health (44–46, 82–84). For example, the research of Veroff, Douvan, and Kulka (85) suggests that depending on the context, what might be considered social network involvement (providing for the welfare of family and friends) is not invariably health-enhancing and can be stressful for many women.

An increasing number of case studies and other investigations do address the question of the variability in obligations and stresses that occur within particular groups (86). For example, Emmons and coworkers (87) evaluated the particular ways in which married, professional women with young children cope with multiple demands. Sorensen and her colleagues (25) evaluated the impact of both occupational experiences and background variables in a large-scale study of both men and women, and found that occupational stress had few implications for risk of coronary heart disease in either men or women. More recently, in a study comparing work, social support, and well-being in both male and female factory workers, Loscocco and Spitze (27) found few gender differences in the effects of working conditions on well-being. These studies are addressed because it is only recently that studies of multiple roles—whether they are case studies, cross-sectional, or even long-term prospective investigations—have been concerned with the specific conditions found within the domain of both home and work. This brings us to the major concern of the present investigation.

INTRODUCING GREATER SPECIFICITY TO
THE STUDY OF ROLES

While researchers know a great deal about multiple roles, we have little information on the particularities and the nature, duration, and intensity of the stresses involved. For example, simply to determine that someone is employed tells us nothing about the hours, conditions, and hazards of work, or whether the exposure to such a job is part-time or full-time. When a detailed assessment of the activities and requirements of the role is lacking, there is no method for assessing whether the fundamental structures of life are producing moderate, mild, or severe demands upon the subjects. For example, an employed woman who has help with the children through a day-care center is not in the same "wife and mother" situation (even if she has the same roles) as a woman who has the same job, the same number of children, and the same marital status, but who lacks such assistance with child care.

In terms of work "role" some jobs are high in resources and benefits such as control, social status, pay, vacation time, and positive organizational climate. Other jobs are by their very nature stressful and debilitating. When all those who are "employed," irrespective of the nature of the exposures involved, are lumped together, then the *results* of such role research would tend to indicate that there is no adverse effect for employment. Certainly a simple dichotomous employment variable (e.g., yes/no) may include such a wide range of exposures that linkages to health endpoints become blurred.

The strength of the multiple role perspective is that it examines the combined influences of more than one structure of daily life. The strength of the work stress perspective is that it examines one domain in terms of specific exposure properties. Both perspectives are important in assessing the totality of daily life stress. In short, in future there may be interest in increasing both the specificity and the scope of investigations, including not merely larger-scale investigations of mental or physical health, but also deeper investigations of the public and the private domains of the lives of many individuals, perhaps extended to document events and patterns over the course of whole lifetimes.

The present investigation, then, is an attempt at what may be a new approach to research—to extend the understanding of home and work beyond simply considering employment status or role occupancy. This investigation seeks to integrate the advantages of a large-scale investigation with the advantages of a greater specificity in the independent variables.

Research Questions

1. Do men and women engage in substantially the same activities in working life and home life? More precisely, is exposure generally the same for both sexes when engaging in the role of spouse, worker, and parent?

2. Is gender in and of itself a predictive variable for psychosomatic strain when adjusting for home and work characteristics?

3. Do the *individual* effects of home and work characteristics differ for men and women?

4. Do the *combined* effects of simultaneous exposure to these characteristics differ for men and women?

RESEARCH METHODS

Study Sample

The conduct of this large study on work stress and health has been extensively described elsewhere (19, 55, 56). The data were obtained from the Swedish Central Bureau of Statistics' (SCB) Survey of Living Conditions (abbreviated ULF in Swedish). This survey was mandated by Swedish Parliament in the early 1970s and has served since that time as the major social accounting system for Sweden. It was designed to investigate the distribution of social resources such as health, income, work environment, education, and housing. The survey relies on objective data and not on personal opinion. Data are collected annually from a series of systematic random samples of individuals born on the 15th of each month, obtained from the National Registry of Births. Our investigation used the 1977 and 1979 years of the ULF. Response rates were 81 percent in 1977 and 89 percent in 1979. The total sample consisted of 12,772 employed workers between the ages of 20 and 65. The 20-year-old age entry criterion was used because the focus of this study was on the combined impact of home responsibilities and work conditions. The 20-year age limit restricted the study group to those who were more likely to have left the home of their parents and to have established their own household and family. In the study sample, 6,010 (47.1 percent) were women and 6,762 (52.9 percent) were men. The sample included equal representation from blue-collar (manual) and white-collar (nonmanual) occupational groups.

Measurement of Home and Work Environment Characteristics

The indicators of work environment characteristics are based on our previous research (19, 55, 56). Items from the work environment component of the ULF were factor analyzed, and five indicators were constructed. Three aspects of the psychosocial work environment were measured: *psychological job demands, work control,* and *workplace social support.* Multi-item indicators of *job hazards* and *physical job demands* were also constructed. The items for each of the five work environment scales are given in the Appendix.

The evaluation of the home environment was an exploratory process based more on theoretical considerations (19) than on previous research, and will therefore be described in greater detail. The first measure, which was termed "home duties," examined a variety of home work demands. Respondents were asked: "If we look back at your situation last week, to what extent did you yourself perform the following home-making activities?"

- Cooking
- Dish-washing
- Housecleaning
- Purchase of groceries and other household items
- Laundry

Response categories were "all or almost all," "about $^3/_4$," "about $^1/_2$," "about $^1/_4$," or "none or almost none." The factor analysis revealed a single factor solution, and the Cronbach's alpha was found to be .95. When the items were summed we observed that the distribution of this variable in the total sample was bimodal. After dividing the total summed score by the number of items, we found that the majority of individuals reported either none or almost none (0–1), or $^3/_4$ or all (3–4). Based on these findings a dichotomous variable was constructed with the score of 1 indicating the performance of $^3/_4$ or more of the housework, and a score of 0 indicating less than $^3/_4$.

To evaluate "home stress" an indicator was constructed from the following question: "If we look back at the situation last week, do you consider your duties in the household to be very burdensome, rather burdensome, or not at all burdensome?" If the respondents indicated that their duties were either very or somewhat burdensome they were given a 1; they were assigned a 0 otherwise.

A child-care demands variable was constructed through combining information that had been asked about each child, and his or her date of birth. "Older children" were those of school age, 7 to 18 years of age, who were living in the home. "Younger children" were preschoolers, from 0 to 6 years of age, also living in the home.

The resources available to parents for child care were also examined. For each child between the ages of 0 to 13 living in the home, the following alternatives were presented. Subjects could indicate more than one alternative if it applied to their situation.

- No day-care resources (the child looks after itself)
- The child goes to school
- Parent at home
- Other relative, friend, etc., cares for child
- Private family day-care
- Municipal family day-care
- Day-care center or kindergarten

A dichotomous variable was constructed that indicated whether parents with children (younger than 13) had *any* form of day-care resources available to them. Those with day-care were assigned a score of 0; those without were assigned a score of 1.

Psychosomatic Strain Measure

A psychosomatic complaints index was constructed by combining six questions that addressed symptoms of fatigue, sleep disorders, headaches, and exhaustion. Respondents were asked whether they had experienced any of the following during the last two weeks; responses were coded either yes = 1 or no = 0:

- Have you often suffered from fatigue?
- Do you have difficulties "getting going" in the mornings?
- Do you suffer from fatigue during the daytime?
- Do you have problems falling asleep?
- Do you suffer from fatigue during the evening?
- Do you suffer from headaches or migraines?

A principal component factor analysis was performed on this set of items, which demonstrated a single factor solution, with all items loading heavily on this factor.

Responses were summed. The Cronbach's alpha was .70. For purposes of analysis the variable was dichotomized, with individuals having one or more symptoms being assigned a 1, and those with no symptoms being assigned a 0.

Additional Measures

A number of other social and demographic variables, indicated in Table 1, were also used in the analysis. Age was dichotomized at less than 40 and greater than or equal to 40. Occupational class was defined as blue-collar (manual workers) and white-collar (office and professional workers). A work time variable was constructed, with greater than 20 hours worked per week assigned a score of 1, and 20 hours or less assigned a 0.

Statistical Analysis

The data were analyzed using the logistic regression programs developed by SAS Institute (88). All variables were dichotomized (based on the distributions observed in the combined male and female sample). The upper quartile of the distribution was defined as the theoretically adverse exposure category for all of the working environment variables and was indicated by 1, with a 0 otherwise. This permits an interpretation of the multivariable odds ratio (OR) as the effect of an independent variable on the odds of the dependent variable in the model, while adjusting for the other terms in the model. All odds ratios presented in Tables 2 to 5 are multivariable odds ratios. Age and occupational class were used as adjustment covariates in the logistic regression analysis and were not examined for interactions with home and work characteristics.

In order to investigate the sex differences in the magnitude or directionality of the associations between environmental variables and psychosomatic strain, sex-pooled logistic regression models were estimated. Particular attention was given in the analysis to detecting the joint effects of combined exposures that introduced an additional level of complexity to the examination of sex differences in the pooled regression analysis. Therefore, both two- and three-way interaction terms were evaluated, including:

1. Two-way interactions involving sex and an additional exposure variable.
2. Two-way interactions involving all combinations of home, work, and home and work exposure interactions.
3. Three-way interactions involving sex and the two-way exposure interactions noted above.

A two-stage model-building strategy was pursued. In the first stage, fully saturated models involving two independent variables, together with sex, were estimated while controlling for age and occupational class. In the second stage, all

Table 1

Sex differences in the frequency distribution of major variables

Variable	Frequency distribution, %						OR, women/men	95% Confidence limits
	Total (N = 12,771)		Women (N = 6,009)		Men (N = 6,762)			
	0	1	0	1	0	1		
≥ 40 Years of age	57.3	42.7	58.9	41.1	55.8	44.2	0.88	0.82–0.94
Blue-collar	45.2	54.8	47.4	52.6	43.3	56.7	0.85	0.79–0.91
Not married	61.5	38.5	58.1	41.1	63.7	36.3	1.22	1.14–1.31
1 or more older child [Older child]	59.9	40.1	57.9	42.1	61.6	38.4	1.17	1.09–1.25
1 or more young child [Young child]	70.5	29.5	71.8	28.2	69.4	30.6	0.89	0.83–0.96
No child care for child under 13 [No child care]	73.5	26.5	77.4	22.6	70.0	30.0	0.68	0.63–0.73
Home duties	69.3	30.7	38.0	62.0	97.1	2.9	54.55	48.90–63.47
Home stress	84.6	15.4	72.5	27.5	95.4	4.6	7.83	7.00–8.76
High job hazards [Hazards]	73.1	26.9	84.6	15.4	62.9	37.1	0.31	0.28–0.34
High physical job demands [Physical]	75.9	24.1	81.6	18.4	70.8	29.2	0.55	0.50–0.60
High psychological job demands [Psychological]	72.8	27.2	72.6	27.4	72.9	27.1	1.01	0.94–1.10
Work time >20 hours/week [Work time]	12.9	87.1	23.8	76.2	3.2	96.8	0.11	0.09–0.12
Low work social support [Social support]	70.2	29.8	64.2	35.8	75.6	24.4	1.73	1.60–1.86
Low work control [Control]	75.0	25.0	72.7	27.3	77.0	23.0	1.25	1.16–1.36
Psychosomatic strain	51.6	48.4	42.7	57.3	59.5	40.5	1.97	1.84–2.12

statistically significant interactions obtained in step 1 were entered into a new model that included the 15 main effect terms. Following the model-building method proposed by Kleinbaum, Kupper, and Morgenstern (89), a backwards stepwise approach was followed with a significance level of less than or equal to .10 being used to retain interaction terms. This higher level of statistical significance has been used to guard against deleting interaction terms from the model that may be of only borderline statistical significance, but of substantive significance as indicated by the magnitude of the odds ratio. The terms in the regression model shown in Table 2 cannot be meaningfully interpreted without calculating the combined exposure odds ratios. In order to facilitate the discussion of the results, Tables 3 to 5 display the odds ratios for the individual and combined effects of work and home characteristics and take into account all of the interaction terms indicated in Table 2.

RESULTS

In Table 1 the relative proportions of the study variables are displayed for the entire study population, and a comparative analysis is performed by sex. The relative odds of being in the adverse category of exposure, represented by the code of 1, was compared for women versus men. Women were *less* likely than men to be over 40, to be blue-collar, to have a preschool child, to have no child care for any of their children under the age of 13, to work more than 20 hours per week, and to have jobs high in hazards and physical demands. Women were *more* likely than men to be unmarried, to have a school-age child, to perform the bulk of home duties, to experience home stress, to have jobs with low social support and low work control, and to report psychosomatic strain. The strongest differences between women and men were found in the domain of home duties and home stress.

Table 2 shows the results of the logistic regression model for psychosomatic strain. The adjusted odds ratios and P values for each main effect term together with those interactions that were statistically significant at a .10 level are reported. It is interesting to note that in the unadjusted analysis reported in Table 1, women have nearly twice the odds of reporting symptoms of psychosomatic strain compared with men. Moreover, in an analysis that adjusted for the effects of age and class the odds ratio remains unchanged at 1.98 ($P < .0001$). However, after considering the effects of work and home characteristic variables and their interaction terms, as indicated in Table 2, the odds ratio for sex drops to 1.00 and is no longer statistically significant ($P = .99$).

As the results displayed in Table 2 indicate, a considerable number of interactions involving sex were found: six two-way interactions and eight three-way interactions. Because of the complexity of the logistic regression model shown in Table 2, we will not attempt to interpret the substantive meaning of the terms shown directly from this table. Rather, the Table 2 logistic model is used to

Table 2

Multivariate odds ratios of the effects of home and work characteristics and their interactions on psychosomatic strain, from a multivariable logistic regression analysis of a pooled sample of Swedish male and female workers; N = 12,771[a]

Variable or interaction	Multivariate OR	95% Confidence limits	P
Intercept	0.80	0.60–1.08	.15
Sex (1 = Female)	1.00	0.72–1.39	.99
Age (1 = 40 years and over)	1.01	0.92–1.10	.90
Class (1 = manual worker)	0.97	0.89–1.06	.49
Not married	1.13	0.99–1.29	.06
Young child	1.00	0.91–1.11	.93
Older child	0.95	0.84–1.08	.41
No child care	0.96	0.84–1.08	.47
Home duties	0.79	0.69–0.90	.00
Perceived home stress	0.38	0.07–1.94	.25
High psychological job demands	1.70	1.56–1.86	.00
Low work control	0.72	0.54–0.97	.03
Low work social support	1.27	1.15–1.41	.00
High physical job demands	1.26	1.12–1.43	.00
High job hazards	1.47	1.30–1.66	.00
Work time (1 = >20 hours/week)	0.53	0.40–0.70	.00
Sex × No child care	1.48	1.12–1.96	.01
Sex × Home stress	6.47	1.24–33.73	.03
Sex × Physical	1.33	1.07–1.65	.01
Sex × Control	1.52	1.22–1.89	.00
Sex × Work time	1.97	1.42–2.75	.00
Sex × Not married	1.45	1.11–1.90	.01
Hazards × Older child	0.79	0.65–0.96	.02
Work time × Control	1.72	1.31–2.27	.00
Not married × Social support	0.86	0.73–1.01	.07
Work time × Home stress	4.57	0.88–23.76	.07
Not married × Older child	1.24	1.04–1.47	.01
Sex × Older Child × Home duties	0.83	0.68–1.00	.05
Sex × No child × Home duties	0.71	0.52–0.97	.03
Sex × Psychological × Physical	0.62	0.47–0.82	.00
Sex × Control × Hazards	0.70	0.52–0.93	.01
Sex × Control × Older child	0.68	0.53–0.87	.00
Sex × Hazards × Older child	2.00	1.45–2.76	.00
Sex × Work time × Not married	0.69	0.53–0.91	.01
Sex × Work time × Home stress	0.17	0.03–0.90	.04

[a]The model was fitted using backwards stepwise deletion of interaction terms not meeting the selection staying criterion of P < .10. All main effect terms were included regardless of the level of statistical significance. The following interaction terms were deleted (the P values in parentheses are from the initial, untrimmed logistic regression model): sex × older child (P = .81); sex × young child (P = .80); sex × home duties (P = 0.21); sex × psychological (P = 0.25); sex × hazards (P = .46); sex × support (P = .23); support × home duties (P = 0.24); work time × hazards (P = 0.19); work time × not married (P = .24); not married × no child care (P = .62); not married × young child (P = .98); sex × support × older child (P = .58); sex × hazards × home stress (P = .39).

Table 3

Sex differences in the multivariate odds ratios of the main effects of
home and work characteristics on psychosomatic strain, from the multivariable
logistic regression model in Table 2[a]

| Variable | Multivariate OR | | P [b] |
	Males	Females	
Not married	1.13	1.64	.01
Young child	1.00	1.00	ns
Older child	0.95	0.95	ns
No child care	0.96	1.42	.01
Home duties	0.79	0.79	ns
Home stress	0.38	2.45	.03
Psychological	1.70	1.70	ns
Control	0.72	1.09	.00
Social support	1.27	1.27	ns
Physical	1.26	1.68	.01
Hazards	1.47	1.47	ns
Work time	0.53	1.04	.00

[a]These main effect multivariate ORs assume that all other exposure variables involved in interactions are fixed to their baseline value of zero. This table should be interpreted in conjunction with Tables 4 and 5, which show the interactions.
[b]ns, not statistically significant, p > .05.

evaluate the sex differences in the main effects (Table 3) and in the combined interaction effects (Tables 4 and 5) of the work and home variables.

Table 3 shows sex differences in terms of the main effects of work and home characteristics on psychosomatic strain. These findings must be interpreted with caution, since the main effects odds ratio for any given variable is that which is obtained when all other variables that interact with it are set to their baseline value of zero, and when adjusting for all of the variables and their interactions shown in Table 2. With this caveat, one finds a number of statistically significant sex differences in the main effects of the work and home characteristics on psychosomatic strain. In all instances where a sex difference was found, women have a higher odds associated with the exposure characteristic than do men. The most pronounced difference was found for the main effect of home stress, where women have an odds ratio of 2.45 compared with the men's odds ratio of 0.38.

The combined effects of joint exposures on psychosomatic strain calculated from the logistic regression model in Table 2 are presented in Tables 4 and 5. Since the effect of the variable low work control is dependent on both sex and the number of hours worked, all combinations involving the control variable are presented in Table 5. In these two tables 60 combined effect comparisons were made, and in only two of these do men have a higher combined exposure odds

Table 4

Multivariate odds ratios for the combined effects of joint exposure to two variables
on psychosomatic strain, based on the sex-pooled logistic regression model in Table 2

		Combined OR	
Variable 1	Variable 2	Males	Females
Home Variables			
Older child	No child care	0.91	1.35
Older child	Home duties	0.75	0.62
Older child	Home stress	0.36	2.34
Older child	Not married	1.33	1.93
No child care	Home duties	0.76	0.80
No child care	Home stress	0.36	3.49
No child care	Not married	1.08	2.32
Home duties	Home stress	0.30	1.94
Home duties	Not married	0.89	1.30
Home stress	Not married	0.43	4.03
Work Variables			
Physical	Psychological	2.14	1.77
Physical	Social support	1.60	2.13
Physical	Work time	0.68	1.75
Psychological	Social support	2.16	2.16
Psychological	Hazards	2.50	2.50
Social support	Work time	0.67	1.32
Hazards	Work time	0.78	1.53
Control	Work time	0.66	1.97
Home and Work Variables			
Older child	Physical	1.20	1.60
No child care	Physical	1.21	2.39
Home duties	Physical	1.00	1.33
Home stress	Physical	0.48	4.12
Not married	Physical	1.42	2.76
Older child	Psychological	1.62	1.62
No child care	Psychological	1.63	2.41
Home duties	Psychological	1.34	1.34
Home stress	Psychological	0.65	4.17
Not married	Psychological	1.92	2.79
Older child	Social support	1.21	1.21
No child care	Social support	1.22	1.80
Home stress	Social support	0.48	3.11
Not married	Social support	1.23	1.79
Older child	Hazards	1.11	2.21
No child care	Hazards	1.41	2.09
Home duties	Hazards	1.16	1.16
Home stress	Hazards	0.56	3.60
Not married	Hazards	1.66	2.41
Older child	Work time	0.50	0.99
No child care	Work time	0.51	1.48
Home duties	Work time	0.42	0.82
Home stress	Work time	0.92	1.99
Not married	Work time	0.60	1.18

Table 5

Influence of hours worked per week on the combined effects of work control
and other variables on psychosomatic strain, based on the sex-pooled
logistic regression model in Table 2

Variable 1	Variable 2	Combined OR	
		Males	Females
Work time >20 hours/week			
Hazards	Control	0.98	2.02
Physical	Control	0.83	3.31
Psychological	Control	1.12	3.35
Social support	Control	0.84	2.50
Older child	Control	0.63	1.27
No child care	Control	0.64	2.79
Home duties	Control	0.52	1.56
Home stress	Control	0.25	4.85
Not married	Control	0.75	3.23
Work time <20 hours/week			
Hazards	Control	1.06	1.13
Physical	Control	0.91	1.83
Psychological	Control	1.22	1.85
Social support	Control	0.91	1.38
Older child	Control	0.68	0.70
No child care	Control	0.69	1.55
Home duties	Control	0.57	0.86
Not married	Control	0.81	1.79
Home stress	Control	0.27	2.68

ratio than women. In six of the 60 comparisons men and women have an *identical* combined odds ratio for psychosomatic strain. In the remaining 52 combined effect comparisons, women have a greater combined odds ratio for psychosomatic strain than do men.

Among the home variables, women have five combined exposures for which the directionality of the association is different from that of men. The largest combined odds ratio sex differences were found for the combinations that included the home stress variable. Fewer differences in combined effects were found among the work variables. The most notable differences were observed in conjunction with the work time variable.

The highest combined odds ratios and the greatest sex differences in terms of combined effects were found in the home and work variable combinations. In all instances women have a greater combined odds ratio than men. The greatest difference was seen in those combinations involving home stress, such as the combined effect of psychological job demands and home stress.

Table 5 presents the combined effects of work control and the other study variables when work time is greater than 20 hours per week and when work time is less than or equal to 20 hours per week. For women, an increase in working hours is associated with an increase in psychosomatic strain, whereas the reverse is true in men. The most powerful finding in Table 5 is that women who work more than 20 hours a week with low control have the highest odds (OR = 4.85) for psychosomatic strain. This combination is also elevated for women working less than 20 hours per week (OR = 2.68).

DISCUSSION

General Observations

Gender is a powerful factor in both the structure and the stress of everyday life. Would studies of role be improved by greater specificity? Yes; it is useful to evaluate the contribution of specific *components* of work and home life to psychosomatic strain. The findings from this investigation show that when the specifics of home and work are evaluated and treated as exposure characteristics, new patterns of association and new insights about the stress process emerge. At a meta-level the present investigation suggests that it is not appropriate to make the a priori assumption that one can generalize from studies of men to conclusions about women. The results argue for a particular stand on the issue of gender: namely, that future studies of gender and health should either analyze and contrast men and women separately or use a sex-pooled approach with gender interaction terms. These observations may be relevant to various aspects of biomedical research, such as the evaluation of risk factors in health outcomes and the study of stress and heart disease.

Before we turn to the specific research questions addressed by the present investigation, the reader is advised that this research is viewed as exploratory. Although the findings largely support the critique presented in the introduction, it is important to distinguish between the types of findings and the statements that may be made concerning them. Certain results replicate previous findings (e.g., that jobs high in demand and low in control produce strain) while other results warrant further scrutiny or replication (e.g., findings concerning the importance of job hazards in psychosomatic strain in women with an older child). Finally, there are results that *may* reflect more the methodological complexities than the specific impact of a particular variable. (This is particularly true in the set of interactions that results from the combinations of gender, work control, and work time.)

Response to Specific Research Questions

Addressing the first question (p. 124): basic differences were observed in the life experience (and therefore in the pattern of exposure to the stresses and the rewards of working and home life) of Swedish men and women. This can be seen most easily in the descriptive statistics: women do most of the housework (62 percent of women do at least $^3/_4$ of the housework, compared with 2.9 percent of the men); 27.5 percent of women experience home stress versus 4.6 percent of the men. There are also differences with respect to working life: 23.8 percent of women and only 3.2 percent of men work 20 hours or less a week, while 29.2 percent of men report physical demands at work, compared with 18.4 percent of women. Finally, with respect to the dependent variable, more than half of women (57.3 percent) report some symptoms of psychosomatic strain, versus 40.5 percent of men.

To turn to the second question, gender is *not* predictive of psychosomatic strain when adjusting for home and work characteristics. It was not expected that the model of the home and work environments and their interaction effects would account for *all* of the excess odds for psychosomatic strain associated with being a woman, partly because there is an extensive literature that explores many different approaches to the question of gender differences in psychiatric and physical morbidity (19, 21, 79–81). To our knowledge this "gender gap" has not been investigated or explained with reference to the *differential distribution* and the *differential effects* of home and work stress. The findings of the present investigation are that when these social environmental contexts are not considered (and only the effects of age and class are adjusted for), women have nearly twice the odds of reporting symptoms of psychosomatic strain compared with men. It should be noted, however, that since several home exposure variables, such as doing most of the housework, are predominantly experienced by women, they may serve as proxy variables for sex. Therefore, the interpretation that differences in home and work exposures account for all of the sex differences in psychosomatic strain can only be made cautiously.

Given this caveat, however, these findings suggest that differential exposure among women to some of the basic structures of daily life could be producing strains that heretofore were believed to be a matter of "sensitivity" or "hardiness" or the "willingness to assume the sick role." An alternative hypothesis is that women and men are exposed to different sets of role-related demands and strains that could be producing related psychosomatic strain and symptoms.

With regard to the third question, it is difficult to discuss individual effects, because of the number of interactions. As noted earlier, the main effects presented in Table 3 are based on the assumption that all other exposure variables involved in interactions are fixed to zero. Given this caveat, some of the main effects indicate clear differences or similarities between men and women. A number of work variables (psychological job demands, social support, and job hazards) and a number of home variables (young child, older child, and home duties) had the same impact on strain for both men and women. However, an equal number of variables showed a different effect for women and men: women who were not married, who had no child care, who reported experiencing home stress, who had low work control and physically demanding work, and who worked more than 20 hours per week had a significantly greater likelihood of psychosomatic strain than did men with the same exposure characteristics.

These results confirm in part the finding reported by Loscocco and Spitze (27) that there are few gender difference in the effects of working conditions on well-being when the measures are confined to psychological demands, hazards, and social support. This example is useful to the major thesis of our research, namely, that research on men, women, and stress has suffered from under-specification. It seems insufficient, both theoretically and methodologically, to exclude unpaid labor in the home from consideration when comparing the effects of occupation upon the health of men and women.

In considering the final question it is important to differentiate between the results of *individual* as opposed to *combined* effects of work and home charac-teristics. The combined effect estimates presented in Tables 4 and 5 incorporate all of the two- and three-way interactions found in the logistic model. One area of similarity between the sexes concerns the combined impact of job demands and social support and being unmarried and caring for an older child.

Marked differences are most evident in combinations involving *both* adverse work and adverse home characteristics. For women home stress is of much more importance in psychosomatic strain than it is for men, especially when there is a lack of resources (e.g., unmarried, and no child care). Men do not appear to be affected by the lack of a spouse or lack of day care. This suggests that the role of spouse and parent involves different stresses and obligations according to gender.

The highest odds ratio was observed in the combination of high home stress and low control in women (working more than 20 hours a week). The odds ratio for women was 4.85, while for men with this combination it was 0.25. Thus for women—but not men—we see preliminary evidence of an accumulative burden mechanism operating. Working more than a modest 20 hours a week does not seem to enhance health for those who are "wives and mothers." It functions as an adverse exposure in women. Given that most women do most of the housework and that only a few men perform these tasks, these findings support some of the more basic contentions presented in the beginning of this chapter: we cannot assess the impact of having multiple roles without understanding the nature and the extent of the stresses involved.

In interpreting the overall patterns of results, we did not expect such major differences in the life experience of Swedish men and women. Men and women exhibit different life patterns with different sets of exposures and different sen-sitivities to these exposures. These findings on the different life patterns of men and women are somewhat surprising since Sweden is among the more eman-cipated of countries for women. Thus they cannot be explained on the basis of official social policy or even widely accepted values. Especially during the 1970s, progressive policies emphasized both social and political equality between the sexes (90–94). Aside from policies that have promoted the entry of women into the work force, the state has provided many social services such as child allowance, day-care and free education, extensive maternity and paternity leave, medical care, and social welfare assistance (90–95). Sweden until recently also had a policy of wage solidarity (guaranteeing that wages are the same for all those who do the same work). Thus Swedish social and economic philosophy does not explain the findings.

The findings are not necessarily generalizable to the United States or other countries. Nevertheless one might suspect that there are lessons to be learned even if exact parallels cannot be drawn to the situation in the United States. The results might be relevant to other countries, not only because one cannot account for the patterns observed by reference to formal policies but because the findings on the time and effort dedicated to paid employment and to unpaid work in the home appear to be remarkably similar in many countries. One can infer that as studies in the United States (83) and most other industrialized countries (95–97) suggest, these results may reflect certain longstanding and deeply rooted conventions: most men work full-time unless they are unhealthy, while women often work part-time if they have young children (and if they are able to); men engage in paid labor but tend not to be engaged in unpaid labor in the home, while for women the reverse is true.

Our research group hopes eventually to determine whether the present findings reflect the problems of coupling traditional patterns of home life with newer requirements for occupational involvement. Certainly these findings suggest that combined exposure to adverse work and home life may result in negative health consequences. Perhaps later researchers can delineate more precisely those factors that characterize good work, good domestic life, and how to achieve a balance between the two.

APPENDIX: INDEPENDENT MEASURES— WORK ENVIRONMENT CHARACTERISTICS

Items from the work environment component of the SCB's ULF were factor analyzed, and the following scales were constructed that measured aspects of the psychosocial work environment.

The *psychological job demands* indicator was constructed from two items:

- Is your job hectic?
- Is your job psychologically demanding?

Work control was measured by an additive scale consisting of a linear composite of the following items, which were scored according to whether the subject never, sometimes, or often had any of the following:

- Influence over the planning of work
- Influence over the setting of the work pace
- Influence over how time is used in work
- Influence over the selection of supervisor
- Influence over the selection of coworkers
- Influence over the planning of work breaks
- Influence over the planning of vacations
- Flexible working hours
- Varied task content
- Varied work procedures
- The possibility of learning new things
- The experience of personal fulfillment on the job

The *workplace social support* scale was constructed based on the dichotomous (yes/no) responses to the following:

- Can you talk to coworkers during breaks?
- Can you leave the job to talk with coworkers?
- Can you interact with coworkers as part of your work?
- Do you see and spend some hours with fellow workers or colleagues outside of work?

Two additional work environment indicators were constructed from a set of dichotomous items that measured other aspects of the work environment. The indicator of *physical job demands* consisted of a linear combination of the following items, which were scored no = 0 and yes = 1:

- Does your work require bent, twisted, or otherwise unsuitable working postures?
- Does your work require heavy lifting?
- Does your work cause you to perspire daily from physical exertion?
- Do you get dirty in your work?
- Do you think your work is safe from the point of view of accident risk?

The *job hazards* scale consisted of items inquiring whether subjects were exposed to and bothered by the following conditions on their jobs:

- Noise
- Heavy shaking or vibrations
- Cold
- Drafts
- Inadequate ventilation
- Bad lighting
- Gas, mist or smoke

REFERENCES

1. Pearlin, L. I. The sociological study of stress. *J. Health Soc. Behav.* 30(3): 241–256, 1989.
2. Moen, P., Dempster-McClain, D., and Williams, R. M., Jr. Social integration and longevity: An event history analysis of women's roles and resilience. *Am. Sociol. Rev.* 54: 635–647, 1989.
3. Aneshensel, C. S., and Pearlin, L. I. Structural contexts of sex differences in stress. In *Gender and Stress*, edited by C. Barnett, L. Biener, and G. K. Baruch, pp. 75–95. Macmillan, New York, 1987.
4. Frankenhaeuser, M. Experimental approaches to the study of human behavior as related to neuroendocrine functions. In *Society, Stress and Disease*, Vol. 1, edited by L. Levi, pp. 22–36. Oxford University Press, Oxford, 1971.
5. Frankenhaeuser, M. Man in technological society: Stress, adaptation and tolerance limits. *Department of Psychology Research Report*, No. 26. University of Stockholm, Stockholm, 1974.
6. Frankenhaeuser, M. Sex differences in reaction to psychosocial stressors and psychoactive drugs. In *Society, Stress and Disease*, Vol. 3, edited by L. Levi, pp. 135–140. Oxford University Press, Oxford, 1978.
7. Frankenhaeuser, M. Pyschoneuroendocrine approaches to the study of stressful person-environment transactions. In *Selye's Guide to Stress Research*, Vol. 1, edited by H. Selye, pp. 46–70. Van Nostrand Reinhold, New York, 1980.
8. Henry, J. P., and Stevens, P. M. The social environment and essential hypertension in mice: Possible role of the adrenal cortex. *Prog. Brain Res.* 47: 263–275, 1977.
9. Henry, J. P., and Stevens, P. M. *Stress, Health and the Social Environment*. Springer, New York, 1977.
10. Gardell, B. Alienation and mental health in the modern industrial environment. In *Society, Stress and Disease*, Vol. 1, edited by L. Levi, pp. 148–180. Oxford University Press, Oxford, 1971.
11. Gardell, B. Autonomy and participation at work. *Hum. Relations* 30(6): 515–533, 1977.
12. Kessler, R. C., and McLeod, J. D. Sex differences in vulnerability to undesirable life events. *Am. Sociol. Rev.* 49: 620–631, 1984.
13. Holmes, T. H., and Rahe, R. H. The social readjustment rating scale. *J. Psychosom. Res.* 11: 213–218, 1967.
14. Dohrenwend, B. S., and Dohrenwend, B. P. *Stressful Life Events: Their Nature and Effects*. Wiley, New York, 1974.
15. Wheaton, B. Where work and family meet: Stress across social roles. In *Stress Between Work and Family*, edited by J. Eckenrode and S. Gore. Plenum, New York, 1990.
16. Friedman, M., and Roseman, R. Type A behavior pattern: Its association with coronary heart disease. *Ann. Clin. Res.* 3: 300–312, 1971.
17. Rose, R. M., Hurst, M. W., and Herd, J. A. Cardiovascular and endocrine responses to work and the risk of psychiatric symptoms among air traffic controllers. In *Stress and Mental Disorder*, edited by J. Barrett. Raven Press, New York, 1979.
18. House, J. S. *Work Stress and Social Support*. Addison-Wesley, Reading, Mass., 1981.
19. Hall, E. M. Gender, work control, and stress: A theoretical discussion and an empirical test. *Int. J. Health Serv.* 19: 725–745, 1989.
20. Haw, M. Women, work and stress: A review and agenda for the future. *J. Health Soc. Behav.* 23: 132–144, 1982.

21. Barnett, R. C., and Baruch, G. K. Social roles, gender and psychological distress. In *Gender and Stress*, edited by R. C. Barnett, L. Biener, and G. K. Baruch, pp. 122–143. Macmillan, New York, 1987.
22. Barnett, R. C., and Baruch, G. K. Women's involvement in multiple roles, and psychological distress. *J. Pers. Soc. Psychol.* 49: 135–145, 1985.
23. Karasek, R. A., and Theorell, T. *Healthy Work.* Basic Books, New York, 1990.
24. LaCroix, A. Z., and Haynes, S. G. Gender differences in the health effects of workplace roles. In *Gender and Stress*, edited by R. C. Barnett, L. Biener, and G. K. Baruch, pp. 96–121. Macmillan, New York, 1987.
25. Sorensen, G., et al. Sex differences in the relationship between work and health: The Minnesota Heart Survey. *J. Health Soc. Behav.* 26: 379–394, 1985.
26. Sorensen, G., and Verbrugge, L. M. Women, work and health. *Annu. Rev. Public Health* 8: 235–251, 1987.
27. Loscocco, K., and Spitze, G. Working conditions, social support, and the well-being of female and male factory workers. *J. Health Soc. Behav.* 31: 313–327, 1990.
28. Passannante, M. R., and Nathanson, C. A. Women in the labor force: Are sex mortality differentials changing? *J. Occup. Med.* 29(1): 21–28, 1987.
29. Kotler, P., and Wingard, D. L. The effect of occupational, marital and parental roles on mortality: The Alameda County Study. *Am. J. Public Health* 79: 607–611, 1989.
30. Brown, G., and Harris, T. *The Social Origins of Depression: A Study of the Psychiatric Disorder in Women.* Tavistock, London, 1978.
31. Finlay-Jones, R. A., and Burvill, P. Women, work and minor psychiatric morbidity. *Soc. Psychiatry* 14: 53–57, 1977.
32. Gore, S. L., and Mangione, T. W. Social roles, sex roles, and psychological distress: Additive and interactive models of sex differences. *J. Health Soc. Behav.* 24: 300–312, 1983.
33. Gove, W. R., and Geerken, M. R. The effect of children and employment on the mental health of married men and women. *Social Forces* 56: 66–76, 1977.
34. Gutek, B., Repetti, R., and Silver, D. Non-work roles and stress at work. In *Causes, Coping and Consequences of Stress at Work*, edited by C. Cooper and R. Payne. Wiley, Chichester, 1991.
35. Kandel, D. B., Davies, M., and Raveis, V. The stressfulness of daily social roles for women: Marital, occupational, and household roles. *J. Health Soc. Behav.* 26: 64–78, 1985.
36. Kessler, R. C., and McRae, J. A. Trends in sex and psychological distress. *Am. Sociol. Rev.* 46: 443–452, 1981.
37. Kessler, R. C., and McRae, J. A. The effects of wives' employment on the mental health of men and women. *Am. Sociol. Rev.* 47: 216–227, 1982.
38. McLanahan, S., and Glass, J. A note on the trend in sex differences in psychological distress. *J. Health Soc. Behav.* 26: 328–336, 1985.
39. Moen, P. The two-provider family. In *Nontraditional Families: Parenting and Child Development*, edited by M. E. Lamb, pp. 13–44. Erlbaum, Hillsdale, N.J., 1982.
40. Moen, P., and Dempster-McClain, D. Employed parents: Role strain, work time and preferences for working less. *J. Marriage Family* 49(3): 579–590, 1987.
41. Pearlin, L. I. Sex roles and depression. In *Life-Span Developmental Psychology: Normative Life Crises*, edited by N. Dalton and L. Ginsburg, pp. 191–207. Academic Press, New York, 1975.
42. Pearlin, L. I. Role strains and personal stress. In *Psychosocial Stress: Trends in Theory and Research*, edited by H. B. Kaplan, pp. 3–32. Academic Press, New York, 1983.

43. Pearlin, L. I., and McCall, M. Occupational problems and marital support. In *The Transmission of Stress Between Work and Family*, edited by J. Eckenrode and S. Gore, Plenum, New York, 1992.
44. Pleck, J. H. Husbands' paid work and family roles: Current research issues. In *Research in the Interweave of Social Roles: Jobs and Families*, edited by H. Z. Lopata and J. H. Pleck, pp. 251–333. JAI Press, Greenwich, Conn., 1983.
45. Pleck, J. H. *Working Wives, Working Husbands*. Sage, Beverly Hills, Calif., 1985.
46. Pleck, J. H., Staines, G. L., and Lang, D. Conflicts between work and family life. *Monthly Labor Rev.* 103(3): 29–32, 1980.
47. Ross, C. E., Mirowsky, J., and Huber, J. Dividing work, sharing work, and in-between: Marriage patterns and depression. *Am. Sociol. Rev.* 48: 809–823, 1983.
48. Thoits, P. A. Multiple identities and psychological well-being: A reformulation and test of the social isolation hypothesis. *Am. Sociol. Rev.* 48: 174–187, 1983.
49. Thoits, P. A. Multiple identities: Examining sexual and marital status differences in distress. *Am. Sociol. Rev.* 51: 259–272, 1986.
50. Turner, R. J. Direct, indirect and moderating effects of social support on psychological distress and associated conditions. In *Psychosocial Stress*, edited by H. B. Kaplan, pp. 105–155. Academic Press, New York, 1983.
51. Alfredsson, L., Karasek, R. A., and Theorell, T. Myocardial infarction risk and psychosocial work environment characteristics: An analysis of the male Swedish work force. *Soc. Sci. Med.* 16: 463–467, 1982.
52. Alfredsson, L., Spetz, L., and Theorell, T. Type of occupation and near-future hospitalization for myocardial infarction and some other diagnoses. *Int. J. Epidemiol.* 14: 378–388, 1985.
53. Baker, D. B. The study of stress at work. *Annu. Rev. Public Health* 6: 367–381, 1985.
54. House, J. S., Robbins, C., and Metzner, H. L. The association of social relationships and activities with mortality: Prospective evidence from the Tecumseh Community Health Study. *Am. J. Epidemiol.* 116: 123–140, 1982.
55. Johnson, J. V., and Hall, E. M. Job strain, work place social support, and cardiovascular disease: A cross sectional study of a random sample of the Swedish working population. *Am. J. Public Health* 78: 1336–1342, 1988.
56. Johnson, J. V., Hall, E. M., and Theorell, T. Combined effects of job strain and social isolation on cardiovascular disease morbidity and mortality in a random sample of the Swedish male working population. *Scand. J. Work Environ. Health* 15: 271–279, 1989.
57. Johnson, J., and Johansson, G. (eds.). *The Psychosocial Work Environment: Work Organization, Democratization and Health*. Baywood, Amityville, N.Y., 1991.
58. Haynes, S. G., and Feinleib, M. Women, work and coronary heart disease: Prospective findings from the Framingham Heart Study. *Am. J. Public Health* 70: 133–141, 1980.
59. Karasek, R. A., et al. Job decision latitude, job demands, and cardiovascular disease: A prospective study of Swedish men. *Am. J. Public Health* 71: 694–705, 1981.
60. Karasek, R. A., Russell, R. S., and Theorell, T. Physiology of stress and regeneration in job related cardiovascular illness. *J. Hum. Stress* 3: 29–42, 1982.
61. Karasek, R. A., et al. Psychosocial Characteristics of Occupations in Relation to Blood Pressure. Unpublished paper. Columbia University, 1982.
62. Karasek, R. A., et al. Job, psychological factors and coronary heart disease. *Adv. Cardiol.* 29: 62–76, 1982.
63. Karasek, R. A., Triantis, K. P., and Chaudhry, S. S. Co-worker and supervisor support as moderators of associations between task characteristics and mental strain. *J. Occup. Behav.* 3: 147–160, 1982.

64. Rose, R. M., Hurst, M. W., and Jenkins, C. D. Health change in air traffic controllers: A prospective study. I. Background and description. *Psychosom. Med.* 40: 142–165, 1978.

65. Kasl, S. V. Changes in mental health status associated with job loss and retirement. In *Stress and Mental Disorder*, edited by R. M. Rose and G. L. Klerman, p. 102. Raven Press, New York, 1979.

66. Schnall, P., et al. The relationship between 'job strain,' workplace diastolic blood pressure, and left ventricular mass index: Results of a case study. *JAMA* 263: 1929–1935, 1990.

67. Theorell, T. Personal control at work and health: A review of epidemiological studies in Sweden. In *Stress, Personal Control and Health*, edited by A. Steptoe and A. Appels. Wiley, Brussels, 1989.

68. Theorell, T., and Floderus-Myrhed, B. 'Workload' and risk of myocardial infarction: A prospective psychosocial analysis. *Int. J. Epidemiol.* 6: 17–21, 1977.

69. Theorell, T., et al. On the interplay between socioeconomic factors, personality and work environment in the pathogenesis of cardiovascular disease. *Scand. J. Work Environ. Health* 10: 373–380, 1984.

70. Theorell, T., et al. Psychosocial and physiological factors in relation to blood pressure at rest: A study of Swedish men in their upper twenties. *J. Hypertens.* 3: 591–600, 1985.

71. Theorell, T., et al. Psychosocial work conditions before myocardial infarction in young men. *Int. J. Cardiol.* 15: 33–46, 1987.

72. Rose, G., and Marmot, M. Social class and coronary heart disease. *Br. Heart J.* 45(1): 13–19, 1981.

73. Jahoda, M. The impact of unemployment in the 1930's and the 1970's. *Bull. Br. Psychol. Soc.* 32: 309, 1979.

74. Warr, P., and Parry, G. Paid employment and women's psychological well-being. *Psychol. Bull.* 91: 498–516, 1982.

75. Gove, W. R., and Zeiss, C. Multiple roles and happiness. In *Spouse, Parent, Worker: On Gender and Multiple Roles*, edited by F. Crosby. Yale University Press, New Haven, Conn., 1987.

76. Radloff, L. Sex differences in depression: The effects of occupation and marital status. *Sex Roles* 1: 249, 1975.

77. Muller, C. Health and health care of employed women and homemakers: Family factors. *Women Health* 11(1): 7–26, 1986.

78. Waldron, I., and Herold, J. Employment, attitudes toward employment, and women's health. *Women Health* 11(1): 79–98, 1986.

79. Waldron, I., and Jacobs, J. A. Effects of multiple roles on women's health: Evidence from a national longitudinal study. *Women Health* 15(1): 3–19, 1989.

80. Verbrugge, L. M. Multiple roles and physical health of women and men. *J. Health Soc. Behav.* 24: 16–30, 1983.

81. Verbrugge, L. M. Gender and health: An update on hypotheses and evidence. *J. Health Soc. Behav.* 26: 156–182, 1985.

82. Pleck, J. H., and Staines, G. L. Work schedules and family life in two-earner couples. *J. Fam. Issues* 6(1): 61–82, 1985.

83. Hochschild, A. (with Machung, A.). *The Second Shift: Working Parents and the Revolution at Home.* Viking Press, New York, 1989.

84. Gove, W., and Geerken, M. The effect of children and employment on the mental health of married men and women. *Soc. Forces* 55: 66, 1977.

85. Veroff, J., Douvan, E., and Kulka, R. A. *The Inner American.* Basic Books, New York, 1981.

86. Eckenrode, J., and Gore, S. (eds.). *Stress Between Work and Family*. Plenum, New York, 1990.
87. Emmons, C.-A., et al. Stress, support and coping among women and professionals with preschool children. In *Stress Between Work and Family*, edited by J. Eckenrode and S. Gore. Plenum, New York, 1990.
88. SAS Institute. *SAS/STAT User's Guide*, Release 6.03 Edition. Cary, N.C., 1988.
89. Kleinbaum, D. G., Kupper, L. L., and Morgenstern, H. *Epidemiologic Research: Principles and Quantitative Methods*. Lifetime Learning Publications, Belmont, Calif., 1982.
90. Ruggie, M. *The State and the Working Woman: A Comparative Study of Britain and Sweden*. Princeton University Press, Princeton, N.J., 1984.
91. Haavio-Manilla, E. (ed.). *Unfinished Democracy: Women in Nordic Politics*. Pergamon Press, Oxford, 1985.
92. Haavio-Manilla, E. Inequalities in health and gender. *Soc. Sci. Med.* 22: 141–149, 1986.
93. Moen, P. *Working Parents*. University of Wisconsin Press, Madison, Wis., 1989.
94. McLeod, D. Why Sweden has better working conditions than the U.S. *Working Life in Sweden*, No. 28. Swedish Information Service, Stockholm, April 1984.
95. Roos, P. A. *Gender and Work: A Comparative Analysis of Industrial Societies*. State University of New York Press, Albany, 1985.
96. Hall, E. M., Johnson, J. V., and Tsou, T. S. Women, occupation and risk of cardiovascular morbidity and mortality, *Occupational Medicine: State of the Art Reviews*, 8: 709–719, 1993.
97. Hall, E. M. Women, work, and health: Employment as a risk factor for coronary heart disease. *Journal of Preventive Cardiology,* 4: 25-30, 1994.

CHAPTER 7

The Interactive Effect of Health Status on Work Patterns among Urban Puerto Rican Women

Ruth E. Zambrana and Marsha Hurst

The relationship between work and health is increasingly the subject of investigations. For example, feminist scholarship in recent years has challenged the model, based on patriarchal conceptions, which dichotomizes work and family roles and has begun to explore the true interrelationships between these roles as well as to develop workable paradigms based on the work-family nexus. Kanter's thorough review of women's work and family roles (1) has been followed by significant Marxist-feminist reanalysis of women's work and family roles in patriarchal capitalist society, including the incorporation of women's home and work roles as crucial elements in both the patriarchal and capitalist structures (2, 3). The women's health movement has concentrated on issues related to the relationship of the effects of the work site on reproductive health, occupational hazards, and the coerced sterilization of women chemical workers (4).

These issues, however, can be treated within the patriarchal work-health nexus, reinforcing concern with individual worker's health rather than the more complete family-work-health interaction. When viewed from a feminist perspective, the whole woman, the physical and mental health of herself and her family, the substance of her work, are all integral parts of her role in the labor force. Women's health research today focuses on the following major issues: (*a*) the individual health of women as workers, particularly as affected by the workplace itself; (*b*) the reproductive and mental health of the woman in the family, with emphasis on her roles as childbearer, child rearer, and less frequently, as home manager; (*c*) the connection between children's health status and women's roles, although there is

Originally published in the *International Journal of Health Services* 14(2): 265-277, 1984.

as yet much less work in this area than in others; and (*d*) the health status of women as a population group compared with men.

The same reexamination of these segmented spheres is required as has begun with segmented work-family role models. Some steps have been made in this direction, notably Nathanson's study of "Social Roles and Health Status among Women" (5), in which she reexamined the well documented poorer self-reported health status among housewives than among employed women, and found that other socially integrating and status conferring factors such as marriage and children, as well as work status and higher education, relate to better health, or at least a more positive perception of physical well-being. Viewed in this perspective, Hurst and Zambrana (6), in a study of Puerto Rican women with dependent children in the New York City area, found erratic work patterns related to socially disintegrating factors: lack of culturally acceptable child care, and family disruption due to health problems of women, their spouses, or their children. The fact that these patterns varied by the occupational status of the woman suggests that better jobs imply more flexibility in terms of child care options and a wider range of acceptable choices, stronger personal and family integration that can more frequently resist the disintegrative effects of health problems, better health status of family members, and more control over the structure of women's employment itself.

Data on employment and health characteristics of low-income Hispanic women are scarce, which makes the understanding of factors related to discontinuous work histories an important area of inquiry. In the area of health status, information on Hispanic women is sorely lacking. For example, a recent review of data, *Women and Health*, (7), advised in one paragraph that data on minority women were needed. Another analysis of "areas of deficient data collection and integration" related to women's health failed to even mention the need to collect data on Latina women or other subpopulations (8). The only published data source on the health of Puerto Ricans (9) deals only with New York City, and mainly with men.

This chapter will report on work-family health relationships among a small sample of Puerto Rican women in New York, and will discuss these findings in the larger context of the status of Puerto Rican women, and within the framework of women's work-family-health relationships.

STUDY METHODS AND SAMPLE CHARACTERISTICS

In-depth interviews were conducted with 40 Puerto Rican women in the New York metropolitan area. The criteria for selection were: women who were working or had formerly worked, between 25 and 45 years of age, and who had parenting responsibilities for at least one dependent child. Network sampling techniques were used to obtain representation in the three broad occupational categories: blue collar, white collar, and professional. Interviews were conducted in both Spanish and English and were designed to obtain data on work history, attitudes toward parenting, availability and use of support systems, and child care options. The analysis was geared toward identifying factors that influenced continuous vs. discontinuous work patterns. A continuous work pattern was defined as steady adult participation in the labor force with breaks of one year or less.

The majority (62 percent) of women were between 30 and 39 years of age, and 20 percent were between 25 and 29 years of age. At the time of the interview, 78 percent of the respondents were living with a spouse or partner in the household.

Roughly equal numbers of respondents from blue-collar (30 percent), white-collar (35 percent), and professional (35 percent) groups were interviewed. Women's occupational status was based primarily on last (or present) job held. All the women had worked during their adult life. However, 65 percent had a discontinuous work history. By occupational status, the most discontinuous work history was found among blue-collar workers (100 percent) and the most continuous work history was among the professional women (64 percent).

By educational status, 27 percent had an average of nine years of schooling, 30 percent of 12 years of schooling, and 43 percent of 18 years of schooling. Women who had less than eight years of education had an average of five children, and professional women (16 years or more of schooling) had an average of one child. These data are consistent with general population trends showing that the more education a woman has, the fewer the number of children.

The average combined family income for blue-collar families was $12,400; for white-collar families, $16,700; and for professional families, $32,000. Women's income alone was considerably less; for example, blue-collar workers averaged $4,905.

RESULTS

Self-Reported Health Events

In this study, 62.5 percent of the sample reported experiencing a major health event in their lives, or that of their children, which did not permit them to continue paid work roles outside the home. Among the health problems reported, 56 percent were related to physical health, 16 percent were mental health problems, and 28 percent were related to health of children. The majority of health problems (over 50 percent) were due to pregnancy and postpartum complications, fertility problems, and the side effects of the long-term use of birth control pills. For those respondents who reported mental health problems, depression or feelings of being overwhelmed with responsibility for children were the most common complaints. Among women who required mental health intervention, marital conflict and/or lack of family support were presenting complaints. Close to 25 percent of women who reported discontinuous work histories indicated that children's health problems were the major reason. Among continuous workers, only 4 percent cited child health problems. Children's problems were usually pulmonary-related, e.g., asthma, bronchitis, and pneumonia, or psychological, e.g., childhood depression. Our data clearly showed that the lower the socioeconomic status of the respondent, the greater the likelihood of reporting a major health event.

The health events of both mothers and children are closely related to income, and to the quality of their lives. Many of the respondents who reported health problems also indicated other social problems such as marital conflict, physical abuse, and feelings of being overwhelmed. Those women who were experiencing more stress in their lives also reported more health-related problems. An important aspect of our study was related to examining those factors which facilitate a woman's ability to maintain herself in the work force. An acute illness or complicated pregnancy, and/or a child's acute or chronic illness episodes, in many instances forced women to leave the work force.

Work-Health Interaction Patterns

Of the respondents who reported a serious health event, 80 percent had a discontinuous work history. Within this group, 36 percent were blue collar, 32 percent white collar, and 12 percent professional. Of the total sample, 50 percent reported health-related problems and also had a discontinuous work history. A close analysis of the relationship between occupational status and work patterns indicates that the lower the occupational status, the more likely there was to be a health problem that increased a woman's chance of leaving the work force.

For both blue-collar and white-collar women, the onset of illness or pregnancy usually meant that they had to leave their jobs or were fired. Clearly the women felt a conflict between their financial need to work and their reluctance to leave sick children with someone else. However, few employers recognized either the women's financial needs or her perceived duty as a mother. As one woman explained:

> I feel guilty leaving my children to go to work especially when they're ill, [but] I was apt to resign or be told straightforward, "Look, we can't deal with you being out so much." At that time my son was getting asthma attacks like four times a week. And very violent ones. . . . [My] work background is very erratic because of the children, the pregnancies, or the illnesses that come up. So each time I left a job it was for health reasons. You can't serve two gods at once.

Similarly, another woman had to leave several jobs when her child was young and frequently ill with tonsillitis:

> I had to leave my job because my daughter got sick. I would have to take off until at least her fever broke and I was able to leave her. As far as they were concerned, if your kid got sick that was your problem.

For the majority of these women, the jobs they were able to obtain were in declining manufacturing sectors of the economy where there was little, if any, responsiveness to the needs of women. Of critical importance was the concern of the women regarding suitable child care for their children if they were ill. Thus, a cyclical process of not earning enough money to pay for child care substitutes if a child was ill and losing their jobs if they were absent was initiated. Low educational status, fewer opportunities in the labor market, and poorer family health worked together to keep these women from regular employment.

For the professional women, however, health problems of mother and/or child did not have a significant impact on the overall work pattern. Twenty percent of the professional women who had a continuous work history also reported a major health problem. In all instances, the women were able to arrange for a leave of absence or for maternity leave or sick leave, or, in the case of a sick child, for personal time. Those professional women who reported a health problem but had a discontinuous work history were most commonly graduate students or consultants during that time, which gave them flexibility in employment status. These professional women, like respondents of other occupational statuses, had taken time off to care for their children .

For respondents as a whole, only a flexible job structure and sympathetic work environment allowed job continuity through periods of family health problems. As one woman remarked:

> I enjoy my present job because the people are understanding. They understand what it means when one of my children is ill, and how important it is for me to be with them.

Poorer health status, particularly among low-income Hispanic families, may help explain the lower labor force participation patterns of Puerto Rican women. Such analysis flows from an awareness of the dynamic interaction between available work, health status, and child care arrangements.

DISCUSSION

Health and Puerto Rican Women

The relationship between poor health, barriers to health care, and low socioeconomic status is well-known (10–12). The Puerto Rican population in mainland United States is predominantly a poor population. In East Harlem, New York City, a typical urban Puerto Rican community, one-third of the population is on public assistance, and in 1980 almost three-quarters of the families earned less than $9000.

With less available primary and preventive care, the Puerto Rican population tends to detect health problems later, when these health problems become more serious and less treatable. Thus, more chronic disability occurs at an earlier age, and more acute episodes that probably could have been avoided take place. In a major government report (13), health status trends among minorities and low-income groups were identified. Racial minorities have almost twice the infant mortality of whites, a higher share of maternity-related and other reproductive health problems, and the highest incidence of acute conditions among lowest-income females. Minorities and low-income persons have higher death rates than the total population for four of the five leading causes of death: heart disease, cancer, stroke, and diabetes.

During 1977, an estimated 2.95 million visits to office-based physicians were made by women 15 years and older, for an average of 3.5 visits per year (14). Only one visit in 10 was made by black women and other non-Caucasian women. The major diagnostic reasons for these visits were diabetes mellitus and hypertension. In general, it has been found that the poor have more health problems than the affluent but do not use a larger share of the health care offered.

Prevalence rates of selected chronic conditions among low-income persons 45 years of age show that non-whites have a higher prevalence of diabetes, asthma, vision impairments, heart conditions, impairments of the back or spine, and arthritis. A recent report on hypertension (15) noted that more women than men have hypertension. The analysis also showed that the lower the level of education and income, the more likely a woman is to have hypertension.

The Puerto Rican population generally suffers the effects of poor nutrition. Complications of childbirth such as toxemia (which can often be prevented or at least detected with early prenatal care, including nutritional guidance and food supplements) are frequent (16). Mortality during the first month and the first year of life is high. One out of every six babies has a low birth weight, the health condition most frequently associated with infant mortality and morbidity. The birth rate and fertility rate among Puerto Ricans is high, though declining, and Puerto Rican women tend to have more children, closer together in years, and at a younger age than other populations.

Children's health also suffers disproportionately from the conditions of urban poverty (17). Childhood asthma is pervasive in the urban Puerto Rican population (18), and caring for the asthmatic child becomes a way of life for many mothers. Among Puerto Rican children, influenza and pneumonia are the third-ranked cause of death (9). Of those respondents who reported a child's health problem, over half were pulmonary-related, i.e., diseases affecting the respiratory tract.

Two surveys conducted among Puerto Rican families in New York City found that serious health problems were prevalent in the sample population. Valle and coworkers (19) found that in 58 percent of the families, one or more members reported serious or chronic illness. The most common ailment among women was gynecological in nature or was connected to children. Twenty-five percent of the families reported that a member had been treated for a mental health disorder, and an overwhelming majority suffered from "nerves." In the study by Goodrich and coworkers (20), 47 percent of the sample indicated they "suffered from nerves." These studies have identified the Puerto Rican population as exhibiting high disability due to the presence of chronic conditions, stressful life circumstances reflected by the "nerves syndrome," and a poor evaluation of their health as reflected in an "understandably greater preoccupation with their health than the average person" (20, p. 43). In a survey conducted by Johnson (21) in 1972, Puerto Rican women perceived their health to be worse than either black or Anglo women in East Harlem, and they were more concerned about their health and that of their families than about any other social or environmental problem. A study in the same neighborhood (17) conducted eight years later indicated a striking concern on the part of minority women with preventive care for themselves as well as primary care for their children. These women admonished themselves for not taking good care of themselves in terms of diet, exercise, and lifestyle, although almost all had regular checkups, including Pap smears and breast examinations.

One of the few studies of the relationships of women's roles to illness behavior (i.e., reporting symptoms and doing something about the symptoms) found that the more roles a woman performed, the more symptoms of illness she reported (22). This was particularly true for women who had three or more children and an ill spouse. However, women with many roles, and particularly working mothers with an ill child, were less likely to decrease normal activity because of symptoms.

Among Puerto Ricans, we have even clearer evidence that employment and unemployment are significantly related to health. In some Puerto Rican neighborhoods, 30 to 40 percent of the adult population is unemployed (23). For men, the primary reason given for not seeking work was poor health, illness, or disability (55 percent). For women, the primary reason was family responsibilities (54 percent), and then poor health (21 percent). Among women who had not worked for at least one year, over two-thirds said the main reason for their joblessness was poor health, illness, or disability.

Puerto Rican Women in the Labor Force

Nationwide, Spanish-origin working women are overrepresented among blue-collar workers (28 percent compared with 14.5 percent of all women) and underrepresented among white-collar workers (48 percent compared with 64 percent of all women). Only 9 percent of employed Spanish-origin women are professionals, while 16 percent of employed non-Spanish-origin women are professionals. The occupational status of Puerto Rican women tends to be even more heavily weighted toward blue-collar work (31 percent in 1978). The largest concentration of Puerto Ricans is in New York City, where both Puerto Rican men and women have had high employment in manufacturing (in 1970, 32 percent of the men and 42 percent of the women, compared with 21 percent of all male and female workers), the declining sector of the city's economy (24).

Changes in the job opportunity structure in New York City, particularly those away from certain kinds of manufacturing in which Hispanic women were traditionally employed, have meant that the Puerto Rican woman has few job opportunities but does not have the upgraded skills now necessary for other employment. While two-thirds of the women in the United States have completed four years of high school or above, only 40 percent of Hispanic women have had this much schooling, and the percentage is less (35 percent) for Puerto Rican women. Between 1960 and 1970, jobs for women with eight years or less of schooling declined by 40 percent, while jobs for women college graduates increased by 64 percent (25, 26). The labor force participation rate of Hispanic women in 1976 lagged behind that of white women by 3.4 percent and that of black women by 7.6 percent. Among Puerto Rican women, there was a 12.4 percent lag behind all Hispanic women. Closely related to this low labor force participation is the increase in the percentage of female-headed households in the Hispanic community. Researchers have found that the growth of female-headed families in the Puerto Rican population is inversely related to labor force participation. In fact, most of the decline in female labor force participation among New York City Puerto Rican women is accounted for by the increase in female-headed families among this group (27).

For all races, single parent status is significantly related to being below the poverty level in socioeconomic status, and being out of the labor force. Being a single parent more than doubles the likelihood of not being able to maintain the family above poverty level. Spanish-origin women who are heads of household, however, are more likely than either blacks or whites to be below the poverty level if they are not in the labor force: 72 percent of Spanish-origin female heads of household who are not in the labor force are below the poverty level (28). Again, the picture is dramatized by the low labor force participation of Hispanic women, particularly single parents. Fewer than 40 percent of Hispanic children in female-headed families have a mother in the labor force, compared to 57 percent of black children and 67 percent of white children with the same family structure (29). A recently completed study (30) of Puerto Rican women who were heads-of-households in New York City concluded, "Puerto Rican female heads-of-households would be well-served by strategies for achieving self-sufficiency."

Health, Employment, and Unemployment

The presumption that a woman's primary place is in the home has meant that little attention has been paid to the effects of female unemployment on women and their families. Men's unemployment is known to affect their physical health. Unemployment among men is acknowledged to be a stressful life event with health consequences: it is associated with increases in uric acid, cholesterol levels, and blood pressure; and more frequent psychological illness and social problems (31). It cannot be assumed that women who are at home are homemakers out of choice. Many are "discouraged workers" who perceive that it is impossible to obtain a job compatible with their other roles (32). When women wish to work and are not working, this causes adverse effects on the family, including not only mental strain on the mother but social and psychological difficulties among children (33). Furthermore, the strain for working women is increased if children are under age six and family income is below $10,000 (34).

Whether women are at home by choice or default, as housewives they are fulfilling an "active occupational role with potential health hazards of its own" (35). Again, we know much less about actual health conditions associated with this role than about reported conditions. However, housewives are more likely than employed women to report having a chronic condition, or to have limited their activity due to a chronic condition (36). A recent analysis of data from the National Longitudinal Survey showed that the extent of women's labor force attachment is clearly related to their self-reported health status, and that "the supply of labor by black women is more affected by self-rated health than that of whites" (37, p. 56). Blacks who rated themselves in good or excellent health were much more likely to have higher labor force attachment ratings than whites of the same education, age, marital, and family status. This difference decreased, however, as self-rated health status became poorer: both black and white women with poor or fair health had significantly lower labor force attachment. The data did not, unfortunately, allow for comparisons with Hispanic women; however, it is probable that the general trend toward lower labor force attachment with poor self-rated health status holds true for Hispanic women as well. For black and Hispanic women, other barriers to job opportunities may be compounded by the prevalence of chronic conditions, particularly ulcers, heart problems, asthma, and persistent urinary tract infections. A study of women's health care experiences in East Harlem showed the overwhelming proportion of presenting complaints to be stress-related (17). National surveys confirm this, showing that for all women, ambulatory care visits are particularly high for abdominal pain, headache, weight gain, obesity, and neurosis (38).

Housework itself may contribute not only to mental stress, but also to certain types of physical illness. Morton and Ungs (35), in a 15-year retrospective study of housewives in one urban area, reported excessive mortality rates for certain types of cancer. These higher rates were not found among paid household workers or among working women who also do housework. Often it is assumed that the "healthy worker effect" found among men applies to women, thus creating a situation in which those women who are not healthy—in this case have cancer—to begin with are found among the homemaker population. However, this phenomenon has not been studied among women and may not apply "because of the existence of the sex-biased category of housewife to which most women not in the labor force belong" (35, p. 352). Certain types of illness, including cancer, may be more prevalent among women who spend more time as housewives because of conditions related to that role itself: multiple carcinogens in the home;

mental stress associated with the homemaker/mother roles; and risk-enhancing behaviors like smoking, coffee drinking, alcoholism, and excessive food consumption more likely to be indulged in by women at home.

By generalizing these illness categories, we come close to the three areas in which to investigate the effects of employment on health: physical, chemical, and biological occupational hazards; social support; and stress (36). For Hispanic women, particularly Puerto Ricans in northeastern urban areas, certain occupational health hazards are most significant. For example, Puerto Rican women who are clerical workers are exposed to certain chemicals such as ozone and methanol from office machinery at possibly hazardous levels. The occupational health hazards of textile work are better known, particularly those such as brown lung or byssinosis common among women working with cotton fibers. In New York City, for example, 42 percent of Puerto Rican women work in manufacturing, particularly garment making. An even greater number of Hispanic women who are unregistered aliens work in the worst "sweat shops" in the City. In these large urban areas, a disproportionately high number of low-level hospital workers are Hispanic. In ghetto areas like East Harlem ("El Barrio"), where large teaching hospitals are located, these hospitals are often the primary source of employment for the neighborhood. Hospital workers suffer from health conditions resulting from their work, ranging from higher rates of infections, frequent back injury, and certain kinds of cancer, to spontaneous abortion from anesthetic gases.

Clearly, there exists a paucity of information on the occupational health hazards faced by Hispanics as a group. Dicker and Dicker (39) conducted a preliminary analysis of eight industrial categories and the distribution of Hispanics among them. They found that 47 percent of all Hispanics work in the top five industrial categories of highest overall relative risk—mining (1 percent), transportation (6 percent), public utilities (6 percent), agriculture (5 percent), and manufacturing (28 percent)—and suggest that research on the last category should be especially emphasized. Occupatonal position and relative risk, however, also vary with social class, health status, and the availability and use of social support.

Social support has a significant effect on health, and has been shown to be associated with decreased risk of illness or death. Previous work by the authors (6) has shown that this support is critical for the employed Puerto Rican mother. In fact, insofar as it is related to the availability of acceptable child care, it can be a determinant in and of itself of work patterns. No studies, however, have compared social support at work and at home for Puerto Rican women; thus, little is known about the interrelationship of social support, work, and health for this group.

Stress may be experienced by both working women and housewives. For the effect of stress to be understood, both stress related to the work role itself—including housework—and stress related to performing multiple roles must be examined. For example, although the jobs of less-educated women may be less stressful, these women more frequently have more responsibilities for their homemaking and mothering roles. Professional women may have more on-the-job stress, but more frequently can purchase services to relieve them of some home responsibilities. A fuller understanding of the relationship between strain and multiple roles and health requires an in-depth analysis of the interplay of economic conditions with the process of how women evaluate their roles and the availability of social support.

CONCLUSIONS

The health needs of the low-income Hispanic woman are not necessarily distinct from those of other members of her class, racial or ethnic group, or sex. However, her position at the low end of the American class, status, and power hierarchies increases the likelihood that she will have serious health needs, and the equally probable chance that those needs will not be adequately met. In fact, the needs of low-income minority women are even greater than straight calculation on the basis of wealth, status, or power would suggest. These women are most likely to be heads of households, to have larger families, to bear the heaviest burden of caring for the health and well-being of all family members, to be in the poorest health themselves, to experience the greatest psychologically induced symptoms or illnesses, and to be at highest medical risk, particularly during pregnancy and childbirth. That these women recognize their health needs and those of their families and work to meet them is not always understood.

Clearly, any effort to increase the labor force participation of Hispanic women must be based on a real understanding of the most significant variables influencing that participation. Since mobility and improved quality of life in the United States are largely attained through the economic system, Hispanic women, more than other American women, are missing opportunities by being outside this system. To equalize their life opportunities, Hispanic women need to have equal access to labor force participation. Thus, understanding the reasons for that lack of participation or access is critical in terms of any policy that strives toward equity. The policy implications of the labor force participation of Hispanic women extend to areas outside the labor market itself. It is clear, for example, that fertility, use of birth control, and spacing of children are related to labor force participation (40, 41). Similarly, education is directly related to labor force participation, and working mothers have been shown to be strong role models for the education and career aspirations of their daughters. Finally, factors related to female labor force participation include the need for child care, residential mobility, and educational background and training, as well as the health status of the woman and her family.

A suggested area of research is to examine the health-related behaviors of mothers with regard to their children for possible differences between working and nonworking mothers. Given the well documented "juggling act" that accompanies the dual role of working and mothering under circumstances of family wellness, we would hypothesize that the working mother compared to the nonworking mother would bias her family health-related behaviors toward wellness in order not to further complicate her life. We might hypothesize, for example, that the working mother would follow more preventive practices than the nonworking mother; that she would be slower to define her children's discomforts (e.g., colds, low grade fevers, stomach aches) as illnesses; that she would use more home and nonprescription remedies for a longer time before seeing or calling a doctor or other health practitioner; that she would rely on telephone communication with health providers more than visits; that she would consider her children to be well sooner after an illness; and that she would, in general, define her own and her children's health status as being healthier than would women who stay home full time.

Future research in the area of the relationship between work and health must take into account a number of complicating factors. First, there is the possibility of the "healthy worker effect," which might mean that women who have healthy children are more likely to work than women who have chronically or periodically ill children. Second, in older children, there is the possibility that their illness-related behavior is learned to some extent and follows a pattern of approved behaviors in the family. Third is the job structure itself and its flexibility or allowance for staying home with sick children, taking time for doctor's visits, and so forth. Fourth, there is the nature of substitute child care, particularly whether the child is exposed to other children in a child care situation, and whether the child is taken from the house to child care or the caretaker comes to the home.

In sum, factors related to employment and health are different depending on race, gender, and class. For example, race and income have been found to be strong discriminant variables in problems of hypertension among employed women (42). Any analysis that fails to take these factors into account will not be able to provide any insightful information which can be used to change existing social conditions for low-income minority women and their families.

REFERENCES

1. Kanter, R. M. *Work and Family in the U.S.: A Critical Review and Agenda for Research and Policy.* Sage Foundation, New York, 1977.
2. Hartman, H. Capitalism, patriarchy, and job discrimination by sex. In *Capitalist Patriarchy and the Case for Socialist Feminism,* edited by Z. R. Eisenstein. Monthly Review Press, New York, 1977.
3. Sokoloff, N. J. Theories of women's labor force status: A review and critique. *Current Perspectives in Social Theory: A Research Annual* 2, 1981.
4. Felkner, M. The political economy of sexism in industrial health. *Soc. Sci. Med.* 16: 3–13, 1982.
5. Nathanson, C. A. Social roles and health status among women: The significance of employment. *Soc. Sci. Med.* 14A: 463–471, 1980.
6. Hurst, M., and Zambrana, R. Parenting and child care in Puerto Rican families: Implications for women's work. *Annals of Political and Social Science,* special volume on "The Young Child and Social Policy," 1982.

7. Moore, E. C. *Women and Health.* United States Public Health Reports Supplement, September-October 1980.
8. Muller, C. Women and health statistics. *Women Health* 4(1): 37–59, 1979.
9. Alers, J. *Puerto Ricans and Health: Findings From New York City.* Hispanic Research Center, New York, 1978.
10. Weaver, J. L. *National Health Policy and the Underserved: Ethnic Minorities, Women and the Elderly.* C. V. Mosby Co., St. Louis, 1976.
11. Davis, K., and Schoen, C. *Health and the War on Poverty.* The Brookings Institution, Washington, D.C., 1978.
12. Dutton, D. Explaining the low use of health services by the poor: Costs, attitudes, or delivery systems? *Am. J. Sociol.* 43: 348–368, 1978.
13. U.S. Department of Health, Education, and Welfare. *Health Stages of Minorities and Low Income Groups.* U.S. Government Printing Office, Washington, D.C., 1977.
14. U.S. Department of Health, Education, and Welfare. Office Visits by Women, the National Ambulatory Medical Care Survey, United States, 1977. *Vital and Health Statistics,* Series 13, No. 45, DHEW Pub. No. (PHS) 80-1796, Public Health Service. U.S. Government Printing Office, Washington, D.C., March 1980.
15. National Center for Health Statistics. Hypertension: United States, 1974. Advance Data, No. 2. U.S. Department of Health, Education, and Welfare, Public Health Service, Health Resources Administration, 1976.
16. Hurst, M., and Zambrana, R. The health careers of urban women: A study in East Harlem. *Signs* 5(3), 1980.
17. Irigoyen, M., and Zambrana, R. The utilization of pediatric health services by Hispanic mothers. In *Work, Family and Health: Latina Women in Transition,* edited by R. Zambrana. Hispanic Research Center, New York, 1982.
18. Rios, L. E. Determinants of asthma among Puerto Ricans. *J. Latin Community Health* 1(1): 25–40, 1982.
19. Valle, M. *What Holds Sami Back? . . . A Study of Service Delivery in a Puerto Rican Community.* Valle Consultants Ltd., New York, 1973.
20. Goodrich, C. H., Olendski, M. C., and Reader, G. G. *Welfare Medical Care: An Experiment.* Harvard Univesity Press, Cambridge, 1970.
21. Johnson, L. East Harlem Community Health Study. Department of Community Medicine, Mount Sinai School of Medicine of the City University of New York, New York, 1972.
22. Woods, N. F., and Hulka, B. S. Symptom reports and illness behavior among employed women and homemakers. *J. Community Health* 5(1): 36–45, 1979.
23. Lecca, P. J., et al. Profile of Health Resources Among Unemployed Puerto Ricans in the U. S. Unpublished manuscript.
24. Gray, L. S. The jobs Puerto Ricans hold in New York City. *Monthly Labor Rev.* 12–16, 1975.
25. U.S. Bureau of Labor Statistics. A Socio-economic Profile of Puerto Rican New Yorkers. Region Report 46, Middle Atlantic Regional Office, 1975.
26. Cooney, R S., and Warren, A. E. C. Declining female participation among Puerto Rican New Yorkers: A comparison with native non-Spanish speaking New Yorkers. *Ethnicity* 6: 281-297.
27. Cooney, R. S., and Colon, A. Work and family: The recent struggle of Puerto Rican females. In *The Puerto Rican Struggle, Essays on Survival in the U.S.,* edited by C. Rodriguez, V. S. Korrol, and J. O. Alers. Puerto Rican Migration Research Consortium, Inc., New York, 1980.
28. *Current Population Reports,* Series P. 60, No. 130, 1979.

29. Grossman, A. S. More than half of all children have working mothers. *Monthly Labor Rev.*, February 1982, pp. 41–43.
30. Morgan, L. S. *Access to Training Programs: Barriers Encountered by Hispanic Female Heads-of-Household in New York City.* Puerto Rican Legal Defense and Education Fund, New York, 1981.
31. Gore, S. The effect of social support in moderating the health consequences of unemployment. *J. Health Soc. Behav.* 19: 157, 1978.
32. Rosen, E. I. Unemployed Women: You Can't Go Home Again. Unpublished manuscript. Wellesley College, 1979.
33. Harrall, J. E., and Ridley, C. A. Substitute child care, maternal employment and the quality of mother-child interaction. *J. Marriage Family* 37: 556–564, 1975.
34. Robeson, E. Strain and Dual Role Occupation Among Women. Ph.D. Dissertation, City University of New York Graduate Center, 1977.
35. Morton, W., and Ungs, T. J. Cancer mortality in the major cottage industry. *Women Health* (4): 343–354, 1979.
36. Waldron, I. Employment and women's health: An analysis of causal relationships. *Int. J. Health Serv.* 10(3), 1980.
37. Maret, E. How women's health affects labor force attachment. *Monthly Labor Rev.* April 1982, pp. 56–58.
38. National Ambulatory Medical Care Survey. U.S. DHEW, 1975.
39. Dicker, L., and Dicker, M. Occupational health hazards faced by Hispanic workers: An exploratory discussion. *J. Latin Community Health* 1(1): 101–107, 1982.
40. Gordon, H. A., and Kammeyer, K. C. W. The gainful employment of women with small children. *J. Marriage Family* 42(2): 327–336, 1980.
41. Groat, H. T., Workman, R. L., and Neal, A. G. Labor force participation and family formation: A study of working mothers. *Demography* 13(1): 115–125, 1976.
42. Zimmerman, M. K., and Hartley, W. S. High blood pressure among employed women: A multi-factor discriminant analysis. *J. Health Soc. Behav.* 23(3): 205–220, 1982.

CHAPTER 8

Sugar and Spice and Everything Nice: Health Effects of the Sexual Division of Labor among Train Cleaners

Karen Messing, Ghislaine Doniol-Shaw, and Chantal Haëntjens

In many countries, women in the paid labor force work at a small number of jobs (1–5). It has been calculated that in order for North American men and women to be distributed randomly across occupational categories, two-thirds of the total working population would have to change jobs (6). In Canada, for example, 55 percent of women work at only 20 jobs, primarily clerical, health care, teaching, waitressing, hairdressing, or assembly line work such as sewing machine operator. Only five occupations are common to the lists of the top 20 men's and women's jobs (7).

Studies done in several countries have shown that women are further segregated into specific tasks within occupations. In the Québec Ministry of Social Affairs, where 73 percent of workers in 1979 were women, an analysis showed that men and women had separate job titles and separate responsibilities at all levels (8). In factories in France (9), Québec (10), Nova Scotia (11), and Norway (12), women and men are in different parts of the production line.

This sexual division of labor is a major factor determining male–female wage differences (5, pp. 41–46; 13, pp. 15–20; 14). For this reason, women are entering nontraditional jobs in increasing numbers. However, desegregation has often been blocked using arguments based on presumed biological differences between the sexes; women are thought to be assigned to specific jobs because they are too exacting, and women are intrinsically weaker and technically less competent than men (13, pp. 35–39; 15). Others have suggested that the sexual division of labor is

Originally published in the *International Journal of Health Services* 23(1): 133–146, 1993.

based not on women's abilities or job characteristics, but rather on the shifting demands of the labor market (1, 16).

The question of whether the sexual division of labor is based on biological differences between the sexes has been approached in two ways. First, the experience of women in nontraditional jobs has been examined. Social barriers to the employment of women in nontraditional jobs have been described (13, 16), but biologically based arguments have also been invoked. Exclusion of women because of their "natural" qualities sometimes appears to be borne out by events in the workplace. In 1982, a group of women brought a case before the Canadian Human Rights Commission asking that women be hired in blue-collar jobs in a railway company. The employer argued that women did not like to do dirty jobs and were unable to do heavy work. The Commission found that the tests used to qualify workers for these jobs were inappropriate, and ordered the company to begin an affirmative action program in order to hire women in nontraditional jobs. However, ten years later, only three of the 20 or so women hired were still employed in this company, whose workforce is over 1,200 (17).

This sequence, in which women attempt to enter nontraditional jobs and are eliminated, may reinforce stereotypes concerning women's strength and aptitudes (18). Addressing this issue, ergonomic analyses of some jobs from which women have been eliminated, including jobs in the railway company mentioned above (17), have revealed that there may be obstacles to women's integration because of the dimensions of working surfaces and tools, resulting in a higher probability of injury for women workers in nontraditional jobs, as well as greater difficulties for women workers in maintaining production (19). Changes in tools and equipment can enable women (and other smaller workers) to perform more safely and efficiently. To some extent at least, difficulties attributed to biological differences may be remedied by job redesign.

A second approach to examining biological differences in job qualifications has been to ask whether women's traditional work is less exacting than men's. Several authors have reviewed the specific physical and technical characteristics of women's work (7, 12, 20). An ergonomic study of data entry work showed that such "unskilled," low-paid work involved a high degree of technical competence whose exercise was not only unrecognized but sometimes had to be hidden from supervisors (21). A study of workers in a cookie factory has shown that technical requirements of women's jobs were unrecognized by both women and men (22).

A fast workspeed is probably the most common characteristic of women's jobs in factories and offices, and a fast overall pace is one of the costs of the "double workday" (19, 23). Women in poultry slaughterhouses make 60 movements per minute; sewing machine operators sew 225 pairs of pants an hour; typists may be controlled by their microcomputers, which scold them if they haven't "produced" a sufficient number of characters in a given time period; hospital workers describe intense time pressures; working mothers rush from job to stores to home (24–26). The physical load resulting from a fast workspeed has been associated with musculoskeletal problems among workers in women's employment "ghettos" (27–29), and the resulting mental load has been associated with stress-related illness (30).

Thus, researchers have suggested that, far from respecting men's and women's biology, the sexual division of labor may have adverse effects on health (31–33). In the course of an ergonomic analysis of train cleaning in France we found a rigid sexual division of labor (34). We present here the results of the analysis and some reflections on the health implications of this sexual division of labor.

The approach that we used, developed by French ergonomists (35), combines observation of work in real-life situations with information obtained from interviews with workers and management. Workers are asked to explain various aspects of their ways of doing their job ("modes opératoires") in the hope that the explanations will reveal technical and physical requirements of their work not apparent in their job descriptions. For example, the data entry clerks mentioned above explained to the research team that they secretly programmed the central computer in order to save time on their jobs (21). Women sewing gloves on an assembly line explained the complexities involved in matching the two halves of a badly cut glove, and researchers were enabled to understand why the physical requirements of this apparently routine undemanding job made it difficult for any but the youngest workers (36). Although such ergonomic studies of a very limited number of workers do not permit generalizations regarding women's work, they can furnish rich detail about the work actually done by some women. We describe here a single job, toilet cleaning, assigned specifically to women. Since we found that there was great resistance to men doing this job, we present it as an example of physical characteristics of a job that can justly be described as "women's work."

MATERIALS AND METHODS

The Cleaning Company

The employer was a cleaning service that had recently signed a contract with the French Société nationale des chemins de fer (SNCF), for a period of three years. The contract requires cleaning of suburban trains according to a schedule determined by the SNCF, which approves the tools and materials used and inspects the trains after cleaning. In France, contracting companies are required to hire the personnel of the previous contractor; thus, the employees' seniority had been acquired with a series of previous employers. During the present study, the employer went bankrupt and its contract was taken over by another branch of the same company.

Access to the site was gained through the recommendation of the occupational health physician. Although the researchers were allowed unlimited observation time, workers were not freed for organized interviews or information gathering.

Conversations and interviews with the latter were always conducted on an informal basis and were held either while working or during coffee breaks.

Study Population

Nineteen men and 17 women were employed on a permanent basis; several people were employed occasionally or for short contracts. The mean age of regular male employees (on December 1, 1990) was 47 ± 9.5 years, and the mean age of the women was 39 ± 9.5 years. Four times as many men as women were over 50. The average seniority of men was 16 ± 7 and of women 8 ± 8 years (Figure 1).

Data Collection

Work was done in shifts. The morning shift (12 to 16 workers) was from 7:30 a.m. to 4:18 p.m.; a group of five to six worked from 8:45 a.m. to 5:33 p.m.; the afternoon shift of 12 to 16 workers was between 2:45 p.m. and 11:33 p.m. Numbers of workers per shift varied according to peak days, and an extra shift was added on Fridays. Our observations were concentrated on the morning shift. Work was observed globally during four two-hour periods, three in the morning and one

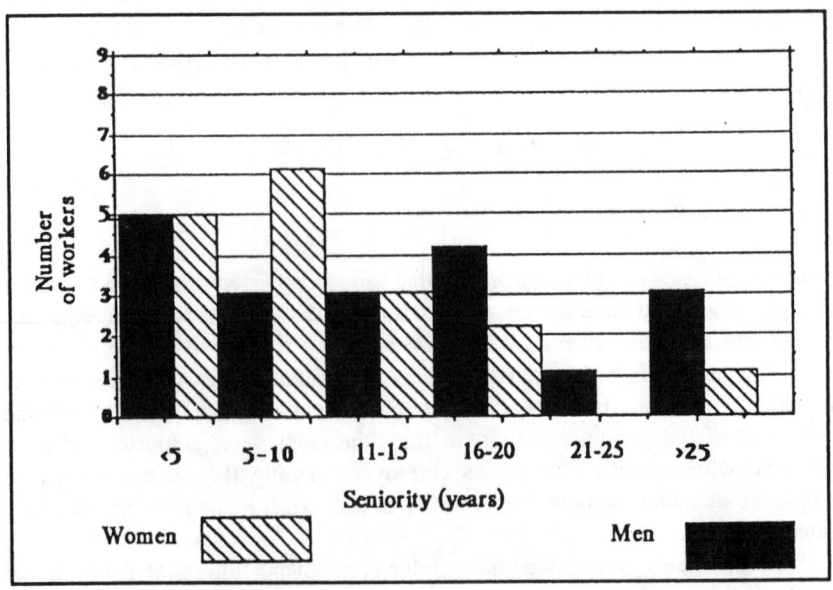

Figure 1. Distribution of seniority, by sex, among French train cleaners.

during the afternoon. In addition, toilet cleaning by three workers was observed systematically for a total of ten hours during morning shifts. Observations of the first five of the ten hours were recorded using paper and pencil (three hours noting actions performed plus two hours noting postures), and the rest of the observations were done using the Psion Organiser II programmed with the Kronos program (patented by Alain Kerguelen), which permits simultaneous recording of several categories at a time. We recorded postures, time per toilet, the state of the toilet, and the state of the water supply. Postures were classified as "standing," "slightly bent," (angle between trunk and legs < 135°), "bent" (angle < 90°), and "crouched" (angle < 45°).

Distances were calculated using the K & E "Thermor" pedometer previously calibrated with the stride of the individual worker and against a measured distance.

Interviews were carried out on work content with the company director, the union representative ("délégué du personnel"), the section head ("inspectrice de chantier"), and the foreman ("chef de chantier"). Conversations about work content and health symptoms took place with the three regular toilet cleaners, and informal conversations occurred with many other employees. In addition, depersonalized compilations of health symptoms existing at the time of any medical interview during the previous five years were supplied by the company's occupational health physician.

Absence records were compiled from the registers of the company for the four months starting September 1990, for all permanent employees. Train schedules were compiled for typical workdays.

RESULTS

Work Organization

The cleaning of suburban trains was organized as follows (workers refer to themselves by the names of their tools or the objects cleaned). The "brush" picked up all objects (newspapers, soft drink cans) from the floor under the seats and the seats themselves, leaving them in the aisle. The "broom" swept the aisle and put all rubbish and dirt into a bag. The mechanized "water cart" drove from car to car and filled the reservoirs for the bathrooms, which were cleaned by the "toilet." The "railings" polished railings and chrome surfaces. The "team leader" dusted after all others had passed. The "foreman" worked out of an office, where he planned the work. If numbers permitted, most cleaning tasks were done by two people who cleaned alternate cars. The cleaning of main line trains was organized in a similar way, with the addition of three tasks: emptying ashtrays, cleaning the bar, and polishing the tray tables at each seat.

The sexual division of labor was clear. The positions of "water cart," "railings," "team leader," and "foremen" were always men; "brush" was mixed; and "broom" was usually a woman. "Toilet cleaners," "ashtrays," "tray tables," and "bar" were always a woman. In fact, strikes were threatened on two occasions when the sexual division of labor was questioned, once when men were asked to clean toilets and once when the company offered to train women to drive the water cart. In both cases the company backed down and the changes were never instituted.

Constraints Associated with These Jobs

Time constraints were very heavy. Twenty to 30 trains were cleaned per shift, concentrating during peak periods. Most of these were suburban trains, which were cleaned in four to 12 minutes, depending on the time available. Time available to clean a train began from the arrival of the train and ended when the first passenger was allowed to embark, ten minutes before departure. Trains often arrived late and time for cleaning was thereby reduced. During the study, a work accident ensued when a "broom," in her hurry to begin cleaning the train, positioned herself next to the steps and was hit in the eye with the briefcase of a disembarking passenger.

The complaint voiced first by all workers asked "What is the principal problem on your job?" was "We run all the time"; this was also the major complaint raised during a five-day strike during the course of the study. Since the trains could arrive on any track and the sequence of tracks was not coordinated with the cleaning schedule, cleaners had to move constantly between different tracks as well as along the 100- to 200-meter long trains. Often, two halves of a train would depart at different times; workers would clean the front half, then clean a train eight or more tracks distant before returning to clean the second half. Pedometer readings for "broom" and "toilet cleaning" gave 22.2 ± 1.6 kilometers per shift.

Health Problems and Absences

In France, the occupational health physician must examine each worker once a year. Table 1 presents the problems reported during the previous five years' examinations of the 19 men and 17 women. Despite the relative age and greater seniority of the men (Figure 1), they reported many fewer health problems, particularly musculoskeletal problems.

Absenteeism was very high among cleaners, averaging 13 percent (number of days absent as percentage of number of days scheduled to work). Absent workers were not replaced, and those present were asked to do the work of those absent. Women's rate of absence was nearly three times that of men (Figure 2), and 76 percent of women were absent at least once during the four month sampling period, compared with 45 percent of men. The reasons for absence were not available from company records.

Absences of women posed a particular problem for toilet cleaning, because men would not be asked to clean toilets. Thus, although three women per shift were

Table 1

Pathologies recorded during annual medical
examinations of French train cleaners, 1985–1990

Pathology[a]	Women (N = 17)	Men (N = 19)
Back pain	7	3
Wrist pain	5	2
Joint pain, upper limb	1	0
Ankle pain	2	0
Knee pain	2	0
Stomach pain	2	5
Circulatory problems		
Heavy legs	11	4
Varicose veins	7	0
Phlebitis	2	2
Asthenia at end of workday	12	1

[a]The same worker could have more than one pathology.

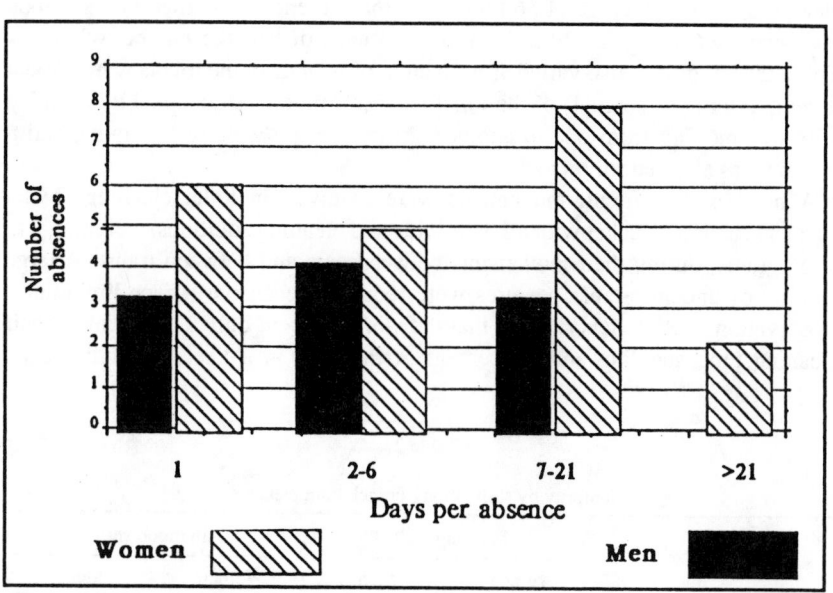

Figure 2. Distribution of absences from work, by sex, among French train cleaners, September–December 1990.

usually assigned to this task, all regularly employed women were assigned to this task at least once during the study period. In the afternoon shift, it was difficult to recruit enough women, because when they acquired seniority they transferred to the morning shift (Table 2), which was easier for them because of family responsibilities. In addition, the company doctor forbade several women with back problems to do tasks that required bending and kneeling, such as toilet cleaning. This contributed to the shortage of women for this task. One 40-year-old woman reported that her foreman refused to accept her medical certificate and threatened her with the loss of her job if she would not clean toilets on a Sunday morning when she was the only woman present.

Characteristics of Toilet Cleaning

Between 180 and 240 bathrooms were cleaned per shift. Workers were required to clean taps, sinks, and mirrors, remove stains from walls, wash floors, and clean toilet fixtures in each cubicle. Two women were normally assigned to cleaning toilets, but there were frequent exceptions. The second toilet cleaner often replaced absent or reassigned colleagues. On weekends and during slack periods, only one toilet cleaner was assigned.

Cleaning time varied between 63 and 108 seconds per toilet as a function of the number of cleaners available. If one worker was available she took 63 seconds to clean each toilet (average of 86 toilets); in the presence of a coworker, she took 108 seconds (average of 30 toilets) to clean each of half the number of toilets. Toilet cleaning time also varied as a function of how dirty the toilets were. About three-quarters (72 percent) of the toilet cleaner's time was occupied by cleaning toilets or moving from one to another, 20 percent by waiting for trains, and 8 percent was allowed for breaks.

A number of difficult movements were involved in toilet cleaning. Toilet cleaners carried a bucket with all their tools and cleaning solutions, weighing 2 to 3 kilograms, during their movements between cars and between trains. A large number of uncomfortable postures were required because of space limitations. Observation of 35 toilets showed that the workers spent only 11 percent of their cleaning time standing and 25 percent of the time in a kneeling or crouched

Table 2

Seniority by shift among French train cleaners

	Morning shift		Afternoon shift	
	Women	Men	Women	Men
Seniority, years	10	15	5	12
Number of workers	12	7	5	11

position. They changed from one position to another once every 3.0 ± 0.2 seconds. Thirty-eight percent of a sample of 317 postural changes involved a displacement for the trunk over an angle of greater than 90° with the legs (between "standing" and "bent," for example).

Among 86 toilets where the operations were noted, very few toilets were cleaned in the same way. Adjustments were constantly made for the type and location of dirt. Angles of attack, scrubbing motions, and sequences of movement were all modified in response to the specific situation encountered in each toilet. In addition, some operations were added or eliminated in response to time constraints, changes in water supply, and the state of the toilet (6).

Toilet cleaners reported feeling disgusted in various situations. In one toilet in five (of 86 sampled), human solid waste had been deposited elsewhere than in the bottom of the toilet bowl, requiring a special effort to scrub it off. On one occasion, a dog defecated on one of the train seats and the "brush" normally assigned to clean the seats called on the toilet cleaner to remove it, resulting in a quarrel over jurisdiction. On weekends, vomitus was frequently found on the floors. No special precautions were taken with this material other than the use of gloves.

DISCUSSION

Characteristics of Women's Work in Train Cleaning

Men's and women's jobs in train cleaning were not compared. However, one job that was exclusively assigned to women, toilet cleaning, had characteristics sometimes thought to be associated with stereotypes of male jobs, that is, it was physically demanding, required technical knowledge, and involved considerable exposure to dirt and filth.

Physical Load

Physical strength is the aspect most often mentioned as a justification of differential job assignment, by both employers and employees (18, 37, 38). In fact, jobs that involve lifting of heavy weights all at once with rest intervals between each lift are most frequently assigned to men, with the exception of patient care tasks in the health care professions and lifting children in day care centers (39). However, it has been shown that traditional women's jobs often involve manipulating a large *total* weight per day. Laundry workers in one study lifted 1,800 kg of wet sheets per day, one by one, and they also pushed or pulled 6,000 kg per day (40). In another factory, sewing machine operators manipulated a total of 3,500 kg per day with their arms and 16,000 kg with their legs (41). Although force was not systematically measured in the present study, the task of toilet cleaning shows a similar pattern of exertion. Workers exert themselves constantly during scrubbing tasks and carry a loaded bucket over long distances, although they do not lift single heavy weights.

The sexual division of labor is often justified by the estimate that women average two-thirds of men's physical strength, based on laboratory tests using psychophysiological testing, in which subjects are asked to lift objects whose weight is increased until the subject reports feeling uncomfortable (42); biomechanical testing, in which dynamic strength is measured by exerting a maximal force against a machine; or physiological testing, in which energy consumption is monitored in relation to exertion (43). However, these tests do not measure suppleness, such as the ability to bend and twist constantly at great speed as in the work of the toilet cleaners, or endurance, such as the ability to keep up a fast work speed throughout the day.

Endurance may be an especially important physical component of women's traditional jobs when the domestic workload is taken into account (44). Although no systematic study of the length of the domestic workday was undertaken in this workplace, a contemporary study revealed that women working full-time in French slaughterhouses do an average of 20 hours of domestic tasks weekly (compared to two hours for the average male coworker) (45). Informal conversations with women train cleaners revealed that most women with families lived outside Paris and commuted up to two and a half hours per day. Several married women said they had exclusive responsibility for domestic tasks; greater female responsibility for these tasks was indicated by the male–female differential in the relationship between shift preference and sex (shown in Table 2). One toilet cleaner spoke of a workday that began at 4 a.m. with making the family breakfast and finished at 9 p.m. with helping the children with their homework.

Technical Competence

A requirement for technical competence is often used to justify assigning men to machine maintenance and surveillance, and women often refuse jobs with machines because of the fear of technical inadequacy (46). However, traditional women's work involves its own requirements for technical competence. As mentioned above (21, 36), hidden qualifications may be involved in apparently routine tasks. In toilet cleaning, technical skill is required to clean a toilet adequately in 63 seconds, while adjusting one's techniques for all the possible locations and types of dirt.

Dirt and Filth

In hospitals, women are assigned to many tasks involving exposure to human excretions. In the home, women have traditionally cared for infants, including changing diapers. The assignment of toilet cleaning in trains to women appears to follow a trend in which dirty jobs are preferentially assigned to women. The fact that a woman was called to clean up the dog excrement although its location made it part of the task of a man illustrates the extent to which this activity was sex-typed.

Biological Basis of the Sexual Division of Labor

The suggestion that the sexual division of labor is based on biological differences between the sexes appears to be supported by the association between women's work and certain job characteristics such as fast movements, repetition, and lack of autonomy (9, 19, 47–49). Men's traditional work, on the other hand, is thought to be heavy and dirty and to require technical knowledge (17–19). The present study shows that toilet cleaning, done by women, involves fast movements and repetition, and thus to some degree bears out this association.

It may be that the type of physical expenditure in traditional jobs is better adapted to the characteristics of the average woman than to those of the average man. Men's larger mean muscle mass facilitates lifting heavy weights. Other parameters of the capacity to do physical work have not yet been fully explored in relation to sex differences. For example, it has been suggested that women have more "fast twitch" fibers than men, and thus might be better suited to work at jobs requiring endurance, although this hypothesis has not been confirmed experimentally (50).

However, this study also shows that requirements for heavy physical labor, technical knowledge, and tolerance of dirt do not prevent jobs from being assigned to women, and may indeed be characteristic of certain jobs considered to be "women's work."

Health and Safety Implications

The health problems observed in this study can be attributed to working conditions poorly adapted to human physiology. Toilet cleaning, done at some time during our study by all 17 women workers, requires walking 20 kilometers per day, cleaning 180 to 240 toilets, spending 49 minutes kneeling or crouched, and changing postures about 5,000 times (200 toilets × 25 posture changes per toilet). We think that illness and fatigue caused by these job requirements could explain the high rate of absence among these women. Although women workers' absences were attributed by various members of the administrative staff to women's family responsibilities, this explanation was not borne out by the fact that women's absences were of relatively long duration (Figure 2). Policies dealing with absences appeared to exacerbate the problem; for example, the fact that absent workers were not replaced meant that the second toilet cleaner was often eliminated. The remaining woman had to cope with a sharply increased workload, which was a result but possibly also a further cause of the high level of absenteeism among women. Although the hypothesis that absenteeism was related to occupational illness could not be verified, since reasons for absence were confidential, it is borne out by the relatively high incidence of various health symptoms, particularly musculoskeletal symptoms, among women workers.

The health problems may reflect combined effects of employment in train cleaning and in the home on women workers. Absence could be due to adverse effects of heavy workload on health and to a reluctance to face such heavy work on any days when the workers are feeling even a bit under the weather.

The sexual division of labor based on male–female biological differences is only one type of worker selection. Older or disabled workers, for example, may be unable to perform certain tasks. Genetic screening has been proposed in order to select workers who may be resistant to toxic chemicals in the workplace. Thus, worker selection is used as a method of promoting efficiency and preventing industrial disease (51). However, it has been argued that the health of all workers may be protected more efficiently by adapting workplaces to a wide variety of physical types than by selecting workers in relation to single, rigidly conceived positions (38). Work would thus be rendered less dangerous for all, irrespective of body type.

Unduly heavy work in train cleaning is not limited to women workers. Many of the other jobs are also extremely demanding. The "brush" works bent over most of the time, the "railings" and "water cart" must occasionally carry heavy loads, and "ashtrays" and "tray tables" require rapid wrist movements that have been suspected of giving rise to carpal tunnel syndrome ("wrist pain" in Table 1). The repetitive character of most of these tasks combined with the awkward movements performed may involve a risk of disability in later life, as has been observed for clothing industry workers (27). Although women train cleaners show a larger proportion of health problems at this time, some of the men may eventually suffer long-term effects of their tasks.

The report submitted to the company and to the employee representative recommended several changes, including better tools, improved conditions for breaks, increases in personnel, and redesign of train bathrooms to facilitate cleaning (34). Workers generally agreed with these recommendations. However, there was much greater resistance to our recommendation to rotate all jobs so that difficult tasks would be shared and to avoid repetitive strain injury. This resistance was heard from both women and men. Similar resistance has been noted to sharing of domestic tasks (52–54). Walkerdine (55) and Cockburn (13) have suggested that changes in sex roles and in sex-based task assignments encounter resistance because of their profound roots in identity and fantasy life as well as their relation to issues of power and dominance. It may therefore be difficult to change the sexual division of labor even though it appears to involve a heavy cost for women train cleaners, and may also involve health effects for their male colleagues.

REFERENCES

1. Bradley, H. *Men's Work, Women's Work*. University of Minnesota Press, Minneapolis, Minn., 1989.

2. Reskin, B. *Sex Segregation in the Workplace.* National Academy Press, Washington, D.C., 1984.
3. Corvi, N., and Salort, M. *Les Femmes et le Marché du Travail.* Hatier, Paris, 1986.
4. Walby, S. *Sex Discrimination at Work.* Open University Press, Milton Keynes, England, 1988.
5. Armstrong, P., and Armstrong, H. *Theorizing Women's Work.* Garamond Press, Toronto, 1991.
6. David, H. *Femmes et emploi: le défi de l'égalité.* Presses de l'Université du Québec, Montréal, 1986.
7. Messing, K. *Occupational Health and Safety Concerns of Canadian Women.* Labour Canada, Ottawa, 1991.
8. Gaucher, D. L'égalité: Une Lutte à Finir. M.A. thesis, Département de sociologie de la santé, Université de Montréal, 1979.
9. Kergoat, D. *Les Ouvrières.* Sycomore, Paris. 1982.
10. Messing, K., and Reveret, J.-P. Are women in female jobs for their health? A study of working conditions and health effects in the fish-processing industry in Québec. *Int. J. Health Serv.* 13: 635–643, 1983.
11. Lamson, C. On the line: Women and fish plant jobs in Atlantic Canada. *Relations industrielles* 41: 145–157, 1986.
12. Kaul, J., and Lie, M. When paths are vicious circles: How women's working conditions limit influence. *Econ. Industr. Democracy* 3: 465–481, 1982.
13. Cockburn, C. *Machinery of Dominance: Women, Men and Technical Know-how.* Pluto Press, London, 1985.
14. Stathan, A., Miller, E. M., and Mauksch, H. O. *The Worth of Women's Work.* State University of New York Press, Albany, N.Y., 1988.
15. Messing, K. Do men and women have different jobs because of their biological differences? *Int. J. Health Serv.* 12: 43–52, 1982.
16. Reskin, B., and Roos, P. A. *Job Queues, Gender Queues.* Temple University Press, Philadelphia, 1990.
17. Courville, J., Vézina, N., and Messing, K. Analysis of work activity of a job in a machine shop held by ten men and one woman. *Int. J. Industr. Ergon.* 7: 163–174, 1991.
18. Ward, J. S. Sex discrimination is essential in industry. *J. Occup. Med.* 20: 594–596, 1978.
19. Courville, J., Vézina, N., and Messing, K. Analyse des facteurs ergonomiques pouvant entraîner l'exclusion des femmes du tri des colis postaux. *Le Travail Humain,* 55: 119–134, 1992.
20. Mergler, D. Rapport-synthèse. Les conditions de travail des femmes. In *Les effets des conditions de travail sur la santé des travailleuses,* edited by J.-A. Bouchard, pp. 215–227. Confédération des syndicats nationaux, Montréal, 1983.
21. Teiger, C., and Bernier, C. Ergonomic analysis of work activity of data entry clerks in the computerized service sector can reveal unrecognized skills. *Women and Health* 18: 67–78, 1992.
22. Dumais, L., Messing, K., Seifert, A. M., Courville, J., and Vézina. Make me a cake as fast as you can: Determinants of inertia and change in the sexual division of labour of an industrial bakery. *Work, Employment and Society,* 7: 363–38, 1993.
23. Kauppinen-Toropainen, K., Kandolin, I., and Mutanen, P. Job dissatisfaction and work-related exhaustion in male and female work. *J. Occup. Behav.* 4: 193–197, 1983.
24. Mergler, D., et al. The weaker sex? Men in women's jobs report similar health symptoms. *J. Occup. Med.* 29: 417–421, 1987.

25. Leppänen, R. A., and Oikinuora, M. A. Psychological stress experienced by health care personnel. *Scand. J. Work Environ. Health* 13: 1–8, 1987.
26. Billette, A., and Piché, J. Organisation du travail et santé mentale chez les auxiliaires en saisie des données. *Santé mentale au Québec* X: 86–98, 1985.
27. Brisson, C., Vinet, A., and Vézina, M. Disability among female garment workers. *Scand. J. Work Environ. Health* 15: 323–328, 1989.
28. Punnett, L. Soft tissue disorders in the upper limbs of female garment workers. *Scand. J. Work Environ. Health* 11: 417–425, 1985.
29. Hägg, G., and Suurküla, J. Relations between shoulder/neck disorders and myoelectric signs of local muscle fatigue in female assembly workers. *Proceedings of the 1984 International Conference on Occupational Ergonomics* 1: 324–327, 1984.
30. Alexander, R. W., and Fedoruk, M. J. Epidemic psychogenic illness in a telephone operators' building. *J. Occup. Med.* 28: 42–45, 1986.
31. Stellman, J. *Women's Work, Women's Health.* Pantheon, New York, 1977.
32. Hunt, V. *Work and the Health of Women.* CRC Publications, Boca Raton, 1978.
33. Chavkin, W. *Double Exposure.* Monthly Review Press, New York, 1984.
34. Messing, K., Haëntjens, C., and Doniol-Shaw, G. L'invisible nécessaire: l'activité de nettoyage des toilettes sur les trains de voyageurs en gare. *Le travail humain,* 55: 353–370, 1993.
35. Guérin, F., et al. *Comprendre le travail pour le transformer.* Editions de l'ANACT, Montrouge, France, 1991.
36. Teiger, C. Les contraintes du travail dans les travaux répétitifs de masse et leurs conséquences sur les travailleuses. In *Les effets des conditions de travail sur la santé des travailleuses,* edited by J.-A. Bouchard, pp. 33–68. Confédération des syndicats nationaux, Montréal, 1984.
37. Ward, J. S. Women at work. Ergonomic considerations. *Ergonomics* 27: 475–479, 1984.
38. Messing, K., Courville, J., and Vézina, N. Minimizing health risks for women who enter jobs traditionally assigned to men. *New Solutions: J. Environ. Occup. Health Policy* 1: 466–471, 1991.
39. Lortie, M. Analyse comparative des accidents déclarés par des préposés hommes et femmes d'un hôpital gériatrique. *J. Occup. Accidents* 9: 59–81, 1987.
40. Brabant, C., Bédard, S., and Mergler, D. Cardiac strain among women laundry workers doing repetitive, sedentary work. *Ergonomics* 32: 615–628, 1989.
41. Vézina, N., and Courville, J. Integrating women into traditionally masculine jobs. *Women Health* 18: 97–118, 1992.
42. Snook, S. H., and Ciriello, V. Maximum weights and work loads acceptable to female workers. *J. Occup. Med.* 16: 527–534, 1974.
43. Aghazadeh, F., and Dharwadkar, S. R. Effect of gender on physical work capacity and strength. In *Trends in Ergonomics/Human Factors,* II, edited by R. E. Erberts and C. G. Erberts, pp. 551–557. Elsevier Science Publishers, Amsterdam, 1985.
44. Tierney, D., Romito, P., and Messing, K. She ate not the bread of idleness: Exhaustion is related to domestic and salaried work of hospital workers in Québec. *Women Health* 16: 21–42, 1990.
45. Messing, K., Romito, P., and Saurel-Cubizolles, M.-J. "Moonlighting" as a Mom: Domestic Workload Should Be Considered when Evaluating the Effects of Shiftwork. Paper presented at the Colloque sur le travail posté de l'Association Internationale d'ergonomie, Paris, July 1991.
46. Cockburn, C. Technical Competence, Gender Identity and Women's Autonomy. Paper presented at the World Congress of Sociology, Madrid, July 9–13, 1990.

47. Molinié, A.-F., and Volkoff, S. Les conditions de travail des ouvriers . . . et des ouvrières. *Economie et Statistique* 118: 25–28, 1980.
48. Kauppinen-Toropainen, K., Kandolin, I., and Haavio-Manila, E. Sex segregation of work in Finland and the quality of women's work. *J. Organizational Behav.* 9: 15–27, 1988.
49. Klitzman, S., et al. A women's occupational health agenda for the 1990s. *New Solutions* 1: 1–11, 1990.
50. Courville, J. Différences biologiques entre les hommes et les femmes et activité de travail. M.Sc. thesis, Department of Biological Sciences, Université du Québec à Montréal, 1990.
51. Hubbard, R., and Henifin, M. S. Genetic screening of prospective parents and of workers: Some scientific and social issues. *Int. J. Health Serv.* 15: 231–251, 1985.
52. Vandelac, L. The New Deal des rapports hommes-femmes: Big deal! In *Du travail et de l'amour*, edited by L. Vandelac. Editions St-Martin, Montréal, 1985.
53. Romito, P. *La naissance du premier enfant,* Chapt. 8. Delachaux et Nestlé, Lausanne, Switzerland, 1990.
54. Le Bourdais, C., Hamel, P. J., and Bernard, P. Le travail et l'ouvrage. Charge et partage des tâches domestiques chez les couples québécois. *Sociologie et sociétés* 19: 37–55, 1987.
55. Walkerdine, V. *Schoolgirl Fictions.* Verso Press, London, 1990.

CHAPTER 9

The Untold Story:
How the Health Care Systems in Developing Countries Contribute to Maternal Mortality

T. K. Sundari

The high maternal mortality rates in most of the developing countries, despite advances in health care, have prompted several studies analyzing the main causes of maternal death and groups at risk, so that medical care can be appropriately directed. However, the role of the health services system itself, both in preventing a woman with a complication in pregnancy or delivery from seeking medical help and in providing a woman who reaches a medical facility with appropriate care, has rarely been looked into. Of the several links in the chain of events that culminate in a maternal death, the role of an inadequate health care system characterized by misplaced priorities seems to be vital. This chapter attempts to put together evidence to this effect, using data from maternal mortality studies in several developing countries.

It is common practice for hospital-based studies on maternal mortality to look into "avoidable factors": factors that, if avoided, could have prevented the maternal death. In a number of cases, the researchers state explicitly that the avoidability of deaths was evaluated by standards realistic under the circumstances prevailing in that country at that time. The discussions in this chapter are based on such accounts.

Originally published in the *International Journal of Health Services* 22(3): 513–528, 1992.

"PATIENT FACTORS," OR INACCESSIBLE
HEALTH SERVICES?

One of the standard categories into which avoidable factors are classified is what are known as "patient factors." Patient factors, as the name suggests, are deemed faulty action on the part of the patient, for which the health care system is not responsible and about which it is helpless to do anything. Table 1 gives an overview of the proportion of maternal deaths attributed to various patient factors in different studies (1–8).

Table 1

Maternal deaths with "patient factor" as an avoidable factor
in selected developing countries

Country: hospital/region (reference no.)	Factor	No. of all maternal deaths (%)	Years
Malaysia: all government health facilities in Krian district (1)	Refusal to go to hospital	95 (10%)	1978–
	Handled by traditional birth attendant and relatives; delayed medical aid	182 (20%)	1981
	Handled by traditional birth attendant alone; no medical aid	164 (18%)	
Vietnam: 22 institutions (2)	Patient not presented	22 (17%)	1984–
	Patient noncompliance	13 (10%)	1985
Pakistan: Civil Hospital, Karachi (3)	Patient's or relations' attitude	85 (67%)	1979–
	Deficient management by traditional birth attendants	11 (9%)	1983
Malawi: Kamuzu Central Hospital, Lilongwe (4)	Patient delay	29 (48%)	1985
Tanzania: Muhimbili Medical Center, Dar-es-Salaam (5)	Delay in arrival	11 (7%)	1983
	Interference with pregnancy	2 (1%)	
India: 41 teaching institutions (6)	Delay by patient or relatives	2,109 (45%)	1978–1981
India: Anantapur district (7)	Lack of early and adequate antenatal care	18 (8%)	1984–1985
	Termination of pregnancy by unqualified personnel	18 (8%)	
Zimbabwe: Harare Maternity Hospital, Harare (8)	Late presentation	8 (16%)	1983
	Refusal of treatment	2 (4%)	
	Unbooked	5 (10%)	

Delayed Arrival or Nonarrival at a Health Facility

Of the various patient factors identified in studies, patients' nonarrival and delayed arrival at a medical facility feature prominently. It is also mentioned in some cases that the patient's and her relatives' attitudes were incorrect, leading to a preference to deliver at home with the help of relatives and/or traditional birth attendants, rather than go to a hospital or health center. Instances of the patient's refusal of treatment are also mentioned. (Delays due to distance and transportation problems are discussed later.)

There may be a number of reasons why women do not seek medical care during pregnancy and delivery. The first of these is probably a lack of awareness of the seriousness of the problem. In Anantapur, India, when family members of women who died were asked if they were aware of the seriousness of the problem, more than one-fifth indicated that they did not comprehend the seriousness of the patient's condition. Of those who knew about the seriousness, the great majority took steps to call a health worker/doctor or to move the patient to a hospital (7). Studies of maternal deaths in the Tangail and Jamalpur districts of Bangladesh indicate that women who developed complications during pregnancy more often received medical help prior to death than women who developed complications during labor and delivery or post partum (9, 10). These studies indicate that the seriousness of complications encountered during pregnancy, and of specific complications such as toxemia that lead to convulsions, is probably more apparent than the seriousness of prolonged labor or postpartum sepsis. This illustrates the failure of the health care system to reach out to the population with important health messages. If women knew how to identify danger signals that call for immediate medical attention, a large majority of them would certainly attempt to reach a health facility.

Poorer and higher parity women remain uncovered by medical services, whereas relatively well-off and lower parity women who are not at any special risk benefit the most (11). Poorer women and women with large families may find it difficult to get away from work at home and on the farms, often at the cost of their lives. In Zaire, for example, 13 of 20 maternal deaths occurred during the first five months of planting and harvest, seasons when the need for women's work in the field can make women reluctant to go to the hospital (12). Lack of available money is, of course, a major deterrent to seeking medical help. That economic factors are an important intervening variable in access to health care is evident from a study in Oran, Algeria, between 1971 and 1980 (13). The maternal mortality rate plunged from 157/100,000 live births in 1971–1975 to 91/100,000 in 1976–1980. One of the reasons for this decline was that after 1974–1975, when fees for medical services were waived in public hospitals, the number of unassisted home deliveries was greatly reduced.

There may be a number of other reasons why women prefer home delivery assisted by a traditional birth attendant or relatives. These include the unfamiliar setting at the health facility where the woman would be attended to by strangers, in the absence of her family and friends and the physical and moral support they offer; the possibility of being attended to by male doctors, unacceptable in some cultures; the nontolerance by hospital staff of cultural practices related to childbirth, such as consumption of special foods and practice of certain rituals; the total lack of sympathy and understanding on the part of health personnel; and not least, the belief that childbirth does not need medical interference. All of these reasons are valid and cannot be ignored or disclaimed.

Failure to Seek Legal Abortion, or Interference with Pregnancy

Another patient factor often mentioned is the failure to seek a legal abortion, or interference with pregnancy. A detailed discussion of the complex issues surrounding why women do not seek legal abortions, or why they interfere with their pregnancies instead of preventing a pregnancy, is beyond the scope of this paper. Some of the underlying reasons may be similar to those that explain why women do not seek medical help during childbirth: not knowing that abortions can be legally obtained, lack of information about where such services are available, and lack of resources. There are, however, many essential differences arising from laws that severely restrict abortions in several countries, and the social, cultural, and religious pressures against seeking an abortion where it may be available. In addition, the degree of privacy afforded by a traditional abortionist may be a factor. The least that can be said is that "failure to seek a legal abortion" cannot be classified neatly as a patient factor for which the woman alone is responsible.

Whatever the reasons for a woman's not going to a medical facility for pregnancy-related problems, the consequences are serious enough to warrant corrective action. To give an example from Kenya, several women who died of maternal causes in the Kenyatta National Hospital between 1972 and 1978 arrived in a poor condition after futile management had been attempted at home for many days (14). This was especially true of women who had illegal abortions. Most of those who died of puerperal sepsis had delivered at home. One patient who had delivered at home with the assistance of a midwife had been treated for nearly a week before she was admitted to the hospital. In Togo, again, women referred to the Centre Hôpitalière Universitaire de Lome during 1977 included many with uterine rupture that had occurred several days earlier at home and had not been detected (15).

Nonuse of Antenatal Care

The next most important patient factor mentioned in studies is the nonuse of antenatal care by pregnant women. This is disturbing given the overwhelming evidence that the lack of antenatal care increases the risk of maternal death.

According to the famous Zaria maternity survey that monitored 22,725 deliveries in Ahmado Bello University Hospital in Nigeria, antenatal care was associated with a reduction in maternal mortality in all age-parity groups (16). In American University of Beirut Medical Centre, Lebanon, the maternal mortality rate for those who had antenatal care was 19/100,000, whereas the rate for those without antenatal care was 197/100,000 (17). In Vietnam, only 34 percent of women who died had attended antenatal clinics, compared with 74 percent in the control group, a statistically significant difference (2).

Early antenatal care is important. In Thailand, mothers who started antenatal care in their first and second trimesters of pregnancy had lower maternal mortality rates than those who did not start antenatal care until the third trimester (18). It is also necessary to make several antenatal visits spread over the gestation period, so that complications that arise at different stages may be identified and followed up. In Zaire (1981–1983) the maternal mortality rate was 250/100,000 live births for those who had made four or more antenatal visits, 270/100,000 for those who had made between one and three visits, and a very high 3,770/100,000 for those who had no antenatal care at all (12). Similarly, in a study of three hospitals in Senegal, 20 percent of the women who died had no antenatal care, compared with only 2 percent in the control group; and only 40 percent of them had made three or more visits, compared with 75 percent in the control group (19).

The case for early and adequate antenatal care is clear. The obstacles to use of antenatal care need to be investigated. There are some clues to the possible reasons for nonuse in these same studies. A community study from Ethiopia found that just as in the case of institutional delivery, it is the better-off and lower parity women who use antenatal care adequately (11). Use of antenatal care decreased with increasing parity, both in hospitals and in the Maternal and Child Health clinics. The extent of nonattendance among the high-risk women who were currently para 5 to para 8 was 35 percent, and that for women who were now para 8+ was 44 percent. Sixty percent of those who did not receive antenatal care had unwanted pregnancies. Women with unwanted pregnancies who did receive antenatal care tended to visit Maternal and Child Health clinics, which were free of cost.

The failure of higher parity women to seek antenatal care may not only result from lack of time and money. They may feel it is unnecessary to seek antenatal care, especially if their earlier pregnancies were problem-free. In the case of unwanted pregnancies out-of-wedlock, hesitation to seek antenatal care is understandable. As for high parity women with unwanted pregnancies, the very reasons for which the pregnancy was unwanted may also impose constraints in seeking antenatal care. The women may also not feel motivated for self-care.

The deficient quality of antenatal care may be another major deterrent. A study of Primary Health Centers in India found that women attending antenatal screening were not screened either for anemia or for high blood pressure or proteinuria to detect the risk of eclampsia (20). This can be a costly shortcoming, as judged from a study in Mozambique: more than 80 percent of the women who died had attended antenatal clinics, and yet there were deaths from preventable causes such as anemia and eclampsia (21, 22). Poor quality of antenatal screening and the indifferent attitude of health personnel in health facilities can destroy women's faith in the usefulness of antenatal care. Dare we blame the women if they decide that it is not worth expending their scarce resources on what may be a futile exercise?

Transportation Problems

In many instances, the late arrival of a patient at a hospital, usually classified as a patient factor, is the result of lack of transportation methods. Poor roads, lack of ambulances or other means of transportation to health facilities, and inadequate means of transporting emergency cases from peripheral to referral hospitals make the essential difference between life and death in most developing countries. In a heart-rending and extreme example from a Tanzanian study, a rural woman had to walk 70 kilometers after the onset of labor to reach a hospital, only to collapse on arrival (23).

Late arrivals and referrals account for a disproportionately large number of maternal deaths in hospitals. The following examples illustrate the magnitude of the problem:

- In Centre Hôpitalière Universitaire de Cocody, Abidjan, Ivory Coast, in 1986, the maternal mortality rate was 2,000/100,000 deliveries for those who had been transferred from within the urban zone, 3,000/100,000 for those who had been transferred from the suburban area, and 6,000/100,000 for those who had been transferred from rural areas (24).

- In the Maternity Hospital, Katmandu, Nepal, 40 percent of the women who died arrived in a very poor condition; 17 percent were unconscious. Forty-five of the 81 deaths (56 percent) occurred within the first day, 38 of them within the first eight hours (25).

- In an Aden Hospital, 73 percent of deaths were of women from rural areas who had to travel a long way. Ten percent of the women who died were dead on arrival, and another 15 percent died within an hour of arrival (26).

- In Zaire, all but two (90 percent) of the women who died were admitted in a critical condition. The most common complication was prolonged labor (greater than 18 hours) due to feto-pelvic disproportion or malpresentation. Sixteen of the 20 women who died had been in labor for more than 18 hours, and nine of these had been in labor for 48 hours. The risk of death was more than 400 times greater for those who had been in labor for more than 48 hours than for those who had labored 12 hours or less. Prolonged labor resulted in a ruptured uterus in 14 cases, which increased the risk of death more than 100-fold (12).

- In Togo, women referred to Centre Hôpitalière Universitaire de Lome during 1977 included cases of uterine rupture that had occurred several days earlier (15).

- In a study of 48 hospitals throughout Tanzania in 1986, 63 percent of the 247 women who died had to travel more than 10 kilometers to the hospital where they eventually died. Of these, 37 percent lived more than 30 kilometers away (27).
- In Krian district, Malaysia, 73 deaths (8 percent) were due to poor transportation methods, and a further seven deaths occurred en route from one hospital to another (1).

When the hospital is far away, not only the distance but also the mode of transport becomes an important determinant of how soon medical help becomes available and, consequently, of survival chances. In Anantapur, India (1984–1985), 41 percent of all maternal deaths occurred at home, and 9 percent en route to a hospital. Of 140 women who were taken to hospital in a serious condition, 96 (69 percent) were transported by public bus, 27 (19 percent) by bullock carts, five (3 percent) by manually drawn rickshaws, and only 12 (9 percent) by motor-driven vehicle or by ambulance. Twenty-four women died on the way to hospital, and another 54 died immediately on arrival (7).

These problems are accentuated when the cause of death is a difficult-to-anticipate complication such as postpartum hemorrhage. In Gambia, where an extremely high maternal mortality rate has been recorded (2,360/100,000 live births), 11 of a total of 15 deaths occurred within four hours after delivery and were associated with hemorrhage or sudden collapse; there were no resuscitation facilities at the nearest dispensary, and the government hospital at Banjul was several hours' journey away, including a ferry crossing of the river Gambia (28).

Weather conditions may also affect the possibility for rapid transportation to hospital. A study covering three hospitals in Senegal found that maternal deaths from hemorrhage and uterine rupture occurred 1.7 times and 3.5 times more frequently in the four wet months between July and October, and suggested that this is probably because of the way rain paralyzes transportation on mud roads and foot paths through which patients have to be transported (19).

All of the patient factors discussed above are a consequence not only of geographic inaccessibility but of the social, cultural, and economic inaccessibility of health services to pregnant women. Could we not consider attributing responsibility for these factors to the patient a case of "victim blaming"?

FAILURES IN THE HEALTH SERVICES DELIVERY SYSTEM

When other obstacles are overcome and women with complications in pregnancy or childbirth finally reach a health facility, there may be yet other problems that jeopardize their chances of survival. Personnel and equipment are scarce, and health facilities are often unable to cope even with the small proportion of affected

Table 2

Maternal deaths with "poor patient management in hospital" as an avoidable factor, selected developing countries

Country: hospital/region (reference no.)	Factors	No. of all maternal deaths (%)	Years
Vietnam: 22 institutions (2)	Delay in diagnosis	68 (53%)	1984–
	Wrong diagnosis	28 (22%)	1985
	Delay in treatment	80 (63%)	
	Wrong treatment	47 (37%)	
	Delay in referral	77 (60%)	
	Inappropriate referral	1 (8%)	
Malawi: Health centers and referral hospitals in Central Region (29)	Medical staff factors	30 (28%)	1977
	Nursing staff factors (includes failure to diagnose, failure to initiate appropriate treatment, delay in referral)	26 (24%)	
Zimbabwe: Harare Maternity Hospital, Harare (8)	Failure to diagnose/delay in diagnosis	4 (8%)	1983
	Failure to operate/ delay in operation	5 (10%)	
	Failure to give appropriate treatment	2 (4%)	
	Poor operative technique	2 (4%)	
	Overtransfusion	2 (4%)	
	Anesthetic problem	1 (2%)	
South Africa: 267 hospitals throughout the country (30)	Delay in diagnosis	11 (1%)	1980–
	Delay in consultation or transfer	25 (3%)	1982
	Judgment errors in diagnosis	11 (1%)	
	Treatment given "too little, too late"	87 (11%)	
	Surgical and anesthetic problems	24 (3%)	
India: 41 teaching institutions (6)	Defective obstetric care	1,525 (32%)	1978– 1981

women who arrive. The quality of care is far from satisfactory, and may be summed up as "doing too little, too late." Table 2 shows the proportion of maternal deaths attributed to various "health service factors" in different studies (2, 6, 8, 29, 30).

Shortage of Trained Personnel

Many countries have a shortage of trained personnel not only at the specialist level, but all down the ladder to the midwife. An extreme example is that of

Gabon, where there is a shortage of trained obstetricians-gynecologists: six of the nine provinces of Gabon do not have the services of a specialist obstetrician. In addition, health centers and even provincial hospitals do not have 24-hour services (31).

Even where the situation is not quite so bad, understaffing of health facilities is a common problem. In Malawi, at Kamuzu Central Hospital, Lilongwe, medical staff were at times required to be at the Central Hospital and the Old Wind Maternity three kilometers away at the same time, and this alone had contributed to maternal death in some cases (4).

Another problem is that staff have inadequate or inappropriate training and cannot cope with obstetrical emergencies. Cameroon is a unique case in point. A hospital study in Yaounde found that the incidence of deaths from ruptured uterus was high not only because of the poor standards of midwives in rural hospitals, but because specialists in referral hospitals were trained abroad and could not handle cases of uterine rupture (32).

Health personnel interviewed in a 48-hospital study in Tanzania stated that, in their opinion, the following were among factors contributing to high maternal mortality (27):

- Scarcity of medical and paramedical personnel, especially in rural areas;
- Poor on-the-job training of health staff at all levels;
- Low salaries, poor working conditions, etc., for health workers, leading to lack of motivation.

The unsatisfactory working conditions of lower-level health workers often tend to be overlooked, but may be a key cause of the scarcity of health personnel so vital to the improvement of coverage of maternal health services.

Lack of Equipment and Facilities

The absence of a blood bank or of facilities for transfusion can be one of the most catastrophic inadequacies in a health facility, and yet is one of the most frequently encountered. A patient with hemorrhage may not survive to reach the referral hospital. In Gabon, a study from Centre Hôpitalière de Libreville mentions that patients suffering from hemorrhage often were kept waiting until a donor with a matching blood group was found, before operative intervention (31). In some studies showing a high incidence of deaths from hemorrhage, absence of a blood bank was often a contributing factor. For example in Vietnam, where 48 percent of maternal deaths in selected hospitals during 1984–1985 were from hemorrhage, lack of blood led to deaths in 46 cases (36 percent) (2). In Kenyatta National Hospital, Kenya, no blood was available for a patient admitted in a highly anemic condition due to postpartum hemorrhage, until she died a day later (33).

Lack of other facilities and equipment is mentioned in many other studies. For example, the study of L'Hôpital Arstride le Dantec, L'Hôpital Principal, and Centre Abbas Ndao in Senegal (1986–1987) found that 70 percent of the 152 maternal deaths were attributable to lack of equipment and facilities (19).

In the hospital at Libreville, Gabon, mentioned above (31), there was over-crowding, with a bed occupancy rate of 130 percent. Supplies of drugs were inadequate, and treatment was delayed until the patient's family bought the drugs from a pharmacy. There were even inordinate delays in transferring the patient to the operative block. In Vietnam, lack of drugs was responsible for 26 deaths (20 percent), and lack of other equipment for 14 deaths (11 percent) (2).

The study of maternal deaths in Kenyatta National Hospital also mentions overcrowding; patients often had to share beds and mattresses, leaving them vulnerable to cross-infection within the hospital. There was not enough clean linen, and even basic equipment such as gloves and antiseptic solution fell short of requirements (33). The lack of basic equipment in conjunction with overcrowding and the scarcity of trained personnel has led to an increase in in-hospital sepsis rates. Sepsis deaths increased from 8 percent of maternal deaths in 1953–1960 to 17 percent in 1961–1971, and stood at 12 percent in 1975–1982 in a hospital study from Durban, South Africa; during this period the maternal mortality rates also rose (34, 35). The reasons for this increase were overcrowding and nonadherence to aseptic and antiseptic principles when doing vaginal examinations, among other things. In Sudan, deaths from puerperal sepsis in the Khartoum Teaching Hospital, Khartoum, increased from 10 percent of all maternal deaths in 1968–1972 to as high as 32 percent in 1978–1982 (36). And in Venezuela, a study in Concepción Palacios maternity hospital, Caracas, covering the period 1939–1974, found that while the maternal mortality rate declined from 196/100,000 live births in 1939–1963 to 125/100,000 in 1964–1972, it subsequently rose to 144/100,000, owing to an alarming increase in post–cesarian section and puerperal sepsis deaths during the last ten years of the study (37).

Lack of equipment is a more acute problem in most peripheral hospitals; the Kenyan study found that of 92 women referred to Kenyatta National Hospital from peripheral hospitals, in 43 cases the anesthetist or the medical officer-in-charge was not available. In 19 of these cases the hospital had no facility for operative delivery, in 21 no blood was available, and in nine cases the hospital had no water or electricity. An added problem was that the hospital admitted high-risk patients when it had no facilities to tackle the problem, or had diagnosed the problem too late, delaying referral (33).

Poor Patient Management

Inappropriate action by health staff in treating patients has been identified in several studies as a factor contributing to maternal deaths.

Delay in diagnosis and treatment and inadequate treatment are often responsible for maternal deaths. There seem to be inordinate delays in initiating treatment even when the patient's condition is critical, for reasons quite apart from lack of equipment and facilities. Crucial decisions are delayed, and not infrequently, wrong decisions are made. Standard procedures for patient management are often absent, which makes it difficult for nursing staff and junior doctors to take appropriate action in emergency cases. Also, decision-making and initiation of sophisticated procedures in hospital settings are frequently concentrated in a small number of senior doctors and specialists, while other members of staff are restricted to carrying out instructions.

A study of Kenyatta National Hospital illustrates some cases of poor patient management. Lack of proper investigations of the etiological causes of infection led to inappropriate choice of drugs and nonresponse of the microorganisms to therapy. Decisions for operative interventions were at times taken too late, and the operations were entrusted to junior doctors. In one instance, a woman admitted for sepsis following abortion had to undergo one colpotomy and two laparotomies within a space of 10 days because the pelvic abscess was not properly drained in the first two procedures. Another instance of patient mismanagement in the same hospital was of two women with ruptured ectopic pregnancies who virtually lost their entire blood volume before they received laparotomy because crossmatching of blood for transfusion was inordinately delayed. Both women died following laparotomy (33).

In another study from the maternity and children's hospital in Saudi Arabia (1978–1980), mismatched blood transfusions were a factor in two of 29 deaths, one from hemorrhage and one from septic abortion (38). Delays in decision-making by the health personnel occurred in two instances: in a case of uncontrollable hemorrhage during cesarean section and in a patient with antepartum hemorrhage, in which case there was delay in deciding about definitive surgery. In another instance the avoidable factor was clinical, namely, combining major surgery with cesarean section in a peripheral hospital with limited facilities. Delay in decision-making and failure to initiate prompt intensive care were responsible for several first-hour deaths in R.M.C. Hospital, Imphal, India (39). In five cases, immediate surgical interventions by experienced obstetricians could have prevented death.

A confidential inquiry into all maternal deaths in Jamaica between 1981 and 1983 gives a very useful analysis of avoidable patient management factors with respect to three major causes of maternal death: hemorrhage, sepsis, and eclampsia (40).

According to this inquiry, some of the factors contributing to deaths from hemorrhage were:

• Delays in midwives' appreciating the extent of blood loss and contacting a doctor;

- Delays in starting and inadequate resuscitative procedures for blood loss, partly due to unavailability of blood or plasma in many of the smaller hospitals;
- Delays in manual removal of the placenta in patients with retained placenta, or attempting this procedure without the necessary preliminary establishment of a reliable intravenous infusion;
- Inadequate use of ergometrine.

In the case of deaths from sepsis the avoidable factors were:

- Inadequate surveillance of body temperature in women with a prolonged first stage of labor, and post delivery;
- Not giving antibiotics to women with prolonged rupture of the membranes;
- Inadequate bacteriological investigations in women with puerperal pyrexia;
- Reluctance to use aggressive treatment with broad-spectrum antibiotics for women with puerperal pyrexia.

Avoidable in-hospital factors that were responsible for deaths from eclampsia included:

- Absence of relevant information on antenatal surveillance symptoms and signs (e.g., weight gain, blood pressure readings) at the time of admission to hospital;
- Inadequate monitoring of patient's blood pressure and urine, particularly on admission and immediately following delivery;
- Delay by hospital staff in initiating appropriate treatment when signs of preeclamptic toxemia were found or the patient had convulsions, the delay being due to lack of coordination among various levels of staff;
- Lack of a clear-cut clinical-therapeutic strategy for dealing with patients with eclampsia.

Problems related to operative techniques and administration of anesthesia also claim a large number of maternal lives, and routinely appear as a cause of death in most hospital studies of maternal mortality. One of the highest rates for maternal deaths from complications of anesthesia has been reported from Ivory Coast (110 deaths/100,000 live births) (41), and high rates of death associated with cesarean sections have been reported from Egypt (222/100,000 live births) (42) and Malawi (142/100,000 live births) (4).

A good proportion of deaths related to complications of cesarean section and anesthesia may in fact be related to the poor condition of the patient prior to the operation. Surgical procedures are often undertaken on emergency admissions as a last recourse, with the knowledge that survival chances are limited. However, the sharp increase in post–cesarean section sepsis in instances such as in Caracas, mentioned above (38), point to faulty in-hospital procedures. In Cuba, again, cesarean delivery was identified as a risk factor associated with maternal death in a study covering the period 1980–1984 (43). Forty-one of the 54 cases of death from sepsis during that period followed a cesarian section, and 13 deaths from complications of anesthesia were also simultaneously associated with cesarean section. In another example from Sudan, a study of all cesarean sections carried out in the Khartoum hospital between 1978 and 1982 found that of 24 maternal deaths following cesarean section (of a total of 140 maternal deaths), only six could be attributed to underlying causes (36).

Clearly, the performance of medical systems in saving maternal lives entrusted to them is far from satisfactory. This is unfortunate, considering the difficulties that women must overcome in order to reach a referral facility. They have to leave their families behind, expend a great deal of money in finding a quick means of transportation, and find a suitable person to accompany them. The person accompanying has to find the means and money to stay in a strange town or city during the period of the patient's treatment. And if the patient should die, quite apart from the fact that it would greatly distress her to be away from family and friends in her last hours, transporting the body back home would prove both difficult and expensive.

We hope that the existence of a number of studies looking into avoidable in-hospital factors in maternal deaths demonstrates a commitment to effecting the required changes wherever possible.

CONCLUSIONS

The prevention of maternal deaths requires far-reaching social and economic changes beyond the confines of the health care system. The factors that make the natural processes of pregnancy and childbirth highly risky and even fatal for poorer women are structural; so are the factors that influence the value women place on their personal well-being, and those that influence their ability to seek health care for themselves. The last depends crucially on resources such as the time, money, and information that women have at their disposal, and whether they have the authority for decision-making.

However, this does not absolve the health care system of its responsibility to make fundamental changes in both the structure and the delivery of health services. From the discussions in this chapter, certain areas stand out as priorities for action. These are presented not as policy recommendations to the medical status quo—whose priorities are, more often than not, determined by the interests of those in power and by their own professional interests—but rather as a proposal for action by health activists.

The starting point of an agenda for action would be to call for a drastic reallocation of national resources with a larger share for the health sector, and a substantial allocation within the health budget for the health care of women, of which maternal health care is one component. The health expenditure of a vast majority of countries falls short of 5 percent of gross national product. Less than half of this is allocated to "primary health care" (a term that has come to be used to define all health care below the secondary and referral levels, as opposed to the principle enunciated in the Alma-Ata Declaration). A minuscule amount of this allocation is spent on maternal and child health care, in which child health and family planning get the lion's share of the resources compared with maternal health. And although it is well known that maternal health cannot be improved without improvement of women's health in general, as far as the health care system is concerned women count only as mothers and have no existence prior to or after a pregnancy and delivery. Also, the disproportionately large share of resources allocated to family planning programs (often a euphemism for population control programs), at the cost of other aspects of maternal health care, can in no way be justified.

Appropriate reallocation of resources for women's health care would have to begin with strengthening health services at the community level. Women who are in greatest need of health care, and who run the greatest risk of maternal death, have the least resources to seek medical help. They can only be reached if services are available close to home, and ideally at their very doorsteps. What is needed is the deployment of thousands of community health workers who are also equipped for maternal health care. Training traditional birth attendants and local women to provide domiciliary care is perhaps one of the best ways to invest resources. However, action in this direction has been disappointing. Far from being one of the cornerstones of the strategy for prevention of maternal mortality and morbidity, it remains a low-priority activity, carried out in a sporadic and haphazard manner.

The next step in appropriate resource allocation would be to equip the first referral levels with the necessary supplies, equipment, and personnel. The World Health Organization guidelines on essential obstetric functions at the first referral level identify eight groups of functions that should be available at a health facility catering to a population of 100,000. Among these are surgical functions such as performing cesarean sections, surgical treatment of severe sepsis, and laparotomy for treatment of uterine rupture; anesthetic functions; and blood-replacement functions. This would bring about an estimated 5 percent reduction in the number of maternal deaths (44).

Shortage of trained personnel is often cited as a major barrier to upgrading first referral facilities. This is usually the result of the strict hierarchy in the division of labor among health personnel, and inflexible notions held by doctors regarding the ethical propriety of entrusting complicated interventions to lower level staff. The Centre Medical Evangelique's Nyakunde, Aba, and Aru hospitals in the Upper Zaire region have successfully overcome such barriers. Here, nurse practitioner surgeons deliver all types of labor, normal or complicated. A study of their performance has shown that the outcome of complicated labor in the hands of the nurse practitioner surgeons is comparable to the outcome of such cases in the hands of physicians (45). Training nursing and midwifery staff to deal with complicated deliveries is clearly a viable option, but may not be welcome to the medical establishment, which would resent such an encroachment on its territory.

There have been a number of such creative interventions aimed at better utilization of scarce resources for maternal health care. In Ekedwani hospital, Malawi, for example, an antenatal waiting shelter was opened for "high-risk" women, to deal with the problem of distances and transport. This greatly reduced the maternal mortality rate, obstetric emergencies having become a thing of the past (46).

The second major area for action is improving the quality of care in health facilities. This involves more than ensuring the availability of equipment and supplies and trained personnel; it also entails making the health services more socially accountable. There should be careful record-keeping, and records should be accessible to the public. Every maternal death and every complicated delivery should be carefully scrutinized. Preventing the recurrence of an "avoidable factor" should be a medical priority. Inappropriate organizational and managerial procedures that cause inordinate delays in instituting care must be challenged: it is not unusual for a patient to be kept waiting while paperwork is being completed or because the person authorized for decision-making is not present. More importantly, seeking health care should cease to be the dehumanizing experience it now is, devoid of respect and consideration or even compassion on the part of health personnel.

The third and perhaps most urgent area for action is to assist and equip those most affected by the problem of high maternal mortality—women (and men) from the most deprived sections of society—to actively participate in demanding the changes outlined above.

The existing state of affairs in the health care system that contributes to high maternal mortality is not the consequence of mere inept planning or poor organizational and managerial capabilities. It is a reflection of the priorities set by an elitist system in which the poor and powerless do not count. We do not expect the demands made in these pages to be handed down from above. They have to be fought for, as part of a much wider struggle for equity and social justice.

REFERENCES[1]

1. Karim, R. Overview of Maternal Mortality in Malaysia and the Application of the Risk Approach Strategy in Maternal Health. Paper presented at the Seminar on Maternal Health, Kemenlerian Kesthatan, Malaysia, 1982.

[1] The unpublished documents in this reference list were referred to from the data base and documentation on maternal mortality maintained by the Division of Family Health, World Health Organization, Geneva, Switzerland.

2. Vietnam, Institute for the Protection of Mother and Newborn. Maternal Mortality in Selected Areas of Vietnam. Paper presented at the Interregional Meeting on the Prevention of Maternal Mortality, Geneva, November 11–15, 1985. Unpublished WHO document no. FHE/PMM/85.9.8.
3. Ahmad, Z. Maternal mortality in an obstetric unit. *J. Pakistan Med. Assoc.* 35: 243–248, 1985.
4. Keller, M. E. Maternal mortality at Kamuzu Central Hospital for 1985. *Med. Q. (Malawi)* 4: 13–16, 1987.
5. Justensen, A. An analysis of maternal mortality in Muhimbili Medical Centre, Dar es Salaam, July 1983 to June 1984. *J. Obstet. Gynaecol. East Central Afr.* 4: 5–8, 1985.
6. Bhasker Rao, K. *Report on the Maternal Mortality Committee of the FOGSI, 1978–1981.* Federation of Obstetricians' and Gynecologists' Societies of India, New Delhi, 1984.
7. Bhatia, J. C. *A Study of Maternal Mortality in Anantapur District, Andhra Pradesh, India.* Indian Institute of Management, Bangalore, 1986.
8. Crowther, C. A. Maternal deaths at the Harare Maternity Hospital during 1983. *South Afr. Med. J.* 69: 180–182, 1986.
9. Alauddin, M. Maternal mortality in rural Bangladesh: The Tangail district. *Stud. Fam. Plann.* 17: 13–21, 1986.
10. Khan, A. R., et al. Maternal mortality in rural Bangladesh: The Jamalpur district. *Stud. Fam. Plann.* 17: 7–12, 1986.
11. Kwast, B. E., et al. *Report on Maternal Health in Addis Ababa.* Swedish Save the Children Federation, Addis Ababa, 1984.
12. Smith, J. B., et al. Hospital Deaths in a High Risk Obstetric Population: Karawa, Zaire. Unpublished document. Family Health International, Durham, 1985.
13. Gana, B., and Louadi, T. *La mortalité maternelle en milieu hôpitalier: le cas d'Oran.* Université d'Oran, Institute de Sciences Sociales, Département de Démographie, Oran, Algeria, 1982.
14. Makokha, A. E. Maternal mortality—Kenyatta National Hospital, 1972–1977. *East Afr. Med. J.* 57: 451–460, 1980.
15. Vovor, M., and Hodonou. Togo. Paper presented at the WHO Regional Multidisciplinary Consultative Meeting on Human Reproduction, Yaounde, December 4–7, 1978.
16. Harrison, K. A. A Review of Maternal Mortality in Nigeria with Particular Reference to the Situation in Zaria, Northern Nigeria 1976–79. Paper presented at the WHO Interregional Meeting on Prevention of Maternal Mortality, Geneva, November 11–15, 1985. Unpublished WHO document no. FHE/PMM/85.9.12.
17. Mashini, I., et al. Maternal mortality in the American University of Beirut Medical Centre (AUBMC). *Int. J. Gynaecol. Obstet.* 22: 275–279, 1984.
18. Rattanporn, P. The Internal Factors Affecting Maternal Mortality. Thesis submitted to the Mahidol University, Bangkok, 1980.
19. Correa, P., et al. Rapport final de l'étude sur la mortalité maternelle à Dakar, Senegal. Causes et mesures a prendre pour l'améliorer. Unpublished report. Dakar, Senegal, 1987.
20. Indian Council for Medical Research. *Evaluation of Quality of Family Welfare Services at PHC Level—Report of 34 PHCs.* New Delhi, 1987.
21. Songade, F. Analise dos casos de mortes maternas ocorridas nosprimeiros 7 meses de 1984. *Boletín Informativo do Servico de Ginecología Obstétrica.* Hospital Central, Maputo, February 1985.
22. Songade, F. Maternal Mortality at Maputo Central Hospital, Mozambique. Paper presented at the FIGO Congress, Berlin, September 1985.

23. Price, T. G. Preliminary reports on maternal deaths in the Southern Highlands of Tanzania in 1984. *J. Obstet. Gynaecol. East. Central Afr.* 3: 103–110, 1984.
24. Berardi, J. C., et al. Evaluation du bénéfice de l'installation d'une structure obstétrico-chiurgicale décentralisée en terme de réduction de la mortalité maternelle et des transferts en Côte d'Ivoire. Unpublished paper, CHU de Cocody, Abidjan, Ivory Coast, 1987.
25. Malla, D. S. Study of Causes of Maternal Mortality in Selected Hospitals in Nepal. Paper presented at the Interregional Meeting on the Prevention of Maternal Mortality, Geneva, November 11–15, 1985. Unpublished WHO document no. FHE/PMM/85.9.9.
26. Ahmed Ali, A. A Review of Maternal Mortality at Abood Maternity Hospital, Aden from 1962–1986. Unpublished paper. Abood Maternity Hospital, Aden, Democratic Yemen, 1987.
27. Murru, M. Hospital Maternal Mortality in Tanzania. Master's Dissertation, Royal Tropical Institute, Amsterdam, 1987.
28. Greenwood, A., et al. A prospective study of pregnancy in a rural area of the Gambia, West Africa. *Bull. WHO* 65: 635–644, 1987.
29. Bullough, C. Analysis of maternal deaths in the Central Region of Malawi. *East Afr. Med. J.* 58: 25–36, 1981.
30. Boes, E. G. M. Maternal mortality in Southern Africa, 1980–82. *South Afr. Med. J.* 71: 158–161, 1987.
31. Nlome-Nze, R., et al. La mortalité maternelle au Centre Hôpitalière de Libreville, Gabon. Unpublished paper, Libreville, Gabon, 1987.
32. Leke, R. J. Outcome of pregnancy and delivery at the Central Maternity, Central Hospital Yaounde. *Ann. Univ. Sci. Santé* 4: 322–330, 1987.
33. Aggarwal, V. P. Obstetric emergency referrals to the Kenyatta National Hospital. *East Afr. Med. J.* 57: 144–149, 1980.
34. Crichton, D., and Knobel, J. The principles of prevention of avoidable maternal death. *South Afr. Med. J.* 47: 2205–2210, 1973.
35. Melrose, S. B. Maternal deaths at King Edward VIII Hospital, Durban. *South Afr. Med. J.* 65: 161–165, 1984.
36. Abbo, A. H. Preventable factors in maternal mortality in Khartoum Teaching Hospital. *Arab Med. J.* 4(11,12): 23–28, 1982.
37. Aguero, O., et al. Mortalidad materna en la maternidad Concepción Palacios, 1939–1974. *Rev. Obstet. Ginecol. Venezuela* 37: 361–366, 1977.
38. Chattopadhyay, S. K., et al. Maternal mortality in Riyadh, Saudi Arabia. *Br. J. Obstet. Gynaecol.* 90: 809–814, 1983.
39. Devi, Y. L., and Singh, J. Maternal morbidity: A ten year study in R.M.C. Hospital, Imphal. *J. Obstet. Gynaecol. India,* 37: 90–94, 1987.
40. Walker, G. J., et al. Maternal Mortality in Jamaica. Paper presented at the Interregional Meeting on the Prevention of Maternal Mortality, Geneva, November 11–15, 1985. Unpublished WHO document no. FHE/PMM/85.9.10.
41. Bohoussou, K. M., et al. La mortalité maternelle au cours de la parturition et la post-partum immédiat. Etude hôpitalière. *Afr. Med.* 25(239): 125–130, 1986.
42. Abdullah, S. A., et al. Maternal Mortality in Upper Egypt. Paper presented at the Interregional Meeting on the Prevention of Maternal Morbidity, Geneva, November 11–15, 1985. Unpublished WHO document no. FHE/PMM/85.9.18.
43. Farnot, U. C. Maternal Mortality in Cuba. Paper presented at the Interregional Meeting on the Prevention of Maternal Mortality, Geneva, November 11–15, 1985. Unpublished WHO document no. FHE/PMM/85.9.13.

44. World Health Organization. *Essential Obstetric Functions at the First Referral Level.* Report of a Technical Working Group, Geneva, June 23–27, 1986. FHE/86.4. Geneva, 1986.
45. Maroja, L. T. The Role of Medical Auxiliaries in Operative Obstetrics in Rural Zaire. Master's Dissertation, Institute of Child Health, University of London, London, 1984.
46. Knowles, J. K. The Antenatal Waiting Shelter as an Important Factor in Reducing Maternal Mortality. Unpublished paper. Ekedwani, Malawi, 1986.

CHAPTER 10

Abortion Policy and Women's Health in Developing Countries

Ruth Dixon-Mueller

In October 1988, physicians and women's health advocates from 35 countries met in Rio de Janeiro at the Christopher Tietze International Symposium on Women's Health in the Third World: The Impact of Unwanted Pregnancies.[1] Recognizing "the appalling wastage of human lives" from unsafe abortion, the symposium concluded with a strong statement urging governments, first, to eliminate all legal constraints to voluntary abortion on health and human rights grounds and, second, to generate the necessary health policies and resource allocations to guarantee safe and accessible procedures to all who need them.

Demographers and health officials estimate that 100 to 200 thousand women in developing countries die every year from the effects of clandestine abortion (1–3). Unsafe induced abortion is responsible for one-quarter to one-half of all maternal deaths in some regions of the world, especially in Latin America. It is clearly time to take a fresh look at international and U.S. abortion policies in the light of their impact on women's lives and health. What is the extent of clandestine abortion in developing countries? What is the nature of the sociocultural environment, the legal environment, and the medical environment in which abortion takes place? What are the consequences to women in developing countries of current international and U.S. abortion policies? Finally, what can be done to eliminate the loss of women's lives and damage to women's health resulting from unsafe abortion?

---

[1]Scientist and activist, Christopher Tietze (1908–1984) published widely on abortion from a medical and human rights perspective. The first International Tietze Symposium was held in conjunction with the meetings of the International Federation of Gynecologists and Obstetricians (FIGO) in Berlin in 1985; the second, in conjunction with FIGO meetings in Rio de Janeiro in 1988. Both symposia were organized by the International Women's Health Coalition in New York.

Originally published in the *International Journal of Health Services* 20(2): 297–314, 1990.

THE PREVALENCE OF CLANDESTINE ABORTIONS

Estimates of the numbers of clandestine abortions in developing countries vary widely. In Brazil, for example, where abortion is legal only to save a woman's life or in cases of rape or incest, social security data covering about 70 percent of the national population report over 200,000 women hospitalized in 1980 for the treatment of complications from illegal abortions (4). Depending on the assumptions one makes about the percentage of all abortion attempts that end in hospitalization, this figure could represent anywhere from 600,000 abortions nationwide (at 50 percent hospitalization) to almost 1.5 million (at 20 percent hospitalization), or even more. Surveys during the 1970s in five Latin American countries found that between 20 and 48 percent of women required hospitalization after their last spontaneous or induced abortion (1).

In Bangladesh, a 1978 study estimated that almost 800,000 illegal abortions were done that year, resulting in the deaths of almost 8,000 women (5). About half of the admissions to gynecology units of major urban hospitals were for abortion complications, as were about one-quarter of pregnancy-related deaths. In 1979, the Government of Bangladesh declared that early menstrual regulation (MR) by vacuum aspiration was not subject to the penal code restricting abortion. By the mid-1980s, a nationally representative survey of MR providers estimated that perhaps 240,000 MRs (as distinct from abortions, which remained restricted to life-threatening cases) were performed yearly, assuming that fewer than one-third were reported (6), in addition to perhaps 200,000 illegal abortions (7). Many women present themselves too late for legal MRs, which cannot be performed later than 10 weeks after the beginning of the last menstrual period. An unknown number of these women resort to clandestine abortion, which becomes especially dangerous in the second trimester. Those women who have no access to MR services continue to use traditional unsafe methods.

Worldwide estimates of clandestine abortion are inevitably even more speculative. A recent guess is a total of 40 to 50 million abortions a year, of which one-quarter to one-third were illegal (8). Earlier estimates range from 40 to 55 million, about half of them illegal (9,10). Unfortunately, these figures are too vague to permit an analysis of trends in the total numbers of abortions worldwide or the proportions that are illegal. In regions such as sub-Saharan Africa where access to contraceptive information and services is limited, however, the demand for abortion is likely to intensify as more women seek ways to control their fertility.

THE LEGAL ENVIRONMENT

According to a recent international review of abortion laws, 76 percent of the world's people live in countries where induced abortion is legal if performed to alleviate a threat to the physical or mental health of the pregnant woman that exceeds the risk normally associated with pregnancy; that is, on broad medical grounds (8). Some of these countries also permit abortion in cases of expected severe physical or mental impairment of the infant (eugenic grounds), when the pregnancy resulted from rape or incest (juridical grounds), or when the effect of childbirth may cause significant social problems to the woman or her family (sociomedical or socioeconomic grounds). Thirty-nine percent of the world's people reside in nations where abortion is available upon request, usually during the first trimester, following which certain restrictions come into force. The procedure is legal on grounds beyond those of reducing a threat to a woman's life in nearly every developed country. In addition, two-thirds of the population of the developing world—including the populations of India and China—live in countries where abortion is permitted at least for broad medical reasons if not for social reasons or on request. Among the most liberal Third World states are India, Taiwan, the Democratic Republic of Korea, Burundi, and Zambia, which allow abortion on social or sociomedical grounds, and the People's Republic of China, Singapore, Vietnam, Turkey, Tunisia, and Cuba, which permit abortion for any reason; that is, on request, although not always free or subsidized.

Nevertheless, one-third of the population of the developing world—more than one billion people—live in countries where abortion is prohibited, or permitted only in extremis to save a woman's life, or in cases of rape or incest. Highly restrictive laws such as these are found in a majority of developing countries, most of them in sub-Saharan Africa, Latin America, and the more fundamentalist Islamic nations.

A pronounced trend can be identified over the past two decades toward the liberalization of abortion laws, especially in Europe, in response to an intensified concern with women's health and social justice (11). In most cases, liberalization has extended eligibility from total prohibition or narrow medical grounds (saving the life of a pregnant woman) to broader health grounds. Some reforms have also extended eligibility to social or sociomedical indications such as serious economic difficulties. Others have made abortion available to women on request within a specified time limit, such as the first trimester. Ironically, many developing countries have maintained highly restrictive abortion laws as a part of their colonial heritage long after their former colonizers liberalized their own laws. Moreover, organized "right-to-life" groups in Western nations that were largely unsuccessful in preventing liberalization in their own countries have allied themselves with conservative forces in some developing nations to try to strengthen restrictive policies there (12). The consequence of this double standard is that women in developing countries who are most in need of safe abortion services because of contraceptive scarcity, failure, misuse, or nonuse are the least likely to have a legal right to safe procedures. Yet as recent international conferences have emphasized, these same women face vastly higher risks than women in industrialized countries of dying of pregnancy-related causes. For a woman in the United States or Canada, for example, the lifetime chance of dying from maternal causes is one in over 6,000; for a woman in sub-Saharan Africa it reaches one in 20 (13).

The legal status of abortion tells only part of the story, of course. Abortion is widely practiced in some countries that have restrictive laws, while in other countries only a small minority of eligible women have access to safe services despite the liberalization of the law. The former category includes a number of "lapsed law" countries such as Mexico, Brazil, Egypt, Nigeria, Thailand, and Indonesia, where abortion is nominally illegal but, according to some observers, readily available (sometimes with the acquiescence of the government) for those who can afford to pay (14).

In countries with restrictive laws, physicians, midwives, and other trained professionals in addition to traditional untrained practitioners or quacks often offer their services in private offices, clinics, a borrowed space, or someone's home despite the threat—at least in theory—of criminal penalties. In the Republic of Korea in 1971, for example, when abortion was legal only on narrow medical grounds, a household survey estimated that about 100,000 illegal abortions were performed in Seoul that year, a ratio of 750 per 1,000 live births (15).

As was the case in the United States prior to the decriminalization of abortion in 1973, governments and local law enforcement agencies often close their eyes to known violations unless they are forced to prosecute because of a formal complaint or a woman's death. Clients themselves are often unaware that they are breaking the law. The 1971 Seoul survey found that approximately 30 percent of respondents did not know that abortion was, in general, illegal at that time (15). Similarly, a 1976 survey of women in five villages in the Philippines found that 57 percent believed that abortion was legal and only 4 percent were unsure, when in fact, abortion was illegal on all grounds with the possible exception of saving the life of a pregnant woman (16).

In countries with more liberal legislation, safe services are sometimes unavailable to a majority of women despite legislation permitting abortion for social or sociomedical reasons or even on request. In India, for example, abortion has been allowed on broad medical and social grounds since the Medical Termination of Pregnancy Act was passed in 1971. "Medical terminations of pregnancy" may be performed only in approved institutions by authorized physicians, however. More than a decade later, in a country with over 160 million women of reproductive age, only 4,600 medical facilities and fewer than 15,000 physicians had received official approval (8). Despite the increase in legal abortions, illegal abortions were estimated at 4 to 6 million yearly because of the shortage of approved hospitals and personnel (1). Two years after abortion was legalized in India on broad medical and social grounds, only 31 percent of married women of reproductive age in a 1973–74 survey of Bangalore City knew about the liberalization (17). As is typically the case, awareness of the law was especially low among women with no formal education.

Other bureaucratic regulations also restrict women's access to safe services where abortion is legal. The written permission of a husband or guardian may be required. Or a woman may be required to obtain authorization from two or even three doctors, which in countries where physicians are scarce is virtually impossible for all but a privileged few. The 1972 abortion law of Zambia, for instance, requires approval by three medical practitioners, including one specialist. Yet in 1975 there was only one physician in Zambia for every 10,000 inhabitants (1). Moreover, the cost of legal abortions performed in hospitals and private clinics can also be prohibitive unless there are subsidies for low-income clients. In the Republic of Korea, a typical charge for a first-trimester legal abortion in Seoul in 1977–78 represented about 10 percent of the monthly earnings of a construction laborer, and for a second-trimester procedure up to 35 percent (15).

The incoming president of the International Federation of Gynecologists and Obstetricians (FIGO) summarized the situation succinctly at a symposium in Rio de Janeiro on unwanted pregnancies. Because "the risks of abortion result not from medical factors but its illegality," he noted, "the logical step to prevent deaths among women who have an unwanted pregnancy is to decriminalize abortion" (4). But whereas the legalization of abortion on request without bureaucratic obstacles is undoubtedly a *necessary* condition for the provision of safe services to all women who need them, it is clearly not a *sufficient* condition. Shortages of facilities and trained providers, combined with the reluctance or refusal of some health professionals, continue to prevent even those women who meet the conditions of eligibility for legal abortion from obtaining safe services in many countries.

According to one legal expert, a major problem in countries with liberal legislation is that governments "are almost invariably reluctant to place health professionals and facilities under positive duties to perform abortions" where the procedure is legal (11). The U.S. experience is a case in point: in 1982, abortions were provided in only 26 percent of all non-Catholic general hospitals and 16 percent of public hospitals (8). In more restrictive regimes, governments are also generally reluctant to clarify through their executive, legislative, or judicial branches the precise conditions under which abortions can legally be performed (11). In these cases, women who do meet eligibility requirements, such as those who are pregnant as a result of rape or incest, or for whom the pregnancy or birth poses grave medical problems, are often not served because medical professionals are reluctant to take the risk in what they perceive as a "chilling" political environment. In both liberal and restrictive regimes, the structure of health care delivery systems and the training and attitudes of health care providers become critically important to the provision of safe services.

THE MEDICAL ENVIRONMENT

Despite international initiatives addressing family planning, maternal and child health, child survival, and safe motherhood, most women in developing countries tend to be marginalized by vertically structured medical institutions that pay little attention to their comprehensive reproductive health needs (18). Problems inherent in the medical environment include lack of access to integrated reproductive health services, and poor quality of care. The World Health Organization estimates that about half of all births to women in developing countries in the mid-1980s were attended by trained personnel, for example (with very wide variations from country to country and between urban and rural settings), and in many countries fewer than one-third of pregnant women visit a trained health worker at least once before childbirth (19). Surveys taken in a number of developing countries for the World Fertility Survey show that fewer than half of all married women in some countries know of a place where they can obtain family planning services (20). With regard to the quality of care, many family planning programs offer little or no personal counseling, method choice, or follow-up care, all of which are associated with user satisfaction and continuation rates, and providers are often more concerned with meeting the targeted numbers of "acceptors" than with meeting the needs of the individual woman (21–24). As a consequence of limited access and poor service quality, many women are left without a contraceptive method at all or with one that is inappropriate and bound to fail. Adolescent girls and unmarried women are not served by most family planning programs as currently structured. The failure to address the comprehensive reproductive health needs of women and girls contributes to the incidence of unwanted pregnancies, especially among individuals at high risk of pregnancy-related disability or death: adolescents, single women with no previous births, and older women of high parity (2).

It is generally acknowledged that to remedy these deficiencies, stronger community-based primary health care services are needed in developing countries (3, 25). The community-based approach to women's reproductive health relies heavily on paramedical personnel such as family planning workers, village health workers, and nurse-midwives for birth control counseling and services, identification and treatment of common reproductive tract infections, basic prenatal and postnatal care, midwifery, and referral of women with high-risk pregnancies to higher level medical facilities, among other activities. Community-based programs counteract the tendency to overmedicalize birth control and childbearing in high-technology centers serving a limited clientele and to overcome clients' fears of seeking treatment. Paramedical personnel are essential where physicians are scarce. When properly trained, they are usually more effective providers of basic health care because they are closer to their clients in social background, are more familiar with the everyday needs and concerns of the people they serve, and specialize in tasks that physicians often consider of little challenge and low prestige (26). The early termination of unwanted pregnancies is one of these tasks.

From the medical viewpoint, the termination of a suspected pregnancy within the first few weeks of a missed period by vacuum aspiration of the uterine lining is safe and relatively simple. Prior to 1970, the medical profession relied primarily on the technique of dilation and curettage for uterine evacuation soon after a missed period. The development in the late 1960s of the Karman syringe and flexible cannula—a simple and cheaply produced plastic instrument—allowed the "induction" or "extraction" of the menses by vacuum aspiration of the uterine lining. The no-touch technique, which reduces the risk of infection, is relatively easy to perform and has low complication rates when done early (27). Menstrual regulation can be performed without anesthesia or sedation by trained paraprofessionals on an outpatient basis in about five to ten minutes. The technique can also be used as a diagnostic tool in cases of excessive uterine bleeding, and for treating women with potentially life-threatening incomplete abortions, either induced or spontaneous, if the pregnancy is of short gestation. The availability of MR services at the primary health care level thus contributes to the reduction of female morbidity and mortality in at least three ways.

The illegality of abortion greatly increases its risks. Not all illegal abortions are unsafe, of course. Some are performed under hygienic conditions by physicians or trained midwives in private offices or clinics. This medicalization of illegal abortion reduces maternal morbidity and mortality, but safe procedures are usually available only for a small minority of women who can afford them. In general, illegal or clandestine abortions are associated with high risks of female death or disability because most are self-induced or performed by unskilled providers using crude methods. Death rates from clandestine abortion in developing countries can reach as high as 400 per 100,000 procedures, according to some estimates, compared with six deaths per 100,000 procedures where abortion is legal (28).

Of special relevance to women in developing countries are the short-term and long-term complications—both physical and emotional—resulting from clandestine procedures. Common physical complications include incomplete abortion requiring evacuation of the uterus, pelvic infection, hemorrhage, shock, poisoning, tetanus, damage to the pelvic organs from mechanical or chemical inserts or from heavy abdominal massage, and secondary sterility (1). The emotional costs include social isolation, panic about what to do, fear of the procedure itself, anxiety about health consequences, resentment of the sexual partner, and shame and humiliation. Where safe abortion is illegal or inaccessible, the time spent experimenting with folk remedies and then searching for a provider increases the danger of complications due to advanced gestation. Women who experience infection, heavy bleeding, or severe pain after an illegal procedure are often reluctant to seek medical help because they believe they have committed a crime. Those who wait too long suffer or die without treatment, while those who do seek medical help are often treated with impatience or contempt in overcrowded maternity wards.

Both the *risks* to women's lives and health and the unnecessarily high costs of treating abortion complications through emergency hospitalization could be significantly reduced by providing early, safe services on an outpatient basis. A hospital study in Thailand in 1977–78, for example, found that women seeking treatment for complications from abortions induced outside the hospital (80 percent of which were self-induced or performed by nonmedical personnel) were hospitalized on average 2.2 days, compared with 0.2 hospital-days on average for women obtaining abortions within the hospital (29). Early MR is cost-effective not only relative to the treatment of septic abortion but also relative to other methods of birth prevention. A study of MR services provided in clinic settings by paramedical personnel in the Bangladesh Women's Health Coalition, for example, found that the cost of an "adjusted birth prevented" through MR was $7.08 (U.S. dollars) for the Coalition clinics, compared with $68.25, $58.10, and $32.20 for other family planning programs that relied primarily on contraception (30). The average cost of providing services to an MR client who left a Coalition clinic with a contraceptive method was $3.75, although clients in most clinics received free services.

The attitudes of physicians and other health care providers also determine the availability of safe services. Even within the constraints of restrictive legislation, medical professionals usually have considerable flexibility to act individually or collectively to provide services. The risk of criminal prosecution or professional censure, however slight, is bound to have an inhibiting effect on some practitioners. But others adopt a broad concept of health or life endangerment, for example, by using WHO's definition of health as "a state of complete physical, mental and social well-being and not merely the absence of disease or infirmity" (11), or by deciding that a woman's life is inevitably endangered if she threatens to resort to a quack if the pregnancy cannot be interrupted. On ethical grounds, some professionals believe strongly that "as medical doctors, we are obliged before any other consideration to attend to the health of our patients and to put their interests before our own," despite one's personal beliefs (31).

Most often, medical professionals and women's health advocates in developing countries with restrictive laws provide safe services because their own attitudes are more liberal than state policy. Physicians practicing in rural Bangladesh, for example, where abortion except for MR is authorized only to save a woman's life, were found overwhelmingly to approve of abortion to protect a woman's health (95 percent) and in cases of premarital pregnancy (79 percent) and rape (66 percent) (32). (Physicians were extremely conservative on the question of abortion for a married woman for reasons acceptable to the physician but without her husband's consent, however; only 12 percent approved.) Nearly half of the physicians interviewed reported performing abortions in the past year, almost all of which would have been illegal.

In contrast, in countries where abortion is legal on health or social grounds or on request, many individual and institutional health care providers refuse to provide the appropriate medical services. Some hold personal religious or ethical values that define abortion on some or all grounds as morally unacceptable or inappropriate. For others, abortion represents a low-status practice lacking in technical challenge or professional or personal rewards. In these settings, a woman's legal "right" to terminate an unwanted pregnancy safely can turn out to be a hollow one indeed.

THE SOCIAL CONTEXT

Cultural definitions of wanted and unwanted pregnancies and of abortion differ sharply among social groups and among individuals according to their gender, marital status, age, religion, caste, class, and ethnicity, among other factors. The termination of certain categories of pregnancy is socially expected or tolerated in some settings and stigmatized in others (33). In Latin America, for example, where abortion is illegal on almost all grounds, a Colombian psychologist points out that women who abort often experience loneliness and guilt because abortion is considered "a dissident act with far-reaching political connotations" (34).

In most pre-industrial societies, women know about a considerable array of "menstrual-inducing recipes" made from ordinary botanical agents, most of them ineffective (35, 36). If these milder methods fail to induce bleeding, a woman may resort to more drastic measures such as inserting leaves, roots, or sticks into her uterus, manipulating the uterus by abdominal massage, or taking more dangerous substances orally, some of them poisons. A woman using such techniques may not define herself as pregnant, however, or the act of bringing on the menses as abortion, until she feels that a fetus is formed, which may be two or three months after a missed period.

The question of whether a particular pregnancy is "wanted" or not is a complicated one. Many pregnancies may have been wanted at the time of conception but unwanted later because of changed circumstances, or wanted by one partner but not the other, or wanted in general but not so soon (37, 38). Some unwanted pregnancies result from unwanted intercourse (rape, incest, emotional or physical coercion), some from unprotected intercourse, others from contraceptive failure. Abortion may be a man's decision with little regard for the woman's wishes. Or a woman may seek to terminate her pregnancy, perhaps surreptitiously, despite her partner's insistence that she bear the child.

Under what conditions is an unwanted pregnancy most likely to be terminated by induced abortion? In a 1975 study of 108 women living in three working-class barrios in Cali, Colombia, who had at least one pregnancy that they described as unwanted at the time of conception, most women reported that it was the response of the lover or husband that was the major determining factor in their decision (39). Most critical was the question of whether the man was willing to accept social and financial responsibility for the child and whether the relationship appeared stable. Abortion is illegal in Colombia except to save a woman's life.

Yet of 123 unwanted pregnancies in the sample, 44 were aborted either spontaneously or with the use of folk remedies, 42 were terminated by surgical intervention, and 37 resulted in live births. Only 28 women made no attempt to interrupt the pregnancy. Women who used major or multiple minor interventions (half of the sample) were significantly more likely to be under 25 years of age, to be single or separated, to be experiencing their first pregnancy, and to have been using a contraceptive when they became pregnant.

Studies in other social settings would doubtless reveal different configurations of events than those described for the women of Cali. Nevertheless, some generalizations pertain. In general, recorded abortion rates are higher in urban areas of developing countries and among the better educated, where knowledge and access are likely to be greater (1). Most illegal abortions in developing countries are performed on married women with several children who wish to stop childbearing or—especially in sub-Saharan Africa—to postpone the next birth. For these women, clandestine abortion is a common method of family planning, a determined effort to space and limit births in the absence of effective and acceptable contraceptive knowledge and services.

Although the absolute numbers are lower, both the proportion of all pregnancies that are unwanted and the proportion of unwanted pregnancies interrupted by abortion are significantly higher among unmarried women. Problems of unwanted pregnancy and illegal abortion are particularly severe for adolescents. According to the incoming president of FIGO, "They have less social support, greater doubts, less financial capacity to pay for an interruption and take longer to realize that they are pregnant. Consequently, they have more severe complications, a higher rate of infection, and greater risk of mutilation and death" (4).

With changing sexual norms and delayed marriage, rates of unwanted pregnancies among single women are rising rapidly in many areas of the world. The phenomenon is particularly noted in sub-Saharan Africa, where the typical patient admitted to an urban hospital for complications of clandestine abortion is likely to be young, usually unmarried, often a student, with no previous births (1). In Mali, for example, only 18 percent of women admitted to hospital for the treatment of complications from induced abortion in 1981–82 were married, compared with 86 percent of women admitted for treatment of spontaneous abortion (40). Four of every ten women admitted for induced abortion were students; 62 percent were reported as having major complications, compared with 16 percent of those with spontaneous abortions. In Thailand, a 1978 survey of rural providers estimated that at least 300,000 illegal abortions were performed that year. Almost half of the rural practitioners who were interviewed stated that they served mostly single women (41). In short, adolescents and unmarried women resort to clandestine abortion in the absence of adequate contraceptive information and services in order to avoid a forced marriage or the social and economic stress of bearing a child out of wedlock, or to remain in school or in a job.

INTERNATIONAL CONFERENCES AND DEBATES

Where abortion has been mentioned at all in the recommendations of major international conferences on maternal and child health, human rights, population, and the status of women, it has usually been in recognition of the need to reduce high levels of maternal morbidity and mortality associated with clandestine procedures. But with a few notable exceptions, participants have been reluctant to endorse publicly the legalization of abortion and the expansion of safe and accessible services as a solution. Although their hesitation may be understandable on political and cultural grounds, it cannot be sustained on scientific or ethical grounds.

International conferences and symposia on child survival have also paid remarkably little attention to the question of whether children who were unwanted by one or both parents at the time of conception are less likely to survive their infancy or childhood than those who were wanted. This question is distinct from that of deliberate infanticide or neglect of children (usually girls) born of the "wrong" sex, which has been analyzed in greater depth. A study in rural Thailand found that children wanted by one or neither parent were twice as likely to die during their first year as children wanted by both parents, after controlling for other factors influencing child survival (42). It is possible that the widely noted higher mortality risks of infants born "too early, too late, too many, or too close" represent in some degree the disguised effects of the pregnancy having been unwanted (43).

Maternal Health Conferences

The International Safe Motherhood Conference held in Nairobi in 1987 drew attention to the effects on maternal mortality and morbidity of early and frequent childbearing combined with the dangers of poorly performed illegal abortions (3). WHO emphasized in its report that services such as evacuation of the uterus for uncomplicated abortion and surgical and medical treatment of sepsis should be among the "essential functions" of a first-referral level medical facility (i.e., above the community health post) (3). But although some participants believed strongly that safe and accessible voluntary abortion services were fundamental to the reduction of maternal morbidity and mortality among Third World women, the conference did not incorporate this sentiment in its formal Call to Action.

Participants at the International Conference on Better Health for Women and Children through Family Planning (also held in Nairobi in 1987) voiced similar concerns with the related health hazards of unwanted pregnancy and adolescent childbearing (28). The preamble to the recommendations for action noted that "it is unethical for scientists and service providers to shut their eyes to this waste of human life" caused by unsafe abortion. Despite the preamble, however, and despite the strong endorsement of safe and accessible services contained in several background papers, the conference concluded only that humane treatment of *septic and incomplete* abortion should be made available regardless of the legal status of abortion in each country (25). Where legal, however, "good quality abortion services should be made easily accessible to all women."

In contrast, the Christopher Tietze International Symposium on Women's Health in the Third World held in Rio de Janeiro in 1988 was more forthright in its recommendations. Declaring that safe, legal, and affordable services for terminating unwanted pregnancies should be available to women in all countries on health and human rights grounds, the symposium issued a statement deploring "the current restrictive policies and pressures, dictated by cultural and religious beliefs and political interests," that were being applied globally and locally to reduce women's access to high-quality reproductive health services and to reproductive choice (44).

Population and Human Rights

The basic right of individuals and couples "to decide freely and responsibly on the number and spacing of their children" has been established in United Nations documents since 1968 (45). In 1969 the General Assembly declared that governments have a corresponding obligation to provide families with "the knowledge and means necessary to enable them to exercise this right" (46). The concept of family planning as a human right has been reaffirmed at the U.N. World Population Conference in Bucharest in August 1974 (47) and the U.N. International Conference on Population in Mexico City in August 1984 (48), among other forums. Noting that "the ability of women to control their own fertility forms an important basis for their enjoyment of other rights," the World Plan of Action adopted at the Mexico City conference affirmed that (49):

> Governments should, as a matter of urgency, make universally available information, education and the means to assist couples and individuals to achieve their desired number of children. Family planning information, education and means should include all medically approved and appropriate methods of family planning, including natural family planning, to ensure a voluntary and free choice in accordance with changing individual and cultural values. Particular attention should be given to those segments of the population which are most vulnerable and difficult to reach.

Does the right to family planning established in these documents include an implied right to abortion? Logically, it does, because in the absence of accessible, acceptable, and universally effective contraception, women do use abortion as an alternative method of family planning to regulate the number or spacing of their children. Opponents of this position have tried repeatedly to define abortion as "not a method of family planning," however, and to exclude it from the debate.

Delegates to the 1974 Bucharest conference avoided the issue by relegating abortion to the morbidity and mortality section of the World Population Plan of

Action, which quietly urged the "reduction of involuntary sterility, subfecundity, defective births and illegal abortions" (47). Although the subject attracted greater attention in Mexico City because of the U.S. policy position, abortion was again mentioned only in the maternal morbidity and mortality section of the plan. But the wording of the recommendation was hotly debated nevertheless. The Plan of Action finally adopted at Mexico City concludes (among other things) that "Governments are urged . . . to take appropriate steps to help women avoid abortion, which in no case should be promoted as a method of family planning, and whenever possible, [to] provide for the humane treatment and counseling of women who have had recourse to abortion" (48). The word "promoted" reflects a compromise with the efforts of the Vatican (which has formal status as U.N. observer) and its conservative supporters to introduce language that would exclude abortion entirely from consideration as a method of family planning (12). The latter amendment was defeated on the grounds that countries have a sovereign right to create their own population and health policies.

From the perspective of women's rights, there is some precedent within the United Nations for including the voluntary termination of pregnancy in the right to family planning. A 1975 study on the relationship between the status of women and family planning concluded that in order to protect the right of individuals and couples to determine the number and spacing of their children, governments must establish the right to terminate an unwanted pregnancy safely, leaving abortion subject only to those regulations surrounding other medical procedures of a similar nature (50). A U.N. Symposium on Population and Human Rights held in Vienna in 1981 declared that "Both the compulsory use of abortion and its unqualified prohibition would be a serious violation of human rights" (51). The three international conferences associated with the U.N. Decade for Women (Mexico City, 1975; Copenhagen, 1980; Nairobi, 1985) were more evasive in their recommendations, however, perhaps in large part because delegates were officially appointed representatives of their governments. Whereas the associated symposia of nongovernmental organizations (held simultaneously) adopted more radical positions representing the views of individual and organizational participants, in the official conferences the principle of reproductive rights beyond the familiar "right to family planning" does not appear in the plans of action adopted at each conference.

UNITED STATES INTERNATIONAL ABORTION POLICY

The tenor of international debate inevitably reflects the policy preferences of individual nations. For the past 20 years or more, the United States has been an influential voice in the population field (52). During the height of U.S. political concern about rapid rates of population growth in developing countries in the late 1960s and early 1970s, the Office of Population of the U.S. Agency for International Development (USAID) funded research to develop and promote safe and effective methods of early pregnancy termination as a basic component of international family planning assistance. A "foremost goal" of USAID research at that time was to develop a safe, postconceptive, once-a-month substance "which, when self-administered on a single occasion, would ensure the nonpregnant state at completion of a monthly cycle" (53). The Office of Population of USAID distributed MR kits to family planning providers in a number of countries as part of its efforts to expand services in the developing world.

In 1973, even as abortion was decriminalized in the United States, the U.S. Congress passed the Helms Amendment to the Foreign Assistance Act of 1961 which prohibited the direct use of foreign aid funds for abortion services in recipient nations. This event marked the beginning of an increasingly restrictive U.S. policy in which organized "right-to-life" groups turned their attention to international arenas. By 1982, USAID announced new restrictions on recipient governments, private voluntary organizations (PVOs), and research institutions, including prohibitions on the procurement or distribution of MR kits and abortion equipment; prohibitions on the training of individuals for the performance of abortion as a means of family planning; and prohibitions on the funding of biomedical research relating to abortion, among other restrictions (54). And in 1984, the Reagan administration broadened its attack on abortion in a manner that sent shock waves through the Mexico City conference. The U.S. delegation announced that "the United States does not consider abortion an acceptable element of family planning programs and will no longer contribute to those of which it is a part" (55, 56).[2] Pledged USAID funds were withdrawn from the U.N. Fund for Population Activities, the major multilateral donor in the population field, and from the International Planned Parenthood Federation, and the definition of abortion-related activities was extended to encompass abortion counseling and referrals whether or not abortion was legal. Moreover, family planning PVOs in developing countries were to be denied assistance even if they used funds from private sources for abortion services, counseling, or referrals, and even if these activities constituted only a small fraction of their total health programs (58).

The Reagan administration's position made no distinction between legal and illegal abortion. USAID's mandated policy was "to separate voluntary family planning which we support from abortion which we oppose" (59). In effect, many PVOs have been forced to choose between offering safe methods of pregnancy termination but losing all USAID funding for their maternal and child health and family planning services, or maintaining their health programs but refusing a

---

[2]The U.S. delegation was headed by former Senator James L. Buckley, President of Radio Free Europe and a strong supporter of a constitutional amendment that would result in banning abortion in the United States (12, 56). The substance and language of the U.S. statement on the relation between population and development was strongly influenced by economist Julian L. Simon, a member of the delegation. Although Simon's pro-growth optimism pervaded the policy statement, his pro-choice position on abortion as a policy consistent with maximizing individual freedoms (57) clearly did not.

woman's request for referral to safe abortion services (14). Despite the declaration that it is "imperative" that population assistance "respect the religious beliefs and culture of each society, and the right of couples to determine the size of their own families" (55), the U.S. policy imposed a narrowly defined position on recipient nations and penalized PVOs that offered safe, legal abortion as a basic component of their health care and family planning services.

CONCLUSIONS

Recent demographic estimates suggest that safe abortion services could prevent from 20 to 25 percent of the half a million deaths each year from pregnancy-related causes, most of them in developing countries (2). Given this startling figure, how can the refusal of so many governments and medical practitioners to consider the termination of unwanted pregnancies as a basic health measure be justified, especially in the face of their professed concern with high levels of maternal morbidity and mortality?

Safe services require that abortion be fully decriminalized, that bureaucratic restrictions such as special approval of physicians be removed, and that all women have access to skilled service providers under affordable conditions. In countries with liberal legislation, accessibility to safe services can be greatly improved if governments enact appropriate health policies and resource allocations for training and services. The curative treatment of incomplete or septic abortion is already considered by WHO as an essential element of medical service at first-referral level facilities. Teaching the simpler preventive techniques of MR to paramedical workers at the community level can almost eliminate the need for emergency treatment, at considerably reduced social, physical, and financial cost.

Where abortion is unlikely to be legalized or liberalized for political reasons, much can still be done to expand current services (11). In countries where abortion is permitted on health grounds, medical professionals can adopt—individually or in their professional associations—the broad definition of health used by WHO that includes mental and social as well as physical well-being. Under more restrictive laws, medical professionals can use a more comprehensive concept of life-threatening pregnancies so that women desperate to terminate an unwanted pregnancy can do so safely.

Government representatives can also clarify the scope of national abortion laws by specifying the circumstances under which the termination of pregnancy can be presumed not to violate prevailing laws. For example, some statutes expressly or implicitly require proof of pregnancy as an element of criminal prosecution. Under such statutes, MR, which is performed early after a missed period, may represent a safe and legal procedure, as in Bangladesh (60, 61). Similar possibilities are raised by the new menstrual-inducing anti-progestin drugs such as RU 486. Governments can also require medical practitioners who are personally unwilling to perform legal abortions to refer eligible candidates immediately to other providers. In addition, judiciaries can be urged to interpret prevailing laws liberally, and law enforcement officials can be slow to prosecute. In many countries safe services are now provided or could quietly be offered to women as a basic health measure in women's centers or in family planning or maternal and child health clinics without substantial risk of prosecution.

More broadly, governments with restrictive laws, and medical institutions with restrictive policies, can reexamine the legal, medical, and ethical principles upon which these restrictions are founded (31, 62). Given the safety of modern methods of pregnancy termination and the dangers of most clandestine procedures, is it appropriate on health grounds to maintain restrictive policies? Given that family planning has been defined in international documents as a basic human right consistent with individual liberty and responsibility, can restrictive policies be justified on human rights grounds? Given the professed commitments of many governments to promoting equality of access to basic social services, is the denial of safe abortion to all women consistent with principles of social justice?

With few exceptions, the international debate on abortion policy and women's health has been dominated by evasiveness and wishful thinking. To avoid direct confrontations that might embarrass participating governments, most representatives at international conferences have not recommended the legalization of abortion and expansion of safe services in developing countries despite the direct and obvious relevance of such measures to women's survival and well-being and to the exercise of their human rights.

Wishful thinking is most apparent in the assumption that the demand for clandestine abortions will fade as contraceptive services become more widely available. There is little evidence to support this view. First, the percentage of couples who are protected by "modern" methods of contraception and sterilization remains extremely low in many countries, especially among the poor, and especially in rural areas. In the late 1970s and early 1980s, only 7 percent of married women in their reproductive years living in the rural areas of 12 African countries were currently using contraception, on average, compared with 20 percent in Asia and 30 percent in Latin America and the Caribbean (20). Many couples cannot hope to have access to effective contraceptive information and services for years to come, and some countries continue to restrict the importation, distribution, and sale of certain contraceptive devices (49). Moreover, organized "right-to-life" groups opposed to the liberalization of abortion laws in developed and developing countries are also active in many countries, such as the Philippines, in opposing artificial methods of contraception that would reduce the number of unwanted pregnancies (63).

The inaccessibility of contraceptive services is often compounded by the lack of choice among methods for those who do seek services, the unacceptability of specific methods or specific service providers, uncertainty about how to use a method, and the fear of contraceptive side effects (64). As a consequence, continuation rates are often low and failure rates high. In the Philippines, for example, a sample of pill users experienced a pregnancy rate of 19 percent in the first year despite a "theoretical" failure rate of about one per 100 women-years of use (2). Demographers have estimated that the rate of accidental pregnancies among contraceptors can be anywhere from under 1 percent to greater than 50 percent, depending on the use-effectiveness and mix of various contraceptive methods in the population. "Given the reality of contraceptive practice," they conclude, "one is faced with the problem of contraceptive failure on a rather large scale. Thus, the requirement for [maternal] health care services (prenatal care, delivery, and abortion services) is raised directly by the needs of the women who have accepted family planning, as well as by the majority who have not" (2).

Moreover, the experience of industrialized countries shows that the demand for abortion often remains high among some subgroups even given widespread contraceptive availability and generally effective use. In France in the early 1980s, there were about 15 legal abortions each year for every 1,000 women in the age group 15 to 44; in Sweden, 18 to 20; in Denmark, 20; in Japan, about 22, in the United States, 24 to 29 (8). These figures represent about 22 to 40 abortions for every 100 live births. For women who hope to limit their childbearing to, say, two children, with perhaps three months of intensive breastfeeding, only 24 months out of a total of approximately 360 months of reproductive life is occupied by gestation and postpartum infertility. Under these conditions, most women involved in sexual unions will be at risk of an unintended pregnancy during over 90 percent of their monthly cycles.

For all of these reasons it is unlikely that the demand for abortion services in most developing countries will decline significantly if and when contraceptive information and services become more widely available. Indeed, the demand for abortion often rises along with contraceptive use, and where it falls, as in Chile, it is never eliminated (65). As the 40 to 45 percent of the total population of many developing countries now under 15 years of age enters its reproductive years and desired family size continues to decline, the number of abortions attempted is likely to increase. The question remaining is whether the majority of Third World women must continue to risk their lives in order to regulate their own fertility, or whether they will be offered safe and affordable services.

REFERENCES

1. Liskin L. S. Complications of abortion in developing countries. *Popul. Rep. [F]* 7, July 1980.
2. Winikoff, B., and Sullivan, M. Assessing the role of family planning in reducing maternal mortality. *Stud. Fam. Plann.* 18: 128–143, 1987.
3. Starrs, A. *Preventing the Tragedy of Maternal Deaths: A Report on the International Safe Motherhood Conference,* Nairobi, Kenya, February 1987. The World Bank, Washington, D.C., 1987.
4. Pinotti, J. A., and A. Faundes. Unwanted pregnancy: Challenges for health policy. *Int. J. Gynecol. Obstet. Suppl* 3: 97–102, 1989.

..

5. Measham, A. R., et al. Complications from induced abortion in Bangladesh related to types of practitioners and methods, and impact on mortality. *Lancet* 1: 199–202, 1981.
6. Begum, S. F., Kamal, H., and Kamal, G. M. *Evaluation of MR Services in Bangladesh.* Bangladesh Association for the Prevention of Septic Abortion, Dhaka, 1987.
7. Khan, A. R., et al. Induced abortion in a rural area of Bangladesh. *Stud. Fam. Plann.* 17: 95–99, 1986.
8. Tietze, C., and Henshaw, S. K. *Induced Abortion: A World Review*, Ed. 6. Alan Guttmacher Institute, New York, 1986.
9. International Planned Parenthood Federation. *Survey of World Needs in Family Planning.* IPPF, London, 1974.
10. Population Crisis Committee. *Population* 9, 1979.
11. Cook, R. J. Abortion laws and policies: Challenges and opportunities. *Int. J. Gynecol. Obstet. Suppl* 3: 61–88, 1989.
12. Finkle, J., and Crane, B. Ideology and politics at Mexico City: The United States at the 1984 International Conference on Population. *Popul. Dev. Rev.* 11: 1–28, 1985.
13. Herz, B., and Measham, A. R. *The Safe Motherhood Initiative: Proposals for Action.* The World Bank, Washington, D.C, 1987.
14. Camp, S. The impact of the Mexico City policy on women and health care in developing countries. *J. Int. Law Polit.* 20: 35–52, 1987.
15. Hong, S., and Tietze, C. Survey of abortion providers in Seoul, Korea. *Stud Fam. Plann.* 10: 161–163, 1979.
16. Flavier, J. M., and Chen, C. H. C. Induced abortion in rural villages of Davite, the Philippines: Knowledge, attitudes, and practice. *Stud. Fam. Plann.* 11: 65–71, 1980.
17. Rao, N. B., and Kanbargi, R. Legal abortions in an Indian state. *Stud Fam. Plann.* 8: 311–315 1977.
18. Germain, A. *Reproductive Health and Dignity: Choices by Third World Women.* The Population Council, New York, 1987.
19. World Health Organization, Division of Family Health. *Coverage of Maternity Care: A Tabulation of Available Information.* FHE/85.1. WHO, Geneva, 1985.
20. United Nations. *Fertility Behaviour in the Context of Development: Evidence from the World Fertility Survey.* U.N., New York, 1987.
21. Bruce, J. *Fundamental Elements of Quality of Care: A Simple Framework.* Programs Division Working Papers No. 1. The Population Council, New York, May 1989.
22. Jain, A. Fertility reduction and the quality of family planning services. *Stud. Fam. Plann.* 20: 1–16, 1989.
23. Ainsworth, M. *Family Planning Programs: The Clients' Perspective.* World Bank Staff Working Papers No. 676. The World Bank, Washington, D.C., 1984.
24. Callen, M. A., and Lettenmaier, C. Counseling makes a difference. *Popul. Rep. [J]* 35, 1987.
25. Black, M. *Better Health for Women and Children through Family Planning: Report on an International Conference Held in Nairobi, Kenya, October 1987.* The Population Council, New York, 1988.
26. Beeson, D., et al. Client-provider transactions in family planning clinics. In *Organizing for Effective Family Planning Programs,* edited by R. J. Lapham and G. B. Simmons. National Academy Press, Washington, D.C., 1987.
27. van der Vlugt, T., and Piotrow, P. T. Menstrual regulation: What is it? *Popul. Rep. [F]* 2, 1973.
28. Sai, F. T., and Nassim, J. The need for a reproductive health approach. *Int. J. Gynecol. Obstet. Suppl.* 3: 103–114, 1989.
29. Chaturachinda, K., et al. Abortion: An epidemiologic study at Ramathibodi Hospital, Bangkok. *Stud. Fam. Plann.* 12: 257–262, 1981.

30. Kay, B. J., and Kabir, S. M. A study of costs and behavioral outcomes of menstrual regulation services in Bangladesh. *Soc. Sci. Med.* 26: 597–604, 1988.
31. Villareal, J. Commentary on unwanted pregnancy, induced abortion, and professional ethics: A concerned physician's point of view. *Int. J. Gynecol. Obstet.* Suppl. 3: 51–56, 1989.
32. Rosenberg, M. J., et al. Attitudes of rural Bangladesh physicians toward abortion. *Stud. Fam Plann.* 12: 318–321, 1981.
33. Devereux, G. *Abortion in Primitive Society.* International Universities Press, New York, 1976.
34. Londono, E. M. L. Abortion counseling: Attention to the whole woman. *Int. J. Gynecol. Obstet.* Suppl. 3: 169–174, 1989.
35. Jochle, W. Menses-inducing drugs: Their role in antique, medieval, and renaissance gynecology and birth control. *Contraception* 10: 428–437, 1974.
36. Newman, L. F. (ed.). *Women's Medicine: A Cross-Cultural Study of Indigenous Fertility Regulation.* Rutgers University Press, New Brunswick, N.J., 1985.
37. Hass, P. Wanted and unwanted pregnancies: A fertility decision-making model. *J. Soc. Issues* 30: 125–164, 1974.
38. Luker, K. *Taking Chances: Abortion and the Decision Not to Contracept.* University of California Press, Berkeley, 1975.
39. Browner, C. Abortion decision making: Some findings from Colombia. *Stud. Fam. Plann.* 10: 96–106, 1979.
40. Binkin, N. J., et al. Women hospitalized for abortion complications in Mali. *Int. Fam. Plann. Perspect.* 10: 8–12, 1984.
41. Narkavonnakit, T. Abortion in rural Thailand: A survey of practitioners. *Stud. Fam. Plann.* 10: 223–229, 1979.
42. Frenzen, P. D., and Hogan, D. P. The impact of class, education, and health care on infant mortality in a developing society: The case of rural Thailand. *Demography* 19: 391–408, 1982.
43. Scrimshaw, S. C. M. Infant mortality and behavior in the regulation of family size. *Popul. Dev. Rev.* 4: 383–402, 1978.
44. Statement of The Christopher Tietze International Symposium on Women's Health in the Third World: The Impact of Unwanted Pregnancy, Rio de Janeiro, Brazil, October 29-30, 1988. *Int. J. Gynecol. Obstet.* Suppl. 3: 175, 1989.
45. United Nations. Final Act of the International Conference on Human Rights, Teheran, April-May 1968, Res. CVIII, Chap. 111, U.N. Document A/CONF.32/41. U.N., New York, 1968.
46. United Nations. General Assembly Resolution 2542, Article 24, CAOR Supp. (No. 30), U.N. Document A/7630. U.N., New York, 1970.
47. Mauldin, W. P., et al. A report on Bucharest: The World Population Conference and The Population Tribune, August 1974. *Stud. Fam. Plann.* 5: 357–395, 1974.
48. Wulf, D., and Willson, P. D. Global politics in Mexico City. *Fam. Plann. Perspect.* 16: 228–232, 1984.
49. Isaacs, S. L., and Cook, R. J. Laws and policies affecting fertility: A decade of change. *Popul. Rep. [E]* 7: 105–151, 1984.
50. United Nations, Department of Economic and Social Affairs. *The Status of Women and Family Planning,* p. 89. U.N., New York, 1975.
51. United Nations, Department of International Economic and Social Affairs. *Population and Human Rights: Proceedings of the Symposium on Population and Human Rights, Vienna, 29 June–3 July 1981,* p. 8. U.N., New York, 1983.
52. Piotrow, P. T. *World Population Crisis: The United States Response,* pp. 175–178. Praeger, New York, 1973.

53. United States Agency for International Development (USAID), Office of Population. *Population Program Assistance: United States Aid to Developing Countries,* p. 14. U.S. Government Printing Office, Washington, D.C., 1974.

54. United States Agency for International Development (USAID). *Popul. Dev. Rev.* 9: 188, 1983.

55. United States. Policy Statement of the United States of America at the United Nations International Conference on Population (Second Session), Mexico D.F., August 6–13, 1984. U.S. Department of State, Washington, D.C., 1984.

56. Fox, G. H. American population policy abroad: The Mexico City abortion restrictions. *J. Int. Law Polit.* 18: 609–662,1986.

57. Simon, J. *The Ultimate Resource,* p. 301. Princeton University Press, Princeton, N.J., 1981.

58. Willson, P. D. Abortion: The new standard for U.S. population aid. *Int. Fam. Plann. Perspect.* 11: 27, 1985.

59. Rosenberg, A. P. *AID Population Policy: The Needs and Rights of Individuals and Families,* Office of Population, U.S. Agency for International Development, Washington, D.C., 1986.

60. Dixon-Mueller, R. Innovations in reproductive health care: Menstrual regulation policies and programs in Bangladesh. *Stud Fam. Plann.* 19: 129–140, 1988.

61. Lee, L. T., and Paxman, J. M. Legal aspects of menstrual regulation. *Stud Fam. Plann.* 8: 273–278, 1977

62. Macklin, R. Liberty, utility, and justice: An ethical approach to unwanted pregnancy. *Int. J. Gynecol. Obstet.* Suppl. 3: 37–50, 1989.

63. Marcelo, A. B. Reproductive Rights and Challenges in the Philippines. Paper presented at the annual meetings of the Population Association of America, Baltimore, March 1989.

64. Bruce, J. Users' perspectives on contraceptive technology and delivery systems: Highlighting some feminist issues. *Technol. Soc.* 9: 359–383, 1987.

65. David, H. Abortion: Its prevalence, correlates, and costs. In *Determinants of Fertility in Developing Countries,* Vol. 2, edited by R. A. Bulatao and R. D. Lee, p. 209. Academic Press, New York, 1983.

Section V
Sexuality, Women's Bodies, and Women's Health

CHAPTER 11

Medical Metaphors of Women's Bodies: Menstruation and Menopause

Emily Martin

It is difficult to see how our current scientific ideas are infused by cultural assumptions; it is easier to see how scientific ideas from the past, ideas that now seem wrong or too simple, might have been affected by cultural ideas of an earlier time. To lay the groundwork for a look at contemporary scientific views of menstruation and menopause, I begin with the past.

It was an accepted notion in medical literature from the ancient Greeks until the late 18th century that male and female bodies were structurally similar. As Nemesius, Bishop of Emesa, Syria, in the fourth century, put it, "women have the same genitals as men, except that theirs are inside the body and not outside it." Although increasingly detailed anatomical understanding (such as the discovery of the nature of the ovaries in the last half of the 17th century) changed the details, medical scholars from Galen in second-century Greece to Harvey in 17th-century Britain all assumed that women's internal organs were structurally analogous to men's external ones (1).

Although the genders were structurally similar, they were not equal. For one thing, what could be seen of men's bodies was assumed as the pattern for what could not be seen of women's. For another, just as humans as a species possessed more "heat" than other animals and hence were considered more perfect, so men possessed more "heat" than women and hence were considered more perfect. The relative coolness of the female prevented her reproductive organs from extruding outside the body but, happily for the species, kept them inside where they provided a protected place for conception and gestation (1, p. 10).

This essay first appeared as Chapter 3 in *The Woman in the Body: A Cultural Analysis of Reproduction* © 1987 by Emily Martin. Reprinted in the *International Journal of Health Services* 18(2): 237–254, 1988, by permission of Beacon Press.

During the centuries when male and female bodies were seen as composed of analogous structures, a connected set of metaphors was used to convey how the parts of male and female bodies functioned. These metaphors were dominant in classical medicine and continued to operate through the 19th century (2, p. 5):

> The body was seen, metaphorically, as a system of dynamic interactions with its environment. Health or disease resulted from a cumulative interaction between constitutional endowment and environmental circumstance. One could not well live without food and air and water; one had to live in a particular climate, subject one's body to a particular style of life and work. Each of these factors implied a necessary and continuing physiological adjustment. The body was always in a state of becoming—and thus always in jeopardy.

Two subsidiary assumptions governed this interaction: first, that "every part of the body was related inevitably and inextricably with every other," and second, that "the body was seen as a system of intake and outgo—a system which had, necessarily, to remain in balance if the individual were to remain healthy" (2, pp. 5–6).

Given these assumptions, changes in the relationship of body functions occurred constantly throughout life, though more acutely at some times than at others. In Edward Tilt's influential mid-19th century account, for example, after the menopause, blood that once flowed out of the body as menstruation was then turned into fat (3, p. 54):

> Fat accumulates in women after the change of life, as it accumulates in animals from whom the ovaries have been removed. The withdrawal of the sexual stimulus from the ganglionic nervous system, enables it to turn into fat and self-aggrandisement that blood which might otherwise have perpetuated the race.

During the transition to menopause, or the "dodging time," the blood cannot be turned into fat, so it was either discharged as hemorrhage or through other compensating mechanisms, the most important of which was "the flush" (3, pp. 54, 57):

> As for thirty-two years it had been habitual for women to lose about 3 oz. of blood every month, so it would have been indeed singular, if there did not exist some well-continued compensating discharges acting as wastegates to protect the system, until health could be permanently re-established by striking new balances in the allotment of blood to the various parts.... The flushes determine the perspirations. Both evidence a strong effect of conservative power, and as they constitute the most important and habitual safety-valve of the system at the change of life, it is worth while studying them.

In this account, compensating mechanisms such as the "flush" are seen as having the positive function of keeping intake and outgo in balance.

These balancing acts had exact analogues in men. In Hippocrates' view of purification, one that was still current in the 17th century (4, p. 50), women were of a colder and less active disposition than men, so that while men could sweat in order to remove the impurities from their blood, the colder dispositions of women did not allow them to be purified in that way. Females menstruated to rid their bodies of impurities.

Or in another view, expounded by Galen in the second century and still accepted into the 18th century, menstruation was the shedding of an excess of blood, a plethora (4, p. 50). But what women did through menstruation men could do in other ways, such as by having blood let (5). In either view of the mechanism of menstruation, the process itself not only had analogues in men, it was seen as inherently health maintaining. Menstrual blood, to be sure, was often seen as foul and unclean (4, p. 63), but the process of excreting it was not intrinsically pathological. In fact, failure to excrete was taken as a sign of disease, and a great variety of remedies existed even into the 19th century specifically to reestablish menstrual flow if it stopped (6).

By 1800, according to Laqueur's important recent study, this long-established tradition that saw male and female bodies as similar both in structure and in function began to come "under devastating attack. Writers of all sorts were determined to base what they insisted were fundamental differences between male and female sexuality, and thus between man and woman, on discoverable biological distinctions" (1, p. 4). Laqueur argues that this attempt to ground differences between the genders in biology grew out of the crumbling of old ideas about the existing order of politics and society as laid down by the order of nature. In the old ideas, men dominated the public world and the world of morality and order by virtue of their greater perfection, a result of their excess heat. Men and women were arranged in a hierarchy in which they differed by degree of heat. They were not different in kind (1, p. 8).

The new liberal claims of Hobbes and Locke in the 17th century and the French revolution were factors that led to a loss of certainty that the social order could be grounded in the natural order. If the social order were merely convention, it could not provide a secure enough basis to hold women and men in their places. But after 1800 the social and biological sciences were brought to the rescue of male superiority. "Scientists in areas as diverse as zoology, embryology, physiology, heredity, anthropology, and psychology had little difficulty in proving that the pattern of male-female relations that characterized the English middle classes was natural, inevitable, and progressive" (7, p. 180).

The assertion was that men's and women's social roles themselves were grounded in nature, by virtue of the dictates of their bodies. In the words of one 19th century theorist (7, p. 190),

the attempt to alter the present relations of the sexes is not a rebellion against some arbitrary law instituted by a despot or a majority—not an attempt to break the yoke of a mere convention; it is a struggle against Nature; a war undertaken to reverse the very conditions under which not man alone, but all mammalian species have reached their present development.

The doctrine of the two spheres—men as workers in the public, wage-earning sphere outside the home and women (except for the lower classes) as wives and mothers in the private, domestic sphere of kinship and morality inside the home—replaced the old hierarchy based on body heat.

During the latter part of the 19th century, new metaphors that posited fundamental differences between the sexes began to appear. One 19th century biologist, Patrick Geddes, perceived two opposite kinds of processes at the level of the cell: "upbuilding, constructive, synthetic processes" summed up as anabolism, and "disruptive, descending series of chemical changes" summed up as katabolism (8). The relationship between the two terms was described in frankly economic terms (8, p. 123):

> The processes of income and expenditure must balance, but only to the usual extent, that expenditure must not altogether outrun income, else the cell's capital of living matter will be lost–a fate which is often not successfully avoided. . . . Just as our expenditure and income should balance at the year's end, but may vastly outstrip each other at particular times, so it is with the cells of the body. Income too may continuously preponderate, and we increase in wealth, or similarly, in weight, or in anabolism. Conversely, expenditure may predominate, but business may be prosecuted at a loss; and similarly we may live on for a while with loss of weight, or in katabolism. This losing game of life is what we call a katabolic habit.

Geddes saw these processes not only at the level of the cell, but also at the level of entire organisms. In the human species, as well as almost all higher animals, females were predominantly anabolic, males katabolic. Although in the terms of his saving-spending metaphor it is not at all clear whether katabolism would be an asset, when Geddes presents male-female differences, there is no doubt which he thought preferable (8, pp. 270–271):

> It is generally true that the males are more active, energetic, eager, passionate, and variable; the females more passive, conservative, sluggish, and stable. . . . The more active males, with a consequently wider range of experience, may have bigger brains and more intelligence; but the females, especially as mothers, have indubitably a larger and more habitual share of the altruistic emotions. The males being usually stronger, have greater independence and courage; the females excel in constancy of affection and in sympathy.

In Geddes, the doctrine of separate spheres was laid on a foundation of separate and fundamentally different biology in men and women, at the level of the cell. One of the striking contradictions in his account is that he did not carry over the implications of his economic metaphors to his discussion of male-female differences. If he had, females might have come off as wisely conserving their energy and never spending beyond their means, males as in the "losing game of life," letting expenditures outrun income.

Geddes may have failed to draw the logical conclusions from his metaphor, but we have to acknowledge that metaphors were never meant to be logical. Other 19th century writers developed metaphors in exactly opposite directions: women spent and men saved. The Reverend John Todd saw women as voracious spenders in the marketplace, and so consumers of all that a man could earn. If unchecked, a woman would ruin a man, by her own extravagant spending, by her demands on him to spend, or in another realm, by her excessive demands on him for sex. Losing too much sperm meant losing that which sperm was believed to manufacture: a man's lifeblood (9).

Todd and Geddes were not alone in the 19th century in using images of business loss and gain to describe physiological processes. Susan Sontag has suggested that 19th century fantasies about disease, especially tuberculosis, "echo the attitudes of early capitalist accumulation. One has a limited amount of energy, which must be properly spent. . . .Energy, like savings, can be depleted, can run out or be used up, through reckless expenditure. The body will start 'consuming' itself, the patient will 'waste away' " (10, pp. 61–62).

Despite the variety of ways that spending-saving metaphors could be related to gender, the radical difference between these metaphors and the earlier intake-outgo metaphor is key. Whereas in the earlier model, male and female ways of secreting were not only analogous but desirable, now the way became open to denigrate, as Geddes overtly did, functions that for the first time were seen as uniquely female, without analogue in males. For our purposes, what happened to accounts of menstruation is most interesting: by the 19th century, the process itself is seen as soundly pathological. In Geddes' terms (8, p. 244),

> it yet evidently lies on the borders of pathological change, as is evidenced not only by the pain which so frequently accompanies it, and the local and constitutional disorders which so frequently arise in this connection, but by the general systemic disturbance and local histological changes of which the discharge is merely the outward expression and result.

Whereas in earlier accounts the blood itself may have been considered impure, now the process itself is seen as a disorder.

Nineteenth century writers were extremely prone to stress the debilitating nature of menstruation and its adverse impact on the lives and activities of women (11). Medical images of menstruation as pathological were remarkably vivid by the end of the century. For Walter Heape, the militant anti-suffragist and Cambridge zoologist, in menstruation the entire epithelium was torn away, "leaving behind a ragged wreck of tissue, torn glands, ruptured vessels, jagged edges of stroma, and masses of blood corpuscles, which it would seem hardly possible to heal satisfactorily without the aid of surgical treatment" (1, p. 32). A few years later, Havelock Ellis could see women as being "periodically wounded" in their most sensitive spot and "emphasize the fact that even in the healthiest woman, a worm however harmless and unperceived, gnaws periodically at the roots of life" (12, p. 284).

If menstruation was consistently seen as pathological, menopause, another function which by this time was regarded as without analogue in men, often was too: many 19th century medical accounts of menopause saw it as a crisis likely to bring on an increase of disease (11, pp. 30–31). Sometimes the metaphor of the body as a small business that is either winning or losing was applied to menopause too. A late 19th century account specifically argued against Tilt's earlier adjustment model: "When the period of fruitfulness is ended the activity of the tissues has reached its culmination, the secreting power of the glandular organs begins to diminish, the epithelium becomes less sensitive and less susceptible to infectious influences, and atrophy and degeneration take the place of the active up-building processes" (13, pp. 25–26). But there were other sides to the picture. Most practitioners felt the "climacteric disease," a more general disease of old age, was far worse for men than for women. And some regarded the period after menopause far more positively than it is being seen medically in our century, as the " 'Indian summer' of a woman's life—a period of increased vigor, optimism, and even of physical beauty" (11, p. 30).

Perhaps the 19th century's concen with conserving energy and limiting expenditure can help account for the seeming anomaly of at least some positive medical views of menopause and the climacteric. As an early 20th century popular health account put it (14, p. 413):

> [Menopause] is merely a conservative process of nature to provide for a higher and more stable phase of existence, an economic lopping off of a function no longer needed, preparing the individual for different forms of activity, but is in no sense pathologic. It is not sexual or physical decrepitude, but belongs to the age of invigoration, marking the fullness of the bodily and mental powers.

Those few writers who saw menopause as an "economic" physiological function might have drawn very positive conclusions from Geddes' description of females as anabolic, stressing their "thriftiness" instead of their passivity, their "growing bank accounts" instead of their sluggishness.

If the shift from the body as an intake-outgo system to the body as a small business trying to spend, save, or balance its accounts is a radical one, with deep importance for medical models of female bodies, so too is another shift that began in the 20th century with the development of scientific medicine. One of the early 20th century engineers of our system of scientific medicine, Frederick T. Gates, who advised John D. Rockefeller on how to use his philanthropies to aid scientific medicine, developed a series of interrelated metaphors to explain the scientific view of how the body works (15, pp. 170–171):

> It is interesting to note the striking comparisons between the human body and the safety and hygienic appliances of a great city. Just as in the streets of a

great city we have "white angels" posted everywhere to gather up poisonous materials from the streets, so in the great streets and avenues of the body, namely the arteries and the blood vessels, there are brigades of corpuscles, white in color like the "white angels," whose function it is to gather up into sacks, formed by their own bodies, and disinfect or eliminate all poisonous substances found in the blood. The body has a network of insulated nerves, like telephone wires, which transmit instantaneous alarms at every point of danger. The body is furnished with the most elaborate police system, with hundreds of police stations to which the criminal elements are carried by the police and jailed. I refer to the great numbers of sanitary glands, skillfully placed at points where vicious germs find entrance, especially about the mouth and throat. The body has a most complete and elaborate sewer system. There are wonderful laboratories placed at convenient points for a subtle brewing of skillful medicines. . . . The fact is that the human body is made up of an infinite number of microscopic cells. Each one of these cells is a small chemical laboratory, into which its own appropriate raw material is constantly being introduced, the processes of chemical separation and combination are constantly taking place automatically, and its own appropriate finished product being necessary for the life and health of the body. Not only is this so, but the great organs of the body like the liver, stomach, pancreas, kidneys, gall bladder are great local manufacturing centers, formed of groups of cells in infinite numbers, manufacturing the same sorts of products, just as industries of the same kind are often grouped in specific districts.

Although such a full-blown description of the body as a model of an industrial society is not often found in contemporary accounts of physiology, elements of the images that occurred to Gates are commonplace. In recent years, the "imagery of the biochemistry of the cell [has] been that of the factory, where functions [are] specialized for the conversion of energy into particular products and which [has] its own part to play in the economy of the organism as a whole" (16, p. 58).

Still more recently, economic functions of greater complexity have been added: adenosine triphosphate (ATP) is seen as the body's "energy currency": "Produced in particular cellular regions, it [is] placed in an 'energy bank' in which it [is] maintained in two forms, those of 'current account' and 'deposit account.' Ultimately, the cell's and the body's energy books must balance by an appropriate mix of monetary and fiscal policies" (16, p. 59). Here we have not just the simpler 19th century saving and spending, but two distinct forms of money in the bank, presumably invested at different levels of profit.

Development of the new molecular biology brought additional metaphors based on information science, management, and control. In this model, flow of information between deoxyribonucleic acid (DNA) and ribonucleic acid (RNA) leads to the production of protein. Molecular biologists conceive of the cell as "an assembly line factory in which the DNA blueprints are interpreted and raw materials fabricated to produce the protein end products in response to a series of regulated requirements" (16, p. 59). The cell is still seen as a factory, but, compared to Gates' description, there is enormous elaboration of the flow of information from one "department" of the body to another and exaggeration of the amount of control exerted by the center. For example, from a college physiology text (17, pp. 7–8):

> All the systems of the body, if they are to function effectively, must be subjected to some form of control. . . . The precise control of body function is brought about by means of the operation of the nervous system and of the hormonal or endocrine system. . . . The most important thing to note about any control system is that before it can control anything it must be supplied with information. . . . Therefore the first essential in any control system is an adequate system of collecting information about the state of the body. . . . Once the CNS [central nervous system] knows what is happening, it must then have a means for rectifying the situation if something is going wrong. There are two available methods for doing this, by using nerve fibres and by using hormones. The motor nerve fibres . . . carry instructions from the CNS to the muscles and glands throughout the body. . . . As far as hormones are concerned the brain acts via the pituitary gland . . . the pituitary secretes a large number of hormones . . . the rate of secretion of each one of these is under the direct control of the brain.

Although there is increasing attention to describing physiological processes as positive and negative feedback loops, so that like a thermostat system, no single element has preeminent control over any other, most descriptions of specific processes give preeminent control to the brain, as we will see below.

In over-all descriptions of female reproduction, the dominant image is that of a signalling system. Lein, in a textbook designed for junior colleges, spells it out in detail (18, p. 14),

> Hormones are chemical signals to which distant tissues or organs are able to respond. Whereas the nervous system has characteristics in common with a telephone network, the endocrine glands perform in a manner somewhat analogous to radio transmission. A radio transmitter may blanket an entire region with its signal, but a response occurs only if a radio receiver is turned on and tuned to the proper frequency . . . the radio receiver in biological systems is a tissue whose cells possess active receptor sites for a particular hormone or hormones.

The signal-response metaphor is found almost universally in current texts for premedical and medical students (19, p. 885; 20, p. 129; 21, p. 115; emphasis added):

> The hypothalamus *receives signals* from almost all possible sources in the nervous system.

> The endometrium *responds directly* to stimulation or withdrawal of estrogen and progesterone. In turn, regulation of the secretion of these steroids involves a well integrated, highly structured series of activities by the hypothalamus and the anterior lobe of the pituitary. Although the ovaries do not function autonomously, they *influence,* through *feedback* mechanisms, the level of performance *programmed* by the hypothalamic-pituitary axis.

> As a result of strong stimulation of FSH [follicle-stimulating hormone], a number of follicles *respond* with growth.

And the same idea is found, more obviously, in popular health books (22, p. 6; 23, p. 6; emphasis added):

> Each month from menarch on, [the hypothalamus] acts as elegant interpreter of the body's rhythms, *transmitting messages* to the pituitary gland that set the menstrual cycle in motion.

> Each month, *in response to a message* from the pituitary gland, one of the unripe egg cells develops inside a tiny microscopic ring of cells, which gradually increases to form a little balloon or cyst called the Graafian follicle.

Although most accounts stress signals or stimuli traveling in a "loop" from hypothalamus to pituitary to ovary and back again, carrying positive or negative feedback, one element in the loop, the hypothalamus, part of the brain, is often seen as predominant. Just as in the general model of the central nervous system, the female brain-hormone-ovary system is usually described not as a feedback loop like a thermostat system, but as a hierarchy, in which the "directions" or "orders" of one element dominate (24, p. 1615; 19, p. 885; emphasis added):

> Both positive and negative feedback control must be invoked, together with *superimposition* of control by the CNS through neurotransmitters released into the hypophyseal portal circulation.

> Almost all secretion by the pituitary is *controlled* by either hormonal or nervous signals from the hypothalamus. . . . The hypothalamus is a collecting center for information concerned with the internal well-being of the body, and in turn much of this information is used to *control* secretions of the many globally important pituitary hormones.

As Lein puts it into ordinary language (18, p. 84):

> The cerebrum, that part of the brain that provides awareness and mood, can play a significant role in the control of the menstrual cycle. As explained before, it seems evident that these higher regions of the brain exert their influence by modifying the actions of the hypothalamus. So even though the hypothalamus is a kind of master gland dominating the anterior pituitary, and through it the ovaries also, it does not act with complete independence or without influence from outside itself . . . there are also pathways of control from the higher centers of the brain.

So this is a communication system organized hierarchically, not a committee reaching decisions by mutual influence. The hierarchical nature of the organization is reflected in some popular literature meant to explain the nature of menstruation simply: "From first menstrual cycle to menopause, the hypothalamus acts as the conductor of a highly trained orchestra. Once its baton signals the downbeat to the pituitary, the hypothalamus-pituitary-ovarian axis is united in purpose and begins to play its symphonic message, preparing a woman's body for conception and childbearing" (22, p. 6). Carrying the metaphor further, the follicles vie with each other for the role of producing the egg like violinists trying for the position of concertmaster; a burst of estrogen is emitted from the follicle like a "clap of tympani" (21, p. 6).

The basic images chosen here—an information-transmitting system with a hierarchical structure—have an obvious relation to the dominant form of organization in our society (25). What I want to show is how this set of metaphors, once chosen as the basis for the description of physiological events, has profound implications for the way in which a change in the basic organization of the system will be perceived. In terms of female reproduction, this basic change is of course menopause. Many criticisms have been made of the medical propensity to see menopause as a pathological state (26). I would like to suggest that the tenacity of this view comes not only from the negative stereotypes associated with aging women in our society, but as a logical outgrowth of seeing the body as a hierarchical information-processing system in the first place. (Another part of the reason menopause is seen so negatively is related to metaphors of production, which I discuss later.)

What is the language in which menopause is described? In menopause, according to a college text, the ovaries become "unresponsive" to stimulation from the gonadotropins, to which they used to respond. As a result the ovaries "regress." On the other end of the cycle, the hypothalamus has gotten estrogen "addiction" from all those years of menstruating. As a result of the "withdrawal" of estrogen at menopause, the hypothalamus begins to give "inappropriate orders" (18, pp. 79, 97). In a more popular account, "the pituitary gland during the change of life becomes disturbed when the ovaries fail to respond to its secretions, which tends to affect its control over other glands. This results in a temporary imbalance existing among all the endocrine glands of the body, which could very well lead to disturbances that may involve a person's nervous system" (27, p. 11).

In both medical texts and popular books, what is being described is the breakdown of a system of authority. The cause of ovarian "decline" is the "decreasing ability of the aging ovaries to respond to pituitary gonadotropins" (28). At every point in this system, functions "fail" and falter. Follicles "fail to muster the strength" to reach ovulation (22, p. 181). As functions fail, so do the members of the system decline; "breasts and genital organs gradually atrophy" (28, p. 598), "wither" (22, p. 181) and become "senile" (21, p. 121). Diminished, atrophied relics of their former vigorous, functioning selves, the "senile ovaries" are an example of the vivid imagery brought to this process. A text whose detailed illustrations make it a primary resource for medical students despite its early date describes the ovaries this way (21, p. 116):

> [T]he *senile ovary* is a shrunken and puckered organ, containing few if any follicles and made up for the most part of old corpora albincantia and corpora atretica, the bleached and functionless remainders of corpora lutia and follicles embedded in a dense connective tissue stroma.

In more recent accounts, it is commonly said that ovaries cease to respond and fail to produce. Everywhere there is regression, decline, atrophy, shrinkage, and disturbance.

The key to the problem connoted by these descriptions is functionlessness. Susan Sontag has written of our obsessive fear of cancer, a disease that we see as entailing a nightmare of excessive growth and rampant production. These images frighten us in part because in our stage of advanced capitalism, they are close to a reality we find difficult to see clearly: broken-down hierarchy and organization members who no longer play their designated parts represent nightmare images for us. One woman I talked to said her doctor gave her two choices for treatment of her menopause: she could take estrogen and get cancer or she could not take it and have her bones dissolve. Like this woman, our imagery of the body as a hierarchical organization gives us no good choice when the basis of the organization seems to us to have changed drastically. We are left with breakdown, decay, and atrophy. Bad as they are, these might be preferable to continued activity, which because it is not properly hierarchically controlled, leads to chaos, unmanaged growth, and disaster.

But let us return to the metaphor of the factory producing substances, which dominates the imagery used to describe cells. At the cellular level DNA communicates with RNA, all for the purpose of the cell's production of proteins. In a similar way, the system of communication involving female reproduction is thought to be geared toward production of various things: the ovaries produce estrogen, the pituitary produces follicle-stimulating hormone and luteinizing hormone, and so on. Follicles also produce eggs in a sense, although this is usually described as "maturing" them since the entire set of eggs a woman has for her lifetime is known to be present at birth. Beyond all this the system is seen as organized for a single preeminent purpose: "transport" of the egg along its journey from the ovary to the uterus (28, p. 580) and preparation of an appropriate place for the egg to grow if it is fertilized. In a chapter titled "Prepregnancy Reproductive Functions of the Female, and the Female Hormones," Guyton puts it all together: "Female reproductive functions can be divided into two major phases: first, preparation of the female body for conception and gestation, and second, the period of gestation itself" (19, p. 968). This view may seem commonsensical, and entirely justified by the evolutionary development of the species with its need for reproduction to ensure survival.

Yet I suggest that assuming this view of the purpose for the process slants our description and understanding of the female cycle unnecessarily. Let us look at how medical textbooks describe menstruation. They see the action of progesterone and estrogen on the lining of the uterus as "ideally suited to provide a hospitable environment for implantation and survival of the embryo" (28, p. 576) or as intended to lead to "the monthly renewal of the tissue that will cradle [the ovum]" (18, p. 43). As Guyton summarizes, "The whole purpose of all these endometrial changes is to produce a highly secretory endometrium containing large amounts of stored nutrients that can provide appropriate conditions for implantation of a fertilized ovum during the latter half of the monthly cycle" (19, p. 976). Given this teleological interpretation of the purpose of the increased amount of endometrial tissue, it should be no surprise that when a fertilized egg does not implant, these texts describe the next event in very negative terms. The fall in blood progesterone and estrogen "deprives" the "highly developed endometrial lining of its hormonal support," "constriction" of blood vessels leads to a "diminished" supply of oxygen and nutrients, and finally "disintegration starts, the entire lining begins to slough, and the menstrual flow begins." Blood vessels in the endometrium "hemorrhage" and the menstrual flow "consists of this blood mixed with endometrial debris" (28, p. 577). The "loss" of hormonal stimulation causes "necrosis" (death of tissue) (19, p. 976).

The construction of these events in terms of a purpose that has failed is beautifully captured in a standard text for medical students (a text otherwise noteworthy for its extremely objective, factual descriptions) in which a discussion of the events covered in the last paragraph (sloughing, hemorrhaging) ends with the statement, "When fertilization fails to occur, the endometrium is shed, and a new cycle starts. This is why it used to be taught that 'menstruation is the uterus crying for lack of a baby' " (29, p. 63).

I am arguing that just as seeing menopause as a kind of failure of the authority structure in the body contributes to our negative view of it, so does seeing menstruation as failed production contribute to our negative view of it. We have seen how Sontag describes our horror of production out of control. But another kind of horror for us is *lack* of production: the disused factory, the failed business, the idle machine. Winner terms the stopping and breakdown of technological systems in modern society "apraxia" and describes it as "the ultimate horror, a condition to be avoided at all costs" (30). This horror of idle workers or machines seems to have been present even at earlier stages of industrialization. A 19th century inventor, Thomas Ewbank, elaborated his view that the whole world "was designed for a Factory" (31). "It is only as a Factory, a *General Factory,* that the whole materials and influences of the earth are to be brought into play" (31, p. 23). In this great workshop, humans' role is to produce: "God employs no idlers— creates none" (31, p. 27). Ewbank continues (31, p. 141):

> Like artificial motors, we are created for the work we can do—for the useful and productive ideas we can stamp upon matter. Engines running daily without doing any work resemble men who live without labor; both are spendthrifts dissipating means that would be productive if given to others.

Menstruation not only carries with it the connotation of a productive system that has failed to produce, it also carries the idea of production gone awry, making products of no use, not to specification, unsalable, wasted, scrap. However disgusting it may be, menstrual blood will come out. Production gone awry is also an image that fills us with dismay and horror. Amid the glorification of machinery common in the 19th century were also fears of what machines could do if they went out of control. Capturing this fear, one satirist wrote of a steam-operated shaving machine that "sliced the noses off too many customers" (32). This image is close to the one Melville created in *The Bell-Tower*, in which an inventor, who can be seen as an allegory of America, is killed by his mechanical slave (32, p. 153), as well as to Mumford's (33) sorcerer's apprentice applied to modern machinery (34, p. 180):

Our civilization has cleverly found a magic formula for setting both industrial and academic brooms and pails of water to work by themselves, in ever-increasing quantities at an ever-increasing speed. But we have lost the Master Magician's spell for altering the tempo of this process, or halting it when it ceases to serve human functions and purposes.

Of course, how much one is gripped by the need to produce goods efficiently and properly depends on one's relationship to those goods. While packing pickles on an assembly line, I remember the foreman often holding up improperly packed bottles to show to us workers and trying to elicit shame at the bad job we were doing. But his job depended on efficient production, which meant many bottles filled right the first time. This factory did not yet have any effective method of quality control, and as soon as our supervisor was out of sight, our efforts went toward filling as few bottles as we could while still concealing who had filled which bottle. In other factories, workers seem to express a certain grim pleasure when they can register objections to company policy by enacting imagery of machinery out of control. Noble reports an incident in which workers resented a supervisor's order to "shut down their machines, pick up brooms, and get to work cleaning the area. But he forgot to tell them to stop. So, like the sorcerer's apprentice, diligently and obediently working to rule, they continued sweeping up all day long" (35, p. 312).

Perhaps one reason the negative image of failed production is attached to menstruation is precisely that women are in some sinister sense out of control when they menstruate. They are not reproducing, not continuing the species, not preparing to stay at home with the baby, not providing a safe, warm womb to nurture a man's sperm. I think it is plain that the negative power behind the image of failure to produce can be considerable when applied metaphorically to women's bodies. Vern Bullough comments optimistically that "no reputable scientist today would regard menstruation as pathological" (36), but this paragraph from a recent college text belies his hope (37, p. 525):

If fertilization and pregnancy do not occur, the corpus luteum degenerates and the levels of estrogens and progesterone decline. As the levels of these hormones decrease and their stimulatory effects are withdrawn, blood vessels of the endometrium undergo prolonged spasms (contractions) that reduce the blood flow to the area of the endometrium supplied by the vessels. The resulting lack of blood causes the tissues of the affected region to degenerate. After some time, the vessels relax, which allows blood to flow through them again. However, capillaries in the area have become so weakened that blood leaks through them. This blood and the deteriorating endometrial tissue are discharged from the uterus as the menstrual flow. As a new ovarian cycle begins and the level of estrogens rises, the functional layer of the endometrium undergoes repair and once again begins to proliferate.

In rapid succession the reader is confronted with "degenerate," "decline," "withdrawn," "spasms," "lack," "degenerate," "weakened," "leak," "deteriorate," "discharge," and, after all that, "repair."

In another standard text, we read (38, p. 624):

> The sudden lack of these two hormones [estrogen and progesterone] causes the blood vessels of the endometrium to become spastic so that blood flow to the surface layers of the endometrium almost ceases. As a result, much of the endometrial tissue dies and sloughs into the uterine cavity. Then, small amounts of blood ooze from the denuded endometrial wall, causing a blood loss of about 50 ml during the next few days. The sloughed endometrial tissue plus the blood and much serous exudate from the denuded uterine surface, all together called the *menstrum,* is gradually expelled by intermittent contractions of the uterine muscle for about 3 to 5 days. This process is called *menstruation.*

The illustration that accompanies this text captures very well the imagery of catastrophic disintegration: "ceasing," "dying," "losing," "denuding," and "expelling."

These are not neutral terms; rather, they convey failure and dissolution. Of course, not all texts contain such a plethora of negative terms in their descriptions of menstruation, but unacknowledged cultural attitudes can seep into scientific writing through evaluative words. Coming at this point from a slightly different angle, consider this extract from a text that describes male reproductive physiology. "The mechanisms which guide the *remarkable* cellular transformation from spermatid to mature sperm remain uncertain. . . . Perhaps the most *amazing* characteristic of spermatogenesis is its *sheer magnitude:* the normal human male may manufacture several hundred million sperm per day" (28, pp. 483–484; emphasis added). As we will see, this text has no parallel appreciation of female processes such as menstruation or ovulation, and it is surely no accident that this "remarkable" process involves precisely what menstruation does not in the medical view: production of something deemed valuable. Although this text sees such massive sperm production as unabashedly positive, in fact, only about one out of every 100 billion sperm ever makes it to fertilize an egg: from the very same point of view that sees menstruation as a waste product, surely here is something really worth crying about!

When this text turns to female reproduction, it describes menstruation in the same terms of failed production we saw earlier (28, p. 577; emphasis added):

> The fall in blood progesterone and estrogen, which results from *regression* of the corpus luteum, *deprives* the highly developed endometrial lining of its hormonal support; the immediate result is *profound constriction* of the uterine blood vessels due to production of vasoconstrictor prostaglandins, which leads to *diminished* supply of oxygen and nutrients. *Disintegration* starts, and the entire lining (except for a thin, deep layer which will regenerate the endometrium in the next cycle) begins to slough. . . . The endometrial arterioles dilate, resulting in *hemorrhage* through the weakened capillary

walls; the menstrual flow consists of this blood mixed with endometrial *debris*. . . The menstrual flow ceases as the endometrium *repairs* itself and then grows under the influence of rising blood estrogen concentration.

And ovulation fares no better. In fact part of the reason ovulation does not merit the enthusiasm that spermatogenesis does may be that all the ovarian follicles containing ova are already present at birth. Far from being *produced* as sperm are, they seem to merely sit on the shelf, as it were, slowly degenerating and aging like overstocked inventory (28, pp. 567–568):

> At birth, normal human ovaries contain an estimated one million follicles, and no new ones appear after birth. Thus, in marked contrast to the male, the newborn female has all the germ cells she will ever have. Only a few, perhaps 400, are destined to reach full maturity during her active productive life. All the others degenerate at some point in their development so that few, if any, remain by the time she reaches menopause at approximately 50 years of age. One result of this is that the ova which are released (ovulated) near menopause are 30 to 35 years older than those ovulated just after puberty; it has been suggested that certain congenital defects, much commoner among children of older women, are the result of aging changes in the ovum.

How different it would sound if texts like this one stressed the vast excess of follicles produced in a female fetus, compared to the number she will actually need. In addition, males are also born with a complement of germ cells (spermatogonia) that divide from time to time, and most of which will eventually differentiate into sperm. This text could easily discuss the fact that these male germ cells and their progeny are also subject to aging, much as female germ cells are. Although we would still be operating within the terms of the production metaphor, at least it would be applied in an evenhanded way to both males and females.

One response to my argument would be that menstruation just is in some objective sense a process of breakdown and deterioration. The particular words are chosen to describe it because they best fit the reality of what is happening. My counterargument is to look at other processes in the body that are fundamentally analogous to menstruation in that they involve the shedding of a lining to see whether they also are described as breakdown and deterioration. The lining of the stomach, for example, is shed and replaced regularly, and seminal fluid picks up shedded cellular material as it goes through the various male ducts.

The lining of the stomach must protect itself against being digested by the hydrochloric acid produced in digestion. In the several texts quoted above, emphasis is on the secretion of mucus (37, p. 419), the *barrier* that mucus cells present to stomach acid (29, p. 776), and—in a phrase that gives the story away—the periodic *renewal* of the lining of the stomach (37, p. 423). There is no reference to degenerating, weakening, deterioration, or repair, or even the more neutral shedding, sloughing, or replacement. As described in an introductory physiology text (38, pp. 498–499):

> The primary function of the gastric secretions is to begin the digestion of proteins. Unfortunately, though, the wall of the stomach is itself constructed mainly of smooth muscle which itself is mainly protein. Therefore, the surface of the stomach must be exceptionally well protected at all times against its own digestion. This function is performed mainly by mucus that is secreted in great abundance in all parts of the stomach. The entire surface of the stomach is covered by a layer of very small *mucous cells,* which themselves are composed almost entirely of mucus; this mucus prevents gastric secretions from ever touching the deeper layers of the stomach wall.

The emphasis here is on production of mucus and protection of the stomach wall. It is not even mentioned, although it is analogous to menstruation, that the mucus cell layers must be continually sloughed off (and digested). Although all the general physiology texts I consulted describe menstruation as a process of disintegration needing repair, only specialized texts for medical students describe the stomach lining even in the more neutral terms of "sloughing" and "renewal" (39). One can choose to look at what happens to the lining of stomachs and uteruses negatively as breakdown and decay needing repair, or positively as continual production and replenishment. Of these two sides of the same coin, stomachs, which women *and* men have, fall on the positive side; uteruses, which only women have, fall on the negative.

One other analogous process is not handled negatively in the general physiology texts. Although it is well known to those researchers who work with male ejaculates that a very large proportion of the ejaculate is composed of shedded cellular material, the texts make no mention of a shedding process let alone processes of deterioration and repair in the male reproductive tract (28, pp. 557–558).

What applies to menstruation once a month applies to menopause once in every lifetime. As we have seen, part of the current imagery attached to menopause is that of a breakdown of central control. Inextricably connected to this imagery is another aspect of the metaphor of failed production. Recall the metaphors of balanced intake and outgo that were applied to menopause up to the mid-19th century, later to be replaced by metaphors of degeneration. In the early 1960s, new research on the role of estrogens in heart disease led to arguments that failure of female reproductive organs to produce much estrogen after menopause was debilitating to health.

This change is marked unmistakably in the successive editions of a major gynecology text. In the 1940s and 1950s, menopause was described as usually not entailing "any very profound alteration in the woman's life current" (40). By the 1965 edition, dramatic changes had occurred: "In the past few years there has been a radical change in viewpoint and some would regard the menopause as a possible pathological state rather than a physiological one and discuss therapeutic prevention rather than the amelioration of symptoms" (41).

In many current accounts, menopause is described as a state in which ovaries fail to produce estrogen. The 1981 World Health Organization report defines menopause as an estrogen deficiency disease (42). Failure to produce estrogen is the leitmotif of another current text (19, p. 979):

> This period during which the cycles cease and the female sex hormones diminish rapidly to almost none at all is called the *menopause*. The cause of the menopause is the "burning out" of the ovaries. . . . Estrogens are produced in subcritical quantities for a short time after the menopause, but over a few years, as the final remaining primordial follicles become atretic, the production of estrogens by the ovaries falls almost to zero.

Loss of ability to produce estrogen is seen as central to a woman's life: "At the time of the menopause a woman must readjust her life from one that has been physiologically stimulated by estrogen and progesterone production to one devoid of those hormones" (19, p. 979).

Of course, I am not implying that the ovaries do not indeed produce much less estrogen than before. I am pointing to the choice of these textbook authors to emphasize above all else the negative aspects of ovaries failing to produce female hormones. By contrast, one current text shows us a positive view of the decline in estrogen production (43, p. 799):

> It would seem that although menopausal women do have an estrogen milieu which is lower than that necessary for *reproductive* function, it is not negligible or absent but is perhaps satisfactory for *maintenance of support tissues*. The menopause could then be regarded as a physiologic phenomenon which is protective in nature—protective from undesirable reproduction and the associated growth stimuli.

I have presented the underlying metaphors contained in medical descriptions of menopause and menstruation to show that these ways of describing events are but one way of fitting an interpretation to the facts. Yet seeing that female organs are imagined to function within a hierarchical order whose members signal each other to produce various substances, all for the purpose of transporting eggs to a place where they can be fertilized and then grown, may not provide us with enough of a jolt to begin to see the contingent nature of these descriptions. Even seeing that the metaphors we choose fit very well with traditional roles assigned to women may still not be enough to make us question whether there might be another way. Here I suggest some other ways that menstruation and menopause could be described.

First, consider the teleological nature of the system, its assumed goal of implanting a fertilized egg. What if a woman has done everything in her power to avoid having an egg implant in her uterus, such as birth control or abstinence from heterosexual sex. Is it still appropriate to speak of the single purpose of her menstrual cycle as dedicated to implantation? From the woman's vantage point, it might capture the sense of events better to say the purpose of the cycle is the production of menstrual flow. Think for a moment how that might change the description in medical texts: "A drop in the formerly high levels of progesterone and estrogen creates the perfect environment for reducing the excess layers of endometrial tissue. Constriction of capillary blood vessels causes a lower level of oxygen and nutrients and paves the way for a vigorous production of menstrual fluids. As a part of the renewal of the remaining endometrium, the capillaries begin to reopen, contributing some blood and serous fluid to the volume of endometrial material already beginning to flow." I can see no reason why the menstrual blood itself could not be seen as the desired "product" of the female cycle, except when the woman intends to become pregnant.

Would it be similarly possible to change the nature of the relationships assumed among the members of the organization—the hypothalamus, pituitary, ovaries, and so on? Why not, instead of an organization with a controller, a team playing a game? When a woman wants to get pregnant, it would be appropriate to describe her pituitary, ovaries, and so on as combining together, communicating with each other, to get the ball, so to speak, into the basket. The image of hierarchical control could give way to specialized function, the way a basketball team needs a center as well as a defense. When she did not want to become pregnant, the purpose of this activity could be considered the production of menstrual flow.

Eliminating the hierarchical organization and the idea of a single purpose to the menstrual cycle also greatly enlarges the ways we could think of menopause. A team which in its youth played vigorous soccer might, in advancing years, decide to enjoy a quieter "new game" where players still interact with each other in satisfying ways but where gentle interaction *itself* is the point of the game, not getting the ball into the basket or the flow into the vagina.

REFERENCES

1. Laqueur, T. Female orgasm, generation, and the politics of reproductive biology. *Representations* 14: 1–82, 1986.
2. Rosenberg, C. E. The therapeutic revolution: Medicine, meaning, and social change in nineteenth-century America. In *The Therapeutic Revolution: Essays in the Social History of American Medicine,* edited by M. J. Vogel and C. E. Rosenberg, pp. 3–25. University of Pennsylvania Press, Philadelphia, 1979.
3. Tilt, E. J. *The Change of Life in Health and Disease.* John Churchill, London, 1857.
4. Crawford, P. Attitudes to menstruation in seventeenth-century England. *Past and Present* 91: 47–73, 1981.
5. Rothstein, W. G. *American Physicians in the Nineteenth Century: From Sects to Science.* Johns Hopkins University Press, Baltimore, 1972.
6. Luker, K. *Abortion and the Politics of Motherhood.* University of California Press, Berkeley, 1984.
7. Fee, E. Science and the woman problem: Historical perspectives. In *Sex Difference: Social and Biological Perspectives,* edited by M. S. Teitelbaum, pp. 175–223. Doubleday, New York, 1976.
8. Geddes, P., and Thompson, J. A. *The Evolution of Sex.* Scribner and Welford, New York, 1890.
9. Barker-Benfield, G. J. *The Horrors of the Half-known Life: Male Attitudes Toward Women and Sexuality in Nineteenth-Century America.* Harper & Row, New York, 1976.

10. Sontag, S. *Illness as Metaphor.* Vintage, New York, 1979.
11. Smith-Rosenberg, C. Puberty to menopause: The cycle of femininity in nineteenth-century America. In *Clio's Consciousness Raised,* edited by M. Hartman and L. W. Banner, pp. 23–37. Harper, New York, 1974.
12. Ellis H. *Man and Woman.* Walter Scott, London, 1904.
13. Currier, A. F. *The Menopause.* Appleton, New York, 1897.
14. Taylor, J. M. The conservation of energy in those of advancing years. *Popular Science Monthly* 64: 343–414, 541–549, 1904.
15. Berliner, H. Medical modes of production. In *The Problem of Medical Knowledge: Examining the Social Construction of Medicine,* edited by P. Wright and A. Treacher, pp. 162–217. Edinburgh University Press, Edinburgh, 1982.
16. Lewontin, R. C. et al. *Not In Our Genes: Biology, Ideology, and Human Nature.* Pantheon, NewYork, 1984.
17. Horrobin, D. F. *Introduction to Human Physiology.* F. A. Davis, Philadelphia, 1973.
18. Lein, A. *The Cycling Female: Her Menstrual Rhythm.* W. H. Freeman, San Francisco, 1979.
19. Guyton, A. C. *Textbook of Medical Physiology.* W. B. Saunders, Philadelphia, 1986.
20. Benson, R. C. *Current Obstetric and Gynecologic Diagnosis and Treatment.* Lange Medical Publishers, Los Altos, Cal., 1982.
21. Netter, F. H. *A Compilation of Paintings on the Normal and Pathological Anatomy of the Reproductive System.* The CIBA Collection of Medical Illustrations, Vol. 2. CIBA, Summit, N.J., 1965.
22. Norris, R. V. *PMS: Premenstrual Syndrome.* Berkeley Books, New York, 1984.
23. Dalton, K., and Greene, R. The premenstrual syndrome. *Br. Med. J.* May 1953, pp. 1016–1017.
24. Mountcastle, V. B. *Medical Physiology,* Ed. 14, Vol. II. C. V. Mosby Co., St. Louis, 1980.
25. Giddens, A. *The Class Structure of Advanced Societies.* Harper & Row, New York, 1973.
26. McCrea, F. B. The politics of menopause: The "discovery" of a deficiency disease. *Social Problems* 31(1): 111–123, 1983.
27. O'Neill, D. J. *Menopause and Its Effect on the Family.* University Press of America, Washington, D.C., 1982.
28. Vander, A. J. et al. *Human Physiology: The Mechanisms of Body Function,* Ed. 4. McGrawHill, New York, 1985.
29. Ganong, W. F. *Review of Medical Physiology,* Ed. 11. Lange Medical Publishers, Los Altos, Cal., 1983.
30. Winner, L. *Autonomous Technology: Technics-out-of-Control as a Theme in Political Thought.* The MIT Press, Cambridge, Mass., 1977.
31. Ewbank, T. *The World a Workshop: Or the Physical Relationship of Man to the Earth.* D. Appleton, New York, 1855.
32. Fisher, M. *Workshops in the Wilderness: The European Response to American Industrialization,* 1830–1860. Oxford University Press, New York, 1967.
33. Mumford, L. *The Myth of the Machine: Technics and Human Development,* Vol. 1. Harcourt, Brace and World, New York, 1967.
34. Mumford, L. *The Myth of the Machine: The Pentagon of Power,* Vol. 2. Harcourt, Brace and World, New York, 1970.
35. Noble, D. *The Forces of Production.* Knopf, New York, 1984.
36. Bullough, V. L. Sex and the medical model. *J. Sex Res.* 11(4): 291–303, 1975.
37. Mason, E. B. *Human Physiology.* Benjamin/Cummings, Menlo Park, Cal., 1983.

38. Guyton, A. C. *Physiology of the Human Body*, Ed. 6. Saunders College Publishing, Philadelphia, 1984.
39. Sernka, T., and Jacobson, E. *Gastrointestinal Physiology: The Essentials.* Williams & Wilkins, Baltimore, 1983.
40. Novak, E. *Textbook of Gynecology*, Ed. 2. Williams & Wilkins, Baltimore, 1944.
41. Novak, E., et al. *Novak's Textbook of Gynecology*, Ed. 7. Williams & Wilkins, Baltimore, 1965.
42. Kaufert, P. A., and Gilbert, P. Women, menopause, and medicalization. *Cult. Med. Psychiatry* 10(1): 7–21, 1986.
43. Jones, H. W., and Jones, G. S. *Novak's Textbook of Gynecology*, Ed. 10. Williams & Wilkins, Baltimore, 1981.

CHAPTER 12

A Critical Historical Analysis of the Medical Construction of Lesbianism

Patricia E. Stevens and Joanne M. Hall

Lesbians are in vulnerable positions as health care clients. In several U.S. investigations (1–6), lesbian clients describe encountering ostracism, invasive questioning, rough physical handling, derogatory comments, breaches of confidentiality, shock, embarrassment, unfriendliness, pity, condescension, and fear in health care situations. Some believe that health care providers' knowledge of their lesbianism could result in neglect, physical endangerment, infliction of pain, or withdrawal of concern should providers harbor negative moral judgments about lesbians. Survey evidence suggests that their fears are legitimate (7–12). Significant numbers of physicians and nurses still consider lesbianism a pathological condition, make attributions of immorality, perversion, and danger to lesbian women, are uncomfortable providing care for lesbian clients, and regularly refuse service to women who are lesbian. Lesbian clients' access to health care services is compromised. As a result of their negative experiences in health care encounters, many lesbians report hesitation in using health care systems and say they delay seeking needed treatment (6, 13–18).

Insensitivity, antagonism, and discrimination toward women, especially lesbian, ethnic/racial minority, and poor women, abound in contemporary health care interactions (19–26). However, these phenomena have not received priority or systematic attention in health services research (27–30). More investigation is needed to understand lesbians' health care experiences, to document the extent of their access to services, to identify conditions that facilitate their utilization of health care systems, and to criticize the interactional, structural, and ideological circumstances that impede their access to and positive experience of health care.

Originally published in the *International Journal of Health Services* 21(2): 291–307, 1991.

Health care experiences of lesbian women cannot be understood apart from the historical construction of medical ideologies that have scapegoated lesbians or the discriminatory aspects of institutional structures that have sustained these ideas over the decades. Lesbianism has been pathologized by the medical profession and condemned by the general public. Lesbians' encounters with health care systems are fraught not only with the repercussions of gender, race, and class stratification, but specifically with the ideological construction of lesbianism as sin/crime/sickness.

Previous research and theory have emphasized individual meanings and interpersonal interactions as they relate to the process of stigmatization, leaving a void in scientific knowledge about the historical origins of particular stigmas, the social structures that maintain them, and the collective efforts by subcultures to transform their stigmatized status (31–33). The projects of this chapter are to illuminate the content of 20th century medical ideologies regarding lesbians and to describe the strategic collective actions lesbians have taken to change stigmatizing diagnostic and treatment situations. An excavation of historical data about medical conceptualizations of lesbianism is undertaken to demonstrate how cultural and medical ideologies throughout the century have reinforced each other to shape lesbians' health care experiences and influence public policies.

LESBIAN EXISTENCE

Lesbians are generally thought to be those women whose primary affectional and sexual attractions are oriented toward women (34). Ponse (35, 36) concluded from her research that some contemporary lesbians see their lesbianism as an essential quality of themselves. However, there is no single lesbian experience, no universal lesbian identity; lesbianism has been constructed in different ways according to historical context. Furthermore, studies in the history of sexuality have documented widely diverse sexual and affectional experiences, gender behaviors, emotions, and identities occurring in various periods, which challenge conventional notions of fixed sexual categories (37–39). Without attempting to explore in detail the concept of lesbian identity per se, the argument presented herein takes as its starting point the observation that a significant number of women in the United States throughout this century have experienced themselves as affectionally and sexually identified with other women. What this has meant in their everyday lives has been affected by their particular historical, sociocultural, political, economic, and embodied life circumstances.

The etymology of the designation, lesbian, can be traced to ancient Greece and the life of Sappho, a writer and teacher of the arts who is among the most revered of Greek lyric poets. The excellence of her poetry, which expresses her primary love for women, motivated efforts to preserve it during religious and political persecutions. Sappho's name, her home on the island of Lesbos, and a few of her verses form a cornerstone of positive meaning inherited by lesbians (40–42).

Lesbian women have lived for centuries under heavy moral, legal, and medical penalties that have forced most to lead hidden, unobtrusive, isolated lives (34, 43–46). There are scarce source materials for historical research about lesbians' lives and few studies exist. There are, however, abundant mines of information about medical conceptualizations of how lesbians lived and what should be done to constrain them. Much of the scholarly analysis that has been done in this area, however, relates the story of medicine's interface with gay men and deals with lesbians only subsidiarily. This state of affairs reflects the larger picture of historical research in general, which is based on notions of historical significance that deny history to women (47, 48).

Society's persistent refusal to acknowledge the existence of lesbians, their numbers in the population, and the variety and intensity of women's emotional and erotic experiences has contributed to their invisibility, even in contemporary times (49). Studies throughout the century have attempted to counter normative assumptions about women's sexual and relational lives by documenting the prevalence of lesbianism. In the 1920s, a national survey of 2200 women by Davis (50) documented that 30 percent of married women and 50 percent of unmarried women had intense emotional relationships with other women. Half of those relationships were also explicitly sexual. Thus 15 percent of married women and 25 percent of unmarried women in the sample reported intense emotional and sexual relationships with women. This seldom-cited investigation by a female researcher presented lesbianism as a common emotional and sexual factor in the everyday lives of women. In a national study of women in the 1950s, Kinsey and his associates (51) conducted 8000 face-to-face interviews about sexual behavior. The researchers found that 25 percent of all the women in their study reported erotic responses to women, while 17 percent stated they had been sexually active with other women. The most recent large-scale study of this sort was conducted in the 1970s. Hite (52) questioned 3000 women about their sexuality in a nationwide survey and found that 17 percent reported sexual involvements with other women. Eight percent of the sample said that they related exclusively with women.

MORAL CONDEMNATION

Moral condemnation of lesbian women has a long history. For centuries, same-sex sexual behavior was seen as a violation of God's nature, a dangerous diversion of energy from the task of human survival. Repression of gay and lesbian sexuality was sustained by an extreme moral fury that lay at the heart of Judeo-Christian cultural foundations. Christians hunted, tortured, and killed gay and lesbian people for 1400 years, from the 3rd through the 17th centuries. The death penalty for male homosexual behavior can be traced back in Judeo-Christian tradition to Leviticus 20:13. Medieval jurists in most Western societies extended the scope of the law against sodomy to include women, based on Romans 1:26, in which Paul condemned women "who did change the natural use into that which is against nature." Legal codes of the 13th century outlawed lesbian sexuality as a "sin against nature," mandating mutilation and burning at the stake (37, 53–55). During the Inquisition, sexual behavior that did not lead to procreation became symbolically associated with heresy, witchcraft, and treason (55, 56). Deviation from any one of medieval society's treasured values, whether it be sexual, social, religious, or political, caused an individual to be suspected of deviating from the others (57, 58). The association of lesbianism with perversity, deviltry, and witchcraft persists today (59).

American colonial attitudes toward male homosexuality and lesbianism are evident in the words of Thomas Jefferson, who in 1779 proposed that, "Whoever shall be guilty of sodomy shall be punished if a man by castration, if a woman by cutting through the cartilage of her nose a hole one-half inch in diameter" (quoted in 60, p. 187). In 19th century America, sodomy was equated with masturbation, both being construed as sinful deviations from procreation. Religious beliefs were incorporated wholesale into medical theories of the period; Benjamin Rush said both sins caused mental and physical illness. Clitoridectomy and blistering of the vulvar area were examples of treatments employed to "cure" masturbation and other "perversions" during this period (61).

Letters and diaries of literate 18th and 19th century women indicate that women among the more privileged classes routinely formed emotionally intense ties with other women that were not an obstacle to heterosexual marriage. These same-sex relationships endured despite separation and geographical distance. The writings reveal a clearly romantic, sensual intimacy between women, which fostered a sense of security and self-esteem. Perhaps because Victorian morality defined women as asexual and spiritual, close female friendships, even erotic friendships, were not stigmatized (62, 63). However, such ties were censured by scientific authorities at the turn of the century through claims that such associations were perverse and sick (64, 65). For instance, in 1898 Mary Wood-Allen, a woman physician, warned against the dangers of female masturbation and "special friendships" with other women (61). The Women's Christian Temperance Union's book of that same year, *What a Young Woman Ought to Know*, rejected women's friendships as perversion and "sex mania" (46, 62).

MEDICALIZATION OF LESBIANISM

At the end of the 19th century new medical-scientific definitions were imposed upon many moral categories of behavior, reinterpreting them as pathologies. A series of medical theories were developed at this time, proclaiming "homosexuality" to be a disease. The 20th century saw the development of technological societies that valued scientific solutions to social problems. Thus religion and state, as institutions of Western social control, relinquished some of their prerogatives to medicine (37, 66–68). Therapeutic response to aberrant same-sex sexual behavior was idealized as a more effective way to restore normality where punitive legal and moral attempts at social control had failed (69).

Medicine's power in the realm of social control stems from its authority to define which behaviors, persons, and things are "normal." Deviance from the normal refers to those behaviors that are defined in particular historical sociopolitical contexts as inappropriate to or in violation of certain powerful groups' conventions. Deviance designations serve political purposes and are created to support and buttress specific status interests at the expense of others (70).

As lesbianism began to be seen as a matter for the physician rather than as the exclusive territory of priests and judges, lesbians became ensnared in an ideological netherworld between immorality and madness. Perceptibly punitive medical interventions tended to "preserve" past moral overtones of "medicalized" problems (68). As Churchill suggested, "In the mass mind there was but a meager distinction, if any at all, between sinfulness and disease. . . . Originally the same devices were used to cleanse the body of illness that were used to purge the soul of sinfulness" (67, p. 29). Medical involvement in the lives of lesbians and gays did not stop religious and legal scrutiny nor make them immune from moral and punitive sanctions. Rather, the pronouncement of lesbianism as a sickness left its negative moral evaluation intact and created a powerful new tool by which to exact women's behavioral conformity.

Homosexuality As Pathology

The medical passion for classification and elaborate description of various forms of deviant sexual behavior served the purposes of making homosexual behavior more recognizable to society and the sanction of lesbians and gays more efficient (37). Late 19th century hereditary theories, such as those of Carl Westphal, Jean Martin Charcot, and Richard von Krafft-Ebing, claimed homosexuality to be a "congenital constitutional weakness," "inborn predisposition to perversion," and "hereditary taint" that could precipitate a full range of dangerous insane and "primitive" behaviors. Confinement in asylums was employed to contain lesbians' and gays' "moral insanity," to protect society from their violence and contaminatory evil (61, 71, 72).

Less contemptuous theories were also developed. In the 1860s, Karl Ulrichs, a German lawyer, began to speak publicly for the human rights of gay men and lesbians. He was strongly opposed, however, and left Germany in the wake of the Prussian invasion. The subsequent unification of Germany extended an anti-homosexual statute, paragraph 175, to all parts of the country (70, 73). In the early 1900s, Magnus Hirschfeld, a German sex researcher, campaigned for the repeal of paragraph 175 of the German penal code. He argued that homosexuals, being endowed with emotional characteristics of the opposite sex, were, using Ulrichs' term a "third sex" (37, 39, 61, 72, 74–76). Ulrichs and Hirschfeld, and British sexologist, Havelock Ellis (77), proclaimed hereditary anomaly to be the cause of homosexuality but emphasized that it was a natural variation rather than a pathology (46, 73, 78, 79). Hirschfeld influenced other sexologists such as Krafft-Ebing and Bloch to soften their positions, and believed that studies about the etiology of homosexuality would hasten decriminalization. But in fact, the search for etiology was itself ultimately cited as evidence that homosexuality was an anomaly, a disease, and a "crime against nature" (72). Thus medicalization appears to have sustained, even intensified, the moral and legal censure of homosexuality.

The emancipatory purposes of some theorists' ideas were all but obscured by the ascendency of the psychoanalytic paradigm, which dominated medical thought on homosexuality in the United States into the 1970s (69, 75). Freud originally contended that homosexuality was a manifestation of universal bisexuality and therefore was an oedipal-level phenomenon. He suggested that homosexuality was not an illness or degradation, but that to remain at this "regressed" stage of psychosexual development into adulthood could deflect the sexual instinct away from its dual purposes of pleasure and procreation (80, 81). Freud later prioritized heterosexuality as a "moral imperative" and depicted homosexuality as a "fixated" state of development, though he continually opposed a disease concept of homosexuality (82). American psychoanalysts, on the other hand, rejected Freud's basic contentions of universal bisexuality and located homosexuality's development at the earlier pre-oedipal stage in psychosexual development. Through these theoretical changes they imputed grave pathology to the condition of lesbianism.

Rado, Bergler, Stekel, Bieber, and Socarides were among the most prolific and influential psychoanalytic theorists on homosexuality in the middle decades of the century (75). They never departed from popular prejudice and proscriptive stereotype. In their multitudinous publications, female and male homosexual behaviors were likened to forgery, treason, drug purveying, addiction, burglary, Nazi cruelty, homicide, and suicide. Lesbians and gay men were considered aggressive, masochistic, destructive, deceitful, neurotic, obsessive, narcissistic, paranoid, and psychotic. They were said to be devoid of happiness, socially crippled, hostile, weak, desperate, self-destructive, and unable to face the responsibilities of adulthood (83–95). Homosexual relations were characterized as demonstrative of "primitive cultures" and medical recommendations called for "civilized societies" to make strict laws against such practices (83, 96).

Medical writings during the first three-quarters of this century portrayed homosexuality as both a disease and a moral corruption. Health care providers and the general public were continually warned about the dangers posed by lesbians and gay men, who were said to be responsible for the rise in crime, murder, racism, societal chaos, and the weakening of the American family (96–100). Psychoanalysts' intellectual rationalizations were invoked to justify irrational hatred and fear and to legitimate discriminatory behaviors toward lesbians and gays (75, 101–103). Their theories of homosexuality provided justification for governmental and private policies of surveillance, blacklisting, and prosecution during the infamous McCarthy years (75). Medical proclamations were pressed into service to vindicate job discrimination (104–106), military exclusion (107–109), expulsion from government employment on the basis of "security risk" (110, 111), immigration and naturalization restrictions (103), and inequalities in housing, public accommodations, child custody, adoption, foster care, association and free speech, insurance coverage, and occupational licensing (112–116).

As Lewes concluded, "Physicians' attack on homosexuals was conducted with an intemperance, ferocity, and lack of empathy that is simply appalling. . . . Equally remarkable was the failure of other physicians to rebuke the offensive stance of more voluble colleagues" (75, p. 239). The sentiments of one psychoanalyst illustrate how objections were constrained. He attacked those advocating the normalcy of homosexuality on the ground that they "are themselves homosexuals" (117). Fear resulting from such "queer-baiting" has deterred many scholars from writing on gay and lesbian topics.

The Kinsey reports (51, 118) were islands of clarity amid a sea of psychoanalytic speculation about male homosexuality and lesbianism. In spite of the Kinsey findings about the prevalence of homosexuality among productive, well-adjusted, nonclinical populations, the psychoanalysts persisted in, and even intensified, their efforts to pathologize homosexuality during the 1950s, 1960s, and 1970s.

Specific Targeting of Lesbians

Lesbians were said to harbor the same sickness and evil found in gay men; however, several medical theories warned of even greater danger associated with female homosexuality. Bergler, who authored more than 300 articles and 24 books about homosexuality during his medical career (75), declared that the numbers of lesbians were far more staggering than those of male homosexuals. He contended that "camouflaged lesbians hiding in marriages" were surreptitiously spreading their "violent hatred," "pathological jealousy," and "masochistic injustice-collecting" (84, pp. 261–265).

Psychoanalytic case studies of lesbians concluded that the "feminine passive attitude" was incompletely developed in such women because of penis envy, hatred of the mother, suicidality, masochistic desires, "uterine fantasies," guilt, fear of disappointment, and sadism (87). Rado (90) claimed that fears of pregnancy and childbirth drove some women to homosexuality. Jones (119) characterized lesbian women as having "extreme oral eroticism." Other manifestations of lesbianism cited in the medical literature included: incapacitating fears of the opposite sex (85), aggressive hatred of a dominating mother (120), infantile fixation (119), and hostility (121). Its implied causes were: fear of responsibility, rape, incest, incest desires, "tomboy" behavior, seduction by older women, masturbation, and fear of dominance (122). Lesbians were specifically described as tragically unhappy and sexually unfulfilled (123). A "cure" for lesbianism suggested by many medical experts was "finding real love with a man" (91, p. 15).

A rigidly stereotypic view of women shapes this medical report of a cosmetological "cure" of lesbianism (83, p. 93):

> She commenced to become more feminine. Instead of a dirty, unbecoming sweater . . . a more attractive one, and . . . little feminine touches, such as a blue chiffon scarf. . . . She finally said she was perfectly normal and inclined to marry her [male] lover. . . . When last seen she wore a canary yellow sweater and a brown corduroy skirt and used cosmetics. She said she had no interest in women sexually and was finding a more womanly job than working at a filling station.

Many medical descriptions legitimated dreadful stereotypes of lesbian women (124), including the following contentions. Half of "female homosexuals" have concomitant schizophrenia, and the other half suffer obsessional phobias, character disorders, psychopathic personalities, or some variety of addiction (93, p. 90). Lesbians are aggressive, hostile, and domineering (97, 120, 121). Besides being "man-haters," homosexual women hate motherhood and children (95, 125). They are self-aggrandizing and behave like "pseudo-men" in order to shock others (117). Lesbians are "brutally sadistic," "blood thirsty," and seek "murderous revenge" (93, pp. 52–56). Lesbians have "violent, brutal sex" (97, p. 170). They fly into "homicidal rages" and sometimes commit murder (97, p. 170).

Why were lesbians perceived to be so dangerous? Ferguson (126) suggests that social and technological changes at the beginning of the 20th century offering women more freedom were perceived as threats to the patriarchy. Urbanization, increased wage and labor opportunities for women, cheap mass-produced birth control, availability of abortion, and liberalization of divorce allowed women to consider options that separated sexuality from marriage, child-rearing, and heterosexuality. Medical ideology was a powerful inhibitory force that sustained women's traditional heterosexual roles by pathologizing nonprocreative sexuality and nontraditional feminine behaviors (62–64).

Lesbianism represented the peril of women's freedom. It was declared a serious intrapersonal disease as well as a drastic social ill, believed to be increasing geometrically with the growing independence of wage-earning women and the rise of feminism (94, 97, 127). The feminist movement itself was accused of exacerbating the contagion of lesbianism. It was believed that "predatory lesbians" abounded in conditions of gender equality, "seducing young girls and causing them to give up the thought of marriage and family life for a life of homosexual enslavement" (97, p. 8). As one physician summed it up, "The real damage from homosexuality lies not in actual sex association but in homosexual attitudes toward life which influence how thousands of women think about men, marriage, and family life" (97, p. 9).

Moreover, emancipatory behaviors and appearances were labeled lesbian and classified as diagnostic signals. The taxonomy of medical symptoms indicative of lesbianism included: casual clothing, short haircuts, lack of cosmetics and "feminine accessories," interest in the women's movement, competition with men, dedication to career, and "unwomanly" work such as skilled labor, business, law, politics, theater, art, science, and writing (83, 93, 94, 97, 100).

Physicians also claimed to be able to diagnose a lesbian based on morphological evidence (93, 96, 99, 128–131). Lesbians were characterized as having wider shoulders, bigger waists, firmer adipose tissue, greater height, firmer muscles, masculine distribution of body hair, smaller uteri, smaller breasts, unusually small or unusually large genitalia, and lower-pitched voices. These physical criteria were proffered as tools of detection, "marks of Cain" (132) constructed by medical science, extending social stereotypes to haunt lesbians at a bodily level.

Published "studies" of lesbianism often relied on speculation, nonscientific literature, and selected cases from psychiatric populations. Caprio's (97) medical treatise on female homosexuality, for instance, drew conclusions about lesbianism from the stories of women prisoners and prostitutes, novels, autobiographical confessions, and tabloid publications such as *My Confessions, Romance Magazine*, and *Coronet* (112). Thus, cross-pollination between professional and popular discourses perpetuated and amplified false, unseemly, bizarre images of lesbian women that continue to influence health care interactions experienced by lesbian clients today.

COLLECTIVE EFFORTS AT DESTIGMATIZATION

For most of the 20th century, lesbians and gay men suffered psychiatric confinement, electroshock treatment, genital mutilation, aversive therapy, psychosurgery, hormonal injection, psychoanalysis, and psychotropic chemotherapy aimed at "curing" their homosexuality (46, 70, 74, 78, 112). Their lives were circumscribed by oppressive medical, legal, political, and religious institutions. In their struggle to resist the exigencies of inferiorization, many lesbians and gays in the early decades of the century looked to the medical profession as a potential compassionate protector (46). They believed it was better to be viewed as sick than as criminal or evil. Therapeutic control initially appeared less coercive than incarceration and damnation (72, 133).

However, in the 1950s a visible emergent lesbian and gay movement, which had been forming in the United States for some decades (134), began to problematize its disenfranchised position. This movement crystallized in the formation of national homophile organizations. The Mattachine Society, One, Inc., and the Daughters of Bilitis attempted to end oppression by educating society about the respectability and competence of lesbians and gays. To an unprecedented extent, these early lesbian and gay rights groups served to unify the many lesbian and gay subcultures. They promoted a positive identity and symbolized a collectivity of lesbian women and gay men who had common concerns and experiences. They educated their constituents about how to cope with hostile environments and provided social support.

In the 1960s it became clearer that accommodation would not end the repression of lesbians and gays. Frank Kameny, an employee terminated in 1957 from his civilian position with the U.S. Army on charges that he was gay, was the first public opponent of the Army's anti-gay policies. He later was instrumental in convincing the homophile movement to adopt a more militant agenda (135). The civil rights movement, opposition to the Vietnam War, and the feminist movement provided a milieu conducive to lesbian and gay liberation efforts. The number of homophile organizations proliferated, and their major focus shifted to activism for civil rights for lesbians and gays (136–140). On June 27, 1969, an incident in a Greenwich Village bar ushered in the modern lesbian and gay liberation movement. Gay and lesbian bar patrons unexpectedly fought back against police during a "routine" gay bar raid. The three day "Stonewall Rebellion" marked a transition in lesbian/gay activism from accommodation to confrontation. This historic moment galvanized self-definition and self-love among lesbian and gay people (135, 137).

In the mid-1960s, the lesbian and gay movement targeted medical diagnostic authority as pivotal to societal exclusion and discrimination. Lesbians and gays began to articulate the burden of humiliation they faced at the hands of medicine's labeling (74, 135, 141–143). For instance, they identified the use of the term "homosexual" as a medical construction, an instrument of oppression, and insisted upon use of cultural terms such as lesbian and gay to designate themselves (144, 145).

With fresh confidence and solidarity, lesbian and gay political organizations in the early 1970s unified their attack on medicine's power over their lives. They utilized organized protests and advanced articulate spokespersons to place persistent and significant pressure upon the American Psychiatric Association (APA) to remove homosexuality from its *Diagnostic and Statistical Manual of Mental Disorders II* (*DSM II*) (69, 146, 147). They presented research evidence on the prevalence of homosexuality (51, 67, 118, 148) and documented the positive psychological adjustment found in nonclinical samples of lesbians and gays (149–152) to refute medical diagnosis of homosexuality. Fueled by lesbian and gay activism, the *DSM II* debate raged vociferously in professional journals and meetings from 1970 to 1974, splitting psychiatry into two camps. Psychiatrists vested in maintaining control over the "disease" of homosexuality charged the APA with capitulating to pressure from lesbian and gay rights groups. The other faction insisted that the conception of homosexuality as disease was based on inadequate science. The result was an unprecedented referendum of the entire APA membership. The mail-in vote succeeded in removing homosexuality per se from the nosology (69, 74, 127, 153).

Most accounts of these events heralded them as the demedicalization of homosexuality, suggesting that medicine had indeed surrendered its position of social control over lesbians and gays. Less well known, however, was the debate three years later during the drafting of the DSM III, in which "ego-dystonic homosexuality" was constructed as a psychiatric disorder. This compromise category allowed for the diagnosis of lesbians and gays who, in the clinical judgment of their physicians, appeared unhappy or distressed about their sexual orientation (147, 154–156). It also sanctioned reorientation therapy in which aversive and other techniques were used in order to produce a shift to heterosexuality (157). This development was protested on ethical grounds by many psychiatrists as well as lesbian and gay communities (158–160). The ego-dystonic label demonstrated lingering psychiatric hostilities toward homosexuality (161, pp. 363–364):

> This new category of psychosexual disorder is restricted to homosexuals; by definition it does not apply to heterosexuals who find their sex lives with members of the opposite sex a source of persistent concern and wish them to be different. . . . The fact that 'ego-dystonic' heterosexuality is not a diagnosis reflects a continuing implicit belief that homosexuality is abnormal.

This later nosological debate was confined to a small circle of physicians who resisted its exposure to public scrutiny and the risk of eroding psychiatry's territorial boundaries and its professional authority over social behavior. Even psychiatrists opposed to the inclusion of a disease category pertaining to lesbians and gay men hesitated to involve the general APA membership and lesbian and gay communities in the negotiations, because of burgeoning social conservatism in the United States and growing sympathy toward the traditional view of homosexuality within the profession. They feared publicity would reopen the dispute over the pathological basis of homosexuality itself (154). Through its quiet maneuverings, medicine once again: "resorted to the codification of social mores while masquerading as an objective science" (156, p. 26).

In May 1987, the APA removed ego-dystonic homosexuality from the revised edition of *DSM III* (162). It maintained a diagnosis, "sexual disorder not otherwise specified," which can be applied in cases where there is "persistent and marked distress about one's sexual orientation" (163, p. 296).

CONCLUSION

The cultural definition of lesbianism as a disease has influenced a long history of scientific inquiry that emphasizes etiology, diagnosis, and cure (164, 165). A relaxation of this perspective in health sciences research was not evident until the 1980s (166). Health and social sciences textbooks continue to label lesbians and gay men deviant and devote much of their discussion to etiological theories of homosexuality (167, 168). Any undertaking that seeks to discover or elaborate the causes of homosexuality prejudicially isolates the experience of being lesbian as an abnormality in need of explanation. It depicts lesbianism as an unhealthy disturbance that requires prevention and treatment (75, 155).

Clearly, the medicalization of lesbianism has been accomplished through its reinforcement of societal prejudices. Depicting behaviors of lesbian women to be both symptoms of disease and causes of social disorder answered institutional demands for social control of women. Indeed, lesbianism has yet to be effectively demedicalized. In the aftermath of the *DSM* debates, medicine simply closed ranks and reconsolidated its power base to prevent any further erosion of its boundaries (169). Psychiatrists became less accusatory about the psychosexual abnormality of homosexuality but retained status as acknowledged experts on the distress of "deviant" sexuality. The theory and research of the 1980s generally did not pathologize homosexuality per se but rather pinpointed developmental and relational aspects of lesbian "lifestyles" as appropriate foci for mental health therapies (170). This "gay-positive" approach tends to depoliticize lesbian identity as a coincidental aspect of the individual, having only to do with a "sexual preference." It also creates a new "pathology" within the heterosexual person, called "homophobia," which blames the individual heterosexual for holding prejudicial attitudes that are actually pervasive in the dominant culture (170).

Deeply entrenched stigmatized meanings about lesbian health remain influential in the education of health care providers, the quality of health care they deliver, their comfort in interacting with clients, and the institutional policies under which they work. The intensity of stigmatizing interactions experienced by lesbians over time has been fueled by moral condemnation, legal proscription, and medical diagnosis and intervention. For nearly a century, lesbians have been characterized by the medical profession as sick, dangerous, aggressive, tragically unhappy, deceitful, contagious, and self-destructive. They have been made to suffer exploitive treatments aimed at curing their homosexuality and have repeatedly been objects of research designed to confirm the pathology of their condition. Such a history underscores the vulnerable position lesbians occupy today as health care clients.

What are the questions clinicians, researchers, and theorists should be asking to demystify ideologies that place lesbians at risk of ostracism, discrimination, misdiagnosis, and attack? How can a more critical analysis of medicine's historical proclamations about lesbians enter into research about women's health, education of health care providers, and health care policy-making? When can a focal shift be made in scholarship and clinical practice so that barriers to and discrimination in health care delivery are problematized rather than blame placed on the gender, sexual orientation, or privatized "coping" skills of individual clients? Without critical investigation and emancipatory changes in health care practice and policy, health care providers will continue to rely on unexamined habits and emotional responses to guide their practices in caring for lesbian women, with all the potential pitfalls of myth, ignorance, and antipathy.

REFERENCES

1. Dardick, L., and Grady, K. E. Openness between gay persons and health professionals. *Ann. Intern. Med.* 93: 115–119, 1980.
2. Johnson, S. R., et al. Factors influencing lesbian gynecological care: A preliminary study. *Am. J. Obstet. Gynecol.* 140: 20–28, 1981.
3. McGhee, R. D., and Owen, W. F. Medical aspects of homosexuality. *N. Engl. J. Med.* 303: 50–51, 1980.
4. Paroski, P. A. Health care delivery and the concerns of gay and lesbian adolescents. *J. Adolesc. Health Care* 8: 188–192, 1987.
5. Smith, E. M., Johnson, S. R., and Guenther, S. M. Health care attitudes and experiences during gynecological care among lesbians and bisexuals. *Am. J. Public Health.* 75: 1085–1087, 1985.
6. Stevens, P. E., and Hall, J. M. Stigma, health beliefs and experiences with health care in lesbian women. *Image: J. Nurs. Scholarship* 20: 69–73, 1988.
7. Harvey, S. M., Carr, C., and Bernheine, S. Lesbian mothers: Health care experiences. *J. Nurse Midwifery* 34: 115–119, 1989.
8. Levy, T. The Lesbian: As Perceived by Mental Health Workers. Doctoral dissertation, California School of Professional Psychology, San Diego, 1978.
9. Mathews, W. C., et al. Physicians' attitudes toward homosexuality: Survey of a California county medical society. *West. J. Med.* 144: 106–110, 1986.
10. Randall, C. E. Lesbian phobia among BSN educators: A survey. *J. Nurs. Educ.* 28: 302–306, 1989.
11. White, T. A. Attitudes of psychiatric nurses toward same sex orientations. *Nurs. Res.* 28: 276–281, 1979.
12. Young, E. W. Nurses' attitudes toward homosexuality: Analysis of change in AIDS workshops. *J. Continuing Educ. Nurs.* 19: 9–12, 1988.
13. Friend, R. A. Sexual identity and human diversity: Implications for nursing practice. *Holistic Nurs. Pract.* 1(4): 21–41, 1987.
14. Gonsiorek, J. C. Mental health issues of gay and lesbian adolescents. *J. Adolesc. Health Care* 9: 114–122, 1988.
15. Good, R. S. The gynecologist and the lesbian. *Clin. Obstet. Gynecol.* 19: 473–482, 1976.
16. Jones, R. With respect to lesbians. *Nurs. Times* 84(20): 48–49, 1988.
17. Raymond, C. A. Lesbians call for greater physician awareness, sensitivity to improve patient care. *JAMA* 259: 18, 1988.
18. Whyte, J., and Capaldini, L. Treating the lesbian or gay patient. *Del. Med. J.* 52: 271–280, 1980.
19. Corea, G. *The Hidden Malpractice: How American Medicine Mistreats Women.* Harper & Row, New York, 1985.
20. Dutton, D. B. Explaining the low use of health services by the poor: Costs, attitudes, or delivery systems? *Am. Sociol. Rev.* 43: 348–368, 1978.
21. Fisher, S., and Groce, S. B. Doctor-patient negotiation of cultural assumptions. *Sociol. Health Illness* 7: 342–374, 1985.
22. Hayward, R. A., et al. Inequities in health services among insured Americans. *N. Engl. J. Med.* 318: 1507–1512, 1988.
23. Pendelton, D., and Bochner, S. The communication of medical information in general practice consultations as a function of patients' social class. *Soc. Sci. Med.* 14A: 669–673, 1980.
24. Roth, J. A. The treatment of the sick. In *Poverty and Health: A Sociological Analysis,* edited by J. Kosa and I. K. Zola, pp. 274–302. Harvard University Press, Cambridge, Mass., 1975.

25. Todd, A. D. *Intimate Adversaries: Cultural Conflict between Doctors and Women Patients.* University of Pennsylvania Press, Philadelphia, 1989.
26. Wallen, J., Waitzkin, H., and Stoeckle, J. D. Physician stereotypes about female health and illness: A study of patient's sex and the information process during medical interviews. *Women Health* 4: 135–146, 1979.
27. Portillo, C. T. Poverty, self-concept, and health: Experience of Latinas. *Women Health* 12: 229–242, 1987,
28. Smith, A., and Stewart, A. J. Approaches to studying racism and sexism in Black women's lives. *J. Soc. Issues* 36(3): 1–15, 1983.
29. Zajac, D. L. Women's health: Problems and options. An overview. *Issues Health Care Women* 4: 287–310, 1983.
30. Zambrana, R. E. A research agenda on issues affecting poor and minority women: A model for understanding their health needs. *Women Health* 12: 137–160, 1987.
31. Ablon, J. Stigmatized health conditions. *Soc. Sci. Med.* 15B: 5–9, 1981.
32. Becker, G., and Arnold, R. Stigma as a social and cultural construct. In *The Dilemma of Difference: A Multidisciplinary View of Stigma,* edited by S. C. Ainlay, G. Becker, and L. M. Coleman, pp. 39–58. Plenum Press, New York, 1986.
33. Plasek, J. W., and Allard, J. Misconceptions of homophobia. *J. Homosex.* 10(1/2): 23–37, 1984.
34. Klaich, D. *Woman Plus Woman: Attitudes toward Lesbians.* Simon & Schuster, New York, 1974.
35. Ponse, B. *Identities in the Lesbian World: The Social Construction of Self.* Greenwood Press, Westport, Conn., 1978.
36. Ponse, B. Lesbians and their worlds. In *Homosexual Behavior: A Modern Reappraisal,* edited by J. Marmor, pp. 157–175. Basic Books, New York, 1980.
37. Bullough, V. L., and Bullough, B. *Sin, Sickness, and Sanity: A History of Sexual Attitudes.* Garland, New York, 1977.
38. D'Emilio, J., and Freedman, E. S. *Intimate Matters: A History of Sexuality in America.* Harper & Row, New York, 1988.
39. Foucault, M. *The History of Sexuality,* Vol. 1: *An Introduction* (trans. R. Hurley). Random House, New York, 1978.
40. Barnard, M. *Sappho: A New Translation.* University of California Press, Berkeley, 1958.
41. Steiner, B. W. From Sappho to Sand: Historical perspectives on cross-dressing and cross gender. *Can. J. Psychiatry* 26: 502–506, 1981.
42. Wysor, B. *The Lesbian Myth.* Random House, New York, 1974.
43. Blackwood, E. Breaking the mirror: The construction of lesbianism and the anthropological discourse on homosexuality. *J. Homosex.* 11(3/4): 1–17, 1985.
44. Cavin, S. *Lesbian Origins.* Ism Press, San Francisco, 1985.
45. Grahn, J. *Another Mother Tongue: Gay Words, Gay Worlds.* Beacon Press, Boston, 1984.
46. Katz, J. *Gay American History: Lesbians and Gay Men in the U.S.A.* Avon Books, New York, 1976.
47. Feinson, M. C. Where are the women in the history of aging? *Soc. Sci. Hist.* 9: 429–452, 1985.
48. Gordon, A. D., Buhle, M. J., and Dye, N. S. The problem of women's history. In *Liberating Women's History,* edited by B. Carroll, pp. 75–92. University of Illinois Press, Urbana, 1976.
49. Wiesen-Cook, B. The historical denial of lesbianism. *Radical Hist. Rev.* 20: 60–65, 1979.

50. Davis, K. B. *Factors in the Sex Life of Twenty-two Hundred Women*. Harper and Brothers, New York, 1929.
51. Kinsey, A. C., et al. *Sexual Behavior in the Human Female*. W. B. Saunders, Philadelphia, 1953.
52. Hite, S. *The Hite Report: A Nationwide Study on Female Sexuality*. Macmillan, New York, 1976.
53. Crompton, L. The myth of lesbian impunity: Capital laws from 1270 to 1791. *J. Homosex.* 6(1/2): 11–25, 1980/81.
54. Eriksson, B. A lesbian execution in Germany, 1721: The trial records. *J. Homosex.* 6(1/2): 27–40, 1980/81.
55. Evans, A. *Witchcraft and the Gay Counterculture: A Radical View of Western Civilization and Some of the People It Has Tried to Destroy*. Fag Rag Books, Boston, 1978.
56. Bullough, V. L. Heresy, witchcraft, and sexuality. *J. Homosex.* 1(2): 183–201, 1974.
57. Karlen, A. *Sexuality and Homosexuality: A New View*. W. W. Norton, New York, 1971.
58. Karlen, A. Homosexuality in history. In *Homosexual Behavior: A Modern Reappraisal*, edited by J. Marmor, pp. 75–99. Basic Books, New York, 1980.
59. Davies, C. Sexual taboos and social boundaries. *Am. J. Sociol.* 87: 1032–1063, 1982.
60. Abramson, H. A. The historical and cultural spectra of homosexuality and their relationship to the fear of being lesbian. *J. Asthma Res.* 17: 177–188, 1980.
61. Bullough, V. L. Homosexuality and its confusion with the 'secret sin' in pre-Freudian America. In *Sex, Society, and History*, edited by V. L. Bullough, pp. 112–124. Science History, New York, 1976.
62. Faderman, L. *Surpassing the Love of Men: Romantic Friendship and Love between Women from the Renaissance to the Present*. William Morrow, New York, 1981.
63. Smith-Rosenberg, C. The female world of love and ritual: Relations between women in nineteenth century America. *Signs: J. Women Culture Society* 1: 1–24, 1975.
64. Faderman, L. The morbidification of love between women by 19th-century sexologists. *J. Homosex.* 4(1): 73–90, 1978.
65. Faderman, L. Love between women in 1928: Why progressivism is not always progress. *J. Homosex.* 12(3/4): 23–42, 1986.
66. Bullough, V. L. Homosexuality and the medical model. *J. Homosex.* 1(1): 99–110, 1974.
67. Churchill, W. *Homosexual Behavior among Males: A Cross-cultural and Cross-species Investigation*. Hawthorn, New York, 1967.
68. Zola, I. K. Medicine as an institution of social control. *Sociol. Rev.* 20: 487–504, 1972.
69. Bayer, R. *Homosexuality and American Psychiatry: The Politics of Diagnosis*. Princeton University Press, Princeton, N.J., 1987.
70. Conrad, P., and Schneider, J. W. *Deviance and Medicalization: From Badness to Sickness*. C. V. Mosby, St. Louis, Mo., 1980.
71. Krafft-Ebing, R. V. *Psychopathia Sexualis*. F. A. Davis, Philadelphia, 1894.
72. Schmidt, G. Allies and persecutors: Science and medicine in the homosexuality issue. *J. Homosex.* 10(3/4): 127–140, 1984.
73. Kennedy, H. C. The third sex theory of Karl Heinrich Ulrichs. *J. Homosex.* 6(1/2): 103–111, 1980/81.
74. Adam, B. D. *The Rise of the Gay and Lesbian Movement*. Twayne, Boston, 1987.
75. Lewes, K. *The Psychoanalytic Theory of Male Homosexuality*. Simon & Schuster, New York, 1988.

76. Mercer, J. D. *They Walk in Shadow: A Study of Sexual Variations with Emphasis on the Ambisexual and Homosexual Components and Our Contemporary Sex Laws.* Comet Press Books, New York, 1959.
77. Ellis, H . *Studies in the Psychology of Sex: Sexual Inversion.* F. A. Davis, Philadelphia, 1901.
78. Katz, J. N. *Gay/Lesbian Almanac: A New Documentary.* Harper & Row, New York, 1983.
79. Robinson, P. *The Modernization of Sex.* Harper & Row, New York, 1976.
80. Freud, S. The psychogenesis of a case of homosexuality in a woman. In *Standard Edition of the Complete Psychological Works of Sigmund Freud*, edited by J. Strachey, pp. 147–172. Hogarth Press, London, 1920.
81. Kinsey, A. C. Historical notes: A letter from Freud. *Am. J. Psychiatry* 107: 786–787, 1951.
82. Murphy, T. F. Freud reconsidered: Bisexuality, homosexuality and moral judgment. *J. Homosex.* 9(2/3): 65–77, 1983/84.
83. Berg, C., and Allen, C. *The Problem of Homosexuality.* Citadel, New York, 1958.
84. Bergler, E. *Homosexuality: Disease or Way of Life.* Hill & Wang, New York, 1957.
85. Bieber, I., et al. *Homosexuality: A Psychoanalytic Study of Male Homosexuals.* Basic Books, New York, 1962.
86. Bychowski, G. The ego of homosexuals. *Int. J. Psychoanal.* 26: 114–127, 1945.
87. Deutsch, H. On female homosexuality. *Psychoanal. Q.* 1: 484–510, 1932.
88. Kaye, H. E., Berl, S., and Clare, J. Homosexuality in women. *Arch. Gen. Psychiatry* 17: 626–634, 1967.
89. Plummer, K. *Sexual Stigma: An Interactionist Account.* Routledge & Kegan Paul, Boston, 1975.
90. Rado, S. Fear of castration in women. *Psychoanal. Q.* 2: 425–475, 1933.
91. Robertiello, R. C. *Voyage from Lesbos: The Psychoanalysis of a Female Homosexual.* Citadel, New York, 1969.
92. Rofes, E. E. *"I Thought People Like That Killed Themselves:" Lesbians, Gay Men and Suicide.* Grey Fox Press, San Francisco, 1983.
93. Socarides, C. W. *The Overt Homosexual.* Grune & Stratton, New York, 1968.
94. Stekel, W. *Bi-sexual Love.* Physicians and Surgeons Books, New York, 1933.
95. Stekel, W. *The Homosexual Neurosis.* Emerson Books, New York, 1946.
96. Henry, G. W., and Galbraith, H. M. Constitutional factors in homosexuality. *Am. J. Psychiatry* 14: 1249–1270, 1934.
97. Caprio, F. S. *Female Homosexuality: A Psychodynamic Study of Lesbianism.* Citadel, New York, 1954.
98. Chideckel, M. *Female Sex Perversion: The Sexually Aberrated Woman As She Is.* Eugenics, New York, 1935.
99. Henry, G. W. *Sex Variants: A Study of Homosexual Patterns.* Paul B. Hoeber, New York, 1948.
100. Morse, B. *The Lesbian: A Frank Study of Women Who Turn to Their Own Sex for Love.* Monarch, Derby, Conn., 1961.
101. Illich, I. *Medical Nemesis: The Expropriation of Health.* Random House, New York, 1976.
102. Shackle, E. M. Psychiatric diagnosis as an ethical problem. *J. Med. Ethics* 11: 132–134, 1985.
103. Szasz, T. S. *The Manufacture of Madness.* Dell, New York, 1970.
104. Bell, A. P., and Weinberg, M. S. *Homosexualities: A Study of Diversity among Men and Women.* Simon & Schuster, New York, 1978.
105. Chafetz, J., et al. A study of homosexual women. *Soc. Work* 19: 714–723, 1974.

106. Levine, M. P., and Leonard, R. Descrimination against lesbians in the work force. *Signs: J. Women Culture Society* 9: 700–710, 1984.

107. Bérubé, A. *Coming Out under Fire: The History of Gay Men and Women in World War II.* Macmillan, New York, 1990.

108. Bérubé, A., and D'Emilio, J. The military and lesbians during the McCarthy years. *Signs: J. Women Culture Society* 9: 759–775, 1984.

109. Williams, C. J., and Weinberg, M. S. *Homosexuals and the Military.* Harper & Row, New York, 1971.

110. Humphreys, L. *Out of the Closets: The Sociology of Homosexual Liberation.* Prentice-Hall, Englewood Cliffs, N.J., 1972.

111. McCrary, J., and Gutierrez, L. The homosexual person in the military and in national security employment. *J. Homosex.* 5(1/2): 115–146, 1979/80.

112. Browning, C. Changing theories of lesbianism: Challenging the stereotypes. In *Women-identified Women,* edited by T. Darty and S. Potter, pp. 11–30. Mayfield, Palo Alto, Calif., 1984.

113. Hitchens, D. Social attitudes, legal standards and personal trauma in child custody cases. *J. Homosex.* 5(1/2): 89-95, 1979/80.

114. Reynolds, W. T. The immigration and national act and the rights of homosexual aliens. *J. Homosex.* 5(1/2): 79-87, 1979/80.

115. Solomon, D. M. The emergence of associational rights for homosexual persons. *J. Homosex.* 5(1/2): 147–155, 1979/80.

116. Vetri, D. The legal arena: Progress for gay civil rights. *J. Homosex.* 5(1/2): 25–34, 1979/80.

117. Aardweg, van den, G. J. M. *On the Origins and Treatment of Homosexuality: A Psychoanalytic Reinterpretation.* Praeger, New York, 1986.

118. Kinsey, A. C., Pomeroy, W. B., and Martin, C. E. *Sexual Behavior in the Human Male.* W. B. Saunders, Philadelphia, 1948.

119. Jones, E. The early development of female sexuality. *Int. J. Psychoanal.* 8: 459–472, 1927.

120. Fenichel, O. *The Psychoanalytic Theory of Neurosis.* W. W. Norton, New York, 1945.

121. Bene, E. On the genesis of female sexuality. *Br. J. Psychiatry* 111: 815–821, 1965.

122. Rosen, D. H. *Lesbianism: A Study of Female Homosexuality.* Charles C Thomas, Springfield, Ill., 1974.

123. Wolff, C. *Love between Women.* Harper & Row, New York, 1971.

124. Simpson, R. *From the Closets to the Courts: The Lesbian Transition.* Viking Press, New York, 1976.

125. Cory, D. W. [pseudonym]. *The Lesbian in America.* Citadel, New York, 1964.

126. Ferguson, A. Lesbian identity: Beauvoir and history. *Women's Stud. Int. Forum* 8: 203–208, 1985.

127. Marmor, J. Overview: The multiple roots of homosexual behavior. In *Homosexual Behavior: A Modern Reappraisal,* edited by J. Marmor, pp. 3–22. Basic Books, New York, 1980.

128. Dickinson, R. L. The gynecology of homosexuality. In *Sex Variants: A Study of Homosexual Patterns,* edited by G. W. Henry, pp. 1069–1130. Paul B. Hoeber, New York, 1948.

129. Dickinson, R. L., and Beam, L. *The Single Woman.* Williams & Wilkins, New York, 1934.

130. Griffith, P. D., et al. Homosexual women: An endocrine and psychological study. *J. Endocrinol.* 63: 549–556, 1974.

131. Kenyon, F. E. Physique and physical health of female homosexuals. *J. Neurol. Neurosurg. Psychiatry.* 31: 487–489, 1968.
132. Shoham, S. G., and Rahav, G. *The Mark of Cain: The Stigma Theory of Crime and Social Deviance.* St. Martin's Press, New York, 1982.
133. Tripp, C. A. *The Homosexual Matrix.* McGraw-Hill, New York, 1975.
134. Lauritsen, J., and Thorstad, D. *The Early Homosexual Rights Movement (1864–1935).* Times Change Press, New York, 1974.
135. D'Emilio, J. *Sexual Politics, Sexual Communities.* University of Chicago Press, Chicago, 1983.
136. Bronski, M. *Culture Clash: The Making of Gay Sensibility.* South End Press, Boston, 1984.
137. Licata, S. J. The homosexual rights movement in the United States: A traditionally overlooked area of American history. *J. Homosex.* 6(1/2): 161–189, 1980/81.
138. Martin, D., and Lyon, P. *Lesbian Woman.* Bantam Books, New York, 1972.
139. Masters, R. E. L. *The Homosexual Revolution: A Challenging Expose of the Social and Political Directions of a Minority Group.* Julian Press, New York, 1962.
140. Weiss, A. *Before Stonewall: The Making of a Gay and Lesbian Community.* Naiad Press, New York, 1988.
141. Abbott, S., and Love, B. *Sappho Was a Right-on Woman: A Liberated View of Lesbianism.* Stein & Day, New York, 1972.
142. Altman, D. *Homosexual Oppression and Liberation.* Avon Books, New York, 1971.
143. Altman, D. *The Homosexualization of America: The Americanization of the Homosexual.* St. Martin's Press, New York, 1982.
144. Adam, B. D. *The Survival of Domination: Inferiorization and Everyday Life.* Elsevier, New York, 1978.
145. Hodges, A., and Hutter, D. *With Downcast Gays: Aspects of Homosexual Self-Expression.* Pomegranate Press, London, 1974.
146. Silverstein, C. Even psychiatry can profit from its past mistakes. *J. Homosex.* 2(2): 153–158, 1976/77.
147. Silverstein, C. The ethical and moral implications of sexual classification: A commentary. *J. Homosex.* 9(4): 29–38, 1984.
148. Ford, C. S., and Beach, F. A. *Patterns of Sexual Behavior.* Harper and Brothers, New York, 1951.
149. Freedman, M. *Homosexuality and Psychological Functioning.* Wadsworth, Belmont, Calif., 1971.
150. Hooker, E. The adjustment of the male overt homosexual. *J. Projective Techniques* 21: 18–31, 1957.
151. Hooker, E. Male homosexuality in the Rorschach. *J. Projective Techniques* 22: 33–54, 1958.
152. Saghir, M. T., and Robins, E. *Male and Female Homosexuality: A Comprehensive Investigation.* Williams & Wilkins, Baltimore, 1973.
153. Green, R. Homosexuality as a mental illness. *Int. J. Psychiatry* 10: 77–128, 1972.
154. Bayer, R., and Spitzer, R. L. Edited correspondence on the status of homosexuality in DSM III. *J. Hist. Behav. Sci.* 18: 32–52, 1982.
155. Goodman, G., et al. *No Turning Back: Lesbian and Gay Liberation for the '80s.* New Society, Philadelphia, 1983.
156. Suppe, F. Classifying sexual disorders: The Diagnostic and Statistical Manual of the American Psychiatric Association. *J. Homosex.* 9(4): 9–28, 1984.

157. Council on Scientific Affairs. Aversion therapy. *JAMA* 258: 2562–2566, 1987.
158. Begelman, D. A. Homosexuality and ethics of behavioral intervention: Paper 3. *J. Homosex.* 2(3): 213–219, 1977.
159. Davison, G. C. Homosexuality and the ethics of behavioral intervention: Paper 1. *J. Homosex.* 2(3): 195–204, 1977.
160. Silverstein, C. Homosexuality and the ethics of behavioral intervention: Paper 2. *J. Homosex.* 2(3): 205–211, 1977.
161. Davison, G. C., and Neale, J. M. *Abnormal Psychology: An Experimental Clinical Approach*, Ed. 3. Wiley, New York, 1982.
162. Harris, S. E. Aversion therapy for homosexuality. *JAMA* 259: 3271, 1988.
163. American Psychiatric Association. *Diagnostic and Statistical Manual of Mental Disorders Revised*, Ed. 3. APA, Washington, D.C., 1987.
164. Morin, S. F. Heterosexual bias in psychological research on lesbianism and male homosexuality. *Am. Psychol.* 32: 629–637, 1977.
165. Schwanberg, S. L. Changes in labeling homosexuality in health sciences literature: A preliminary investigation. *J. Homosex.* 12(1): 51–73, 1985.
166. Watters, A. T. Heterosexual bias in psychological research on lesbianism and male homosexuality (1979–1983): Utilizing the bibliographic and taxonomic system of Morin (1977). *J. Homosex.* 13(1): 35–58, 1986.
167. Adam, B. D. The construction of a sociological 'homosexual' in Canadian textbooks. *Rev. Can. Sociol. Anthropol.* 23: 399–411, 1986.
168. Newton, D. E. Representations of homosexuality in health science textbooks. *J. Homosex.* 4(3): 247–254, 1979.
169. Pasnau, R. O. The remedicalization of psychiatry. *Hosp. Community Psychiatry* 38: 145–151, 1987.
170. Kitzinger, C. *The Social Construction of Lesbianism.* Sage, Beverly Hills, Calif., 1987.

Section VI
Women and AIDS

CHAPTER 13

More than Mothers and Whores: Redefining the AIDS Prevention Needs of Women

Kathryn Carovano

In the spring of 1989, while I was working in Lima, Peru, a group of feminist women organized a meeting so that I could talk with them about women and AIDS. We talked a lot about the risks to women and about what they thought could be done, and we got into a discussion of options: the condom and non-penetrative sex. Frescia, a health educator there, told me this story:

> We had just finished a health promotion program with a group of women and we asked them to fill out an evaluation form. One of the women who was very good during the training was taking a long time to finish the questionnaire, so I asked her if she was having trouble with it. She told me that she was having a hard time reading it, so I asked her if maybe she needed to use glasses. She said yes, that she had had her eyes tested ten years ago, and the doctor had prescribed glasses for her. She had bought a pair but lost them a few months later. To explain why she had never gotten a new pair she said, "My husband told me that I was so stupid that he would never buy me another pair of glasses." So just imagine this woman asking her husband to use a condom or consider having nonpenetrative sex.

Around the world, women are at increasing risk for AIDS. At the root of this risk is women's lack of control over their bodies and their lives. As Herbert Daniel (1), a writer and activist living with AIDS in Brazil has pointed out, "Like every other epidemic, AIDS develops in the cracks and crevasses of society's inequalities. We cannot face the epidemic if we try to hide the contradictions and conflicts which it exposes."

Originally published in the *International Journal of Health Services* 21(1): 131–142, 1991.

As the AIDS epidemic continues to unfold, we are being forced to confront once again one of society's more glaring inequalities—the inequality of the sexes. The relative lack of control by women in relation to men, particularly in the context of sexual relations, places them at increasing risk for AIDS. Those women with the least control, generally poor women of color, are those who face the greatest risk. In order to develop effective AIDS prevention programs, we must confront the challenges that this "crack" exposes and develop programs that give women control over their sexuality and over their own lives. A first step toward developing prevention programs for women is to recognize that women are primarily at risk for AIDS because they are sexually active, and that their sexual activity goes beyond the simplified realms of sex for procreation or sex for money. Sex for some is for pleasure. And for many women, sex is simply part of survival.

Throughout the world, women's sexual identities have long been defined on the basis of their reproductive capacity and, to a lesser degree, their involvement in commercial sex. Motherhood legitimizes a woman's sexuality—and very often her life—while prostitution provides women with a means of survival, though with a heavy stigma. Women in many societies have traditionally been identified sexually as either mothers or whores, "good girls" or "bad girls." In examining current AIDS prevention efforts for women, one finds that this dichotomy dominates and is being utilized as a framework to identify the risks posed to and by women. Many societies regard the sensuous, sexual woman as "bad" and, in essence, only "bad girls" are perceived to be at risk for AIDS. "Good girls" in contrast, are viewed as asexual or their sexuality is relegated to the socially sanctioned realm of sex for procreation, which is seen as unrelated to HIV transmission. Both "mother" and "prostitute" are definitions for women that are based on their relationships to others; "As women we are so often defined by who leans on us. Being needed names us" (2). In the context of AIDS, these definitions reflect the needs of men and children, and it is in their relationship to the HIV-infected woman that she becomes a concern or threat. The focus on these particular identities, "mother" and "prostitute," among the many that define women leads one easily to the hypothesis that efforts to prevent AIDS among women have been the result not of a concern for women, but rather a concern that is primarily about protecting the health of men and children.

The impact of this thinking is reflected by the fact that to date, most AIDS prevention programs for women have been designed exclusively to reach women in the sex industry. Women engaged in prostitution have been identified as one of the principal "reservoirs" for HIV and, as such, a "risk group" that threatens the "general population." Faced with increasing numbers of children at risk for AIDS as a result of rising infection rates among women, new programs are also being formulated to target prenatal women. Unfortunately, those women—and they are most of us—who do not fall into one of these limited spheres are being largely ignored by program planners and implementing agencies working in AIDS prevention. Not surprisingly, the numbers of AIDS cases reported among women continue to grow at alarming rates.

THE EPIDEMIOLOGY OF AIDS AMONG WOMEN

According to the World Health Organization, of the estimated 600,000 people who developed AIDS in the 1980s, over 150,000 were women. During the next two years, 500,000 more people will develop AIDS and of these, 200,000 are expected to be women. In other words, more women are expected to become ill with AIDS during 1990 and 1991 than developed AIDS during the last decade (3).

These figures are alarming as they stand, yet the actual number of women who have died or are living with AIDS is undoubtedly far greater even than these numbers convey. Underreporting of AIDS cases is a recognized problem throughout the developing world, and underreporting of cases among women is a problem everywhere. Problems of reporting cases among women result from factors as varied as women's lack of access to health care, the exclusion of "female diseases" in the diagnostic criteria for AIDS, and the persistent attitude among many physicians that "good girls don't get AIDS." Despite these problems, data still show that women around the world are being diagnosed with AIDS in ever increasing numbers and most of them are poor women of color, whether they are living in Newark, Bangkok, Nairobi, or Rio de Janeiro.

In the United States, the proportion of the total AIDS cases occurring among women rose from 7 percent of cases reported before 1985 to 11 percent of cases reported during the first half of 1989 (4). In Frankfurt, West Germany, the percentage of HIV-infected patients who are women rose from 4 percent in 1984 to 25 percent in 1988 (5). Throughout much of sub-Saharan Africa, women represent 50 percent or more of AIDS cases, and similar ratios have been reported in some parts of the English-speaking Caribbean. Studies conducted among pregnant women have revealed seroprevalence rates of 10.5 percent in Port au Prince, Haiti, and 24 percent in Kampala, Uganda (3). In Latin America and Asia, women currently make up a small but growing percentage of reported cases. The growth of pediatric AIDS cases reveals the ripple effect of HIV infection in women; according to James Grant (6), Director General of UNICEF, over 90 percent of pediatric AIDS cases are the result of perinatal transmission. AIDS accounts for up to one-third of all deaths to children in some African cities, and in some parts of New York City, one of every 100 babies is born with HIV infection (7). UNICEF has projected that the average infant mortality rate in ten East and Central African countries will rise from a current rate of 164 deaths per 1000 to 185 per 1000 by the year 2000; prior to the introduction of HIV, these rates had been projected to fall to 130 per 1000 during the next decade. In addition, UNICEF has estimated that in these countries, as many as 5 million children will have lost their parents to AIDS by the end of the decade (6). A survey conducted in 1989 in the Rakai district of Uganda—the region hardest hit by AIDS—found that 23,351 children had already lost one or both parents, the majority of them to AIDS (8).

These alarming statistics indicate the need to develop AIDS prevention programs that provide information and sexual empowerment to all sexually active women. The remainder of this chapter will look at the risks that AIDS poses to specific segments of the population of women, beginning with young, adolescent women.

ADOLESCENT WOMEN

If knowledge were power, then adolescent women would probably be among the least powerful—and in fact they are when it comes to their ability to protect themselves against HIV infection.

The guiding philosophy in dealing with adolescent sexuality in many cultures is "if you don't talk about sex they won't do it." This logic, however, is critically flawed. Adolescents are sexual beings at varying stages of self-awareness and understanding. Many of them do and will continue to engage in sexual intercourse despite lack of access to any accurate information about sex. Unfortunately, if you do not talk to them, they will almost undoubtedly also engage in "unsafe sex." Sex can and does occur without much understanding; "safe" sex requires an ability to distinguish between risky and nonrisky sexual activities *and* an ability to choose safer sex.

Whether or not you talk about it, teens clearly are having sex. Many women—and most men—have their first sexual relations prior to marriage, usually during their teens, and most often those first encounters are unprotected. Research in family planning has revealed that the quality of reproductive health information is generally low among adolescents. This is a reflection in part of the lack of social acceptance of providing sex education and contraceptive services to teens in many countries. In the developing world, contraceptive services are often available only to married women, and in some situations, only to women who have already borne one or more children (9).

In most of the world's countries, births to women under 20 represent a significant proportion of all births; in Swaziland a study conducted in 1985 reported that over 30 percent of children were born to women between 15 and 19 years of age (10). According to evidence from the World Fertility Survey, the average fertility rate for women aged 15 to 19 in developing countries is 8.7 percent of the global total (11, Table 21, p. 33). High levels of adolescent pregnancy and teenage abortions reported in Japan (12), Nigeria (13), and Baltimore, Maryland (14), reflect the reality of high levels of sexual activity and low levels of correct contraceptive use among adolescents.

Given the sexual practices of teens, the threat of AIDS cannot be ignored. In the United States in 1989, 26.3 percent (n = 4,306) of the AIDS cases reported among females occurred among women between 20 and 29 years of age (15). Given the long incubation period for AIDS, the majority of these women may very well have been infected during adolescence. A survey conducted in 1988 in a New York City shelter found that 18 percent of the girls in the study tested positive for HIV antibody (16). In some African cities where infection rates among sexually active adults have reached 30 to 40 percent, the risk of exposure through sexual contact is extremely high. Young women tend to have their first sexual encounter later than their male peers, hence even their first contact could place them at risk for HIV. In Uganda, older men are reportedly looking to young school girls instead of prostitutes for "AIDS-free sex" (17).

AIDS prevention programs for adolescent women and girls, in school, while increasingly common in developed countries, are still extremely rare in the developing world. The need for such programs is critical, though given the very early school drop-out rates of many girls in developing countries, school-based programs alone are not enough. On average, 44 percent of ever-married women in the developing world have received no formal education and of those who have, only 7 percent have ten or more years of schooling (11, p. 217). Out-of-school programs will be critical in reaching young minority women in many developed countries as well.

Adolescent women, like everyone else, need to be given information that offers them choices and is based on an understanding of their sexual behavior. Studies of adolescents who have received sex education have shown that they are not likely to engage in sex any sooner or any more frequently than their uninformed peers, but they are more likely to use contraceptives (18). Sex education and AIDS information is not an aphrodisiac, but rather a basic tool for adolescent health and survival. To deny adolescents access is to leave them powerless and at high risk for HIV.

"WOMEN OF REPRODUCTIVE AGE"

The first woman to be diagnosed with AIDS in Mexico (in 1985) was a 52-year-old housewife living in Mexico City; her only known "risk" behavior was having unprotected sexual intercourse with her husband (19). The vast majority of women with AIDS and HIV infection are between the ages of 20 and 45 and are frequently referred to as "women of reproductive age." As neglected as young women have been, even more neglected are women over 20. Although these women are generally better informed about sexuality and family planning and perhaps more able to make mature choices about their sexual behavior, they are also at increasing risk for AIDS and yet remain largely uninformed. To date, this group—if not involved in prostitution—has probably received the least attention of all sectors of society.

The primary reason for the lack of programs for this population is the false notion that these women are not at risk. These are the "good girls" who are generally perceived to be loyally monogamous or asexual and hence not at risk for HIV. Only when pregnant or considering pregnancy are most women in this population directly confronted with their potential risk of contracting AIDS, and generally in the context of society's concern for their unborn children. Many women with HIV infection in both developed and developing countries learn that they are infected only after one of their children is diagnosed with AIDS; in the United States an estimated 60 percent of HIV-infected women find out about their seropositive status only once their children are diagnosed with AIDS (20). Routine screening of prenatal women is increasingly becoming the norm in many developed countries, including the United Kingdom, where legislation passed in November 1989 makes it a requirement for all pregnant women (21).

Ironically, despite the identification of this population as "women of reproductive age," the only advice given is that if they perceive themselves to be at risk, they should protect themselves from AIDS using methods that prohibit conception. The limited means available to prevent the sexual transmission of HIV have exposed the contradiction between disease prevention and women's reproductive roles. As discussed earlier, condoms and nonpenetrative sex are currently the only means available to sexually active men and women to prevent HIV transmission. In addition to providing protection against the sexual transmission of HIV, both methods also inhibit conception, an added advantage for some, but a critical flaw for those wishing to conceive.

Noreen Kaleeba (22), Director of the AIDS Support Organization in Uganda, made real this dilemma when she described her experience counseling a young woman considering pregnancy. Her client's reasons for not adopting measures to protect herself from HIV despite recognizing her potential risk included the following: "Babies and condoms don't go together, nonpenetrative sex is no sex at all for a man, and it is a woman's responsibility to bear a child." Motherhood brings status, security, and validation to many women's lives. In many cultures women are told that the purpose of their existence is to bring forth new life, especially male, and that their value depends on bringing it forth (23, p. 159).

In many cultures, there is no social place for women who are unable or choose not to have children. "Because there is no alternative social or personal identity for women separate from parenting, women's risk of infection is greater" (24). In other words, as long as there is no valid role for women who choose not to parent children, measures to prevent HIV infection that negate the importance of that role will have only limited impact. To provide women exclusively with HIV prevention methods that contradict most societies' fertility norms is to provide many women with no options at all. The need for research and development of an effective virucide to prevent HIV transmission without impeding reproduction is critical if we are to provide a real choice to many women.

Women need to be able to protect themselves from HIV without being forced to forfeit the option to bear children. In an ideal world, mutually faithful monogamy would allow women to protect themselves and have healthy children, but this is not the reality of relationships for most of the world's population. To force women to rely on abstinence, nonpenetrative sex, condoms, female condoms, and potentially even spermicides is to ignore the importance placed on women's reproductive roles.

WOMEN IN THE SEX INDUSTRY

In January 1990, the *Prensa Libre*, a leading newspaper in Guatemala, published a plea to national police from the regional health director of Esquintla to undertake a national search for a young Salvadoran woman who had left the city. The article provided her name, a description of her appearance, and information about where she had most recently worked. The justification for the search: the young woman in question was a prostitute who had tested positive for HIV. The objective of the search: to find this woman and put her under "medical surveillance" in order to control the further spread of HIV in Guatemala.

Throughout the world, AIDS prevention programs have been developed targeting women in the sex industry. While there are many programs that have been developed with the clear intention of protecting women working in what is potentially a high-risk trade, there are also countless cases of scapegoating and abuse. Prostitutes have repeatedly been referred to as "reservoirs for transmission" and blamed for "spreading AIDS." This is a reflection of the "bad girl" vision of woman as temptress, while men are simply viewed as innocently responding to natural urges. Prostitutes are seen as encouraging men to stray, hence they are held responsible for their own and others' disease. It is worth noting that despite this portrayal of prostitute-as-vector, as of January 1989, in the United States, ". . . there [had] been no documented cases of men becoming infected through contact with a specific prostitute" (25).

Prostitution has existed in every society for which there are written records and continues to exist as a result of sexual double standards that limit women's economic options and means of sexual expression. It is, by definition, the exchange of sexual services for money or goods, and thus logically, most women who enter voluntarily into prostitution do so primarily for economic reasons (26). As Simone de Beauvoir (27, p. 620) points out in *The Second Sex*:

> The truth is that in a world where misery and unemployment prevail, there will be people to enter any profession that is open; as long as a police force and prostitution exist, there will be policemen and prostitutes, more especially as these occupations pay better than many others. It is pure hypocrisy to wonder at the supply that masculine demand stimulates; that is simply the action of an elementary and universal economic process.

According to a report in the *New African*, economic problems compelled many Ghanaian women to seek income through prostitution; these women currently constitute the population at highest risk for AIDS in Ghana (28).

Considerable effort has been focused on developing AIDS prevention programs targeting women in the sex industry. To date, this work has involved five principal approaches, which can be summarized as follows:

- Methods that truly seek to provide women with information and tools that will allow them to protect themselves, or at least give them a better chance at doing so.
- Methods that seek to evade the risk posed by HIV by providing sex workers with job training and alternative employment opportunities.
- The harassment and/or arrest of women as a means of theoretically eliminating prostitution.
- Routine HIV antibody testing of legally or semi-legally registered prostitutes.
- Combinations of one or more of these approaches.

Of these approaches, only the first has proven appropriate or effective in preventing the spread of AIDS to prostitutes. The others either scapegoat women, are unrealistic, or overlook prostitutes entirely to focus instead on the protection of male clients. A common flaw found in almost all efforts thus far is a lack of focus on the education of both clients and/or noncommercial partners, and a lack of recognition that not all sex is "work."

Women involved in prostitution face many of the same challenges in their intimate—as opposed to commercial—sexual relations as do their "nonworking" peers (29). Efforts to promote behavior change among prostitutes have shown that the greatest area of resistance is in women's relationships with their steady and/or noncommercial partners. "Although most prostitutes [in the United States] expect to use condoms with their customers, most do not use them with their primary partners" (25). Additionally, numerous studies have shown that, more frequently than not, prostitutes are mothers as well as whores. A survey conducted among 100 female sex workers in metropolitan Manila found that 31 percent of them were married and 62 percent were supporting children; 14 percent were raising children with no support from their spouse or family (30). A survey of 47 women in Nairobi, Kenya, found that all of them had at least one child, though 95 percent were unmarried (31). Approaches that negate the mother—and lover—in the whore have not been and will not be effective in preventing the further spread of HIV to women.

The first step toward developing effective prevention programs for women in the sex industry must be a recognition of the diverse population of women involved in prostitution and the complexity of their lives. Women's situations vary depending on multiple factors such as number of dependents, age, legal status, general health and appearance, where they work (e.g., street, brothel, bar), drug-use practices, voluntary or forced involvement in prostitution, and sexual behavior. Many of these factors will affect the degree of control that sex workers experience in their sexual encounters and will determine whether it is more appropriate to provide training in safe sex negotiation or condom use techniques that will leave clients unaware.

For those women who choose or are forced to work in the sex industry, the risk posed by AIDS is potentially high and the need for information and skills great. "Women in general and sex workers in specific have little trust in the 'good intentions' of outsiders" (32), and programs that include sex workers in their design and implementation have proven most likely to succeed.

REPRODUCTIVE DECISION-MAKING FOR WOMEN LIVING WITH HIV AND AIDS

As HIV continues to spread among women, the need for prevention and support programs for women and their children with HIV disease is also growing. HIV-positive women need to have access to quality information about HIV transmission and disease management. They also need to receive quality counseling that will assist them to make informed choices about future sexual behavior and fertility.

Women with HIV disease need to understand the potential risk of pregnancy and repeated exposure to HIV to their own health. Studies remain inconclusive on the issue of the effect of pregnancy on an HIV-infected woman's health, though the majority suggest that it may have little impact. In addition, women need information about the risk of transmitting the virus to their unborn children. Current estimates of vertical transmission rates range from 30 to 50 percent (33), a risk that may or may not be deemed acceptable to an HIV-infected woman and/or her partner. One popular anecdote is of a poor, black seropositive woman who upon being accused by her physician of making an irresponsible decision in choosing to bear a child responded: "Fifty percent is the best odds I've been given since I was diagnosed as carrying this virus" (34). Perception of risk is relative, and on the basis of a woman's or couple's view of this risk, they must be free to choose whether or not to bear children.

Throughout the world, millions of women who are subfertile or infertile live in dread of divorce or social ostracism because they cannot bear children (9, p. 6). "Women's status as childbearer has been made into a major fact of her life. Terms like 'barren' or 'childless' have been used to negate any further identity" (23, p. 11). The argument that suggests that HIV-positive women should not bear children identifies them, in essence, as barren.

In many parts of the developing world in particular, women make reproductive decisions with a view to children as security investments. Studies have shown that "the higher the level of infant mortality, the greater fertility necessary to achieve the [security] goal" (35). As infant mortality levels increase as a result of HIV, we may witness more rather than fewer births to women with HIV disease. A survey conducted among 58 women with HIV infection in Kinshasa, Zaire, supports this possibility by documenting that 71 percent wanted more children within the next two years and 5 percent were already pregnant (36). In Port au Prince, Haiti, a study found that pregnancies were as common among HIV-infected women as among a control group of uninfected women (3). The argument that HIV-infected women should receive "directive counseling" to avoid or terminate pregnancy denies the complexity and real importance of motherhood in many women's lives.

For HIV-infected women who choose to bear children or who have already delivered children who are infected with HIV, health care programs need to be integrated to provide concurrent care for women and children. If a woman has to travel to two separate clinics to receive care for herself and her child, the woman's health can be expected to suffer. Women have traditionally given priority to their children's health care needs over their own, and there is no evidence to suggest that AIDS has changed this pattern (37).

CONCLUSION

Women of all ages are primarily at risk of contracting AIDS through sexual contact with an infected partner. Most women currently lack needed information, tools, and the power over their own bodies and lives to enable them to reduce their risk. A review of available data leaves a feeling that we must find a "magic bullet" that will give women the technological means to protect themselves, or there must be a revolution to finally give women equal control over sexual decisions.

Women are more than mothers and whores, and the core issue is about "women's right to be sexual, to separate sexuality from procreation" (23, p. xvii) and to be in control of their own sexual decision-making. For those women who do not seek to conceive, condoms and nonpenetrative sex do exist as potential alternatives. However, the general problem of powerlessness and lack of control by women in sexual decision-making is highlighted when considering either option, particularly condoms. Women who attempt to introduce condoms into a relationship are often perceived as overly "prepared" for sex, not trusting of their partner's fidelity, unfaithful themselves, or even HIV-infected (38, 39). For women in the sex industry, a condom may mean accepting a lower fee for service or blurring the distinction between work and love. For all women, condoms and nonpenetrative sex, unlike most other contraceptive technologies available today, both require male cooperation, which implicitly means male control. Women tend to choose contraceptive methods that their male partners are not "inconvenienced" by and often are not even aware of. Evidence from the World Fertility Survey of current contraceptive users shows that the mean level of pill use is 31 percent throughout the developing world, a rate that far exceeds that of any other modern method, including condoms, which are reportedly used by only 7 percent of the population (11, p. 146). From family planning we know that while many men support controlling the size of their families, few assume primary responsibility for the prevention of pregnancy.

Alternative, women-controlled preventive technology is critically needed, but in the meantime, prevention education programs are also needed that begin to make all sexually active women aware of their potential risk for AIDS. Studies conducted in the United States have shown that while women are relatively knowledgeable about AIDS and endorse condoms as an important way to prevent the spread of HIV, they do not use them, in large part because they do not perceive *themselves* to be at risk (40). This lack of risk awareness, which is certainly not unique to U.S. women, is largely a reflection of the false notion that women are not at risk—a perception that must be challenged if effective programs are to be developed.

Efforts to prevent the spread of AIDS to women must therefore focus on empowerment, on the "repossession by women of our bodies" (23, p. 285), which will require both social reform and technological support. Acknowledging the risks faced by women and providing them with targeted prevention information are desperately needed, but alone will not enable many women in both developed and developing countries to protect themselves from HIV infection. Supporting efforts to develop women-controlled preventive technology that provides women with real choices is also critical, given the reality of many women's lives.

In order to be effective, AIDS prevention programs for women must be developed in a context of understanding the social and economic barriers that result in the powerlessness that characterizes many of the women affected by AIDS in both the developing and the developed world. It is time to go beyond the simple vision of women as either mothers or whores to a recognition of the diversity of women's sexual roles and the risks they face, often for reasons that go far beyond their individual control. The "risk group" approach tends to deny the multiple factors that place women at risk of contracting HIV and to ignore the complexity of implementing change in many women's lives. To ensure this understanding, the women being targeted must be involved at every stage of policy and program development. Only then can women's needs begin to be understood and met in ways that will allow them to effectively protect themselves from AIDS.

REFERENCES

1. Daniel, H. *Vida Antes da Morte/Life Before Death*, p. 37. Escritorio e Tipografia Jaboti Ltda, Rio de Janeiro, Brazil, 1989.
2. Moskowitz, F. *A Leak in the Heart: Tales From a Woman's Life*, p. 99. David R. Godine, Boston, 1985.
3. Mann, J. Women, Mothers, Children and the Global AIDS Strategy. Paper presented at the International Conference on the Implications of AIDS for Mothers and Children, Paris, November 27, 1989.
4. Current trends: First 100,000 cases of AIDS—United States. *MMWR* 38: 561–563, 1989.

5. Staszewski, S. Epidemiology of HIV Infection in Women from Frankfurt Area. Poster presented at the Fifth International Conference on AIDS, Montreal, June 7, 1989.
6. Grant, J. UNICEF's Present Policy and New Approaches. Paper presented at the International Conference on the Implications of AIDS for Mothers and Children, Paris, November 27, 1989.
7. New York State Department of Health. *Status Report: HIV Seroprevalence Study.* Albany, N.Y., July 1988.
8. U.S. Department of State. Pediatric AIDS Prevention Under FY90 Child Survival FRA. Unclassified Cable. American Embassy, Kampala, Uganda, December 5, 1989.
9. Germain, A., and Ordway, J. *Population Control and Women's Health: Balancing the Scales,* pp. 1–15. International Women's Health Coalition, Washington, D.C., June 1989.
10. Gule, G. Z. *Youth Education and Services for Health and Family Life: Situation Analysis in Swaziland,* p. 28. International Planned Parenthood Federation, Africa Region, July 1985.
11. United Nations. *Fertility Behavior in the Context of Development: Evidence from the World Fertility Survey.* New York, 1987.
12. Hayashi, K. Adolescent sexual activities and fertility in Japan. *Bull. Inst. Public Health* 32(2–4): 88–94, 1983.
13. Nichols, D., et al. Sexual behavior, contraceptive practice and reproductive health among Nigerian adolescents. *Stud. Fam. Plann.* 17: 110–116, 1986.
14. Governor's Task Force on Teen Pregnancy. *A Call to Action: Final Report, Governor's Task Force on Teen Pregnancy, State of Maryland,* p. 56. Annapolis, September 1985.
15. Centers for Disease Control. AIDS cases by sex, age at diagnosis, and race ethnicity, reported through June 1898, United States. In *HIV/AIDS Among Racial and Ethnic Populations,* p. 3. Atlanta, June 1989.
16. Foley, M. J. Women health policymakers: Interview with Dr. Mathilde Krim. *The Network News* (National Women's Health Network) 13(6): 52, 1988.
17. Ojulu, E. Ugandan prostitutes are now wiser. *New African,* September, 1988, p. 34.
18. Youth in the 1980s: Social and health concerns. *Popul. Rep [M]* 12: M-349–M-388, 1985.
19. Lifshiz, A. Inmunodeficiencia adquirida en un sujeto de bajo riesgo: primera mujer en Mexico. In *Revista Medica.* Instituto Mexicano de Seguro Social, Mexico, June 1986.
20. Low income minority women and AIDS. *The Network News* (National Women's Health Network) 13(5): 6, 1988.
21. Sherr, L. Changes in the Impact of AIDS on Obstetrics Staff. Paper presented at the International Conference on the Implications for AIDS for Mothers and Children, Paris, November 29, 1989.
22. Kaleeba, N. Management of Mothers, Children and Families in Developing Countries. Paper presented at the International Conference on the Implications of AIDS for Mothers and Children, Paris, November 28, 1989.
23. Rich, A. *Of Woman Born: Motherhood as Experience and Institution.* W. W. Norton, New York, 1976.
24. Reid, E. Women and AIDS. In *National AIDS Bulletin,* pp. 20–23. Australian Federation of AIDS Organizations, August 1988.
25. Cohen, J. Overstating the risk of AIDS: Scapegoating prostitutes. *Focus: A Guide to AIDS Research* 2(4): 1–2, 1989.
26. Alexander, P. On Prostitution, pp. 1–20. Unpublished monograph. The National Task Force on Prostitution, February 1987.

27. de Beauvoir, S. *The Second Sex*. Random House, New York, 1952.
28. Yeboah-Afaria, A. Ghananian prostitutes fight AIDS with condoms. *New African*, January 1989, p. 54.
29. Worth, D. Sexual decisionmaking and AIDS: Why condom promotion among vulnerable women is likely to fail. *Stud. Fam. Plann.* 20: 297–307, 1989.
30. MacDonald, G. KAP Survey of a Purposive Sample of Male and Female Sex Workers in Metropolitan Manila, the Philippines. Internal AIDSCOM Monograph. Academy for Educational Development, Washington, D.C., January 1989.
31. Katsivo, M. N. Social Characteristics and Sexual Behavior of Women in the High Risk Behavior Category. Paper presented at the Fifth International Conference on AIDS, Montreal, June 7, 1989.
32. Stephens, C. Women Working as Prostitutes: Participatory/Consensus-Based Planning for the Provision of Mobile, Prevention, Risk-Reduction, and Seroprevalence Activities. Paper presented at the Fifth International Conference on AIDS, Montreal, June 8, 1989.
33. Hauer, L. B. Pregnancy and HIV Infection. *Focus: A Guide to AIDS Research* 4(11): 1–2, 1989.
34. Arras, J. D. HIV Infection and Reproductive Decisions: An Ethical Analysis. Paper presented at the Fifth International Conference on AIDS, Montreal, June 6, 1989.
35. Cain, M. Women's status and fertility in developing countries: Son preference and economic security. *World Bank Staff Working Paper, No. 682, Population and Development Series*, No. 7, pp. 1–68. World Bank, Washington, D.C., 1984.
36. Hassig, S. Contraceptive Utilization and Reproductive Desires in a Group of HIV-Positive Women in Kinshasa. Paper presented at the Fifth International Conference on AIDS, Montreal, June 7, 1989.
37. Riley, M. Project Director, Children's HIV & AIDS Model Program (Project CHAMP), Children's National Medical Center/Academy for Educational Development, Washington, D.C. Personal communication, May 9, 1990.
38. Worth, D., and Rodriguez, R. Latina women and AIDS. *SIECUS Report* 15(3): 5–7, 1987.
39. Bledsoe, C. The Cultural Meaning of AIDS and Condoms for Stable Heterosexual Relations in Africa: Recent Evidence from the Local Print Media. Paper presented at IUSSP Seminar, Kinshasa, Zaire, February 27, 1989.
40. Valdiserri, R. O., et al. The relationship between women's attitudes about condoms and their use: Implications for condom promotion campaigns. *Am. J. Public Health*, 79: 499–501, 1989.

CHAPTER 14

Women and AIDS in Zimbabwe: The Making of an Epidemic

Mary T. Bassett and Marvellous Mhloyi

The AIDS epidemic in Africa, first reported in 1983 among patients from Central Africa who sought medical care in European centers (1), has now reached major proportions. In some urban areas, the prevalence of infection by HIV, the human immunodeficiency virus, in the adult population is approaching 20 percent (2–4). The burden on health services is already being felt: in Ivory Coast, where the first person with AIDS was diagnosed as recently as 1985, over 40 percent of hospitalized patients in the capital city are seropositive (5). Popular concern about the disease reflects these figures. In Uganda, where the wasting syndrome "Slim Disease" was described in the early 1980s, a community-based survey found AIDS to be identified as the number one health problem. Affecting young people who have successfully survived the risks of death in early childhood, AIDS is causing deaths in an economically important age group (15 to 45 years) that was previously relatively protected from mortality. Perinatal transmission threatens hard-won gains in the reduction of infant mortality. Though dwarfed by the big killers—malnutrition and parasitic and bacterial infections—AIDS is having an important and still-evolving effect on health, and poses a substantial threat to present and future generations.

Efforts to halt the epidemic of AIDS in Africa will fall short if we fail to consider the diverse components, both social and biological, that contribute to its spread. Drawing on our joint experience as a clinician/epidemiologist and a social scientist in Zimbabwe, we will explore how current patterns of AIDS transmission in our country—and in Africa more generally—are driven by a combination of factors stemming from the intersection of traditional culture with our colonial legacy and present-day political economy. In particular, we will examine how

Originally published in the *International Journal of Health Services* 21(1): 143-156, 1991.

social conditions have shaped the course of AIDS through their effects on sexual relationships within and outside fast-changing family structures. By focusing on the particular situation of women in Zimbabwe, and by highlighting how the epidemic is perpetuated by patterns of trade, migrant labor, and sexually transmitted diseases, we hope to suggest a broader framework for comprehending and preventing AIDS in Africa.

UNDERSTANDING AIDS IN AFRICA:
THE DIFFERING EXPLANATIONS

Early in the epidemic, investigators working in Africa noted that AIDS was occurring about as often in women as in men. This was in striking contrast to the pattern seen in North America and Europe (now called "Pattern 1"), where male predominance reflected the fact that the initial major risk group in these regions was homosexual men. The different epidemiological profile of AIDS in central and eastern Africa, however, supported the hypothesis that heterosexual intercourse was the major mechanism of transmission in these parts of Africa. Because of the subsequent large numbers of infected women, perinatal transmission also took on significant public health importance. It is generally estimated that these two mechanisms—heterosexual intercourse and perinatal transmission—account for 80 percent of AIDS cases in Africa. In Zimbabwe, where blood supplies have been screened for HIV-1 since 1985, the proportion attributable to these two routes of spread is certainly even higher. Blandly labeled "Pattern 2," this pattern of spread has been regarded as ominous and threatening ever since it was first described.

Since the initial studies of AIDS in Africa, our appreciation of the modes of transmission has expanded, but the basic framework remains unchanged: AIDS in Africa is a sexually transmitted disease with no special risk groups. In this chapter we suggest that an understanding of the full dimensions of the AIDS outbreak in Africa, what Jonathan Mann (6) has described as the "third epidemic," requires that the discussion be broadened. We need to go beyond the supposedly neutral terms of "risk group" and "risk factor" to examine the social context in which the epidemic has taken hold and is spreading. Any epidemic sustains itself largely because of the social organization that supports its propagation, not simply because of the biological characteristics of the "causative agent." In the case of HIV, the single most important biological feature, from a public health point of view, is the long period (years) of asymptomatic infection during which transmission can occur. Although lethal, HIV is relatively noninfectious: who gets infected and who does not has more to do with socially determined behavior than with pathogenicity. Just as much as HIV is a requirement for the AIDS epidemic, so too are the social relations that mold, even determine, the setting of each individual's exposure and susceptibility to infection.

What is it about Africa that explains its particular mass pattern of disease? Behind the "how" of transmission lies a "why" which haunts the understanding of

AIDS in Africa. Addressing these issues has important implications for control of the epidemic. In this chapter we focus on the more difficult question of "why," in part because we believe much of the "how" has already been explained. Our central thesis is that the stage on which this epidemic is unfolding has been set by the social realities of Africa: the migrant labor system, rapid urbanization, constant war with high levels of military mobilization, landlessness, and poverty.

In Africa, traditional cultures are filtered through the facts of colonization and the market economy, both of which have transformed traditional family roles. The history of social misery and dispossession under colonialism has left its stamp on the facts of everyday life: how the family is organized, the role of women, and the role of men. In this sense, the traditional cultures of precolonial societies no longer exist. Instead, culture represents an adaptation of tradition to the changing society. In recent years, the world economic crisis has eroded many of the social gains of independent African countries. This, in broad strokes, is the setting in which the AIDS epidemic is occurring.

The heterosexual transmission of AIDS in Africa poses a frightening specter to the West. Although heterosexual transmission had been identified in North America prior to the description of AIDS in Africa (7), the number of such cases was small and, though growing, remains small. Western explanations for the heterosexual pattern in Africa have been marked by both media hysteria and scientific racism. Images of the dark continent, harboring dangerous diseases, inhabited by people whose social interactions are propelled by sexual frenzy, have long been engraved in the Western view of Africa. Eminent scientists proclaimed the origin of the epidemic to be Africa before data to substantiate their hypothesis were definitive (8). Work on genetic markers for susceptibility rapidly found its way into print (9). Even data on cranial capacities, a relic of eugenic science, were trotted out to explain African susceptibility (10).

This cultural assault, coupled with the fear of loss of needed foreign currency in tourist revenues and investment, was followed by an unfortunate delay in, and even suppression of, the African public health response to the AIDS outbreak. To admit the existence of the AIDS epidemic became tantamount to admitting the inferiority of African ways of life. This was particularly galling when it was clear that the vast majority of cases were initially diagnosed in the United States. The weight of numbers has now stripped away African preoccupation with the intrigues of international science. Researchers in Africa, in both the social and biological sciences, with the support of their governments, have turned their attention to the ways in which the epidemic can be slowed.

WOMEN AND AIDS IN AFRICA:
REASONS FOR PARTICULAR CONCERN

In this chapter our focus is particularly on women. This emphasis derives from several concerns. First, women in Africa are being portrayed as the dangerous vectors of the AIDS outbreak. For example, in terms of epidemiological investigations, this has meant an emphasis on study of female prostitutes to the exclusion of other women. The devastating level of infection documented in some groups of women who sell sexual services is wrongly interpreted to mean that without them, the epidemic would not be occurring. Usually, as Padian (11) has pointed out, all we know is that these women, infected by their clients, are experiencing the brunt of the epidemic. Usually, because we have not identified or studied the men who use prostitutes, we do not know the extent of HIV infection among this group of men. Although it is plausible that female prostitutes contribute to the spread of HIV, we do not know the extent to which the propagation of the epidemic depends upon them.

If not depicted as a dangerous source of infection, women are of interest to those conducting AIDS research or designing interventions mainly when in their pregnant state. Numerous surveys record the prevalence of HIV infection among prenatal women. Information on the extent of infection in this group is important for charting the course of the epidemic. Still, the image of women becomes one of contaminated vessels bearing condemned babies. Because of the shorter natural history of infection in children, a woman may be identified as seropositive because of a sick child, before she herself shows signs of being ill. This reinforces the notion that the mother is solely responsible for the child's serostatus.

These negative portrayals alone are reason enough to examine the position of women in this epidemic. Dangerous precedents exist for the curtailment of women's rights in the face of outbreaks of other sexually transmitted diseases (12). But the position of women is important for still other reasons. The limited control that women have to determine their own lives forms parts of the social substrate of the current epidemic, as we will describe in more detail. The subordination of African women in patrilineal societies places them at a special disadvantage with regard to their ability or willingness to intervene and reduce their own risk of HIV infection. For many women, faced with divorce or dire poverty on the one hand and the risk of HIV infection on the other, the choice becomes one of "social death" or biological death. No one involved in caring for HIV-infected women in Zimbabwe, and presumably elsewhere, can fail to be struck by the limited options women have in negotiating their sexual relations.

Appreciation of these constraints should inform our efforts in developing intervention strategies. In many settings, women in the younger age groups are actually experiencing higher levels of infection than men. In Zaire, women have a higher prevalence of HIV infection until the age of 35 (13). In Ghana, among those diagnosed with AIDS, women outnumber men (14). Ghana's female predominance, Neequaque (14) suggests, may result from women returning home to Ghana when they are ill, after having engaged in sex work in neighboring Ivory Coast.

Unfolding behind these statistics are family tragedies with wrenching human dimensions:

- An elderly woman is carried into the clinic by her daughters. She is wasted by chronic diarrhea which, compounded with severe peripheral neuropathy, has left her unable to walk. She has been tested for HIV but has not been informed of her diagnosis. In privacy, she is told that she has AIDS and that her prognosis is poor. Does she want to go home or come into hospital? "I will go home," she says. Should we discuss the diagnosis with her children? "Are they in danger?" she asks. No. Then she will keep it to herself. And her husband? Well, he comes around only now and then, and she is staying with her elder daughter. What does he do for a living? He is a long-distance truck driver. "He provided well for the family," she says, "driving up and down and bringing us money and bringing us AIDS." She thanks us for explaining what is happening to her and goes home.
- A young woman of 24, her pretty face scarred by a rash, comes to the clinic with her 1-year-old child, the third born. The child is well dressed, for clinic day. He clings to his mother. I pat his head and feel his neck: he has enlarged lymph nodes and looks small for his age. She asks, "Can I please have another HIV test?" Her husband sent her and the boy home to her parents when told of her HIV status. He will only take her back if the test is negative. He is not providing any support. No, he refused testing, saying he is fine. The first two children are fine, they have been kept by the paternal grandmother. She has not seen them in six months.
- A women in her mid-30s, divorced and caring for her two children, frankly states that she supplements her income by having "friends." The children are brought in for testing: they are negative. They are living with their maternal grandparents, she supports them. Can she get her partners to use condoms? She has tried and they refuse. What arrangements can she make for the children if she gets sick? She shakes her head: "My children will suffer."

These cases illustrate that, in Africa, as everywhere, women are the caregivers. They take the larger responsibility for the maintenance of family health and care of the sick. Women are caring for the sick children, sick husbands, and sick relatives who have AIDS. Care for a sick child must carry on in the face of her own illness and an uncertain future for (usually) both parents (15). How can we support this role? Will traditional coping mechanisms within the extended family hold up?

In their role as caregivers and as consumers of family planning techniques, women may be more accessible than men to health care providers. But as a locus of change in this epidemic, women may have the most limited options. Prescriptions to control the spread of AIDS must take into account these constraints and include efforts to increase women's options.

TRACING THE SPREAD OF AIDS IN AFRICA:
THE ROLE OF TRADE, MIGRANT LABOR, AND URBANIZATION

The path of the AIDS epidemic among both women and men in Africa cannot be understood apart from the realities of commerce and civil strife. Data suggest that the epidemic first became established in the central African countries of Zaire, Ruwanda, and Burundi. Early sporadic cases may have been identified as early as the 1960s in Zaire (16), with the epidemic form beginning to appear in the mid-1970s. AIDS was next identified in Uganda, to the east, and in Zambia, to the south. Following the routes of trade and population movement, the epidemic soon spread even further east, to Kenya and Tanzania, and also further south, to Zimbabwe and Malawi. Together, these countries form the large hinterland of South Africa's labor reserve. That infection travels in the wake of trade is shown by the experience of the small town of Kasensero in southern Uganda, located along the truck route to the capital of Kampala. Recent reports suggest that up to half of all deaths in this town are attributable to AIDS (17). Undoubtedly the tremendous social disruptions experienced during Uganda's recent war-torn years have also contributed to the spread of the virus.

Within Zimbabwe, data support a north-to-south spread. In 1985, for example, 3 percent of blood donors in the northern city of Harare were seropositive, compared with 0.05 percent in the city of Bulwayo, to the south. South Africa, the southern tip of the continent, continues to report low rates of infection (below 5 percent), but the doubling time of the incidence of infection is six months (18). While no evidence of HIV seropositivity was found in 1987 among attenders at a South African clinic for the treatment of sexually transmitted diseases (STDs), by 1988 the prevalence had risen to 1.1 percent among women and to 0.6 percent among men (19).

The populous west coast of Africa, belonging to a different axis of trade and commerce connections than east-central Africa, has been affected by AIDS more recently. For example, Nigeria—where one in five Africans live—has relatively few cases of AIDS. But seroprevalence data suggest that the virus is present in the Nigerian population: one survey found that about 1 percent of prostitutes were infected (20). In addition, the identification of a second human immunodeficiency virus (HIV-2) in Senegal in 1985 adds another dimension to the epidemic in west Africa.

In all, 43 of Africa's 50 countries have reported cases of AIDS to the World Health Organization. Some 80 percent of these cases have occurred in nine nations at the center of the epidemic; these countries account for about one-sixth of Africa's population (21). But it would be shortsighted to describe the epidemic as geographically limited. Once HIV is present in a population, the incidence of infection can undergo exponential spread. In Zimbabwe, blood donor data suggest a rapid rise in HIV infection in recent years. In 1985, an average of 2.3 percent of donations tested positive on a single ELISA (enzyme-linked immunosorbent assay), but the figure in some urban areas five years later exceeds 15 percent. In Ivory Coast, the prevalence rose from 1 to 4 percent in two years (22); among prenatal women in Lilongwe, Malawi, it rose from 3 percent in 1986 to 18 percent in 1989 (23); in Bangui, Central African Republic, it rose from 2 percent in 1985 to 7 percent in 1989 (24). In the absence of aggressive intervention efforts, rapid spread of the virus seems likely.

Researchers often remark that HIV infection seems to be an urban rather than a rural problem (25). Much of Africa's population presumably should be protected, since the majority (from 60 to 90 percent) still is rural. But data suggest that significant rates of infection nonetheless are occurring in rural areas: 12 percent in a community sample in rural Uganda (26), 4.9 percent in a sample including prenatal women and donors from rural Tanzania (27), and 3.2 percent among hospital patients in rural Zimbabwe (28). Sparing of these regions seems a function more of the level of technological development (roads, bus transport, etc.) than of any "cultural barriers" to infection due to the strength of "traditional" values in rural areas. Undisrupted traditional culture simply no longer exists, particularly in regions where migrant labor was forcibly introduced at the turn of the century. At present, rates of urban migration in Africa are the highest in the world. In Zimbabwe, which has a good infrastructure and where movement between town and rural areas is frequent, many researchers do not expect the rural–urban gradient to be sustained. The history of Zimbabwe serves as an example of the role of recent colonial history, particularly in the settler colonies, in establishing the social context of the epidemic.

UNDERSTANDING THE EPIDEMIOLOGY OF AIDS IN ZIMBABWE: THE POLITICAL ECONOMY OF FAMILY STRUCTURES

Zimbabwe became independent in 1980 after a long and bitter war against the settler regime that left at least 20,000 dead (29). Its period of colonization lasted nearly a century. White "pioneers" in search of gold entered the territory from South Africa in the 1890s. The final uprising in opposition to the European incursion was defeated in 1897. When gold failed to materialize, the settlers turned to agriculture, and the expropriation of African lands rapidly followed. Land alienation served the dual function of expanding the commercial agricultural sector and creating a labor pool among the now landless peasants. The forced entry of African men into the cash economy was furthered by the introduction of a hut tax that required cash payment. By the 1930s, the law of the land decreed that whites—who comprised less than 5 percent of the population—own half of the land, while the original inhabitants—who comprised 95 percent of the population—be relegated to the remaining half. This "other half," then called the "Tribal Trust Lands" and now called the "communal areas," consisted of the least arable lands.

Prior to the colonial period, traditional Zimbabwean societies were patrilineal (30). Marriage was, and is today, accompanied by payment of a bride-price in compensation to the wife's family for loss of her labor and reproductive capacity, and also as a token of esteem and affection from one family to another. In Zimbabwe, the bride-price has taken on new economic meaning in a market economy. Payment is substantial and may take years to complete. In precolonial times, women returned to their natal family only if divorced. The commitment implicit in married life was not to male sexual fidelity, but to financial support of the wife and offspring (who became part of the male lineage). If wealth permitted, men could have more than one wife. These additional wives did not displace the older wives, who instead maintained their status as senior wives and also could share in the labor of more junior wives. Having multiple wives, however, is beyond the financial capability of most men: according to a 1982 study, under 5 percent of married women in Zimbabwe were in polygamous unions (31).

Patriarchal values parallel the patrilineal system of inheritance and dominated Zimbabwe's traditional societies. Women's entitlement was limited, but it was not nonexistent. For example, women were entitled to the earnings of their own handwork, to plots on which to grow family foods, and to certain gifts of motherhood (30). These limited protections were further curtailed during the colonial period, when European settler society introduced its own patriarchal values. Codification of European-identified "traditional" law reduced women to perpetual minority status in the guardianship of either their fathers or their husbands. Property rights were extremely limited, as were rights even to their own children. Surveys in the early 1980s showed that about half of households in rural areas of Zimbabwe were de facto headed by women (32). But responsibility does not translate into control. Women did not become owners of either land or the products of their labor. While many of the legal barriers to women's equality were overturned in a series of laws passed after Zimbabwe's independence in 1980, decades of legally entrenched social inequality will take time to overcome.

Barriers to women's equality in Zimbabwe, however, stem not simply from patriarchal values but also from the land hunger created by European expropriation. Severe overcrowding in the most unproductive areas meant that women rarely were awarded land in their own right. As men left to work in the towns and on large-scale farms and mines, women and families were left behind to manage as subsistence farmers. Rural women's labor also increased, as it extended to tasks originally performed by men. A study of a peasant woman's "typical" workday suggests that it extends from 4:30 a.m. until 9 p.m. In 1982, of an estimated 780,000 families in the peasant sector, nearly a third (235,000) operated on this split-family strategy (33).

As family separation became a feature of life, the rules of sexual relationships outside marriage also changed. Husbands formed other liaisons in town. These relationships might even supersede the rural wife, leading to divorce or a reduction in remittances. The impact on the rural families left behind could be catastrophic. Loss of cash income from the towns placed women-headed households at a far higher risk of having malnourished children; in one study, the risk was found to increase sixfold (34). The rural income might even be used to supplement urban expenses. Those men who could not afford to maintain urban wives opted for more casual arrangements. These multiple relationships, often referred to as modern-day versions of polygamy, actually differ considerably from the polygamous unions of Zimbabwe's traditional culture, described above.

In sharp contrast to the practice of polygamy in the precolonial era, the multiple relationships that arose in the urban setting of the colonial and postcolonial Zimbabwean society are not rare: they are practically universal. Obviously, this has required a change in where both women and men live, as well as in their patterns of sexual interaction. Although urban female migration initially was restricted both legally and by the lack of employment prospects, some women migrated to meet the demand for sexual services created by the artificial settlement of men without their families. An urban woman, particularly one divorced or unmarried, became almost synonymous with a prostitute. This stereotype is strong and has found its way into the AIDS control program. An early poster depicted a woman in a miniskirt and high-heeled boots, dragging on a cigarette, and the caption exhorted men to remain faithful to their families. (The poster concept, we are told, was developed by women!)

In Zimbabwe, as in other parts of Africa (35, 36), the exchange of sex for money or for other goods and services covers a broad range of arrangements. Many are not socially considered to be prostitution. Some of these women sell single sexual encounters. Probably more common are situations in which men pay for ongoing sexual and domestic services. These may range from sporadic payments to stable live-in partnerships. The definition of a prostitute therefore becomes somewhat arbitrary. Women who live apart or are divorced from their husbands may supplement their low incomes with gifts from male friends. Most would not enter into liaisons without financial compensation, and none would consider themselves prostitutes. In addition, some women who work as seasonal laborers support themselves off-season by selling sex. Others sell sex to meet a specific obligation, such as school fees. Younger women, even those of school age, may trade sex for the status of an older lover who can give them otherwise inaccessible goods or experiences (meals in hotels, riding in an expensive car, and so on). These men are popularly known as "sugar daddies." Finally, employed women may be forced to exchange sex for job security.

Popular belief holds that these patterns are well established in towns, but rural life also offers the opportunity for commercial sex. Rural "growth points" (rudimentary business centers), army camps, and similar locations provide the setting for such exchanges to occur. It is also widely believed that some urban women, particularly professional women, are both willing and have the opportunity to "balance the score" with their errant husbands. Whatever the extent of this practice, strong social sanctions exist against women engaging in extramarital sex. Although hardly any data exist on contemporary sexual relations in Zimbabwe, it seems safe to state that few women feel they are in the position to have sexual relations without some sort of benefit, whether social (including marriage) or material. For the vast majority of women, sexual relationships occur in the context of marriage (37, Table A.2.2, p. 65). By the age of 20 to 24 years, 75 percent of women in Zimbabwe have been married, in line with the traditionally sanctioned requirement that childbearing occur within marriage.

AIDS AND SEXUALLY TRANSMITTED DISEASES IN ZIMBABWE: AN IMPORTANT CONNECTION

The changing nature of marital and extramarital sexual relationships in Zimbabwe has profoundly influenced patterns of transmission of not only AIDS, but other STDs as well. The link between these STDs and AIDS is twofold. Serving as a marker of sexual activity outside the family unit, the presence of STDs indicates likely areas where AIDS may spread. In addition, data suggest that STDs may be a cofactor for HIV infection (15, 38), as discussed below.

At present, STDs are common in Zimbabwe. Last year, over 900,000 cases of STDs were treated nationwide (39). With the population estimated at 10 million (and assuming one case per person), this averages out to treatment of nearly one-quarter of the adult population! Popular ideas about STDs suggest that little stigma is attached to male infection. Having an STD is almost a rite of passage into manhood, proof of sexual activity: "A bull is not a bull without his scars." Consistent with both data and belief, a study on HIV infection among male factory workers found that a history of prior STD was common among both seropositive and seronegative men: 100 and 75 percent, respectively (40). Other risk factors, now documented in numerous studies of AIDS in Africa, were also more common in the HIV-positive group, e.g., multiple partners, a history of payment for sex. What was unexpected was the high prevalence of high-risk activities among the seronegative men: 40 percent reported an STD in the previous year, and the majority (67 percent) had paid money for sex. Seropositive men were more likely than seronegative men to report a history of genital ulcer. In the light of these data, one can hardly characterize the seronegative comparison group as "low risk."

Many investigators now believe that the enhanced risk of heterosexual transmission of AIDS in Africa may largely be explained by high rates of concurrent infection with another STD (15, 38, 41). Of particular concern is chancroid, an STD that is common in Africa but not in the West. In Zimbabwe, about half of genital ulcer disease is due to chancroid. The important role of such ulcers in HIV transmission is biologically plausible. Both disruption of the mucosal barrier and the presence of HIV-infected white blood cells would explain the increased likelihood of infection. In our clinic in Harare, where we have been seeing patients referred for HIV infection for a number of years, we found that among those couples in which the male partner was the index case, a history of genital ulcers was three times more likely among men in couples where HIV infection was concordant rather than discordant (15).

The focus on genital ulcers as an important cofactor for HIV transmission has both positive and negative features. While it offers new approaches for intervention programs, it also shifts emphasis from the broader social context of STD occurrence to more narrow medical concerns. Certainly any intervention that results in reduced rates of STDs, such as increasing public awareness about the availability of treatment for STDs, will also mean a diminution of HIV transmission. It is said that some women now inspect men for signs of genital ulcer before agreeing to have sex, a strategy that may be particularly useful for women engaged in commercial sex. The focus on genital ulcer also is appealing because it seems to eliminate all of the value-laden issues that accompany interpretation of other risk factors, such as multiple partners and prostitute contact. Zimbabwe's Ministry of Health has generated protocols for STD treatment, and the nation's independence made access to medical care effectively universal. Nonetheless, the number of cases of STDs in Zimbabwe increases yearly. To reduce the problem of HIV transmission to the problem of controlling genital ulcer is to search for a "technological fix" that fails to address the social factors that jointly underlie both problems.

As suggested by our work in Harare (15), it is against this background of high rates of STDs that AIDS transmission occurs, and in most cases it is the male partner who introduces HIV infection into the family unit. In our clinic, we ask married patients to bring their spouses. About half of the partners eventually appear for screening. The main reason that other partners do not come is because they live elsewhere, usually in the rural areas. Among the initial 75 couples, reported risk factors for AIDS were more prevalent among men that women, who universally denied having multiple partners. Only in two couples was the wife seropositive and the husband seronegative. In both cases, the wife had an identifiable risk factor (blood transfusion, first marriage to a partner who died of an AIDS-like illness). Although we do not know the duration or timing of infection in the couples we have studied, the paucity of female-positive/male-negative couples supports our impression that wives are most often placed at risk by their husbands. Moreover, because women in general are more likely to use health services than men, referral patterns seem unlikely to explain the small number of women as the index cases.

We are seeing more women now, usually referred because of HIV-related illness in a child. Often the mother has been tested without the involvement of the husband. Increasingly, the husband declines screening and sometimes rejects the mother and child. These are the realities of AIDS experienced by women in Zimbabwe.

AIDS PREVENTION IN AFRICA:
PROSPECTS FOR THE FUTURE

We have discussed how sexual relationships in Zimbabwe and, by extension, other parts of sub-Saharan Africa are far more complex than the term "promiscuous" implies. To halt the current epidemic spread of AIDS, we will have to reckon with these patterns as we encourage changes in individual behavior—so far the only universally available "weapon" to combat this disease. The fact that historically produced social conditions have created situations that promote behavior which we now call "high risk" should not be taken to mean that this behavior is inevitable, or that only a complete social transformation will permit meaningful interventions to reduce transmission of HIV. Instead, our point is that the pattern of sexual relations, which places many people at risk for HIV infection, is not due to some "natural proclivity" of African men or to some inherent feature of "human nature," but is social in origin, and so can be changed. In Zimbabwe, the twin legacies of the patriarchy and colonialism seem the most important factors in shaping family structure, sexual relations, and the risk of HIV infection. If we do not take this into account, we cannot hope to develop specific and effective interventions to halt the spread of AIDS.

A first and urgent step in AIDS prevention is to ensure that people are provided with information and resources necessary to diminish their chance of being infected by HIV. As far as possible, the public health campaign should be rooted in organizations that people know and trust. Schoepf and coauthors (42) report that in Zaire, people initially joked that AIDS was an "imaginary syndrome invented by Europeans to discourage African lovers." This attitude betrays a distrust of outside prescriptions for changes in sexual behavior, prescriptions that were initially seen as part of population control programs. Clinics, schools, and the radio are all natural places for information to be made available. In settings where the government is not trusted, other organizations become particularly important: the trade union movement, women's groups, grassroots organizations—all need to be convinced of the importance of adding AIDS prevention to their agendas.

The campaign should bring information about HIV transmission and prevention into everyday life in forms accessible to a population in which many people are illiterate and a biological understanding of disease is virtually absent. A series of articles on AIDS in Zimbabwe's national newspaper in 1987 was replete with such terms as "killer lymphocytes," "T4 cells," and the like, and required a university-level biology background. Decades of experience in health education can be brought to bear on developing methods of getting across information about AIDS in ways that are popular, nonjudgmental, and hopeful. For example, a leading musician here recently came out with a song about AIDS, as have musicians in Zaire, Uganda, Zambia, and elsewhere.

For most people, celibacy or a single lifetime partner are not realistic options. Efforts should therefore focus on reducing transmission. In practice this means limiting the number of partners and using condoms. Condoms cost only a few cents each, but providing them in adequate numbers to the sexually active population of the continent will still run into millions of dollars. Most African governments are facing cuts in social expenditures as a result of structural adjustment, and many cannot afford the cost of condoms or, indeed, the overall public health campaign. International aid will continue to be vital in AIDS control.

Adopting the use of condoms is more complicated than learning how to use them (42). While the distribution, and presumably use, of condoms appears to be increasing (43), a recent national survey of Zimbabwean men found that only 35 percent said they had ever used condoms (44). Most viewed condom use as appropriate for prostitutes, but not within marriages or other stable arrangements. As we have suggested, women are in a weak position to dictate how sex takes place. As seroprevalence increases and individuals are more likely to know personally someone with AIDS, more women may be willing to risk abuse or divorce to reduce their risk of infection. Further complicating matters is the fact that many women want to have children. Clearly acceptable alternatives to condoms need to be found that allow women to control use and possibly permit conception. Some possibilities have been outlined by Stein (45).

Unfortunately, we have little direct experience with such a broad public health program. So far, attention in Zimbabwe has focused on individual counseling and case identification. Blood donors who test positive are not informed of a "problem" (unless they ask) and are permitted to continue to donate blood (which subsequently is discarded). Research activities have been subject to careful and lengthy scrutiny. Posters about AIDS on clinic walls are now three years old. The pace is picking up, but progress is slow. Reports from other centers (46, 47) support some optimism about people's ability to change high-risk behaviors.

We have had ample time to reflect on the social implications of the AIDS epidemic. We have agonized as we see patients who are infected and who had no knowledge of their risks. Fathers as well as mothers suffer when their children become sick or, though seemingly well, carry a death sentence in their small bodies. For all the hardships of womanhood in Africa, there is no doubt that children are universally cherished. To protect their future may be the strongest incentive in the campaign to reduce HIV transmission.

REFERENCES

1. Clumeck, N., et al. Acquired immunodeficiency syndrome in African patients. *N. Engl. J. Med.* 310: 492–497, 1984.
2. Nationwide community-based serological survey of human immunodeficiency virus type 1 (HIV-1) and other human retrovirus infections in a central African country. Rwandan HIV seroprevalence study group. *Lancet* 1: 941–943, 1988.

3. Carswell, J. W. HIV infection in healthy persons in Uganda. *AIDS* 1: 223–227, 1987.
4. Malbye, M., et al. Evidence for heterosexual transmission and clinical manifestations of human immunodeficiency virus infection and related conditions in Lusaka, Zambia, *Lancet* 2: 1113–1115, 1986.
5. DeCock, K. M., et al. Rapid emergence of AIDS in Abidjan, Ivory Coast. *Lancet* 2: 408–411, 1989.
6. Mann, J. M. Social, cultural and political aspects: An overview. *AIDS* 2(Suppl.): S207–S208, 1988.
7. Harris, C., et al. Immunodeficiency in female sexual partners of men with the acquired immunodeficiency syndrome. *N. Engl. J. Med.* 308: 1181–1184, 1983.
8. Sabatier, R. *Blaming Others: Prejudice, Race, and Worldwide AIDS.* The Panos Institute, Washington, D.C., 1988.
9. Eales, L. J., et al. Association of different allelic forms of group specific component with susceptibility to and clinical manifestations of human immunodeficiency virus. *Lancet* 2: 277–283, 1987.
10. Rushton, J. P., and Bogaert, A. F. Population differences in susceptibility to AIDS: An evolutionary analysis. *Soc. Sci. Med.* 28: 1211–1220, 1989.
11. Padian, N. Prostitute women and AIDS: Epidemiology. *AIDS* 2: 413–419, 1989.
12. Schoepf, B. G. Methodology, Ethics, and Politics: AIDS Research in Africa for Whom? Unpublished manuscript.
13. Quinn, T., et al. AIDS in Africa: An epidemiologic paradigm. *Science* 234: 955–963, 1986.
14. Neequaque, A. R., Osei, L., and Mingle, A. A. Dynamics of HIV epidemic: The Ghanian experience. In *The Global Impact of AIDS*, edited by A. Fleming and M. Carballo, pp. 9–15. Alan R. Liss, New York, 1988.
15. Latif, A. S., et al. Genital ulcers and transmission of HIV among couples in Zimbabwe. *AIDS* 3: 519–523, 1989.
16. Sonnet, J., et al. Early AIDS cases originating in Zaire and Burundi (1962–1976). *Scand. J. Infect. Dis.* 19: 511–517, 1987.
17. Hooper, E. AIDS in Uganda. *Afr. Aff.* 86: 469–477, 1987.
18. Schapiro, M., Crookes, R. L., and O'Sullivan, E. Screening antenatal blood samples for anti-human immunodeficiency virus antibodies by a large pool enzyme-linked immunosorbant assay system: Results of an 18 month investigation. *S. Afr. J. Med.* 76: 245–249, 1989.
19. *Annual Report of the Medical Research Council*, p. 17. South Africa, 1988.
20. Mohammed, F., et al. HIV infection in Nigeria [letter]. *AIDS* 2: 61–62, 1988.
21. Chen, J., and Mann, J. M. Global patterns and prevalence of AIDS and HIV infection. *AIDS* 3(Suppl. 1): S247–S252, 1989.
22. Mann, J. M. Global AIDS in the 1990s. Unpublished document. Global Program on AIDS/Dir/89.2. World Health Organization, Geneva, 1989.
23. Liomba, N. G., et al. Comparison of Age Distribution of Anti-HIV-1 and AntiHBc in an Urban Population from Malawi. Abstract No. W.G.027. Fifth International Conference on AIDS, Montreal, 1989.
24. Somse, P., et al. Les aspects épidémiologiques des affections lieés aux VIH1 et 2 en République Centrafricaine. Abstract No. W.G.028. Fifth International Conference on AIDS, Montreal, 1989.
25. Turshen, M. *The Politics of Public Health*, pp. 219–241. Rutgers University Press, Rutgers, N.J., 1989.
26. Kenegeay-Kayondo, J. F., et al. Anti-HIV Seroprevalence in Adult Rural Populations in Uganda and Its Implication for Preventive Strategies. Abstract No. T.A.P. 111. Fifth International Conference on AIDS, Montreal, 1989.

27. Dolmans, W. M. V., et al. Prevalence of HIV-1 antibody among groups of patients and healthy subjects from a rural and urban population in Mwanza region, Tanzania. *AIDS* 3: 297–299, 1989.
28. Mertens, T., et al. Epidemiology of HIV and hepatitis B virus (HBV) in selected African and Asian populations. *Infections* 17: 4–7, 1989.
29. Stoneman, C. *Zimbabwe's Inheritance.* St. Martin's Press, New York, 1982.
30. Batezat, E., and Mwalo, M. *Women in Zimbabwe*, pp. 9–12. Sapes Trust Jongwe Printers, Harare, Zimbabwe, 1989.
31. Central Statistical Office. *Report on Demographic Socio-economic Survey of the Communal Lands. Permanent Sample Survey Unit Programme (ZNHSCP). Report No. 1 to 5.* Zimbabwe, 1984/85.
32. Riddell, R. *Report of the Commission of Inquiry into Incomes Price, and Conditions of Service.* Government of Zimbabwe, Harare, 1982.
33. Callear, D. *The Social and Cultural Factors Involved in Production by Small Farmers in Wedza Communal Area, Zimbabwe*, p. 22. Division for the Study of Development, UNESCO, Paris, 1982. [Cited in reference 37.]
34. Thiesen, R. J. *Agro-economic Factors Relating to the Health and Academic Achievement of Rural School Children.* Tribal Areas of Rhodesia Research Foundation, Salisbury [Harare], 1975. [Cited in reference 37.]
35. Day, S. Prostitute women and AIDS: Anthropology. *AIDS* 2: 421–428, 1989.
36. Larson, A. Social context of human immunodeficiency virus transmission in Africa: Historical and cultural bases of east and central African sexual relations. *Rev. Infect. Dis.* 2: 716–731, 1989.
37. UNICEF. *Children and Women in Zimbabwe: A Situation Analysis.* Government Printers, Harare, Zimbabwe, 1985.
38. Cameron, D. W., et al. Female to male transmission of human immunodeficiency virus type 1: Risk factors for seroconversion in men. *Lancet* 2: 403–407, 1989.
39. Secretary for Health. *Annual Report, 1988.* Government Printers, Harare, Zimbabwe, 1989.
40. Bassett, M. T., et al. HIV Infection in Urban Men in Zimbabwe. Abstract No. Th.C.581, Sixth International Conference on AIDS, San Francisco, 1990.
41. Kreiss, J. K., et al. AIDS virus infection in Nairobi prostitutes: Spread of the epidemic to East Africa. *N. Engl. J. Med.* 314: 414–418, 1986.
42. Schoepf, B. G., et al. AIDS in society in Central Africa: A view from Zaire. In *AIDS in Africa*, pp. 211–235. The Edwin Mellen Press, Lewiston, N.Y., 1988.
43. Condom use on the increase. *The Herald* (Harare, Zimbabwe), September 6, 1989, p. 1.
44. Mbivzo, M., and Adamchak, D. J. Condom use and acceptance: A survey of male Zimbabweans. *Cent. Afr. J. Med.* 35: 519–558, 1989.
45. Stein, Z. HIV prevention: The need for methods women can use. *Am. J. Public Health* 80: 460–462, 1990.
46. Ngugi, E. N., Plummer, F. A., and Simonsen, J. N. Prevention of transmission of human immunodeficiency virus in Africa: Effectiveness of condom promotion and health education among prostitutes. *Lancet* 2: 887–890, 1988.
47. Ngugi, E. N., and Plummer, F. A. Health outreach and control of HIV infection in Kenya. *J. Acquired Immunodeficiency Syndromes* 6: 566–570, 1988.

Section VII
Gender, Social Policy, and Women's Lives

CHAPTER 15

The Feminization of Poverty:
Myth or Reality?

Martha E. Gimenez

The "feminization of poverty" is currently a phenomenon of great concern to the government, social scientists, politicians, and feminists of all political persuasions. This phrase attempts to capture the essence of the following facts: in the United States, the fastest growing type of family structure is that of female-headed households and, because of the high rate of poverty among these households, their increase is mirrored in the growing numbers of women and children who are poor; almost half of all the poor in the United States today live in families headed by women. In 1984, 16 percent of all white families, 25 percent of all families of Spanish origin,[1] and 53 percent of all black families were headed by women (1, p. 5). In the same year, the poverty rate for white, Spanish-origin, and black female-headed households was 27.1 percent, 53.4 percent, and 51.7 percent, respectively (1, p. 12). Poverty affects not only young and adult women with children but also older women; in 1984, the median income of women aged 65 years and over was $6,020 (while it was $10,450 for men in the same age category), and 15.0 percent of all women aged 65 and over had incomes below the poverty line (2, p. 158). The poverty of women is reflected in the poverty of

---

[1] Both "Spanish-origin" and "Hispanic" are, for political, theoretical, and methodologieal reasons, highly problematic labels. They misrepresent the determinants of the disproportionate poverty rate among people of Mexican and Puerto Rican origin and/or descent, and obscure the qualitative differences between U.S. minority groups and Spanish and Latin American immigrants. Throughout this chapter, I chose to use "Spanish-origin" because, unlike "Hispanic," it is a simple descriptive label that does not create the presumption of some kind of "Hispanic" race or culture. Readers interested in this issue should consult the January 1987 issue of the *American Journal of Public Health,* in which the political and methodological problems inherent in the "Hispanic" label are thoroughly examined.

Originally published in the *International Journal of Health Services* 19(1): 45–61, 1989.

children. There are almost 13 million poor children in the United States; 52 percent of them live in families headed by women, and the poverty rate for white, black, and Spanish-origin children living in female-headed households is 46 percent, 66 percent, and 71 percent, respectively (1, pp. 32–33).

The facts and figures documenting the increased immiseration of women and children can be found in many recent and important publications (1–3), together with analyses that put forth the notion that it is women, *as women*, who are peculiarly vulnerable to poverty. Poverty is being feminized, and this idea is nowhere expressed more clearly than in an often quoted statement from the President's National Advisory Council on Economic Opportunity (1981) (1, p. 7):

> All other things being equal, if the proportion of the poor in female-householder families were to continue to increase at the same rate as it did from 1976 to 1978, the poverty population would be composed solely of women and their children before the year 2000.

Critics have rightly pointed out that the statement suggests that "by the year 2000 all of those men who are presently poor will be either rich or dead" (4, p. 6). While those who quote this statement acknowledge that society does not keep still, that poverty affects men also and falls more heavily among nonwhites, nevertheless, the main thrust of the analysis of present trends continues to interpret them as the "feminization of poverty."

Is this a theoretically adequate notion? What can we learn from it? What are its shortcomings? Does it adequately convey the nature of the processes it describes? Is the "feminization of poverty" a real phenomenon or a mystification that obscures the unfolding of other processes? These are some of the questions I will seek to answer in this chapter. I will examine, from the standpoint of Marxist feminist theory, the strengths and shortcomings of current explanations to establish whether recent changes in the size and composition of the poor population, growth in female-headed families, and the increased vulnerability of women to poverty can be adequately understood as the "feminization of poverty."

FACTORS ACCOUNTING FOR
THE FEMINIZATION OF POVERTY

The definition of a social phenomenon shapes the questions that can be asked about its possible determinants and, of course, the questions in turn shape the answers. In this case, it is unavoidable to center such questions around women: why are women more likely to be poor than men? Why are female-headed households and families more likely to be poor? Why is the number of those households and families increasing? This leads researchers to focus on factors that are specific to the situation of women in modern society, and conclude that women, as a group and regardless of class, are more vulnerable to poverty than men and that, consequently, women's poverty has different causes than the poverty of men. These are some representative statements of this view (2, p. 25; 3, p. 9; 5, p. 12):

> While there is clearly much truth to the statement that race and class have been major determinants of poverty in this country, women as a group, including middle and sometimes even upper-middle class women, have recently become far more vulnerable to poverty or near poverty than their male counterparts. . . . It is clear that some of the key causes of poverty among women are fundamentally different from the causes of poverty among men.

> . . . there is a fundamental difference between male and female poverty: for men, poverty is often the consequence of unemployment and a job is generally an effective remedy, while female poverty often exists even when a woman works full-time. . . . Virtually all women are vulnerable—a divorce or widowhood is all it takes to throw many middle class women into poverty.

> Race may well be the principal determinant of poverty in this country. . . . And it is redundant to say that class causes poverty . . . to account for a trend that specifically involves women, we need an explanation in which gender is the determining factor . . . to explain the feminization of poverty we have to invoke some of the things that many women have in common—such as motherhood and low paying jobs . . . looking at commonalities, we are not attempting to dissolve differences, but to understand how gender—as one factor—can affect one's economic status.

The conceptualization of women *as a group* or a primary focus on gender characterizes most discussions of the feminization of poverty. Census data do not differentiate between social classes; researchers have information about income, sex, racial, and ethnic categories of analysis, and this reinforces the tendency to frame the discussion in terms of statistical rather than theoretically significant categories of analysis. The determinants of women's poverty, it is therefore implied in the analysis, are factors that affect all women and place all women at risk.

What are these factors? Changes in mortality and marriage rates, divorce and separations, and out-of-wedlock births contribute to the increase in female-headed households (1, pp. 38–42). Women's higher life expectancy contributes to the increasing number of women over 65 years of age living alone, and a substantial proportion of these women are poor. Younger women become heads of households through out-of-wedlock childbearing, separation, divorce, or the decision to live alone while they work and postpone marriage until they consider it appropriate.

Needless to say, while young and old single women are found among poor female-headed households, the majority of these households consists of women and their children. Poor young women, particularly minority women, are more likely to become single mothers, and teenage motherhood is perhaps one of the most important correlates of poverty. The level of child support that women receive from their children's father is very low; the majority receives none and

significance, are devalued and time-consuming, and interfere with women's full participation in the labor force. The domestic division of labor thus interacts with the sex-segregated nature of occupations to restrict the economic and educational opportunities of women. The negative effects of this situation become more salient once women become single heads of families (see, for example, 2, pp. 25–35).

As the preceding discussion indicates, the feminization of poverty is associated with many interrelated structural and ideological variables. Stallard and associates sum up the determinants of the feminization of poverty as follows (3, p. 51):

> [It] is a direct outgrowth of women's dual role as unpaid labor in the home and underpaid labor in the workforce. The pace has been quickened by rising rates of divorce and single motherhood, but the course of women's poverty is determined by the sexism—and racism—ingrained in an unjust economy.

It would seem that recent literature has produced not only a detailed description but also some plausible and, some may even say, obvious explanations of the feminization of poverty. That this is really the case, in spite of the impressive documentation and well-developed arguments, is not as self-evident as it may seem. The identification of the determinants of the feminization of poverty in sexism, racism, and the operation of the economy does not really tell us much beyond that which is empirically obvious and observable. What is questionable is the meaning given to the trends: are we witnessing the feminization and the minoritization of poverty or something else? I will introduce some additional facts and figures about poverty to highlight the complexity of these issues, and the problems inherent in the "feminization of poverty" perspective.

WHO ARE THE POOR?

A recent analysis of poverty in the United States indicates that, while it is the case that women are more likely to be poor than men and that, in absolute numbers, in 1983 there were more poor women (20,084,000) than men (15,182,000), "*the female share of the overall poverty population was the same in 1983 as it was in 1966 (the earliest available data) 57 percent*" (6, p. 18, emphasis added). Poverty trends since 1983 have modified this conclusion only slightly. Between 1983 and 1986, the female share of the poverty population increased slightly from 57.0 percent to 57.6 percent (9, p. 30).

The female and male shares of the poverty population from 1966 to 1985 show remarkable stability: the female share increases gradually, rising to 59.1 percent in 1978, declining to 57 percent in 1983 and 1984, rising to 57.6 percent in 1986 (Table 1). If only adults over 21 are considered, in 1983—*as it was in 1966*— women comprised 62 percent of the poor (6, p. 18); this percentage increased to 62.1 percent in 1984, 62.7 percent in 1985, and 64.2 percent in 1986 (9, p. 30; 10, p. 28; 11, p. 27).

Mortality differentials increase the numbers of older women living alone; 27.7 percent of the 6.7 million women aged 65 and over who in 1983 lived as "unrelated individuals" were below the poverty level; in 1984, the number of women in that category increased to 6.8 million, but the percentage below the poverty level declined to 25.2 percent (10, p. 29; 12). By comparison, in 1984, 20.8 percent of "unrelated males" aged 65 and over fell below the poverty level. The differences between the poverty rate of younger "unrelated" women and men is small: "at ages 25–34 in 1983 . . . the rate was 15.3 percent for men and 15.0 percent for women" (6, p. 18). In 1984, the comparable rates were 12.7 percent for men and 13.5 percent for women (10, p. 29).

As indicated in Table 1, the overall poverty rate increased between 1978 and 1983 (from 11.4 percent to 15.2 percent), declining to 14.4 percent in 1984 and 13.6 percent in 1986. Between 1978 and 1983, poverty increased faster for the 18 to 44 age category (70 percent) than for the 45 to 64 or the 65 and over age categories (26 percent and 14.8 percent, respectively). *Taking into account male/female differences, between 1978 and 1983 the number of poor men increased faster than the number of poor women at all ages (51.6 percent versus 38. 7 percent), ages 18 to 44 (93.3 percent versus 56.9 percent), and ages 45 to 64 (33.0 percent versus 22.5 percent).* Among those aged 18 and under, the percentage increase for males and females was relatively similar (40.0 percent versus 38.1 percent); only among those 65 and over was the percentage increase in the number of poor women slightly higher (15.7 percent versus 12.7 percent) (6, p. 14).

Given the mortality differentials between the sexes, it is to be expected that poverty among the elderly would increase faster for women; on the other hand, the fact that poverty increased faster for men in the other age groups, particularly among those between 18 and 44 years of age, is somewhat surprising, because of the public and scholarly concern with the "feminization of poverty," which gives the impression that the growth of poverty has been primarily among women and that men have been less affected by the structural transformations of the economy. In actuality, between 1978 and 1983 the increase in poverty affected primarily younger people, particularly men. For example, the number of men aged 18 to 44 below the poverty level almost doubled between 1978 and 1983, increasing from 2,832,000 to 5,474,000. One could make a case for considering age, rather than sex, the defining feature of current poverty trends.

It may be argued that the higher percentage change in male poverty between 1978 and 1983 is an artifact of the particular years chosen to make a comparison. O'Hare's (6) analysis reflects the sharp fluctuations associated with the 1981–82 recession. However, an examination of the average annual percentage changes in the number of men and women below the poverty level between 1975 and every year until 1985, for all ages, shows a greater increase in male poverty in every year from 1982 on. At ages 18 to 44, there is a higher rate of increase in male poverty for every year from 1979 on. The lower proportion of men below the poverty level makes percentage changes in male poverty higher than they would have been had

Table 1

Male-female share of the poverty population, by age and sex, 1966–86[a]

Year	Poverty rate	Poverty population (1000s)	All ages		Age 18–44[b]		Age 45–64		Age 65+	
			%F	%M	%F	%M	%F	%M	%F	%M
1966	14.7	28,490	57.1	42.0	16.3	11.5	9.4	5.8	11.5	6.5
1967	14.2	27,764	57.5	42.5	16.4	11.3	9.5	5.5	12.7	6.7
1968	12.8	25,371	57.5	42.5	16.7	11.2	8.4	5.6	11.9	5.8
1969	12.1	24,270	57.6	42.4	16.8	11.0	9.5	5.7	13.0	6.7
1970	12.6	25,516	57.4	42.6	17.2	12.6	9.4	5.4	12.3	6.0
1971	12.5	25,549	58.0	42.0	18.6	12.6	9.4	5.6	11.7	5.0
1972	11.9	25,031	58.3	41.7	19.5	12.6	9.5	5.5	10.8	4.5
1973	11.1	22,958	58.0	42.0	20.1	12.4	9.4	5.7	10.0	4.6
1974	11.2	24,294	57.2	42.5	20.2	13.3	9.0	5.4	9.4	4.2
1975	12.3	25,878	57.8	42.2	18.8	11.1	8.7	5.6	8.9	3.9
1976	11.8	24,978	58.5	41.5	19.5	11.7	9.1	5.2	9.3	4.0
1977	11.6	24,721	58.2	41.8	19.8	11.5	8.9	5.5	9.0	3.9
1978	11.4	24,497	59.1	40.9	20.4	11.6	8.9	5.4	9.3	3.9
1979	11.7	25,345	58.4	41.6	19.8	11.8	8.9	5.4	9.9	4.3
1980	13.0	29,272	58.3	41.7	21.1	13.2	8.1	4.9	9.5	3.8
1981	14.0	31,822	58.1	41.9	21.6	14.0	8.1	4.9	8.7	3.4
1982	15.0	34,398	56.9	43.1	21.8	14.8	7.9	5.0	7.7	3.2
1983	15.2	35,266	57.0	43.0	22.2	15.5	7.6	5.0	7.5	3.0
1984	14.4	33,700	57.0	43.1	22.0	15.2	7.8	5.3	7.0	2.8
1985	14.0	33,063	57.2	42.8	22.4	15.0	7.6	5.2	7.6	2.9
1986	13.6	32,370	57.6	42.4	22.8	14.1	7.7	4.9	7.7	3.0

[a]Sources: Bureau of the Census. Supplementary report on the low income population: 1966–1972. *Current Population Reports*, Series P-60, No. 95, July 1974. Characteristics of the low income population: 1973. *Current Population Reports*, Series P-60, No. 98, January 1975. Characteristics of the population below the poverty level, 1974–1983. *Current Population Reports*, Series P-60, No. 102, January 1976; No. 106, June 1977; No. 115, July 1978; No. 119, March 1979; No. 124, July 1980; No. 130, December 1981; No. 133, July 1982; No. 138, March 1984; No. 144, March 1984; No. 147, February 1985; and No. 152, June 1986. Money income and poverty status of families and persons in the United States: 1985. *Current Population Reports*, Series P-60, No. 154, August 1986 and No. 157, July 1987. U.S. Government Printing Office, Washington, D.C.

[b]Statistics for 1966–74 are for ages 16 to 44.

sex ratios been closer to unity.[2] On the other hand, the higher percentage changes in male poverty cannot be dismissed lightly as statistical artifacts; and it must be remembered that male poverty is an important correlate of female poverty. The sharp increases in male poverty between 1978 and 1983 were real and seem to have lingered on after the "economic recovery" that followed the 1981–82 recession; they reflect the vulnerability of men to unemployment at times of rapid economic decline, whereas women tend to work in "recession-proof" sectors of the economy (16; 17, p. 11).

As indicated earlier, the proportion of men and women in the 18 to 44 age group who become poor has been steadily increasing. While in 1983 the poverty rate was 8.7 percent (up from 6.4 percent in 1978) for families with a householder aged 45 to 64 and 14.2 percent (up from 10.2 percent in 1978) for families with a householder aged 25 to 44, it was 29.5 percent (up from 18.5 percent in 1978) for families with a householder under 25 (6, p. 13). In 1984, the poverty rate for householders under 25 was practically unchanged at 29.4 percent, while the rate for householders aged 25 to 44 declined slightly to 13.2 percent (10, p. 14).

The faster increase in the poverty rate of younger workers of both sexes indicates that the working class is experiencing substantial downward mobility (6, pp. 13–14; 18). The increase in the poverty of children, usually linked to the increase in the number of female-headed families, is actually the result of the increase in poverty among young adult workers; while in 1983, 49 percent of poor children lived in female-headed households, 81 percent of children in poor families lived in families with a householder under 45. Between 1978 and 1983, 4 million children under 18 joined the poverty population, and only 25 percent of them lived in female-headed households (6, pp. 13–17).

Real average earnings of young male workers aged 20 to 24 have declined 30 percent since 1973. A comparison between the earnings of men who turned 30 in 1973, and in 1983, shows that the average real income of the older men kept up with inflation while that of the younger men declined 35 percent (19, p. 10). Income inequality among young men is related to education; those without a college degree are reduced to taking whatever the economy offers them, which, in these days, are jobs that pay relatively little. While college attendance by low-income men is declining, the gap in earnings between college graduates and high school dropouts is growing: "in 1973, the average earnings of a 20- to 24-year-old

---

[2]The lower proportion of poor men in the population below the poverty level might be partially correlated with sex differential mortality. This is a complex issue that cannot be fully examined here, but some pertinent observations can be made. Occupationally-caused mortality and disability are disproportionately high among working-class men and women (13, 14). Death rates among working males aged 15 to 64 are considerably higher than among females of the same age. Death rates from accidents and violence are also exceedingly high for younger males, particularly for blacks (15). As mortality varies inversely with socioeconomic status, it is reasonable to suppose that death rates for occupational accidents, disease, and violence are likely to be higher for working-class men than the reported rates, which do not take class differences into account.

male high school dropout were three-quarters of the earnings of a college graduate. By 1984, this fraction dropped to two-thirds" (19, p. 11).

In the light of this information, it must be acknowledged that the "feminization of poverty" is only one important dimension of a broader process that also affects men, children, and the elderly in different degrees and for reasons that are fundamentally interrelated. *Just as an exclusive focus on "women" leads to a one-sided analysis that seems to give lesser importance to other dimensions of poverty, it would be equally misguided to focus on the poverty of "men" or of "young adult workers."* These are simple descriptive categories that describe the composition of the poor population, but cannot serve as the basis for developing a theoretical analysis of the meaning of present poverty trends. Poverty is, further-more, only a descriptive concept that does not help us understand the nature of the phenomena captured by these and many other statistics and statistical reports.

An important statement critical of the "feminization of poverty" perspective convincingly argues that it offers an inaccurate empirical and political analysis of the situation because it ignores, for all practical purposes, the class differences between women and the common basis for class, racial, and ethnic solidarity between men and women (4). Because the focus of analysis is the poverty of women as women, their class and race are not considered as crucial in determining their poverty as the fact that they are women. It is the case, however, that not all women are in danger of becoming poor; only those who are working class or members of racial and ethnic minorities are thus threatened. Many women are becoming richer and, of course, ruling-class women have never been at risk of becoming poor (4, p. 2). Poverty is not a phenomenon affecting primarily women; it is a structural component of the capitalist economy that affects people regardless of age and sex and falls disproportionately upon minorities. It is racism, not sexism, that determines who works in the worst sectors of the economy. Racism excludes large numbers of minority men from employment and the possibility of forming families, thus changing the conditions faced by working-class women of color in ways that the "feminization of poverty" perspective cannot adequately account for, as long as it views all women as an oppressed class (4, 8, 17, 20).

The critique of the "feminization of poverty" interpretation of current trends presented above does indeed identify important issues for further theoretical and empirical investigation. These insights, as well as those presented previously, have to be connected to their underlying capitalist structural determinants in production and reproduction, to understand more clearly the significance of these empirically observable phenomena. This process entails the examination of the relationship between capitalist structures, processes, and contradictions, which are not readily observable, and empirically observable changes in the size and com-position of the poverty population. *It is my contention that the feminization of poverty is an important dimension of a larger process: the immiseration of the working class brought about by the profound structural changes undergone by the U.S. economy during the 1980s.* It would be beyond the limits of this chapter to do justice to the complexity of these issues; the remarks that follow ought to be taken as tentative statements that will provide guidelines for future theoretical and empirical investigation.

BEYOND WOMEN AS A CATEGORY OF ANALYSIS: CLASS DIFFERENCES AMONG WOMEN AND THEIR IMPACT ON THE POVERTY OF PROPERTYLESS WOMEN

The feminization of poverty perspective focuses mainly on the poverty of women as women. This starting point introduces problems in understanding why some women become poor, while others do not. In this section, I will argue that gender-related factors are relevant correlates (not determinants) of poverty only among women whose class location already makes them vulnerable to poverty. If no class differences (in the Marxist sense) are taken into account in the analysis of the feminization of poverty, it does appear as if it were caused primarily by sexism. It is necessary, therefore, to examine the concept of social class and explore its implications for the life chances of women in different social classes.

From the standpoint of Marxist theory, class is a relation between people mediated by their relationship to the means of production. Ownership of means of production, even in a modest scale, gives political and economic control over others, and economic independence. Lack of means of production places workers—male and female—in a dependent situation, vulnerable to the decisions taken by those who, in controlling capital, control their access to the conditions indispensable for their physical and social daily and generational reproduction: employment. Changes in the occupational structure and quantitative and qualitative changes in the demand for labor divide the propertyless class in terms of occupation, income, and education, which are precisely the building blocks with which the average person and most social scientists construct socioeconomic status categories.[3] This is the material basis for the common-sense division of people into a variety of "classes," in a ranking that ranges from "the poor" and the "lower class" at the bottom, to the "upper class" at the top, with the "working class," "middle class," and "upper-middle class" in between. This is an empiricist understanding of social class that mystifies the sources of women's poverty; it is a simple ordering or gradational concept of class, that focuses only on the different power and resources individuals bring to the sexual and economic markets (21, 22).

---

[3]I am aware of the complexity of the issue of class and class structure within Marxist and neo-Marxist theory. Nevertheless, for the purposes of developing my argument, I consider it enough to point out the crucial differences between classes defined at the level of production relations and classes defined at the level of market relations. If relationship to the means of production is overlooked, it is possible to argue that most women, regardless of social class, could become poor; if the impact of propertylessness is taken into account, it becomes obvious that it is the working-class women who are at the greatest risk of becoming poor.

It is a central contention in my argument that, if the social class location of women (not their socioeconomic status) is taken into account, it becomes obvious that it is not sex but class that propels some women into poverty.

1. *Capitalist women and petty bourgeois women are not at risk of becoming poor.* Being a capitalist or a petty bourgeois women entails, theoretically, having capital of one's own and, therefore, a source of income independent from marriage or from paid employment. Women who own wealth are unlikely to become poor from gender-related factors, though inheritance practices and family accumulation strategies might deny them full control of their property.

Of the top wealth-holders with gross assets of $300,000 or more in 1982, 39.3 percent (1.85 percent of the total female population) were women. Between 1985 and 1986, the proportion of women aged 21 and over in the poverty population rose 1.5 percentage points (from 62.7 percent to 64.2 percent); in the same period of time, the number of women workers (full- and part-time) earning more than $35,000 increased 32 percent; those earning between $50,000 and $75,000 increased 34.5 percent, while the number of full-time women workers earning more than $75,000 increased 55.4 percent. As some women fell into poverty, others certainly became more affluent, although only 3.2 percent of all women workers—1,841,000—earned more than $35,000 a year, and only 0.3 percent of full-time working women earned more than $75,000 (9, p. 19; 15, p. 447). Women earning over $35,000 a year are certainly far less likely to fall into poverty if they become single mothers, divorce, or separate. On the other hand, if they lose their jobs, *lack an independent source of income,* and are unable to find a job with similar pay, they will experience downward social mobility and might even become poor. Patterns of income distribution and wealth ownership indicate the existence of extreme socioeconomic status differences (income-based) and class differences (based on wealth ownership) among women, which constitute the underlying material basis for the notion that virtually all women are vulnerable to poverty: that is so because most women (and most men as well) are propertyless.

2. *Propertyless women (and propertyless men) are always at risk of becoming poor.* As economist Ferdinand Lundberg trenchantly observed (23, p. 23):

> . . . anyone who does not own a substantial amount of income-producing property, or does not receive an earned income sufficiently large to make substantial regular savings or does not hold a well-paid securely tenured job is poor. . . . by this standard at least 70% of Americans are poor, although not all of these are by any means destitute or poverty stricken.

Propertyless women may attain, at the level of market relations, through family-transmitted advantages (e.g., real estate property, higher education) and/or marriage, a socioeconomic status that appears to place them above the working class. When it is argued that the feminization of poverty places all or most women at risk, including "middle-class" and "upper-middle-class" women, a very important observation is made that does not apply to women across social classes. The often made statement, "most women are just a man or a divorce away from poverty," reflects the conditions of existence of most *propertyless* women whom the capitalist organization of production and reproduction makes dependent on marriage and/or employment for economic survival.

Working-class women with substantial "human capital" of their own are still a tiny minority; they and women with stable jobs face a lower probability of poverty than women with less skills or with precarious working conditions. Data on women's income and employment indicate that the vast majority of propertyless women are working class, not only in terms of their location in the relations of production (i.e., they are propertyless and depend on a wage or salary for the economic survival of themselves and their families) but also at the level of socioeconomic stratification (i.e., the vast majority of women work in low-paid, low-status, blue- or white-collar jobs). Of the 39,214,000 women who worked full time in 1986, 72.3 percent earned less than $20,000; 32.3 percent earned less than $10,000 (9, p. 19). On the other hand, there are more men than women in "middle-class" and "upper-middle-class" occupations and in the better paid skilled blue-collar jobs. Consequently, most women experience some form of "upward mobility" through marriage and, if they lack skills or resources of their own, are likely to return to their previous place in the socioeconomic structure in case of separation, divorce, or widowhood.

Most of the "social mobility" that propertyless men and women experience in their life time is not social class mobility in the Marxist sense (e.g., changing from being propertyless to becoming petty bourgeois, small or big capitalist, etc.) but occupational mobility. It is important to realize that men and women can experience mobility at the market level while remaining, at the same time and whatever their socioeconomic status may be, located in the working class or propertyless class. Intraclass differences (i.e., within the propertyless class) in the socioeconomic status and individual resources men and women bring to the market is at the core of women's greater vulnerability to poverty and the transformation of marriage into the major source of economic survival for vast numbers of women.[4]

The feminization of poverty is a market-level structural effect of intra-class differences in male and female socioeconomic status and mobility; it is fundamentally a class issue although it is experienced and analyzed as an effect of sex and race discrimination. Sexism and racism unquestionably intensify the effects of economic changes upon the more impoverished layers of the working class (4, 17). Nevertheless, the ultimate determinant of individuals' relative vulnerability to poverty is their class location: "if sexism [and, I add, racism] were eliminated,

---

[4]Intraclass differences in the market resources of propertyless men and women reflect, in turn, differential patterns in the intergenerational transmission of socioeconomic status, which, in turn, are determined by the articulation of production and reproduction within the propertyless class, a topic that cannot be examined here.

there would still be poor women (and poor non-whites). The only difference is that women (and non-whites) would stand the same chance as men (and whites) of being poor" (17, p. 11).

THE IMMISERATION OF THE WORKING CLASS

Capital is indifferent to the reproduction of the working class as a whole; the extent to which workers can have access to the means necessary for their own reproduction and that of the future generation of workers is very much constrained by the demand for different kinds of labor power. The demand for certain kinds of skilled labor power may lead not only to good wages and salaries but also to special subsidies such as public and private funding for the development of special training and educational programs and, sometimes, the establishment of day care facilities at the place of work. In general, however, the social and physical reproduction of the working class on a daily and generational level is left to the ingenuity of the workers themselves. Those whose skills are no longer needed or whose birth in the reserve army of labor deprived them of the opportunity of developing any skills are left behind in poverty.

In the United States, the working class has suffered enormous setbacks in the last 15 years, reflected in high rates of unemployment, an overall decline in real wages, the demise of the "family wage" for most workers, and qualitative changes in the economy and the organization of work that have significantly reduced the number of full-time, skilled, and relatively well-paid blue-collar male jobs that constituted the backbone of the U.S. "middle class." The "new poor" include not only working-class women but a substantial number of working-class men and their families as well. According to a 1982 survey of the U.S. Conference of Mayors, the "new poor" were created by economic decline, high unemployment, and cuts in federal programs: "[they are] people who are losing their jobs, exhausting their financial resources, exhausting their unemployment benefits and losing their hopes" (24, p. 129). According to the Bureau of Labor Statistics (25, pp. 24–25):

> . . . only 65% of the 3.8 million experienced workers aged 25 to 54 laid off between 1979 and 1983 were employed in January of 1984, some 25% were still unemployed, and 10% had dropped out of the labor force altogether. They averaged 23 weeks of unemployment and only half of them earned as much after their reemployment as they had earned before.

In such times of economic crisis, the illusory nature of "middle-class" and "upper-middle-class" statuses is clearly revealed when social class reasserts itself through the powerlessness and untold suffering heaped upon men, women, and children by unemployment, underemployment, and cuts in social services.[5]

---

[5]See Richard Parker (26) for an excellent discussion of the distorted way in which social class is commonly perceived by social scientists and the general public.

A number of indicators suggest that recent changes in the U.S. economy have had a more negative impact on the employment situation of male workers than on that of female workers: "since 1982, the gain in real earnings for women has been higher than for men. Between 1982 and 1986 women's median earnings rose by 9.8 percent. This increase compares with a 5.5 percent increase in men's earnings" (9, p. 2). According to another study (27, emphasis added):

> [M]ore than half of the 8 million net new jobs created between 1979 and 1984 in the U.S. paid less than $7,000 a year while the number of jobs paying $28,000 or more actually fell . . . *the biggest losers in the changing job market have been white men while the biggest winners have been white women* . . . since 1979, nearly 97 percent of net employment gains among white men have been in the low wage stratum (incomes below $7,012) . . . during the same period, white men have experienced a net loss of 1 million jobs paying $28,000 or more in 1984 dollars. Among white women, 42 percent of the 5 million net job gains fell into the median income range (incomes between $7,012 and $28,048) and 13.7 percent into the $28,000 or above category.

The significance of this information becomes clearer when one takes into account the fact that the official poverty line for an average family of four was $10,178 in 1983 (6, p. 6) and $11,000 in 1985; this means that more than half of the jobs created between 1979 and 1983 did not cover even the minimum costs of the physical reproduction of workers unless those earning such a low wage had a working spouse.

The sex ratio of the population of full-time workers (24,099,000) who in 1986 earned less than $10,000 (below the 1986 poverty threshold for a family of four, $11,203) was 0.90. The sex ratio of those earning less than $20,000 in 1986 (52.2 percent of full-time workers) was 0.95 (9, p. 19). In 1986, among full-time male workers, 45.5 percent earned less than $20,000 and 23.2 percent earned between $20,000 and $29,999 (comparable percentages for full-time women workers are 72.3 and 19.3 percent) (9, p. 19). While men earn more than women and a larger proportion of full-time male workers earn more than $30,000 a year, the information provided above indicates that the vast majority of working men (almost 70 percent) earn rather modest incomes.

The Bureau of Labor Statistics predicts the largest job growth between 1984 and 1985 for jobs mainly at the top (e.g., lawyers, physicians, and surgeons) and bottom of the occupational hierarchy (e.g., orderlies, nursing aides, janitors and cleaners, waiters and waitresses, etc.), with relatively few in the middle (e.g., blue-collar supervisors, registered nurses, computer programmers) (15, p. 394); as noted elsewhere (19, p. 10):

> [S]ince 1973 . . . one of the fastest growing occupations for men has been sales, increasing by 114 percent through 1986 . . . between 1973 and 1986, the number of blue collar workers . . . increased by only 4.4 percent. In contrast, men's employment in service occupations—for example, security guards, orderlies, waiters, day care workers, and janitors—increased by 36.7 percent.

Hence, the notion that the poverty of men can be easily remedied with a job while women are poor even if they work full time (3, p. 9) is not entirely accurate. Male poverty increased at the same time that the "feminization of poverty" was taking place. In the light of these trends, it is obvious that full employment policies not only would be insufficient to reduce the poverty of women (5, p. 12) but would not necessarily keep most men out of poverty or near-poverty conditions.

CONCLUSION

The data discussed earlier in this chapter show that the sex ratio of the poverty population has changed little since 1966; its age composition, however, did change. Today, the majority of the poor are children under 18 and adults under 44 (Table 1). While in absolute numbers, there are more poor women than poor men, the dramatic increase in poverty between 1978 and 1983 was felt more heavily among men than among women. Since 1983, the modest decline in poverty has also been more rapid among men than among women.

Theoretically, these trends are empirical indicators of the immiseration of the working class. The essence of this argument is that people do not fall into poverty because of their age, sex, or racial/ethnic characteristics, but because of their social class. Age, sex, and ethnic/racial groups are not socially homogeneous; they are divided in social classes that, in turn, are stratified on the basis of income, education, and occupation. The fact that poverty falls disproportionately upon the young, women, and minorities does not invalidate the analysis; those who become poor share a common relationship to the means of production that cuts across age, sex, and racial/ethnic differences.

Sexism and racism are important in determining who gets the worst jobs or is most likely to be affected by unemployment (4). But sexism and racism are not unchanging entities standing on an independent material base; they are shifting structural effects of capitalist processes of labor allocation designed to increase profit margins and enhance economic and political control over the working class. The general determining dynamics of poverty are, from this standpoint, located in general capitalist processes that racialize, ethnicize, and sexualize the work force on national and world-system levels (processes whose ideological, political, and legal effects, in turn, perpetuate them through time, endowing them with a deceptive universality and antiquity) (28, 29). The specific determinants of recent poverty trends, on the other hand, are to be found in the interplay between the historical effects of sexism and racism and recent political and economic changes that have drastically altered the economic structure in the United States. Some sectors of the capitalist class, to become competitive at the international level, are lowering the average price of labor; cuts in wages, union busting, right-to-work laws, "give backs," cuts in social services, and recent changes in immigration laws that allow the legalization of undocumented workers under certain conditions are all efforts aimed at cheapening the overall costs of labor (7, 18).

Lacking access to the material conditions for their physical and social reproduction on a daily and generational level, over 32 million members of the working class below the poverty level barely survive under the restrictive conditions imposed by the welfare state. Altogether, over 43 million people live below 125 percent of the poverty level; this includes 9.4 million families (45.8 percent headed by women) and 15.5 million children under 18 (51.1 percent of which live in families headed by women) (9, p. 28). Nutrition levels and health among the poor have deteriorated; between 1982 and 1985, the food-stamp program was cut by $7 billion and child-nutrition programs by $5 billion. In spite of the large number of people below the poverty level, only 19 million receive food stamps: 12 million children and 8 million adults suffer from hunger (30).

Lack of access to the basic material conditions necessary for physical and social reproduction on a daily and generational basis threatens the intergenerational reproduction of the working class among all races, particularly among racial and ethnic minorities. The immiseration of the working class culminates in the breakdown of its intergenerational reproduction; poor parents, particularly poor single mothers, are placed under conditions that deprive them of their ability to reproduce people with marketable skills. This situation may be "functional" for the economy, insofar as the demand for skilled and educated workers is not likely to rise dramatically during the near future. From the standpoint of the working class and minorities in particular, this is a very serious situation that civil rights, better educational opportunities, and measures designed to help women combine work and parenting, *in themselves*, cannot possibly solve. Wilson (31, 32) wrote of the "declining significance of race" and the need to recognize the primarily economic and class-based determinants of the poverty and deprivation of most black Americans; by the same token, *the recent increase in male and female poverty should alert us to the declining significance of sex as a cause of women's poverty*. The feminization of poverty reflects the fact that women are more than half of the U.S. propertyless class and that the standard of living of this class has noticeably declined in the last 10 years (for a thoughtful statement about the need to overcome the limits of an exclusive focus on sex, to the detriment of class and race as sources of women's oppression, see 33).

The media, social scientists, politicians, and activists give—depending on their specific concerns, political agendas, and theoretical commitments—greater importance to different sectors of the poor: the notoriety of the "feminization of poverty," the poverty of minorities, the elderly, or children contrasts with the relative silence about the erosion in the standard of living and the growing poverty of the working class. It is important to uncover the correlates of poverty pertinent to each of these sectors, but to the extent that the analysis stops there, it can lead to the development of theoretically flawed explanations and policies that pit the interests of women against the interests of men, the young versus the old, whites versus nonwhites. Stress upon the poverty of those who are disproportionately poor produces a misleading perception of poverty as something that affects mainly women, the elderly, ethnic/racial minorities, and welfare recipients, and something that could, theoretically, be effectively dealt with by measures addressing the needs of women workers, civil rights enforcement, and welfare reforms. In fact, most of the poor are white (69 percent in 1986); most of the poor between the ages of 22 and 64 are working or looking for work, and only 35 percent of poor families receive welfare benefits (6, p. 4); only 10.5 percent of the elderly aged 65 and over are poor, and 55 percent of the poor who live in families do not live in families headed by women (11, pp. 22–24). Furthermore, of the 2,530,000 families between poverty level and 125 percent of the poverty level, only 27.2 percent are headed by women (10, pp. 25–26).

To speak of the immiseration of the working class does not entail the adoption of a mindless economic reductionism nor the callous denial of the plight of minorities, women, children, and the elderly. It simply entails the recognition of the fact that those sectors of the poor population, including men, do not live as isolated individuals but are linked to each other through common relations of production and reproduction. The fate of each sector is tied to the fate of the others because they are all part of the same social class, just as the fate of individuals is tied to the fate of those with whom they share kinship or emotional and social bonds. People are "an ensemble of social relations" (34, p. 198) and cannot be meaningfully understood in isolation from those relations that give them their historically specific place in the world they live in. It is not by reducing people to age, sex, racial, or ethnic categories that poverty and its determinants can be best understood; people are poor or become poor because they are subject to common socioeconomic and political processes that deprive them of access to their material conditions of existence, tear families apart, or make family formation impossible for vast numbers of working-class men and women, particularly those who are also members of racial and ethnic minorities. Placed in its historical context, the feminization of poverty is a real, important, albeit partial dimension of a vast process of social transformation resulting in a drastic decline in the overall level of wages and standard of living of the U.S. working class; a significant increase in the size of the reserve army of labor and its pauperized sector; the intensification in the proletarianization of women;[6] and the undermining of the material conditions necessary for the maintenance of "middle-class" and even "upper-middle-class" illusions, and for the intergenerational physical and social reproduction of

---

[6]This process is not equivalent to the "feminization of the proletariat" (5, p. 12). For demographic reasons (high male mortality), women have always been more than half of the proletariat, whether they were aware of it or not. I refer here to the erosion of "middle-class" and "upper-middle-class" statuses among growing numbers of propertyless women. It is also true that working women are concentrated in the more poorly paid jobs and the demand for female (and male) cheap labor is increasing. These trends can be best understood not in demographic terms (giving emphasis to the sex or age composition of the proletariat), but as effects of current processes of wealth concentration and class proletarianization.

the lower strata of the working class (particularly the racialized, ethnicized, and feminized sectors).

REFERENCES

1. Rodgers, H. T., Jr. *Poor Women, Poor Families.* M. E. Sharpe, New York, 1986.
2. Sidel, R. *Women and Children Last—The Plight of Poor Women in Affluent America.* Viking, New York, 1986.
3. Stallard, K., et al. *Poverty in the American Dream: Women and Children First.* South End Press, Boston, 1983.
4. Alliance Against Women's Oppression. *Poverty: Not for Women Only—A Critique of the Feminization of Poverty.* AAWO Discussion Paper No. 3, September 1983.
5. Ehrenreich, B. Making poverty a woman's issue. *Dollars and Sense,* Special Issue on Women and Work, 1987.
6. O'Hare, W. P. Poverty in America: Trends and new patterns. *Population Bulletin,* Vol. 40, No. 3. Population Reference Bureau, Washington, D.C., 1985.
7. Piven, F., and Cloward, R. A. *The New Class War.* Pantheon, New York, 1985.
8. Center for the Study of Social Policy. The flip side of black families headed by women: The economic status of black men. In *The Black Family,* edited by R. Staples, pp. 232–238. Wadsworth, Belmont, 1985.
9. Bureau of the Census. *Current Population Reports,* Series P-60, No. 157. Money, Income, and Poverty Status of Families and Persons in the United States: 1986. U.S. Government Printing Office, Washington, D.C., 1986.
10. Bureau of the Census. *Current Population Reports,* Series P-60, No. 152. Characteristics of the Population Below the Poverty Level: 1984. U.S. Government Printing Office, Washington, D.C., 1986.
11. Bureau of the Census. *Current Population Reports,* Series P-60, No. 154. Money, Income, and Poverty Status of Families and Persons in the United States: 1985. U.S. Government Printing Office, Washington, D.C., 1986.
12. Bureau of the Census. *Current Population Reports,* Series P-60, No. 147. Money, Income, and Poverty Status of Families and Persons in the United States: 1984, p. 41. U.S. Government Printing Office, Washington, D.C., 1985.
13. Berman, D. M. *Death on the Job: Occupational Health and Safety Struggles in the United States.* Monthly Review Press, New York, 1978.
14. Chavkin, W. (ed.). *Double Exposure: Women's Health Hazards on the Job and at Home.* Monthly Review Press, New York, 1984.
15. Bureau of the Census. *Statistical Abstracts of the United States: 1987.* U.S. Government Printing Office, Washington, D.C., 1986.
16. Smith, J. All crises are not the same: Households in the U.S. during two crises. In *Work Without Wages: Comparative Studies of Housework and Petty Commodity Production,* edited by J. Collins and M. E. Gimenez, p. 3. SUNY University Press, New York, 1988.
17. Sparr, P. Re-evaluating feminist economics: Feminization of poverty ignores key issues. *Dollars and Sense,* Special Issue on Women and Work, 1987.
18. Harrington, M. *The New American Poverty,* pp. 46–48. Penguin, New York, 1984.
19. Even young men feel the pinch. *Dollars and Sense* 131: 10–11, 1987.
20. Staples, R. Beyond the black family: The trend toward singlehood. In *The Black Family,* edited by R. Staples, pp. 99–105. Wadsworth, Belmont, 1985.
21. Ossowski, S. *Class Structure in the Social Consciousness.* The Free Press, New York, 1963.

22. Weber, M. Determination of class situation by market situation. In *Class, Power, and Conflict*, edited by A. Giddens and D. Held, pp. 60–61. University of California Press, Berkeley, 1982.
23. Lundberg, F. *The Rich and the Super-Rich.* Bantam, New York, 1969.
24. Problems of the unemployed. In *Employment in America*, pp. 129–155. *Congressional Quarterly*, Washington, D.C., 1983.
25. Rose, S. J. *The American Profile Poster.* Pantheon, New York, 1986.
26. Parker, R. *The Myth of the Middle Class.* Liveright, New York, 1972.
27. Bluestone, B., and Harrison, B. Most jobs in the U.S. low paying. *Daily Camera*, December 10, 1986.
28. Wallerstein, I. *Historical Capitalism.* Verso, London, 1983.
29. Wallerstein, I. The Construction of Peoplehood: Racism, Nationalism, Ethnicity. Mimeographed paper, Fernand Braudel Center for the Study of Economies, Historical Systems, and Civilization, SUNY-Binghamton, New York, 1985.
30. Brown, J. L. Hunger in the U.S. *Sci Am.* 256(2): 37–41, 1987.
31. Wilson, W. J. *The Declining Significance of Race.* University of Chicago Press, Chicago, 1978.
32. Wilson, W. J. The black community in the 1980s: Questions of race, class, and public policy. In *From Different Shores: Perspectives on Race and Ethnicity in America*, edited by R. Takaki, pp. 233–240. Oxford University Press, New York, 1987.
33. Thorton Dill, B. Race, class, and gender: Prospects for an all-inclusive sisterhood. In *From Different Shores: Perspectives on Race and Ethnicity in America*, edited by R. Takaki, pp. 204–213. Oxford University Press, New York, 1987.
34. Marx, K., and Engels, F. *The German Ideology.* International Publishers, New York, 1969.

CHAPTER 16

Women and Children at Risk: A Feminist Perspective on Child Abuse

Evan Stark and Anne H. Flitcraft

In this chapter we examine the link between woman battering and child abuse from a feminist perspective. Viewing child abuse through the prism of woman battering reveals that both problems originate in conflicts over gender identity and male authority. Male authority is directly expressed in violent control over women and children. But just as important is the construction of clinical knowledge that distorts how women are perceived and subordinates their needs.

While a feminist approach to woman battering has gained some currency in mainstream thinking, feminists have had comparatively little impact on how child abuse is understood or managed. In part, this is because the view is widely shared that child abuse results from some combination of maternal pathology/inadequacy and "environmental stress." Where child abuse occurs against a background of "family violence," the presumption is that the violence is transmitted intergenerationally. A man who was beaten as a child now beats his wife. Then, unable to cope, she uses the child as scapegoat. Politics—including the politics of family life—play no role in this analysis.

In marked contrast to this emphasis, Gertrude Williams (1) suggests that sexism and pronatalism have taught these women that motherhood is the only fulfilling activity. Breines and Gordon (2) note a number of other gender-related issues, including the fact that women are primary parents, the lack of well-paid work alternatives to mothering, and the inadequacy of sex education (as well as contraceptive methods) leading to a large number of unwanted pregnancies.

Originally published in the *International Journal of Health Services* 18(1): 97–118, 1988.

Neither the conventional wisdom nor the nascent feminist analysis resolves these key questions:

1. Are men or women primarily responsible for child abuse?
2. What is the typical context for child abuse? Part of the answer to this question involves the link to battering and part lies in establishing whether the behavior of abusing parent, regardless of gender, reflects some combination of pathology and stress (the dominant view) or a political struggle for control.
3. How do child protective services respond to battered women whose children are abused? The issue here is how women are "known" in clinical settings as well as how they are treated.
4. How do clinical interventions affect the dynamics in abusive relationships?
5. How can the current approach be improved?

The data examined in the first part of this chapter bear on the first three questions. We then sketch a theoretical framework that may account for the evidence and explain the effects of current interventions, and conclude with an examination of current and proposed policy in child abuse.

THE ARGUMENT

Interestingly, even work that considers gender accepts the claim that child abuse is primarily a female crime. To the contrary, we argue, surveys and hospital and medical examiners' records indicate that men may be the typical child abusers, particularly when serious injury is involved (3–6). Similarly unfounded is the belief that battered mothers or mothers of abused children are "sick." In fact, while a significant minority have multi-problem backgrounds, the typical context for child abuse is a battering relationship for which the woman bears little responsibility. Widespread beliefs that women are responsible for child abuse and that child abuse results from environmental stress or family pathology justify interventions—such as therapy for mothers—that exacerbate the gender inequities from which battering and child abuse stem in the first place. Holding women responsible for child abuse and targeting their inadequacies as parents as the cause can deepen a woman's resentment toward her child and constrain her to behave in gender-stereotyped ways that seriously increase her risk in a battering relationship.

The problem goes beyond faulty assumptions and misguided policies and treatment strategies. In fact, law, social service practice, and psychological theory hold women "responsible" for child abuse even when a male assailant is clearly identified and is also battering the mother. This singular emphasis on women and their traditional roles converges with battering in the home. One result is that women experience gender identity as a vehicle for male domination, what we term "patriarchal mothering," and their consequent resentment can often become violent.

CHILD ABUSE: GENDER POLITICS OR FEMALE PATHOLOGY?

Mothers or Fathers?

A classic vignette of the physically abused child has been that of an under-nourished infant with multiple musculoskeletal trauma inflicted at different times by his or her depressed mother. Child abuse has been variously traced to maternal violence or neglect in the family of origin (7), current psychological dynamics such as role reversal (8), a lack of parenting skills (9), poverty or other environmental deprivations (6), the absence of needed institutional supports (10), or some combination of provocation, psychological predisposition, and environmental "trigger" events (11). But whether female psychology or a malfunctioning family system is emphasized, whether "destructive, disturbed mothers" are perceived or merely "sad, deprived, needy human beings," the fact that abuse results from a breakdown in appropriate mother-child bonding is taken as self-evident. The normative character of female domesticity and mothering is an unquestioned presumption in child psychology, pediatric medicine, and children's services. Thus the social consequences of adopting these images in problem solving remain unexamined.

But are most child abusers women? Representative sample surveys indicate that fathers may be as likely as or more likely than mothers to abuse children. Gil (6) estimates that 40 percent of the children in a national survey were abused by fathers, and an American Humane Society survey concluded that males were the assailants in 55 percent of reported cases of child abuse (3). Smaller surveys have produced somewhat different results, estimates of abuse by fathers running as low as 25 percent (12). Even this is remarkable given the division of child-care responsibilities and the proportion of children raised by single women.

While the percentage of abusing males is disputed, there is little doubt that, if a man is present, he is many times more likely to abuse the child than is the mother. For example, national survey data indicate that men were responsible for two-thirds of reported incidents in which men were present (6), probably an under-estimate of male responsibility. Surveys measure single acts without taking their consequences into account and cannot distinguish documented from alleged abuse or identify abuse resulting in severe injury or death. Of equal importance, punitive welfare regulations and fear of violence lead many women to conceal relationships with men.

A recent study of hospital and medical examiners' records indicates that men, not women, are primarily responsible for serious child abuse. In comparing the records of child abuse cases for two time periods, 1971–73 and 1981–83, Bergman, Larsen and Mueller (4) report that while the incidence of hospitalized cases has not changed, the proportion of severe injuries has increased dramatically. Also increasing is the proportion of known male perpetrators reported, rising from 38 percent to 49 percent for all cases, and from 30 percent to 64 percent for the severe cases. Meanwhile, for all cases the proportion of female perpetrators has decreased from 32 percent to 20 percent, and for severe cases from 20 percent to 6 percent. Fully 80 percent of the fatal cases in the most recent group are attributed to men, and 20 percent are "unknown." None are attributed to women. Finally, if a male perpetrator is identified, there is a 70 percent chance that the child's injury is severe, up from 25 percent a decade earlier. The authors (4) wisely suggest that the apparent increase in severe abuse by men—and a corresponding decline in cases categorized as "unknown"—reflects a growing willingness to report "male friends," not an actual shift in violence.

Battering and Male Control

Earlier work shows that child abuse occurs disproportionately in battering relationships, although it may be a relatively rare event overall (13–16). But how central is battering in child abuse? Is it merely one of many background factors? Or does its frequency as an etiological factor point to a common cause? And, in the latter case, is this cause inherited violence or current deficits? Or is female independence the root issue, as feminist theory suggests, whether it is the batterer or the abused woman who assaults the child?

Evidence is strong that male control over women, not female pathology, environmental "stress," or family history, leads to battering (17). Battered women experience a disproportionate risk of mental illness, alcoholism, and other problems only *after* the onset of abuse and frustrated help-seeking (16, 18), indicating that violence breeds psychopathology, not the reverse. Differences in battering by social class, race, and employment status are small (17). By contrast, "fights" typically center on gender issues (such as sex, housework, child care, and women's right to money and wage work) (19); rates of male violence against women who are single, separated, or divorced are actually higher than against married women (17); and the nature and pattern of assaultive injury strongly suggest the violence is directed at a woman's gender identity (including her sexual identity) and is neither impulsive nor random (13, 18, 20).

Have batterers "learned" their behavior from their own abuse as children? Although this belief is widely shared, its empirical support comes mainly from second-hand or anecdotal reports, psychiatric studies of unrepresentative or deviant populations (such as presidential assassins), and vague notions of childhood abuse. Thus a leading psychiatric authority on intergenerational transmission defines "abuse" and "neglect" as a "lack of empathetic mothering" (7) or "a variety of less than ideal responses of the caretaker (usually the mother) to the infant," which leads to "a lack of confidence or trust" in the child as an adult (21). The single random survey tracing abuse in the family-of-origin to current male violence finds "a clear trend for violence in childhood to produce violence in adult life" (22). But the actual data show the reverse. While boys experiencing violence as children are disproportionately violent as adults, 90 percent of all children from violent homes and even 80 percent from homes described as "most violent" do not abuse their wives. Conversely, a current batterer is more than twice as likely to have had a "nonviolent" than a violent childhood (7, p. 3) and seven times more likely to have had a nonviolent than a "most violent" childhood. Reviewing studies in this genre, Kaufman and Zigler (23) conclude that no more than 30 percent of those who experienced or witnessed violence as children are currently abusive, an estimate we believe is too high.

Medicine and Battering

Violence is only one dimension of the male control that entraps women in battering relationships. The other dimension is the response when abused women seek help. Although woman abuse is second only to male-male assault as a source of serious injury to adults (and is a major cause of death among younger black females), clinicians rarely identify the problem, minimize its significance, inappropriately medicate and label abused women, provide them with perfunctory or punitive care, refer them for secondary psychosocial problems but not for protection from violence, and emphasize family maintenance and compliance with traditional role expectations rather than personal safety (13–16, 24). Battering—the ongoing entrapment of women—is broken down into its medical symptoms (e.g., injuries, complaints, and psychosocial reactions to stress) and then the symptoms are reinterpreted so that the violence appears to result from rather than cause a woman's multiple problems. Within the health care system, women are increasingly isolated by inappropriate medication (such as tranquilizers), labels, psychiatric maintenance, and punitive interventions. And this process supports their being locked ever more tightly into relationships in which ongoing abuse is virtually inevitable.

In effect, clinical interventions manage the efforts of battered women to resist and escape domination, not domination itself. The political dimensions of battering are concealed behind a picture of "chaotic" families that need help "coping." "Restored functioning" is typically equated with getting the woman to better manage family conflict, usually by suppressing her own need for autonomy and development and by resuming traditional domestic responsibilities. As battering progresses through a range of increasingly severe psychosocial problems, abused women may come to know themselves as they are known. Thus, like their clinicians and their assailants, battered women in psychiatric facilities deny their problem, minimize its importance, or blame themselves (25).

Child Abuse: Responsible Mothers and Invisible Men

Can child abuse be understood as an extension of this entrapment process, as a problem rooted in the politics of gender inequality, occasioned by male violence and aggravated by the institutional response?

In contrast to battering, where sexist interpretations and practices confront a grassroots political movement, in the child abuse field, stereotypic and patronizing imagery of women goes unchallenged. One result is that men are invisible. Another is that "mothers" are held responsible for child abuse, even when the mother and child are being battered by an identifiable man.

Despite the evidence that men are a significant subset of abusive parents, there are few articles in the child abuse literature specifically on men. In a recent literature review, for instance, Martin (26) could identify only two individual case reports about men. Even in the minority of studies that consider both parents, women are the only source of direct information, no attempt is made to control for gender or to differentiate parental behavior and/or motivation by sex, and "abusing parent" is often a euphemism for mother.

Men are equally invisible in programs for abusing parents. Starting with images of appropriate gender behavior such as mother-child bonding, interventions proceed as if noncompliance with these norms reflects a character deficit that puts mother and child at risk. Varying combinations of parent education, counseling, peer pressure, and sanctions are used to instill appropriate maternal behavior, presumably so that the mother will adequately care for and protect the developing child.

Broad moral conceptions of women's "responsibility" for violence are incorporated in state regulations that define the mother's battering as a failure of her protective function. In New York State, for instance, an abusing parent includes one who "allows to be created a substantial risk of physical injury to the child," and this is frequently interpreted to mean allowing a child to witness violence against the mother. In Connecticut as well as many other states, women are interviewed by child protective services in determining foster placements, but not men, a practice undoubtedly linked to high rates of child abuse in foster homes.

Two decades of experience and thousands of monographs and programs offer no convincing evidence that child abuse has been reduced, let alone prevented, by this broad approach to mothering. But if child abuse is primarily a male crime and is rooted in subordinating women in gender-stereotyped roles, then the current emphasis on mothering may actually aggravate the problem it is designed to solve.

If violence is evoked by struggles around traditional sex roles, the practical result of reenforcing these roles may be to restrict a woman's perceived options, increase her vulnerability to violence, decrease her capacity to protect her children from violence, exacerbate her own frustration and anger, and increase the probability that she will be destructive to self and others, including her children. This is what feminist theory leads us to expect. In this case, the best way to prevent child abuse is to protect women's physical integrity and support their empowerment. At a minimum, this implies close collaboration between child protective services and community-based shelters and a shift in child protection away from parenting education, therapy, and the removal of children. The question of whether the child-protection establishment would be receptive to this approach is examined later ("Conclusions").

BATTERING AND CHILD ABUSE: A STUDY

The disproportionate association of child abuse with battering is well established. Our earlier work (14, 17) indicates that battered women in a medical population are six times more likely than nonbattered women to have a report of child abuse (or "fear of child abuse") listed on their medical records (6 percent versus 1 percent). In their national survey of domestic violence, meanwhile, Straus and associates (22) found that abused women were 150 percent more likely to use severe violence with their children than were nonabused women. And after questioning women in a British shelter, Gayford (27) reported that 54 percent of abusive husbands and 37 percent of abused wives had also abused their children. From the vantage of its effect on children, exposure to parental violence may itself be counted as a form of "abuse."[1] Hilberman and Munson (13) report that one-third of 209 children exposed to marital violence exhibited somatic, psychological, and behavioral dysfunctions. Meanwhile, in his local medical practice, Levine (29) found that difficulty coping with children was a common presentation of woman battering. He suggests that the child's reaction depends on how violence is experienced. If the batterer's relation to the children is nonviolent, their response is limited to psychiatric problems. But in instances where children attempt to intervene and are, in turn, used as scapegoats and beaten by the batterer, they become more aggressive in their other relations.

It is possible that although children are at risk for abuse in battering relationships, battering is a relatively minor etiological factor in child abuse. This study identifies the importance of battering in the etiology of child abuse, examines whether the identity of the assailant and the parent held responsible are the same, assesses the role of disposition, and asks whether battered mothers have a distinctive psychiatric profile.

Study Population

At Yale-New Haven Hospital, the medical records of children suspected of being abused or neglected are specially marked or "darted" and the children are referred for investigation and disposition to a special hospital "Dart Committee."

---

[1] But Rosenbaum and O'Leary (28) found no differences for male children among violent, discordant, and satisfactorily married couples on the Behavior Problem Checklist. Interestingly, while they found no more behavioral problems in abused children than in those who had not been abused, 70 percent of the children whose mothers had been victims of spouse abuse were above the mean for a normative sample, suggesting that the psychological consequences of spouse abuse may be more serious for children than those of child abuse.

The study population includes the mothers of all children referred to the hospital Dart Committee for suspicion of abuse and/or neglect between July 1977 and June 1978, 116 mothers in all. Dart Committee reports on children were matched to the medical records of their mothers, and the mothers were then classified as battered or nonbattered based on their adult trauma history and the risk classification described below. The analysis of medical records was supplemented by data from family background notes in Dart Committee reports.

Methodology

The trauma screen employed in the study was designed to identify abuse in a population that had not been explicitly identified as battered and to generate sufficiently large groups of abused and nonabused women to permit statistical analysis and comparison. Each adult hospital visit prompted by trauma after the age of 16 was reviewed, and women were assigned to a "battering risk group" according to the following criteria:

- *Positive*: At least one episode in the woman's trauma history was attributed to assault by a male family member or male intimate.
- *Probable*: At least one episode in the trauma history was an assault (kicked, beaten, stabbed, etc.) but no personal etiology was indicated. (Note that muggings and anonymous assaults were *not* included in category.)
- *Suggestive*: At least one episode in the trauma history was *not* well explained by the recorded alleged etiology.
- *Negative*: All episodes in the trauma history were well explained by the recorded injury, including those sustained in muggings, anonymous assaults, etc.

Data were gathered on (*a*) the significance of battering in families experiencing child abuse, (*b*) the identity of perpetrators, (*c*) whether mothers who are battered come disproportionately from problem homes (as some research suggests), and (*d*) whether current dispositions respond appropriately to the family situation.

Findings

Prevalence and frequency of battering. Of the 116 women, 52 (45 percent) had a trauma history that indicated battering and another 6 (5 percent) had a history of "marital conflict," though it was impossible to tell from their trauma history or other medical information whether they had been abused. Twenty-nine women (25 percent) presented "positive" episodes, an additional 18 (16 percent) were "probables," and five (4 percent) were "suggestive." Fifty-eight women (50 percent) had no documented trauma history indicating abuse and no record of "marital conflict." This frequency of at-risk women (45 percent) is 2.4 times greater than the frequency of battering among women presenting injuries to the surgical service (19 percent) and twice as great as the frequency of battering in the prenatal clinic (21 percent), making this the highest at-risk population yet identified. This information is summarized in Table 1.

The 52 abused women presented a total of 217 injury episodes during their adult histories, for a mean of 4.2 trauma presentations per woman. Women in the positive group averaged 4.9 episodes each, while those in the probable and suggestive groups averaged 3.4 and 2.6 episodes. By contrast, women in the negative group averaged only 1.1 injury episodes, as one would expect in a "normal" population. Interestingly, the 1.8 trauma episodes averaged by the six mothers with a history of "marital conflict" fell somewhere between the suggestive and negative groups (Table 1). Conceivably this group constitutes a battering risk category outside the purview of an identification method based solely on the trauma history. At any rate, for battered mothers as for battered women generally, abusive assault is an ongoing process, not an isolated incident.

Family History

A frequent claim is that the link between battering and child abuse reflects a multiproblem family history that includes violence or other serious problems. This was explored by drawing information on alcoholism, violence, "chaos" or "disorganization," suicide attempts, and incest, common indicators of a high-risk family history, from social services notes in the medical record and from Dart

Table 1

Number of trauma episodes among battered and nonbattered mothers of abused children

Mother's battering risk group[a]	N	No. of episodes in risk group	Mean no. of trauma episodes per woman
Positive	29	143	4.9
Probable	18	61	3.4
Suggestive	5	13	2.6
Total at-risk	52	217	4.2
Marital conflict	6	11	1.8
Negative	58	64	1.1

[a]See text for details of risk groups.

Committee files. To strengthen the conservative bias, women with a history of "marital conflict" were included with "negatives."

As shown in Table 2, a significant subpopulation of these 116 mothers came from high-risk families of origin. It is evident, however, that abused mothers do not typically come from multi-problem backgrounds, are far less likely to come from a background that includes incest and/or alcoholism, and, perhaps most important, are no more likely to have a family background that includes violence. In sum, battered mothers of abused children cannot be distinguished by a background of family disorganization and, if anything, are less likely than nonbattered mothers in this group to have such a background.

Reason for "Dart"

Most children are "darted" because a clinician believes that they are "at risk" of abuse, neglected, or injured under "suspicious circumstances," or because the mother needs "support" to help her cope. As indicated in Table 3, only a minority are darted because of documented physical abuse. However, children whose mothers have a positive history of being battered are twice as likely as the children of nonbattered mothers to be darted for actual abuse. Interestingly, they are also more likely to be darted because "mother needs support." At best, this represents a tacit recognition of the battered mother's predicament since in almost no instance is "abuse" or "battering" actually noted.

The mothers in this study were selected because their children were darted in 1977–78. Thus it is not surprising that virtually all their trauma visits preceded the

Table 2

Problems in the family histories of mothers of abused children

Problem	No. among mothers in the at-risk[a] groups, N = 52	No. among mothers in the negative and marital conflict risk groups, N = 64
Alcoholism	6 (12%)	12 (19%)
Violence	9 (17%)	10 (16%)
Suicide attempts	5 (10%)	7 (11%)
Incest	1 (2%)	4 (6%)
Chaotic family	12 (23%)	12 (19%)

[a]Includes the positive, probable, and suggestive battering risk groups.

Table 3

Reasons for "dart"[a]

Mother's battering risk group	N	Mother needs support	Neglect and/or suspicious injury	Abuse
Positive	29	15 (50%)	5 (18%)	9 (32%)
Probable	18	6 (33%)	8 (44%)	4 (22%)
Suggestive	5	2 (40%)	2 (40%)	1 (20%)
Total at-risk	52	23 (44%)	15 (29%)	14 (27%)
Marital conflict and negative	64	29 (46%)	23 (35%)	12 (19%)

[a]See text for explanation of this term.

child's referral. The fact that battering is the context within which child abuse develops for these women cannot be generalized to other populations of women. Conceivably, mothers currently classified as nonbattered will be abused in the future. However, since a longer history of assault is associated with "positive" women whose children are also most likely to be physically abused, child abuse seems to appear after a pattern of battering is established, an issue taken up in the Discussion.

Identity of the Abuser

Dart Committee reports give the identity of the parent allegedly responsible for abusing the child. For families in which the mother is battered, the father or father substitute is more than three times more likely to be the child's abuser than in families of nonbattered mothers. Approximately 50 percent of darted children of at-risk women are abused by the male batterer, 35 percent are abused by the mother who is also being battered, and the rest are abused by others or by "both."

Removal of the Child

Of children darted for all reasons, almost one-third are removed from homes where mothers are being battered. This is significantly higher than the percentage of children removed for all reasons from families with nonbattered mothers. Does this simply reflect the greater likelihood, documented above, that children of battered mothers will be physically abused? To control for this possibility, we compared the disposition only for cases in which the children have been allegedly neglected or in which the mothers needed support. Here too, if the mother was battered, the child was far more likely to be removed from her home than if she was not. Whatever the rationale for disproportionately removing children from battered mothers, the effect is obviously punitive.

Discussion

The findings support an analysis of child abuse as a component of female subordination. Even a highly conservative definition of battering requiring that at least one abusive injury be serious enough for hospital treatment reveals that 45 percent of these young mothers are battered and another 5 percent are experiencing "marital conflict." The documented prevalence of battering in this population is greater than in any other group yet identified, including emergency surgical patients, female alcoholics, drug abusers, women who attempt suicide, rape victims, mental patients, women filing for divorce, or women using emergency psychiatric or obstetrical services (15, 17). These women have already presented an average of four injury episodes to the hospital, only slightly fewer than the far older emergency room sample, corroborating our suspicion that child abuse in these relationships represents the extension of ongoing violence and is an intermediary point in an unfolding history of battering. Not only are the children of battered mothers significantly more likely to be physically abused than neglected, for instance, but the batterer also appears to be the typical source of child abuse, not a mother "overwhelmed with problems." The data shed little light on the dynamics of child abuse in battering homes. Again, however, the battering clearly predates the child abuse and, even when the battered mother is the abusive parent, she is less likely to have had a violent or "disorganized" family-of-origin, both facts suggesting that "transmission" involves the extension of the same unresolved conflict that elicits battering. The mothers divide into women with a problematic family history whose children are suspected of "neglect," and battered women whose background appears comparatively nonproblematic. In either case, the popular stereotype of the mother "predisposed by her history" to be battered and to abuse her child is a convenient fiction with little relation to documented cases.

To those familiar with the literature on child abuse, the clinical response to families in which mothers are battered will come as no surprise. As is the literature, the records of battered mothers are silent about physical abuse and the children's records rarely mention the man's violence. Instead, the mother's failure to fulfill her feminine role is emphasized ("mother needs support coping"). Here too, as in the clinical response to battering or in the literature on child abuse, women are held responsible when things go wrong. Even when we control for danger to the child, battered mothers are more likely to lose their children than nonbattered mothers.

Behind the ultimate threat—that a woman will lose her child—providers require periodic displays of nurturance and homemaker efficiency as prerequisites for basic family supports. In many cases, the mother does not report the abusing male and the caseworker lists the source of violence as "unknown" or "other." This may be because the woman defines the worker as her adversary, is afraid of the batterer's retaliation, or fears the withdrawal of welfare benefits if her relation with an unrelated man is discovered.

Ironically, since there are no therapeutic modalities to deal with men, foster placement—a punitive intervention as far as the mother is concerned—is more likely when a man is battering the mother and child. Not only are the mothers who pose least danger to their children most likely to lose them, but they may also lose access to whatever meager resources resulted from agency concern. With foster placement, the therapeutic focus shifts from the natural parents onto the child and his or her new milieu, while the underlying problems—including any violence toward the mother—are ignored (30).

In summary, and contrary to the prevalent view in the field, men are primarily responsible for child abuse, not women; battering is the typical context for child abuse, not maternal deficits; battered mothers whose children are abused are not distinguished by a family background of violence or psychopathology; and the response of the child abuse system—including neglect of the violence, support for mothering, and removal of the child to foster care—are ineffective at best and punitive at worst. In the next section, we place these findings in a feminist framework and link them to the dynamics in violent relationships.

A FEMINIST APPROACH TO BATTERING AND CHILD ABUSE

Feminists approach the family as a system characterized by inequity, conflict, and contradiction. As a structure of male domination, it shapes intersubjective life into rigid gender identities to which real needs are subordinated (31). At the same time, the family must also provide the interpersonal and emotional support needed for subjective differentiation, autonomy, and independence (32, 33). The link of battering to child abuse can be defined by this dilemma. Autonomy is not attainable within rigid gender roles. Thus it is both inevitable that women will struggle to expand their options, including the option to engage openly in conflict, and appropriate for them to do so (34). Nevertheless, many men respond to these struggles violently, often seeking to subjugate children as well as their mothers.[2]

Women's growing independence and the withering of ideological supports for power based on gender make violence ever more central to male privilege in the

---

[2]Baker-Miller writes "inequality generates hidden conflict around elements that the inequality itself has set in motion" (31, p. 14). The relevant point is that in the context of gender inequality, every "fight" concerns both the issue at hand and the larger—and usually unspoken—issue of inequality or "who will decide who will decide." In many battering relationships, once violence ensues, this larger political dimension grows in importance in direct proportion to its suppression, so that both sides attribute an importance to disagreements that appears inappropriate to outsiders. One goal of feminist intervention is to bring this hidden political dimension to the fore, to support the woman's (and incidentally the batterer's) perception that "the issue is not the issue."

home. One consequence is that women's health utilization is increasingly emblematic of their larger political situation. How medical and social services receive the myriad consequences of violence, including child abuse, is therefore crucial to women's political fate as well as their health.

Ideologically, battering and child abuse are connected by the presumption that women's responsibilities as wives and mothers supercede their personal needs and social rights, including their need for independence and physical safety. By normalizing these responsibilities through theories of women's character and mother-child bonding, psychology provides the health and social services with a rationale for making the delivery of vital resources contingent on women's acceptance of this ideology. By subsuming a woman's personal development to the stability of her family and the well-being of her children, both family stability and children's welfare are jeopardized.

The Knowledge of Mothers

Until recently, the child protection bureaucracy, including pediatrics, has dominated the field from which data on child abuse are produced. As a result, the knowledge base and practice of child protection form two dimensions of a single moral paradigm in which women's presumed propensity for nurturance and mothering is sacrosanct. It follows that women are and should be held responsible for abuse whether or not they actually assault (or neglect) their children.

The psychological knowledge of women as mothers has been largely developed through observational and interpretative studies that remove parenting from its political context. The structure, substance, and intensity of women's involvement with their children is obviously affected by pronatalist ideology, the absence of adequate daycare or health benefits, punitive welfare policies, and job, housing, and wage constraints. Not surprisingly, housewives subjected to these constraints exhibit high rates of situational depression (35), and behind housewife depression lie "high levels of anger and conflict towards husband and children in families" (36). But on the videotapes of middle-class parent-child interaction used to support theories of mother-child bonding, these environmental factors are invisible (37). With the social and historical content of women's lives omitted, the intersubjective takes on an illusory comprehensiveness. Divorced from the factors that isolate mother with child, their reliance on one another appears to derive from inner principles (rather than external necessities), hence the conclusion: women have an innate propensity for "bonding." In this way, women's work as mothers is normalized and therapeutic management is justified for those who refuse or fail to perform this work.

The methodological short-sightedness that dominates research in maternal and child health may seem relatively benign. But the administration of the resulting "knowledge" is not. The normalization of mothering and the extension of patterns presumed to typify middle-class (i.e., "healthy") families to assessments of behavior among working-class, minority, or poor women is the ground on which pediatrics, social, and protective services shift child abuse from the realm of politics to pathology and "re-cognize" the violent suppression of women and children as a deficit in women's ability to parent. Thus, pediatric texts, popular advice literature, and psychological research "blame mother" when things go wrong (38–41). Child abuse is alternately interpreted as a failure or an exaggeration of the maternal function, a lack of parenting skills, or an inappropriate dependence on or resentment of a vulnerable other. If a man harms the child, this is because the mother is not present when the child returns from school, because adults other than the mother care for the child when ill, or because working mothers make unsatisfactory care arrangements (42, 43). In a London survey, More and Davy (cited in reference 26, p. 294) are explicit:

> In the 20 cases where the father or step-father had hit the child, the following pattern emerged. . . . In 7 of these cases, the mother's behavior acted as a trigger for the assault. Either she had provoked her husband in some way and then made sure—perhaps by going out—that the child got the full weight of the anger produced, or she had complained to her husband about the child's behavior (sometimes, perhaps to take the spotlight off herself in an explosive situation).

Interestingly, holding women responsible for male violence (both against themselves and their children) reinforces the batterer's common tendency to deny or externalize responsibility for the assault.

Patriarchal Mothering: The Practice

The knowledge of mother-child bonding, of mother's responsibility for abuse, and of how violence evolves across generations of pathology is taken as self-evident by child rescue workers and is unreflectively incorporated into child protection. The administrative practices that follow include parent aides, homemaker services, "hot lines," Parents Anonymous, hospital-based outpatient therapy classes, comprehensive crisis intervention, shelter programs, and, if these fail, foster placement and/or legal prosecution. In each case, the governing assumption is that the parenting role needs "support" and that the "family unit" has dissolved into a structure of pathology that must somehow be managed by institutional and/or state intervention if its protective functions are to be restored.

The identification of responsibility for child abuse with rigid notions of women's role behavior engenders both conflict between agency representatives and women perceived as deviant mothers and growing resentment among women toward their children. Mothers are defined as people without needs of their own, who do or do not live up to their child's expectations and needs as service providers view them. When women's behavior differs from the projected expectations, service providers become frustrated and seek rationales to "help women shape up." One such rationale is provided by "retrospective reinterpretation." Deviance from perceived gender norms is transformed into disease by locating characteristics of abnormality in a women's environment or history. Once so identified, a woman becomes a so-called "customer" of social services and each subsequent deviant act, no matter how common among women in similar situations, occasions ever more rigid case management, usually through some combination of "support" and therapy. Although peer treatment is widely touted as an alternative to traditional medical therapies, peer groups similarly interpret conflicts in social identity as an illness. Thus Parents Anonymous insists that child abuse stems from a problem that is "within us as a parent," that the woman is "a destructive, disturbed mother." Not surprisingly, women offered therapy and support parenting instead of protection and food stamps transfer some of their anger toward their caseworkers and some to their children (44).

The Battered Mother's Dilemma

Battered women cannot fully protect their children from the assailant. To protect themselves from child services, however, they pretend they can. In encounters with the caseworker, both sides know that the woman's behavior is a charade. Homemaking can hardly be "normal" when daily life is punctuated by male violence. "Home-visits" thus become exercises in mutual impression management. If the source of the trouble is obvious (e.g., the woman answers the door with a black eye) or the woman threatens to reveal it, the caseworker reminds her directly or by implication that a failure in maternal responsibilities could easily lead to the child's removal.

This situation creates a profound dilemma. The woman cannot protect her child unless she is protected. But if she asks for protection for herself, her child may be removed. In the matrix of power in which the woman finds herself, one way to seek aid is by drawing attention to her problems with her child whether or not these are particularly significant. As a result, she may project an image of herself as "unable to cope," hoping that, by accommodating the preconceptions of child protection, she will be given the supports she needs to protect herself. This is a dangerous game.

Another facet of the battered mother's dilemma is whether to expose the assailant's behavior and lose her child or conceal it and risk further child abuse. Here, being a good mother (having her child removed to safety) means admitting to being "bad" (i.e., to being battered). The effects of exposure are often tragic. Apart from the risk to children in foster care, the effects of foster placement on a battering relationship can include a depressive reaction; self-blame and a reduction in a woman's survival defenses; the internalization of anger formerly directed at the child scapegoat and attempted suicide; an escalation in abuse since the batterer has also lost a scapegoat; and pregnancy to prove readiness for a new child and to compensate for depression.

Patriarchal Mothering: The Lived Experience

But the dilemma goes deeper still. If women's situation were simply paradigmatic of "the weak and the governed," to borrow Elizabeth Janeway's phrase, then the complex system constructed to manage their behavior would be largely superfluous. Women confront male domination as active subjects, legally free and independent, struggling to shape reality to their needs. The women who are videotaped are not mere pawns, therefore, but their initiative has been displaced so that they must fulfill their gender identities through their relation to their children. As Foucault, Lacan, and the French feminists have shown, sexism in liberal societies rests less on open bias than in privileging certain definitions of feminine behavior within which women must both find themselves and survive. As the limited meanings through which women and children understand their experience are internalized, women may come to know themselves as men would have them known, i.e., in this case, to become locked into the knowledge of themselves as mothers.

In the laboratory, mother-infant bonding is observed devoid of its political context. As woman abuse evolves into "battering," women may experience the same diminished sense of themselves in relation to the social as is projected by the psychological paradigm. Just as they experience the mothering role as alien, it also feels as if it is all there is. Administrative transactions foster and aggravate role closure by simultaneously encouraging women to view the world through the prism of motherhood and to ask whether a "good mother" would have an abusing partner. This becomes a double bind when structural constraints leave a woman no alternative but to define herself through mothering. Forced to choose between liking herself as abused or deciding she is "bad," she develops a peculiar myopia to the political reality of her predicament, denying her own battering and living in a kind of fool's paradise of power "over" her children while at the same time feeling completely powerless or "overwhelmed." Child-abusing women themselves "yearn for good mothering" (7); they suffer low self-esteem because of a felt incongruence between how they view themselves and how they would like to be (45) and turn to their children for company and nurturance ("role reversal") (7, 11). Researchers trace these characteristics to a "breakdown in the maternal affection system" (7). However, at least in homes where women are also being assaulted, quite the contrary process is at work. Here women strive for selfhood ("how they would like to be") and nurturance ("good mothering") within the constraints of the mothering role, in part because children are the only source of nurturance in violent homes and in part because, as they define their options within a world bounded by a male *telos,* battered women lose access to the strains of resistance and initiative through which to establish themselves as something other than "his."

Thus, the matrix of power in which she is situated finds a parallel in a narrowing of the cognitive frame through which the battered mother perceives the world. Where she formerly sought control and autonomy to supplement nurturance and dependence, "mothering" must now mediate the impulse to power through the practice of nurturance and dependence, a process central to what we term patriarchal mothering. In any case, it is her restriction to mothering, not its abandonment, that may lead the battered woman to violence against her child.

There is an additional pathway by which the administrative response to woman and child abuse links the knowledge of women as mothers to their child abuse. We have seen that prevalent interventions to stop child abuse, like the response to battering, are inattentive to the woman's needs, holding her responsible for the child's predicament and making her rights as a parent contingent on her surpressing her own urge to self-development and survival. The autonomy she seeks to escape her assailant—getting a job, going to night school, moving in with friends—may provide the grounds for a judgment of "neglect" or removing her child to foster care. But if she stays at home, she and her child become more vulnerable to the batterer and her resentment at blocked opportunities builds. Whereas one reconciliation of this double bind is to deny her abuse, another is to hold the child responsible for the man's violence. By using the child as scapegoat, she momentarily reconciles the dilemma in which loving the child, being a "good mother," means putting herself at risk. But if the child is "bad," then its removal and her independence can be effected simultaneously with a minimum of internal conflict. Here too, child abuse is a "survival" strategy evoked by entrapment.

CHILD PROTECTIVE SERVICES AND THE PROSPECTS FOR REFORM

Policy Reform: Past Experience

How has the child protective establishment responded to the "news" about battering? The evidence is disheartening.

Internal pressure to acknowledge battering has been building in the child abuse field for almost a decade. For instance, while the American Humane Society championed the involuntary service approach to mothers throughout the 1950s and 1960s (46), by 1977–78, 20 percent of its child abuse reports from the field were accompanied by descriptions of wife abuse (3). Meanwhile, the team approach in hospital settings focused on the mother's "stressful environment."

Outside the child abuse field, the challenge to child rescue is framed within legislation and funding decisions that prioritize "spouse abuse" or "family violence." Child rescue lacks an activist base and, as a result, child savers tread a thin line between the narrow definition of child abuse needed to access political agendas and the broad concern with equity needed to placate the wider social welfare community (46). Moreover, shrinking social service resources exacerbate the contradictions between reformist rhetoric ("supporting families in trouble") and a narrowly protectionist practice (foster placement), engendering distrust within the larger liberal community.

The response to these pressures has been to deny their legitimacy and, more recently, to accommodate battering by rationalizing and broadening the punitive conception of mothering. When the Battered Women's Movement was still embryonic, the child protective establishment rejected battering as an issue simply to retain the economic status quo. As one prominent child policy maker asked (47, p. 8):

> Can we assume that new funding on a relatively large scale will be forthcoming? If not, we should [ask] . . . who will [be] winners and who losers, since it will be necessary to redistribute a limited pie. That redistribution will obviously be at the perceived expense of child abuse and neglect agencies.

But a broader jurisdictional appeal was needed for the welfare community (47, p. 8):

> We should ask whether the conceptual joining of these problems is likely to affect . . . the approach to families in which violence occurs. . . . At a time when a concerted effort is underway to move away from a punitive approach to parents who maltreat their children [there is a prevalent view] that violence against spouses is essentially a police problem. . . . Will joining the two issues result in an attitudinal and institutional retrogression to a reliance on punishment?

As the child protectionists feared, a shift in funds and media interest away from child rescue accompanied the growing recognition of battering. However, alongside the Battered Women's Movement emerged a new stratum of professionals and researchers specializing in "family violence" but fully willing to accommodate the child protectionists within a broader conceptual scheme in which the emphasis on child rescue is retained and supplemented by a more catholic perspective on "environmental" factors. In this schema, for instance, the link of battering to child abuse proves the importance of a primal injury to children (including child sexual abuse) and lends support to the claim that the family (termed a "cradle of violence") requires the same sort of social service policing as crime on the street (22). Again, "policing the family" becomes a euphemism for managing mothers. Indeed, having learned of the dangers to children when women are battered, child protective services in many states are seeking power to remove the battered woman's child if she fails to get a protective order against her assailant.

Proposals for Reform

Proposals for reforming child protective services run the gamut. Neoconservatives argue that to protect privacy, interventions should be limited to cases of documented physical abuse (48). By contrast, left-liberal child savers insist that the stigma of child abuse be eliminated altogether and that, instead, an "ecological definition" (which includes the child's "moral and social environment") be used to determine children at risk. Newberger (49), for example, normally a staunch critic of the punitive biases implicit in the helping response, proposes that we consider a variety of potential harms to the child—including poisoning, accidents, and the deprivation of medical care— "in the matrix of his developmental process, the family, neighborhood and helping environment."

Neoconservative proposals to limit interventions to the minority of cases in which physical abuse is documented offer a viable framework for a sharply curtailed protective establishment, on balance an attractive prospect. The neoconservatives view family intervention as a latent or aberrant function of vague laws and overzealous administrators (to be replaced by clear laws and hard-headed bureaucrats). But they fail to conceptualize this pattern in political terms, and hence never confront the possibility that managing mothers is the intended rather than the accidental consequence of child protection. In this case, restrictive policies may narrow the range of women who are controlled, but will still not protect children.

Liberal policy proposals shift attention from explicit violence to "the security of the environment" in which the child is raised. The environment rather than the woman is blamed and the woman is offered counseling and support. Although removing the stigma of abuse, it naively approaches clinical management as otherwise unproblematic, while extending the jurisdiction of treatment for the woman to a range of ills—such as the lack of medical coverage or a landlord's code violations—which she has even less control over than the batterer's violence. In practice, the ecological definition revives the old association of abuse with poverty. Thus investigators in Massachusetts are instructed that "An example of a home which poses a low risk to a child is one which is clean, with no apparent safety hazards such as exposed wiring or rodent infestation, and structurally sound" (cited in reference 49, p. 16). Like other models of multiple causation, the ecological picture can become so intricate that in trying to grasp the complexity of the relations between the physical, social, and interpersonal environments, we lose sight of the one event about which something immediate can be done: the political subordination of women and children in the home. More pointedly, in justifying access to nonabusing mothers (the majority of the current caseload) by a system whose means are almost exclusively punitive, the probability of removing children from battering or impoverished relationships would be dramatically increased.

CONCLUSIONS

From Entrapment to Empowerment

For many abused women, when assault combines with a history of frustrated, even punitive, help-seeking, the result is entrapment in a syndrome of escalating pathology. Isolated within the relationship and blocked from without from pursuing alternatives to it, the battered woman's self-development proceeds within an ever narrower realm, including the constricted realm of the mother-child relationship, and resentment and anger mount alongside the suppressed need for independence and autonomy. Multiple suicide attempts, homicidal rage, and violence against vulnerable others, including children, may result.

A similar process of entrapment is the typical context for child abuse. Men are the typical child abusers and, in almost half of all child abuse cases, are battering the woman as well. But whichever parent abuses the child in a battering relationship, the woman confronts a continuum of control extending from the violence at home through labeling and punitive clinical interventions at the hospital to sanctions and "support for mothering" from protective services. Even when the battered woman sacrifices the child (hoping the batterer will hit the child instead of her) or beats the child herself, the real source of her rage is entrapment in an enforced association of rigid gender roles and personal identity.

The imposition of "parenting skills" replaces the positive valence of motherhood with formal obedience and mounting rage. The obligations of mothering reappear as rules imposed by an alien force, depriving the woman of the very "responsibility" and sense of control over her environment that protective services claim to instill. Anger emerges as a defense against helplessness, and child abuse as a desperate way to exert control in the context of little or no control. But though rage is a "political emotion," to paraphrase Teresa Bernandez (34), it is often expressed symptomatically: resistance to mind control may evoke dissociation; resistance to isolation, imaginary companions, and resistance to guilt and shame, a "false self" that performs chores obediently, even cheerfully (50). Or, rage may find direct expression in killing the assailant.

If battering is the major context for child abuse and female independence is the basic issue for both, female empowerment is the best means to prevent child abuse. Empowerment primarily includes three components: (a) advocacy (to protect and expand women's entitlements); (b) collective support (to overcome estrangement and provide the political base for change); and (c) control. At a minimum, enhancing control implies that the battered mother can select the option she feels best suits her situation, even when she has abused the child.[3] A woman may choose to remain in a violent relationship of course, but in general, empowerment is impossible while the woman and child are accessible to the batterer.

These principles are anathema to a child welfare establishment that sees itself as advocating for children, but not their mothers; views politics as beyond the scope of treatment and protection; defines the mother as an "involuntary" client; and relies on a therapeutic or humanistic approach wholly lacking the means to limit,

---

[3]Extraordinarily complex ethical and liability issues are involved in a decision to support a battered woman, even when she has previousiy put the child at risk or may do so, in a shelter environment, e.g., during the process of empowerment. Even in the worst case, however, this is preferable to the present practice of sacrificing the battered mother to rescue the child (often to a worse fate), and so restricting the mother's options that further child abuse and battering are virtually ensured.

let alone prevent, male violence. By contrast, safety and empowerment guide the shelter movement's response to battering and are gradually being extended to an understanding of children. Many shelters now employ "child advocates," some run groups for mothers and children (51, 52), and virtually all have "no violence" rules as a precondition for residence. In Connecticut, meanwhile, the Division of Children and Youth Services has subcontracted to battered women's shelters for services to families in which mother and child are abused. Still, however central shelters may become in dealing with "family violence," the problem of providing for the long-term security and autonomy of women and children is far too vast to be solved by even so vital a community-based service as this.

Cooperative arrangements between shelters and the child welfare establishment can succeed only if there is mutual recognition that the autonomous women's movement—and the institutional alternatives it creates for battered women—is the safest place for children. In its emphasis on equity and its political analysis of social ills, its community base, its willingness to take responsibility for problems few want to tackle, the excitement it communicates, and its capacity to dramatize issues and to mobilize constituencies, the Battered Women's Movement in particular can win over large segments of the social welfare audience from the child savers.

Acknowledging that child abuse originates in the politics of gender in no way diminishes personal responsibility for violence. To the contrary, as women are released from rigid role stereotypes and become more comfortable with their social power, they will be better able to accept real responsibility for the range of unresolved, ambivalent, and angry feelings all mothers share.

As the evidence of the common roots of battering and child abuse was first becoming clear, the Region II Director of the National Center on Child Abuse and Neglect issued this warning (47, p 9):

> Perhaps the dynamics of child abuse, wife abuse and husband beating and rape are interrelated in ways that lend themselves to a common form of intervention. Are we prepared to follow the implications of this linkage? . . . We are unlikely to end with the intrafamilial dynamics of violence. . . . The discussion will almost certainly be extended to a systematic examination of the social causation of all forms of family violence.

It is to be hoped that this fear will prove prophetic.

REFERENCES

1. Williams, G. Toward the eradication of child abuse and neglect at home. In *Traumatic Abuse and the Neglect of Children at Home*, edited by G. Williams and J. Money, pp. 588–605. Johns Hopkins University Press, Baltimore, 1980.
2. Breines, W., and Gordon, L. The new scholarship on family violence. *Signs: Journal of Women and Culture in Society* 8(3): 490–531, 1983.

3. American Humane Society. *National Analysis of Official Child Neglect and Abuse Reporting.* Denver, 1978.
4. Bergman, A., Larsen, R. M., and Mueller, B. Changing spectrum of serious child abuse. *Pediatrics* 77(1): 113–116, 1986.
5. Stark, E., and Flitcraft, A. Woman-battering, child abuse and social heredity: What is the relationship? In *Marital Violence*, edited by N. K. Johnson, pp. 147–171. *Sociological Review Monograph*, No. 31. Routledge and Kegan Paul, London, 1985.
6. Gil, D. *Violence Against Children: Physical Child Abuse in the United States.* Harvard University Press, Cambridge, Mass., 1973.
7. Steele, B., and Pollack, C. A psychiatric study of parents who abuse infants and small children. In *The Battered Child*, edited by R. Helfer and C. Henry Kempe, pp. 103–147. University of Chicago Press, Chicago, 1976.
8. Kempe, R., and Kempe, C. H. Assessing family pathology. In *Child Abuse and Neglect: The Family and the Community*, edited by R. Helfer and C. H. Kempe. Ballinger, Cambridge, Mass., 1976.
9. Newberger, C. B., and Newberger, E. The etiology of child abuse. In *Child Abuse: A Medical Reference*, edited by N. F. Ellerstein, pp. 11–20. John Wiley and Sons, New York, 1981.
10. Newberger, E., and Bourne, R. E. The medicalization and legalization of child abuse. *Am. J. Orthopsychiatry* 48(4): 593–606, 1978.
11. Helfer, R F. Basic issues concerning prediction. In *Child Abuse and Neglect: The Family and the Community*, edited by R. E. Helfer and C. H. Kempe. Ballinger, Cambridge, Mass., 1976.
12. Baher, E., et al. *At Risk: An Account of the Work of the Battered Child Research Department.* National Society for Prevention of Cruelty to Children. Routledge and Kegan Paul, Boston, 1976.
13. Hilberman, E., and Munson, K. Sixty battered women. *Victimology: An International Journal* 2(3-4): 460–470, 1977/78.
14. Stark, E., and Flitcraft, A. Personal power and institutional victimization: Treating the dual trauma of woman battering. In *Post-Traumatic Therapy*, edited by F. Ochberg. Bruner and Mazel, New York, 1987.
15. Stark, E. The Battering Syndrome: Social Knowledge, Social Therapy and the Abuse of Women. Doctoral dissertation, Department of Sociology, State University of New York, Binghamton, 1984.
16. Stark, E., Flitcraft, A., and Frazier, W. Medicine and patriarchal violence: The social construction of a "private" event. *Int. J. Health Serv.* 9(3): 461–493, 1979.
17. Stark, E., and Flitcraft, A. Violence among intimates: An epidemiological review. In *Handbook of Family Violence*, edited by V. N. Hasselt et al. Plenum Press, New York, 1987.
18. Stark, E., et al. *Wife Abuse in the Medical Setting: An Introduction for Health Personnel.* Monograph No.7. Office of Domestic Violence, Washington, D.C., 1981.
19. Dobash, R. E., and Dobash, R. *Violence Against Wives.* Free Press, New York, 1979.
20. Rosenberg, M., Stark, E., and Zahn, M. A. Interpersonal violence: Homicide and spouse abuse. In *Maxcy-Rosenau: Public Health and Preventive Medicine*, Ed. 12, edited by J. M. Last, pp. 1399–1426. Appleton-Century-Crofts, New York, 1985.
21. Steele, B. F. Violence within the family. In *Child Abuse and Neglect: The Family and the Community*, edited by R. E. Helfer and C. H. Kempe. Ballinger, Cambridge, Mass., 1976.
22. Straus, M., Gelles, R., and Steinmetz, S. K. *Behind Closed Doors: A Survey of Family Violence in America.* Doubleday, New York, 1980.

23. Kautman, J., and Zigler, E. Do abused children become abusive parents? *Am. J. Orthopsychiatry* 57(2): 186–193, 1987.
24. Kurz, D., and Stark, E. Health education and feminist strategy: The case of woman abuse. In *Feminist Perspectives on Wife Abuse*, edited by M. Bograd and K. Yllo. Sage, Beverly Hills, Calif., 1987.
25. Carmen, E. H., Rieker, P. P., and Mills, T. Victims of violence and psychiatric illness. In *The Gender Gap in Psychotherapy, Social Realities and Psychological Processes*, edited by P. P. Rieker and E. H. Carmen, pp. 199–213. Plenum Press, New York, 1984.
26. Martin, J. Maternal and paternal abuse of children: Theoretical and research perspectives. In *The Dark Side of Families: Current Family Violence Research*, edited by D. Finkelhor et al., pp. 293–305. Sage, Beverly Hills, Calif., 1983.
27. Gayford, J. J. Wife battering: A preliminary survey of 100 cases. *Br. Med. J.* 25: 194–197, 1975.
28. Rosenbaum, A., and O'Leary, D. Children: The unintended victims of marital violence. *Am. J. Orthopsychiatry* 51(4): 692–699, 1981.
29. Levine, M. Interparental violence and its effect on the children: A study of 50 families in general practice. *Med. Sci. Law* 15(3): 172–183, 1975.
30. Green, A. Societal neglect and child abusing parents. *Victimology: An International Journal* 11(2): 285–293, 1977.
31. Baker-Miller, J. *Toward a New Psychology of Women*. Beacon Press, Boston, 1976.
32. Chodorow, N. J. Gender, relation and difference in psychoanalytic perspective. In *The Future of Difference*, edited by H. Eisenstein and A. Jardine, pp. 3–20. Rutgers University Press, New Brunswick, N.J., 1985.
33. Flax, J. Mother-daughter relationships: Psychodynamics, politics and philosophy. In *The Future of Difference*, edited by H. Eisenstein and A. Jardine, pp. 20–41. Rutgers University Press, New Brunswick, N.J., 1985.
34. Bernardez, T. Women and Anger, Cultural Prohibitions and the Feminine Ideal. Paper presented at Learning from Women: Theory and Practice, Boston, April 1987.
35. Brown, G. W., and Harris, T. *Social Origins of Depression—A Study of Psychiatric Disorder in Women*. Tavistock, London, 1978.
36. Weissman, M. The depressed mother and her rebellious adolescent. In *Children of Depressed Parents: Risk, Identification and Intervention*, edited by H. Morrison. Grune and Stratton, New York, 1983.
37. Henriques, J., et al. *Changing the Subject: Psychology, Social Regulation and Subjectivity*. Methuen, London, 1984.
38. Howell, M. C. Pediatricians and mothers. In *The Cultural Crisis of Modern Medicine*, edited by J. Ehrenreich. Monthly Review Press, New York, 1979.
39. Ehrenreich, B., and English, D. *For Her Own Good*. Anchor Books, New York, 1979.
40. Caplan, P., and Hall-McCorguodale, I. The scapegoating of mothers: A call for change. *Am. J. Orthopsychiatry* 55(4): 610–613, 1985.
41. Caplan, P. Mother blaming in major clinical journals. *Am. J. Orthopsychiatry* 55(5): 345–353, 1985.
42. Garbarino, J., and Sherman, D. High risk neighborhoods and high risk families: The human ecology of child maltreatment. *Child Dev.* 51(1), 1980.
43. Robertson, B. A., and Juritz, J. M. Characteristics of the families of abused children. *Child Abuse and Neglect* 3: 861, 1979.
44. Kott-Washburne, C. A feminist analysis of child abuse and neglect. In *The Dark Side of Families*, edited by D. Finkelhor et al., pp. 289–293. Sage, Beverly Hills, Calif., 1984.
45. Rosen, B. Self-concept disturbance among mothers who abuse their children. *Psychol. Rep.* 43: 323–326, 1978.

46. Nelson, B. *Making an Issue of Child Abuse: Political Agenda Setting for Social Problems.* University of Chicago Press, Chicago, 1984.
47. National Center on Child Abuse and Neglect. *Child Abuse and Family Violence.* U.S. Children's Bureau, Washington, D.C., 1978.
48. Besharov, D. J. Right versus rights: The dilemma of child protection. *Public Welfare* 43(2): 19–46, 1985.
49. Newberger, E. Child abuse. In *Source Book: Surgeon General's Workshop, Violence and Public Health.* Leesberg, Va., 1985.
50. Herman, J. Sexual Violence. Paper presented at Learning from Women: Theory and Practice, Boston, April 1987.
51. Rhodes, R. M., and Zelman, A. B. An ongoing multifamily group in a women's shelter. *Am J. Orthopsychiatry* 56(1): 120–131, 1986.
52. Alessi, J. J., and Hearn, K. Group treatment of children in shelters for battered women. In *Battered Women and Their Families: Intervention Strategies and Treatment Programs,* edited by A. R. Roberts. Springer, New York, 1978.

CHAPTER 17

Older Women in the Post-Reagan Era

Terry Arendell and Carroll L. Estes

Gender and minority status are crucial in explaining differences in the economic and health issues confronted by the aged. Significantly, the situation of older women is a result not of old age, but of lifelong patterns of socioeconomic and gender stratification in the larger society. The social origins of the disadvantaged status of older women are not mysterious; they reside in the institutions and structures of the family (the informal sector), the labor market, and the state and its social policy (both parts of the formal sector). Each of these areas has received independent study; however, the consequences for older women flow from the complex and often subtle interrelationships among and across these social institutions (1). Women's family roles, particularly their caregiving, directly impinge upon their economic status. Not only does economic status directly affect access to health care, but social class and socioeconomic status have repeatedly been shown to be strongly linked to health status as measured by mortality, disability, chronic illness, and institutionalization (2–6).

Because of the structural embeddedness and complexity of these institutional arrangements and interrelationships that adversely affect women, the resolution of older women's economic and health issues cannot be achieved by providing services alone. While a more comprehensive and integrated health and social service delivery system is needed for older females, this need is shared by all individuals who are asked to provide caregiving up and down, within and between the generations in the growing number of three and four generational families. Although state support of access, availability, and financing of services remains vitally important, changes in service provision alone will do little to address the

Originally published in the *International Journal of Health Services* 21(1): 59–73, 1991.

gendered division of labor and the capitalist mode of production that have played a pivotal role in socially creating the jeopardized situation in which older women find themselves. The analytical framework proposed here acknowledges the link between income and health needs in a life course perspective, delicately balancing health and well-being. For women, this raises the need for broad-based solutions that address sex, race, and age discrimination in the labor market, unequal pay for comparable worth, and the invidious quality of income security programs for older women that are predicated on ideological and inaccurate assumptions, wage discrimination, and a lifetime of devalued caregiving work.

A key element of women's precarious economic status in old age is their family responsibility across the lifespan for which they bear a significant and continuous burden of work. Lodged primarily in what has been socially constructed as the private sphere of the family, women have been responsible for providing care and nurturing both the very young and the very old in a social and political context that romanticizes but provides no financial remunerations for their caring activities. Because caring takes place within millions of individual family units, it is neither recognized nor valorized because of the historic neglect and devaluation of women's unpaid labor, and the ideological dichotomy between the "public" and "private" in which the family is defined as private, autonomous, and self-sufficient. As a result, the place of women and children in the gendered division of labor and the costs of caring activities tend to be ignored and obscured. Although women have entered the wage labor force in unprecedented numbers over the last two decades, the wage differentials between men and women have not improved or changed significantly in the past 30 years, a significant number of women hold part-time jobs, and most wives remain economically dependent on husbands (7).

In old age, many women discover that the structural conditions and the normative expectations that have promoted and maintained their economic dependence converge, resulting in poverty or near-poverty and economic uncertainty. Indeed, poverty is the central problem facing older women (8).

The aged are not a homogeneous population, despite recent reports asserting the economic gains made by the elderly. While there has been a decline in the overall rate of poverty among the aged in the past 15 years, major pockets of poverty and conditions of economic hardship persist (7, 9, 10). Indeed, because so many aged persons are near poverty (150 percent of the poverty level and below), the proportion of aged who are poor and near-poor is larger than the combined proportion of nonaged who are poor and near-poor (7). Well over 50 percent of older women will find themselves facing economic hardships.

DEMOGRAPHIC CHARACTERISTICS

The older population is disproportionately female: nearly 60 percent of all Americans 66 years and older, and nearly 70 percent of those 80 and over, are female. Because women typically outlive their husbands, fewer than 40 percent of older women are married, whereas nearly 80 percent of older men are married and live with their wives. Marital status—especially being widowed but also being divorced or separated—is a primary explanation for the high percentage (41 percent) of older women who live alone (7). These gender differences in marital status and living arrangements for older women are significant because women's economic status in later life (as well as throughout the lifespan) is directly related to marital status.

Life expectancy, both at birth and at age 65, is higher for women than men. In 1986, total remaining life expectancy for men at age 65 was estimated at 14.4 years, while that for women was estimated at 18.7 years. For those born in 1986, life expectancy was estimated at 71.3 years for males and 78.3 years for females. Though improvements in mortality rates have been shared by both males and females over the last three decades, women have experienced more rapid improvements for most leading causes of death. Yet, proportionately more elderly women are limited in their activities of daily living than men, and elderly women visit physicians more frequently and use more days of hospital and nursing home care than men (11). Older women have more acute and chronic conditions than men and these diseases limit their activity, but they are seldom life-threatening (12, 13). Women also bear a greater burden of health care costs than men; older women's health care expenditures constitute 63 percent of the total of the elderly's health care costs, although women make up 59 percent of the population (11).

The availability of adult children, particularly daughters, to give care is the significant factor in keeping the frail and disabled elderly out of residential care (14, 15). Indeed, researchers have found that "the critical variable in the elderly's living arrangement was not the degree of the elderly's functional impairment but rather the access to family care" (15). Some 1.3 million elderly persons reside in institutions, three-quarters of whom are women (7). Several factors account for this phenomenon: women live longer than men, and older women have a higher prevalence of chronic disability and are less likely than men to have a spouse from whom to receive care. Because the majority of older men have living spouses, they typically receive informal care from their wives; "females [depend on] care from offspring and relatives" (16). The importance of such family support in preventing institutionalization is shown in the statistic that persons living alone who are single, divorced, or separated have a ten times greater probability of being institutionalized than those who are married (17).

Based on demographic projections, the greatest growth in the potential population in need of long-term care is for unmarried females aged 75 and over, with the largest increase (both absolute and relative) projected for the population of women over age 85 (16). The oldest old—generally women—can, and will, be disadvantaged not only by increasing infirmity, but also by outliving their close relatives.

ECONOMIC STATUS OF THE AGED: A GENDER STORY

It is a myth that the old are financially well-off and that their economic status has been achieved at the expense of the young. The best illustration of this point is the case of older women. Older women were 59 percent of the elderly population and 71 percent of its poor in 1984 (18). Significantly, over half of all older women live marginally close to, if not actually below, the poverty level (7, 19). In 1987, the median annual income was $11,854 for older men and $6,734 for older women. Even using the low official poverty line of $5,447 a year ($105 a week for a single individual), older women have almost double the poverty rate of older men (7). Additionally, significant racial differences exist in the economic status of older women. Being old, female, and a member of a minority group represents a "triple jeopardy" (18, 20). More research, especially longitudinal studies, needs to be conducted to fully identify the nature and extent of jeopardy.

Women's poverty in old age is significantly related to their marital status, added to the cumulative effects of wage discrimination and their unpaid work. Unmarried women between the ages of 65 and 69 receive approximately 40 percent of the total income of their married counterparts (7). The substantial differences in poverty rates between married and unmarried older women reflect the economic vulnerability of a large majority of older women. Most women outlive their husbands, and for most women widowhood is accompanied by a dramatic fall in overall income. Further, these economic problems are compounded with age. With increasing age, there is a real drop in income, such that the oldest elderly have the lowest money incomes. Medical expenditures increase with age. People aged 85 and older were found in 1984 to have an average income that was 36 percent less than that of people aged 65 to 69, while Medicare costs of elders aged 80 and older were 77 percent higher than those of elders 66 to 69 years of age (21). The "oldest old" tend to be female and, with increasing age, women are more likely to be widowed and in a precarious economic circumstance.

The impoverishment of women, however, is not unique to old age. Indeed, women of all ages are at risk of being poor, as denoted by the concept of "the feminization of poverty." Factors in the impoverishment of women include: the effects of wage discrimination and occupational segregation; lack of comparable pay; the increase in numbers of female-headed households; child care costs; inequitable divorce statutes and the extensive noncompliance with support orders; the "widow's gap" in Social Security; the rapid increase in numbers of displaced homemakers who are especially disadvantaged in reentering the employment sector as a result of both ageism and sexism; the inadequacy of social programs; cutbacks in domestic programs; increased health care costs; and biases in pension and retirement programs for the aged (22–26). Due to a combination of these various social processes, women are actively being pushed into low-income and poverty conditions. It should be noted here that the feminization of poverty and the marginality of older women cannot be fully understood without taking race into account. As Dressel (27) has shown, a comprehensive explanation of economic inequality and impoverishment, as well as the situation of older women within it, requires attention to the complex interrelations between gender, race, and class. This is particularly important for policy and programmatic actions, since policies designed to address female poverty alone will be insufficient to address the economic issues of older black women and older women of other racial–ethnic groups.

FACTORS IN THE ECONOMIC GENDER GAP

Older women's low income status reflects the culmination of a lifetime of secondary economic status. Contemporary wage and social policies are still based on the underlying assumption that women are economically dependent on a wage-earning male head-of-household, who theoretically shares with his wife and other dependents his higher earnings, retirement pension, and other employment-related benefits. The eligibility rules for public entitlement programs reflect the male model of work (28) and male patterns of labor force participation. The non–means-tested entitlement programs such as Social Security give men greater access to benefits and reward continuous participation in the primary labor force, while the more penurious means-tested and state-variable social assistance programs, including Supplemental Security Income (SSI), primarily support women (29).

Thus, public and private sector policies have contributed to the perpetuation of both the gender-structured wage and public pension systems. Most women are employed in secondary jobs, receiving substantially lower wages and fewer work-related benefits (for example, health insurance coverage and retirement pensions) than their male counterparts, and women's earnings continue to average approximately three-fifths of those of men. Older women's incomes average even less. Women who invested the majority of their efforts and time in homemaking and caring for children—traditional women's roles that are socially expected—discover in old age or when they divorce or are widowed in mid-life that they are economically penalized for having performed these traditional gender role activities. As displaced homemakers these women, who expected continued economic security in their marriages, find themselves living in conditions of genuine economic hardship, victims of sexism, ageism, wage discrimination, lack of recent employment experience, and inadequate (if any) spousal support after divorce or inadequate widow's benefits after a husband's death.

The increase in numbers of mid-life and older women who suddenly need to be self-supporting after having been economically dependent in marriage is due largely to the high rate of divorce. Over one-third of the more than one million divorces annually occur between couples married ten or more years, and 20 percent of all divorces involve couples married 15 or more years. The divorce rate among couples of long-term marriages and among those middle-aged or older continues to rise (23, 30). Divorce has profound, often lasting, effects on women's standard of living. Studies show that men recover economically from divorce, and in fact, improve their financial status after divorce. Women, however, generally experience no such recovery—unless they remarry, which few women over age 40 do (23, 30, 31). While the economic effects of divorce adversely affect women of all ages, mid-life and older women have even fewer options for reversing the downward mobility prompted by divorce than do younger women (22, 23). "The dramatic increase in divorce, especially in marriages of long duration, predicts an increase in the number of older women living alone and in poverty in the next generation" (8).

Widowhood also puts some women in the status of displaced homemakers. The average age at which a woman becomes widowed in the United States is about 56, yet no Social Security widow's benefits are available until age 60 (32, 33). The time between becoming widowed and turning age 60, referred to as the "widow's gap," is a time of desperate economic uncertainty for many widowed women. Coupled with the unfavorable labor market for mid-life and older reentry women, the lack of economic protection pushes many widowed women—who were economically secure during marriage—into harsh and unremitting economic conditions.

There are essentially no public funds available for providing temporary support to women, without minor children, who suddenly lose their economic base. Displaced homemakers themselves qualify for no unemployment compensation, since their family and home work is unpaid labor. They do not qualify for Social Security disability benefits. Despite the increased numbers of displaced homemakers, now estimated at nearly 11.5 million American women (70 percent of whom are over age 55) (34, p. 37), no programs have been initiated to provide economic support for these women, no matter how desperate their economic situations. Federal cuts in employment and training programs have brought these programs to their lowest funding levels in 15 years (35). Women attempting to reenter the employment sector during mid-life or later years are directly harmed by the lack of training programs.

Sources of Income

Women's disadvantaged economic status in old age is directly related to the sources of income available to them, primarily Social Security benefits, asset income, private pension benefits, and employment earnings. These income sources are themselves directly related to women's earlier family and work activities and women's secondary status in the employment and policy sectors.

Dependency on Social Security as the primary, or often only, source of income is a major factor in older women's precarious economic standing. One in three unmarried older women receiving Social Security depends on it for more than 90 percent of her income (36). In 1987, the average old age Social Security benefit was $6,924 annually for men and $5,292 for women (34, p. 28). Not only are women's Social Security payments less, but women rely to a much greater extent than do men on Social Security as their primary, and often only, source of old age income.

The gender inequities of the Social Security program and its disadvantages for women are well documented (26, 36). Income inequalities throughout the basic social structure of society, based on gender and class status, are both reproduced and reinforced through the Social Security program. Because Social Security is modeled on an insurance scheme, wage earners who remain attached to the labor force throughout their adult years until retirement age—usually men—secure relatively greater protection through this public pension system. Women's lower earning records and interrupted work histories—for parenting and caring of older dependents—and their consequent economic dependency on husbands result in their lower Social Security benefits. Further, over 70 percent of women take early retirement at age 62, either to care for elderly family members or because of ill health, and so receive reduced monthly benefits. Yet, even though most women who reach age 62 will live another two or more decades, their Social Security benefits remain at the lower amount. The average Social Security monthly benefit paid to retired men in 1987 was $577, compared with $441 paid to retired women, $265 paid to dependent wives, and $342 paid to widows (37).

Several Social Security reforms of the 1980s will adversely affect women, including those who will enter old age in the coming years: (a) the 1983 and other intermittent periods during which Social Security cost of living adjustments (COLAs) have been frozen, even for limited periods of time (for example, it has been projected that a delay in the COLA for only one year would bring 500,000 more elderly, mostly women, below the poverty level); (b) the gradual increase of the retirement age to 67 and the stepped-up penalties for early retirement (which nearly three-quarters of older women take); (c) the termination of the widow's benefit when the youngest child reaches age 16 rather than 18; (d) the phase-out of student benefits for children of retired, disabled, or deceased workers, all of which affect older women; and (e) the elimination of the minimum Social Security benefit (which earlier had been only $122 per month) for persons retiring after January 1982, which further disadvantages the poorest women by removing them from the respectability of Social Security coverage and forcing many to seek public assistance in the form of SSI (7). The major policy changes that are likely to positively affect older women were in the pension reforms, particularly those of 1984 and 1986 that reduced the time for pension vesting (from ten to five years) and required the signature of the pensioner spouse who wishes to receive higher pension benefits during his lifetime by resigning the rights to a pension for the surviving spouse. In addition, one of the few remaining provisions of the repealed Catastrophic Coverage Act was a provision on spousal impoverishment to protect a minimum income and assets for spouses of those who are institutionalized in nursing homes.

Income from private pensions does not compensate for women's low Social Security payments. Only about 13 percent of older women receive income from private pensions and, even then, the amounts received are less than half the amounts received by men. According to Moon's (38) estimate, women's pensions averaged 59 percent of men's in amount. Women's lower earnings and intermittent attachment to the wage labor force contribute to their lower pension coverage. As noted, many women who become widowed or divorced are inadequately protected with regard to legal claim to their husband's accrued pension funds, even though the "pension accrued by the working spouse is often the single largest asset of an older married couple" (39). Assets contribute relatively little to older women's overall income. Even though approximately one-half of the older population receives income from assets, most people receive very small amounts of asset income, and the proportion of total income that it represents is low (26). Evidence indicates that individuals whose lifetime incomes are high will accumulate more assets than those whose incomes are relatively low. This means that women, whose lifetime incomes are significantly lower than men's and whose economic status depends primarily on their marital status, are not likely to benefit from asset income during old age. Only 7.2 percent of older women improved their economic status through employment in 1986, and the majority of these women had only part-time employment (7). Thus, the total amounts of income derived by older women from pensions, assets, and employment generally do not significantly add to Social Security benefits. Most older men, however, rely on a combination of income sources and are relatively secure in their economic status.

Income Supports for the Very Poor

The SSI program is a federal–state cash assistance program for the poor aged, blind, and disabled. Eligibility for SSI benefits requires extreme poverty and almost no assets (a maximum of $2,000). Nationally there are four and a half million beneficiaries, about three-quarters of whom qualify on the basis of age. Three-quarters of the aged SSI recipients are women—not surprisingly, given the much higher poverty rate of older women compared with men (7). The income assistance provided through the SSI program is so minimal that its recipients remain below the poverty level (40). The monthly federal benefit level for SSI for aged persons living alone was $354 in 1988, and only 26 states supplemented this amount (but at a very limited level, averaging about $1.00 a day) (34, p. 28). In nominal dollars, this supplementation has been cut 16 percent since 1980, and it has been eroded by an estimated 40 percent due to inflation (34). Further, SSI benefit levels discriminate against single individuals by setting the maximum federal benefit level at 76 percent of the poverty line for individuals (mostly women) and at 90 percent of the poverty line for couples. Eligibility requirements for SSI are so rigid that, once a woman becomes a beneficiary, few options exist for moving off this program (14, 41), and it is estimated that only half of those eligible for this assistance receive it. Further, state Medicaid programs have tightened eligibility requirements in the last decade, contributing to a decline in the proportion of poor who are eligible for Medicaid, from 63 percent in 1975 to 40 percent in 1987. Among the aged, an even lower percentage of those below the poverty level are covered, and the percentage of poor aged (again, largely women) in the Medicaid program has also declined (39, 42).

The deleterious economic status of older women of the future must remain a serious cause for concern, particularly in view of the projections of the Commonwealth Fund (43) that, by 2020, the percentage of older men living alone who are poor or near-poor will decline rapidly (from 38 to 6 percent), while the proportion of poor and near-poor older women will change little (declining from 45 to 38 percent).

HEALTH CARE

A large body of data has consistently shown that social class and health are correlated, with the poor and near-poor most compromised. Older women's lower incomes are coupled with ill health and the likelihood of increased need for medical care. Medical and health care costs have increased for older women owing to higher patient cost-sharing and the greater need for care with age. As aggregate medical care costs continue to rise, publicly financed health programs have been faced with growing constraints. Yet, older women's available income remains relatively fixed and will fall with the death of a spouse. It has been well documented that Medicare meets only 44 percent of the elderly's health care costs (44, 45). However, a recent study showed that, while Medicare meets about 44 percent of the health care expenditures of elderly married couples, it meets only about 33 percent of these costs for an elderly single woman (45). This is easily understood in the context of Medicare's acute care policy that, on average, pays out more in both Part A (hospital) and Part B (physician) benefits to men than to women, and shortchanges women in terms of the chronic illness care they need (46).

Few private insurance dollars (less than 16 percent) go to health services for the aged (25). Since most private health insurance coverage is a benefit of employment, those who are unemployed, retired, or low-wage casual employees are not likely to have private health insurance coverage. "The lack of health insurance is most common among those least able to afford the consequences of poor health or lack of preventive health care" (25). Further, since women's marital status is a more significant predictor of their health insurance coverage than is their own employment status, older women lose access to health coverage when they lose their spouse through death or divorce (47). Since older women make up the majority of the older poor and those who are not married, it is women who are least able to cover out-of-pocket expenses or to afford supplementary private insurance coverage.

Because of escalating health care costs, aged persons actually expend a greater share of their income on health care costs now than they did prior to the enactment of Medicare (36, 40). A Congressional report in March 1984 stated that the average out-of-pocket costs for doctors' bills was "virtually the same for older persons with incomes under $5,000 as for those few older persons with incomes of $36,000 and up" (24). Older women, who are at greater risk for chronic disability and disadvantaged economic status, bear a heavier out-of-pocket burden for health care costs, in terms of both absolute dollars and proportion of income expended. An elderly married couple paid about 9 percent of its income on direct out-of-pocket payments and health insurance premiums in 1986, compared with the almost double out-of-pocket expenses paid by single elderly women (over 16 percent of their incomes) (45). Most older men are in couples, whereas most older women are not. Further, single women's spending increases proportionately with age, with monthly out-of-pocket expenses being greater for the oldest old. Although the average income of people aged 85 and older is 36 percent less than the income of people aged 65 to 69, Medicare costs for those over 80 have been shown to be 77 percent greater than for those between 65 and 69 (21).

Older women must purchase supplementary medical insurance (Part B premiums for physicians' services and Medigap coverage to cushion the cost of hospital and physician deductibles and copayments not covered by Medicare), or else they must pay out-of-pocket for the costs that are not covered by Medicare directly. Out-of-pocket and cost-sharing expenses for all elderly receiving hospital and physician services increased substantially in the 1980s. Obviously, low-income individuals are handicapped the most by these changes. Aged recipients of SSI cash assistance may qualify for publicly financed health coverage through the Medicaid program, but the eligibility requirements of many states are more restrictive than those for SSI (48). Thus, many who are poor and near-poor are denied this health coverage (35, 49). Over $15 billion were cut from the Medicaid program between 1980 and 1987. Medicaid cuts were implemented through reductions in the federal share of the costs and incentives provided to states to constrain expenditures and access in this program for the poor. One result has been that the variability among the states in their eligibility and utilization has increased, as the percentage below poverty who are covered by Medicaid has declined (50, 51).

No publicly financed health coverage exists for nondisabled American adults prior to their eligibility age for Medicare (age 65), unless they are economically destitute or qualify as medically needy under Medicaid. Women below age 65 and past the years of raising minor children cannot qualify for Medicare coverage unless they are disabled. Given that displaced homemakers are more likely to have no private health insurance, since most of it is a benefit of husbands' employment, divorced women are twice as likely as any other group to be without any kind of health insurance coverage (47). Recent legislation (COBRA) has been adopted to require employers to offer conversion plans to retain health insurance for women for a limited time period (18 months) following widowhood or divorce, but they must be able to afford to purchase it (paying both their own and their employer's share of the insurance). Following this, women attempting to obtain *new* coverage will be particularly disadvantaged if they have preexisting medical conditions because of the exclusions that insurers typically impose. Lack of money and the presence of certain medical conditions simply preclude access to private health insurance for many unmarried mid-life and older women. In future years, not only are more women likely to enter old age already poor, but—without major health reform—more women will enter old age without having had access to adequate preventive medical care during important periods earlier in their lifetimes.

Several limited advances have occurred in health care policy that are of import to older women. These include the ability to extend health insurance coverage under COBRA, the inclusion under Medicare of coverage for Pap smears, and the requirement that, for the elderly poor, Medicaid programs cover copayments, deductibles, and premiums. However, the continuing omission of long-term care coverage under Medicare is particularly damaging for women since they are asked to provide 80 percent of these services, and the individual costs of women's doing so have begun to be documented.

CAREGIVING, WOMEN, AND IDEOLOGY: THE CONSEQUENCES

The 1980s have been marked by an ideological revolution in which the New Right that was forged promoted a simultaneous revival of the free market (under neoliberalism) and a return of the (now-mythical) patriarchal autonomous family (under neoconservatism). The former ideological strain is distinctly oriented toward a "minimalist state" in being hostile to anything that may impede the (natural) order of the market (and its natural superiority). The latter appeals to authority, allegiance, tradition, and to "nature." "A corollary . . . is that the [traditional nuclear] family is central to maintaining the state" (52). Because this New Right model "squares the circle between an intellectual adherence to the free market and the emotional attachment to authority and imposed tradition" (53), it melds the interests of capitalism and patriarchy. Further, the New Right has reminded us that the primary, if not the only, justification for government intervention is the national defense and law enforcement.

Natural rights individualism is the "ideological cement" binding together contemporary neoconservative and neoliberal ideas and U.S. politics (54, p. 232), supporting principles of self-help based on economic initiative and productivity, individual autonomy, and voluntary association. The difficulty in restoring "both the giant corporation and the autonomous family . . . to their 'rightful place' in American life [requires] . . . faith and patriotism" (54, p. 237), but it is a project whose stunning success is one of the most significant hallmarks of Ronald Reagan's presidency. Reagan's ideological project was operationalized through a policy agenda designed to promote both privatization of the welfare state and the isolation of the "family" from "society" (55). Privatization policies promote the belief that the "proper" and best form of health and social services to the elderly is nongovernmental. In U.S. health and social policy, privatization has operated hand-in-glove with the increased informalization of care bolstered by the rhetoric of family responsibility. The message once again was that women workers should return home to care for their elderly (56); yet there was a contradictory message that those who do not achieve labor market participation on the male model will not be helped by the state. Phrases such as the "sandwich generation," the "daughter shortage," the "baby dearth" were bemoaned, yet policymakers remained firm in their refusal to move toward a long-term care policy and beyond reaffirmations of the need for continuing family support (57).

As a consequence, every American woman can expect to spend 18 years of her life helping an aging parent and 17 years caring for children (57). It has been estimated that over 27 million days of unpaid caregiving are provided for older Americans every week. Women's caregiving directly affects both their economic status and health in old age. These effects again point to the structural conditions that contribute to women's lower socioeconomic status and to the direct and indirect economic costs of caregiving. The women who give care to their disabled spouses may have to drain their savings and assets acquired during the marriage, "spending them down" on their spouse's or parent's needs. Family labor—more precisely, women's unpaid labor—is viewed as free labor (if recognized as labor at all). Yet, it is in government's interest to secure as much of this free work as possible since it relieves the government of the costs of having to provide adequate long-term care. It is noteworthy that "over 40 percent of adult offspring participating in one survey reported that the time spent on caregiving tasks was equivalent to the time required by a full time job" (15).

Additionally, there are "opportunity costs"—costs that may well be the greatest economic expense of caregiving. The women who take early retirement or otherwise modify their employment to provide care lose not only wages and wage-related benefits, but also additional Social Security credits. Studies suggest that changing work patterns and even quitting work are common coping strategies of caregivers (58). Data from the Informal Caregivers Survey, a component of the larger National Long Term Care Survey, indicate that a majority of caregiving women had either reduced their paid working hours, rearranged their work schedules, taken time off without pay, or quit their jobs to resolve conflicting demands of caregiving and employment (59). Caregiver women jeopardize their own sources of income for their later years: Social Security and private pension benefits are directly tied to wages and employment patterns. In these ways, female caregivers' own economic dependency is reproduced. Because a total of only five years can be dropped out from the averaging of accrued Social Security credits, women who quit their employment to caretake (either their children or elders) directly affect their future Social Security benefits, and perhaps even their eligibility. These caregiving women find themselves in a no-win situation: they are expected to provide care to their husbands or elderly relatives, yet public policy economically penalizes them for doing so. Because the majority of older women's economic situations are precarious, at best, the added costs from caregiving are significant.

Caregiving carries high physical health risks (58, 60). Physical labor, sometimes excessive, is part of caregiving, and disabled persons need various kinds of assistance. Since many caregivers themselves are old, or approaching old age (59), they too are vulnerable to, and may be experiencing, chronic ailments. Older women have more health problems than do older men (11, 12), yet it is women who do most caregiving work. Additionally, there are somatic outcomes of high levels of stress: high blood pressure, fatigue and exhaustion, and greater susceptibility to physical illness are some of the physical health risks (12). Lack of respite and relief from responsibilities, lack of assistance in performing physical tasks, and emotional fatigue and overload thwart a caregiver's recovery from illness (61). Their physical health is also endangered by a lack of preventive health care resulting from inadequate financial resources, time, and attention to the onset of disabilities (58, 60).

UNSETTLED FUTURE

Social policies are shaped largely by requirements of the economy and the politics surrounding it. Women's position as female workers, caregivers, and beneficiaries of public policies continues to be systematically unequal to that of men. By failing to address these structural inequities, social policies perpetuate, both directly and indirectly, the disadvantaged economic and health situation of older women throughout old age.

Under the politics and fiscal trenchment of the 1980s, the position of women has been undermined, and there has been a distinct shift of resources away from women to men and from minorities to whites. The most important elements of the Reagan legacy for older women (57) are: (a) intensified commodification and medicalization of care for the aging in ways that are consistent with capitalist expansion of the medical-industrial complex (62); (b) the continuing refusal of the State to provide meaningful long-term care benefits to the elderly and disabled; (c) the accumulation of multiple pressures on a beleaguered network of traditionally nonprofit home and community-based health and social service providers, thinly stretched by the demands of very sick and very old patients discharged from the hospital earlier than ever before (63) and a growing population of oldest old (85 and over); and (d) the use of policies to promote family responsibility and increase the informalization of care. These efforts to restore and regulate family life (primarily women) are congruent with the deep concerns of the state and capital to minimize state costs for the elderly, and concerns of the New Right to restore patriarchal family arrangements to assure a continuing supply of women's free labor essential to the reproduction and maintenance of the work force (64).

The Reagan Administration's resistance to a federal policy solution to the problem of long-term care and its unstated policy of informalization must be understood as part of a larger austerity strategy in the context of the state's need for women (regardless of their labor force participation) to continue to perform large (and increasing) amounts of unpaid servicing work (28).

The economic and health situations of older women require deep structural and policy changes that redress inequities and provide access to basic resources, including Social Security, housing, health and long-term care, and broad-based social reforms aimed at ending the social and economic inequities experienced by women. The economic and health issues confronted by aging and aged women will challenge the very structure of our social institutions. In conclusion, some points warrant reemphasis. The relationship between the private and public spheres has a profound effect on the economic and health condition of women. This effect will vary across different critical periods of older women's lives as their overall health status declines and available financial and social resources become more limited. The opportunity for responding to these increasing needs varies, not only by gender, but by class and race.

The austerity imposed on publicly funded programs has redirected attention away from the prior decade's concern for increasing access to a comprehensive system of health and social services. Today, the greater emphasis upon individual self-reliance, private insurance, and the ability to save for and purchase health care makes the issue of an adequate income policy more important than ever. Health must be regarded in the broad sense to include well-being and not merely the absence of disease. Thus, women's income issues cannot be ignored in the health policy debate. Public commitment to a strong state role remains essential because of the deep structural origins and potential solutions to the problems identified here. Key issues for older women are not only state policies that provide adequate income, health, and long-term care, but also policies that abridge (and compensate for) the gendered division of labor and lifelong discrimination that women experience.

REFERENCES

1. Estes, C., Gerard, J., and Clark, A. Women and the economics of aging. *Int. J. Health Serv.* 14: 55–68, 1984.
2. Marmot, M. G., Kogevinas, M., and Elston, M. A. Social/economic status and disease. *Annu. Rev. Public Health* 8: 111–135, 1987.
3. Dutton, D. B. Social class, health and fitness. In *Applications of Social Science to Clinical Medicine and Health Policy*, edited by L. H. Aiken and D. Mechanic, pp. 31–62. Rutgers University Press, New Brunswick, N.J., 1986.
4. Butler, L. H., and Newacheck, P. W. Health and social factors relevant to long term care policy. In *Policy Options in Long Term Care*, edited by J. Meltzer, F. Farrow, and H. Richman, pp. 38–77. University of Chicago Press, Chicago, 1981.
5. Kane, R. A., and Kane, R. L. *Long Term Care: Principles, Programs, and Policies.* Springer, New York, 1987.

6. Luft, H. S. *Poverty and Health: Economic Causes and Consequences of Health Problems*. Ballinger, Cambridge, Mass., 1978.
7. United States Bureau of the Census. *Statistical Abstract of the United States, 1988. National Data Book and Guide to Sources*. U.S. Government Printing Office, Washington, D.C., 1989.
8. King, N., and Marvel, M. *Issues, Policies, and Programs for Midlife and Older Women*, p. 44. Center for Women's Policy Studies, Washington, D.C., 1982.
9. Schultz, J. *The Economics of Aging*. Van Nostrand Reinhold, New York, 1985.
10. Stone, R. *Recent Developments in Respite Care Services for Caregivers of the Impaired Elderly*. The Institute for Health and Aging, University of California, San Francisco, July 1985.
11. Rice, D., and Estes, C. Health of the elderly: Policy issues and challenges. *Health Aff.* 3: 25–49, 1984.
12. Verbrugge, L. Women and men: Mortality and health of older people. In *Aging in Society: Selected Reviews of Recent Research*, edited by M. Riley, B. Hess, and K. Bond. Lawrence Erlbauns Association, London, 1983.
13. Rice, D. Sex differences in mortality and morbidity: Some aspects of the economic burden. In *Sex Differentials in Mortality: Trends, Determinants, and Consequences*, edited by A. Lopez and L. Ruzicka. Department of Demography, Canberra, Australia, 1983.
14. Vladeck, B. *Unloving Care: The Nursing Home Tragedy*. Basic Books, New York, 1980.
15. Feldblum, C. Home health care for the elderly: Programs, problems, and potential. *Harvard J. Legislation* 22: 194–254, 1985.
16. Manton, K., and Soldo, B. Dynamics of health changes in the oldest old. *Milbank Mem. Fund. Q. Health Soc.* 63: 252, 1985.
17. Butler, L., and Newacheck, P. W. Health and social factors relevant to long term care policy. In *Policy Options in Long Term Care*, edited by J. Meltzer, F. Farrow, and H. Richman, pp. 38–77. University of Chicago Press, Chicago, 1981.
18. Minkler, M., and Stone, R. The feminization of poverty and older women. *Gerontologist* 25: 351–357, 1985.
19. Grad, S. Incomes of the aged and nonaged, 1950–82. *Social Security Bull.* 47(6), 1984.
20. Markides, K. S., and Mindel, C. H. *Aging and Ethnicity*, pp. 31–35. Sage, Beverly Hills, 1987.
21. Torrey, B. Sharing increasing costs on declining income: The visible dilemma of the invisible aged. *Milbank Mem. Fund Q. Health Soc.* 63: 385–387, 1985.
22. Arendell, T. *Mothers and Divorce: Legal, Economic, and Social Dilemmas*. University of California Press, Berkeley, 1986.
23. Arendell, T. A review: Women and the economics of divorce in the contemporary United States. *Signs: Journal of Women in Culture and Society*, Winter 1987.
24. Coalition on Women and the Budget. *Inequality of Sacrifice: The Impact of the Reagan Budget on Women*. National Women's Law Center, Washington, D.C., March 1984.
25. Kasper, A., and Soldinger, E. Falling between the cracks: How health insurance discriminates against women. *Women Health* 8: 77–93, 1983.
26. Rix, S. *Older Women: The Economics of Aging*. Women's Research and Education Institute of the Congressional Caucus for Women's Issues, Washington, D.C., 1984.
27. Dressel, P. L. Gender, race, and class: Beyond the feminization of poverty in later life. *Gerontologist* 28: 177–180, 1988.
28. Sassoon, A. S. Women's new social role: Contradictions of the welfare state. In *Women and the State*, edited by A. S. Sassoon, pp. 166–167. Hutchinson, London, 1987.

29. Quadagno, J. Race, class, and gender in the U.S. welfare state: Nixon's failed Family Assistance Plan. *Am. Sociol. Rev.* 55: 11–28, 1990.

30. National Center for Health Statistics. *Monthly Vital Statistics Report.* U.S. Department of Health and Human Services, Washington, D.C., 1985.

31. Weitzman, L. *The Divorce Revolution.* The Free Press, New York, 1985.

32. U.S. Senate Special Committee on Aging. *Aging America: Trends and Projections, 1985–86.* U.S. Department of Health and Human Services, Washington, D.C., 1986.

33. Markson, E. *Older Women: Issues and Prospects.* Lexington Books, Lexington, Mass., 1985.

34. Families U.S.A. Foundation. *Three Year Report (1986–1987–1988).* Washington, D.C., 1989.

35. United States Congress. *Problems of Working Women.* Hearing before the Joint Economic Commissions, April 4. U.S. Government Printing Office, Washington, D.C., 1984.

36. Women's Equity Action League (WEAL). *WEAL Facts: Letter To the Editor, Equity for Women.* Washington, D.C., 1985.

37. Social Security Bulletin. *Annual Statistical Supplement, 1988.* U.S. Department of Health and Human Services, Social Security Administration, Washington, D.C., 1988.

38. Moon, M. Economic Issues Facing a Growing Population of Older Women. Paper presented at the American Sociological Association, New York, September 1986.

39. United States Senate, Special Committee on Aging. *The Future of Medicine.* U.S. Government Printing Office, Washington, D.C., 1983.

40. United States Congress. *An Analysis of the President's Budgetary Proposals for Fiscal Year 1986.* Congressional Budget Office, U.S. Government Printing Office, Washington, D.C., February 1986.

41. Crystal, S. *America's Old Age Crisis: Public Policy and the Two Worlds of Aging.* Basic Books, New York, 1982.

42. Estes, C. Long-term care and public policy in an era of austerity. *J. Public Health Policy* 6: 464–475, 1985.

43. Commonwealth Fund Commission on Elderly People Living Alone. Testimony of Karen Davis, Director, to House of Representatives, Select Committee on Aging. *Report on The Quality of Life for Older Women: Older Women Living Alone.* U.S. Government Printing Office, Washington, D.C., 1988.

44. National Health Law Program. *In Poor Health: The Administration's 1985 Health Budget.* Los Angeles, 1985.

45. ICF, Inc. *Medicare's Role in Financing the Health Care of Older Women.* Submitted to the American Association of Retired Persons, July 1985.

46. United States Department of Health and Human Services, Health Care Financing Administration, Division of Program Statistics. Unpublished data for 1984.

47. Berk, M., and Taylor, A. Women and Divorce: Health Insurance Coverage, Utilization, and Health Care Expenditures: National Health Care Expenditures Study. Paper presented at the Annual Meeting of the American Public Health Association, Dallas, November 1983.

48. Estes, C., et al. *Organizational and Community Responses to Medicare Policy: Consequences for Health and Social Services for the Elderly. Project Summary.* The Institute for Health and Aging, University of California, San Francisco, 1985.

49. Davis, K., and Rowland, D. Uninsured and underserved: Inequities in health care in the United States. In *Securing Access to Health Care 3.* Presidential Commission for the Study of Ethical Problems in Medicine and Biomedical and Behavior Research. U.S. Government Printing Office, Washington, D.C., March 1983.

50. Holahan, J. F., and Cohen, J. W. *Medicaid: The Trade-Off Between Cost Containment and Access to Care*. Urban Institute, Washington, D.C., 1984.
51. Darling, H. The role of the federal government in assuring access to health care. *Inquiry* 23: 286–295, 1986.
52. Levitas, R. Competition and compliance: The utopias of the New Right. In *The Ideology of the New Right*, edited by R. Levitas, p. 93. Polity Press, Cambridge, Mass., 1986.
53. Edgar, D. The free or the good. In *The Ideology of the New Right*, edited by R. Levitas, pp. 74–75. Polity Press, Cambridge, Mass., 1986.
54. O'Connor, J. *Accumulation Crisis*. Basil Blackwell, New York, 1984.
55. Myles, J. Personal communication, March 1989.
56. Binney, E. A., Estes, C. L., and Humphers, S. Informalization and Community Services for the Elderly. Paper presented at the American Sociological Association, San Francisco, 1989.
57. Estes, C. L. The Reagan legacy: Privatization, the welfare state, and aging. In *States, Labor Markets, and the Future of Old Age*, edited by J. Myles and J. Quadagno. Temple University Press, Philadelphia, 1991.
58. Brody, E. Parent care as a normative family stress. *Gerontologist* 25: 19–29, 1985.
59. Stone, R., Cafferata, G., and Sangl, J. *Caregivers of the Frail Elderly: A National Profile*. National Center for Health Services Research, Rockville, Md., 1986.
60. Bader, J. Respite care: Temporary relief for caregivers. *Women Health* [*Special Issue*] 10(2/3): 39–52, 1985.
61. Corbin, J., and Strauss, A. Issues concerning regime management in the home. *Ageing and Society* 5: 249–265, 1985.
62. Estes, C. L., and Binney, E. A. The biomedicalization of aging: Dangers and dilemmas. *Gerontologist* 29: 587–596, 1990.
63. Wood, J. B., and Estes, C. L. The impact of DRGs on community-based service providers: Implications for the elderly. *Am. J. Public Health* 80: 840–843, 1990.
64. Abramovitz, M. *Regulating the Lives of Women*, pp. 349–379. South End Press, Boston, 1988.

Contributors

TERRY ARENDELL is Associate Professor of Sociology at Hunter College/City University of New York in the Department of Sociology. She completed her doctoral degree at the University of California, Berkeley, in the Department of Sociology in 1984 and then did a postdoctoral National Institute of Aging postdoctoral fellowship at the University of California, San Francisco, in the Department of Sociology and Institute for Health & Aging. Her primary research area is contemporary divorce and changing gender and family relationships. She is the author of *Mothers and Divorce: Social, Legal, and Economic Dilemmas* and *Fathers Living with Divorce*. She has taught at the University of California, Davis, Hobart and William Smith Colleges, Cornell University, and the University of Wisconsin-Madison.

MARY BASSETT trained as a physician and epidemiologist. Since 1986, she has taught at the University of Zimbabwe Medical School where she is a senior lecturer in Community Medicine. Her current AIDS-related activities include a school-based adolescent AIDS prevention program.

IRENE H. BUTTER received her Ph.D. in economics from Duke University in 1960. Specializing in the economics of human resources in health, she has published on the international mobility of doctors and a variety of policy-related manpower issues. Her current research includes: gender differentiation in the health workforce, impending surpluses in selected health occupations, and issues related to maternal and child health, including alternative childbirth options. Her teaching includes courses in health manpower planning, gender, race and ethnicity in health, and applied policy analysis.

EUGENIA S. CARPENTER, M.P.P., is president of Gini Associates, a consulting firm located in Ann Arbor, Michigan, and emeritus research faculty member of the University of Michigan School of Public Health. Her graduate studies at the University of Michigan were in public policy and political science. In her academic and consulting career, she has been principal investigator for studies on the education of health professionals, physician distribution, regulation of health professionals and health facilities, cost and quality of state Medicaid programs, health care for the indigent, strategic planning, feasibility, and organizational studies of public health and social service agencies. She has served on advisory boards and commissions on a variety of health and regulatory issues at the state and national levels.

KATHRYN CAROVANO is a senior program officer at the Center for Communication Programs of The Johns Hopkins University working on the AIDSCOM Project, in Washington D.C. In this capacity, she is involved in the development, monitoring, and evaluation of AIDS prevention communication programs in Latin America and is also responsible for AIDSCOM's Women and AIDS initiative. Prior to joining AIDSCOM Ms. Carovano worked at the Overseas Development Council, where she was engaged in research and writing on U.S. foreign policy toward the developing world, with a focus on AIDS policy. Ms. Carovano received her M.A. in International Relations from the Johns Hopkins School of Advanced International Studies in 1985, and her B.A. from Middlebury College in 1982. She has carried out research and written on foreign policy in Latin America, and is currently involved in work focusing on women and AIDS in the United States and elsewhere.

GHISLAINE DONIOL-SHAW is a research engineer at the Laboratoire Techniques, Territoires, Sociétés de l'école Nationale des Ponts et Chaussées and is associated with the Centre National de la Recherche Scientifique in France. She specializes in ergonomics research concerning the impact of technological evolution on employment and working conditions. Her present projects focus on working conditions in subcontract work particularly in nuclear power stations, and on equal opportunities for women. She also teaches ergonomy at the post-graduate level.

LESLEY DOYAL is Professor of Health Studies at the University of the West of England. She has published extensively on health policy and politics and acted as a consultant to WHO on women's health issues. She is joint editor (with Jennie Naidoo and Tamsin Wilton) of *AIDS: Setting a Feminist Agenda* from Taylor and Francis, 1994, and her latest book, *What Makes Women Sick? Gender and the Politics of Health*, is forthcoming from Macmillan in 1994.

SUZANNE ENGLAND is Associate Professor at the University of Illinois at Chicago and director of the Project for the Study of Families, Health and Social Policy. She is an author of *Wages for Caring* (with Linsk, Keigher, and Simon-Rusinowitz), and has published a number of articles on policies and practices related to illness and disability. Currently she is collaborating with humanities scholars and practicing social workers and using literary, biographical, and clinical narratives to better comprehend how dilemmas stemming from the socially constructed aspects of disability and caregiving are expressed in personal stories.

CARROLL L. ESTES, Professor of Sociology, is Chairperson of the Department of Social and Behavioral Sciences, School of Nursing, University of California, San Francisco, and is Director of the Institute for Health and Aging, University of California, San Francisco. Dr. Estes, whose Ph.D. is from the University of California, San Diego, conducts research on aging policy, long-term care, fiscal crisis, and new federalism. She is the author of *The Decision-Makers: The Power Structure of Dallas* (1963) and *The Aging Enterprise* (Jossey-Bass, 1979), and co-author of *Fiscal Austerity and Aging* (Sage, 1983) and *Political Economy, Health and Aging* (Little Brown, 1984).

ELIZABETH FEE is Professor of History and Health Policy in the Department of Health Policy and Management at the Johns Hopkins School of Hygiene and Public Health in Baltimore, Maryland. She is author of *Disease and Discovery : A History of the Johns Hopkins School of Hygiene and Public Health, 1916–1939* (1987), editor of *Women and Health* (1983), and co-editor of *AIDS: The Burdens of History* (1988), *A History of Education in Public Health* (1991), *The Baltimore Book: New Views of Local History* (1991), *AIDS: The Making of a Chronic Disease* (1992), and *Making Medical History: The Life and Work of Henry E. Sigerist* (forthcoming, 1995). She teaches courses in health policy, history of public health, and women's health and is contributing editor of the *American Journal of Public Health.*

DR. ANNE FLITCRAFT, M.D. is Associate Professor of Medicine at the University of Connecticut and Co-Director of the Domestic Violence Training Project, an award winning program that provides domestic violence education to health care professionals. Dr. Flitcraft has received numerous honors for her work on behalf of battered women including the Elizabeth Blackwell award from the American Medical Women's Association (AMWA).

MARTHA E. GIMENEZ is Associate Professor of Sociology at the University of Colorado at Boulder. She received her Ph.D. from the University of California, Los Angeles in 1973. Dr. Gimenez is the co-editor of *Work Without Wages: Comparative Studies of Domestic Labor and Self-Employment* and has published numerous book chapters and articles in *Gender & Society, Science & Society, The Insurgent Sociologist, The International Journal of Women's Studies,* and other journals. Her areas of specialization include Marxist theory, social stratification, feminist theory, and population studies.

CHANTAL HAËNTJENS is an occupational health physician with expertise in ergonomics. She is employed by the Association des Centres Medico-sociaux in Paris.

ELLEN M. HALL is an Assistant Professor of Behavioral Sciences at the Johns Hopkins School of Hygiene and Public Health. She received her Ph.D. in psychosocial environmental medicine from the Karolinska Institute in Sweden. She has helped direct a cooperative Swedish-American Research Group that studies work organization, stress, and health. She has worked in the occupational health field since the early 1970s and has held positions at the Environmental Protection Agency, the Occupational Safety and Health Administration, and various trade unions. Currrently her research activities focus on studying the combined effects of total paid and unpaid work activity on women's health, and the impact of gender-dependent career trajectories on work stress exposure over the life course.

JOANNE M. HALL, R.N., Ph.D., is a Postdoctoral Fellow in the School of Nursing at University of California, San Francisco. She is supported by a National Research Service Award Individual Postdoctoral Fellowship from the National Institute for Nursing Research at the National Institutes of Health. Her current research endeavors are in the areas of prevention and recovery from alcohol problems in women, survival of childhood abuse in adolescent girls and women, and psychosocial health needs of marginalized women. She has published widely on women and alcohol problems, lesbian health, women and work, and feminist research methodologies.

MARSHA HURST, a political scientist, is a faculty associate at the Center for the Study of Women and Society at the City University of New York's Graduate Center. She earned her doctorate at Columbia University in 1972, taught government at John Jay College of the City University of New York for six years, and was a National Institute of Mental Health postdoctoral fellow in community medicine and medical sociology at the Mount Sinai School of Medicine.

BONNIE J. KAY is a health systems analyst specializing in issues related to the health of women and their children. Dr. Kay is presently self-employed as a consultant. She has held faculty positions at the University of Michigan School of Public Health, and at the Georgia Institute of Technology where her teaching areas included health economics, regional planning, applied policy analysis, project design and evaluation. Dr. Kay has directed studies on cost, project design and evaluation, quality and availability of health services in the United States and abroad in the area of women's reproductive health. She has served as a consultant to governmental and private local, state, national and international organizations.

SHARON M. KEIGHER is Associate Professor and Director of the Social Work Program at the School of Social Welfare, University of Wisconsin-Milwaukee. Her research interests include homelessness and the elderly, the housing problems of older women, and cross-national and state-level analysis of policies affecting informal caregivers of the elderly and disabled. She is a co-author of *Wages for Caring: Compensating Family Care of the Elderly* (Praeger, 1992) and author of *Housing Risks and Homelessness Among the Urban Elderly* (Haworth, 1991).

NANCY KRIEGER is an epidemiologist at the Division of Research of the Kaiser Foundation Research Institute, Oakland, California, and lecturer in the Epidemiology Program of the School of Public Health at the University of California at Berkeley. Her research focuses on issues of race, class, gender, and health, particularly breast cancer; other work concerns the history and theoretical underpinnings of epidemiology. She is co-author of *The Politics of AIDS* (1986) and co-editor of *AIDS: The Politics of Survival*, Baywood, 1994.

MARSHA LILLIE-BLANTON is an Assistant Professor in the Department of Health Policy and Management at the Johns Hopkins School of Hygiene and Public Health. Her research and teaching interests are in the areas of substance abuse, minority health, and access to care. Prior to joining the Johns Hopkins faculty, Ms. Lillie-Blanton worked as a Senior Health Policy Research Analyst with the U.S. General Accounting Office. Ms. Lillie-Blanton received her Doctorate of Public Health degree from the Johns Hopkins University.

NATHAN L. LINSK, Ph.D. is Associate Professor at the Jane Addams College of Social Work at the University of Illinois at Chicago. Linsk has been Director/ Principal Investigator for the Midwest AIDS Training and Education Center, a six state health professional training project funded by the U.S. Public Health Service Health Resources and Services Administration. Linsk's work with family caregiving issues, staff training and development of service models for care provision to dependent populations has included home-based care programs, long-term care reform, case management systems of development and research on development of dementia units as Principal Investigator for an Alzheimer's Disease Family Care Center in a Chicago-based university-affiliated teaching nursing home. Current research and training includes cross cultural work in eastern Europe, where he has headed the Romanian American AIDS HIV Prevention Project, and long-term care research about HIV and nursing homes and HIV and the elderly.

EMILY MARTIN is Mary Garrett Professor of Arts and Sciences in the Department of Anthropology at The Johns Hopkins University, Baltimore, Maryland. She taught previously at Yale University and the University of California, Irvine. Her areas of research include the culture of medicine, the anthropology of science, and the ethnography of gender, work and politics in the United States. Her major publications include: *The Cult of the Dead in a Chinese Village, Chinese Ritual and Politics,* and *The Woman in the Body: A Cultural Analysis of Reproduction,* which won the Eileen Basker Memorial Prize of the Association of Medical Anthropology. *Flexible Bodies: Tracking Immunity in America from the Days of Polio to the Age of AIDS* is forthcoming in June, 1994.

ROSE MARIE MARTINEZ, Sc.D. is an Assistant Director of Health Financing and Policy Issues for the U.S. General Accounting Office (GAO). Ms. Martinez directs evaluations and analyses of health policy issues as requested by the Congress. Prior to joining GAO, Ms. Martinez directed health policy research at the Instituto Regional de Estudios de Salud y Bienestar Social in Madrid, Spain. Ms. Martinez holds a Doctor of Science Degree from The Johns Hopkins School of Hygiene and Public Health.

KAREN MESSING received her B.A. in Social Relations from Harvard University and her Ph.D. in biology from McGill. She was also trained in ergonomics at the Conservatoire national des arts et métiers in Paris. She is Professor of Biological Sciences at the University of Québec in Montréal, Canada. Since 1990, she has directed CINBIOSE, the Center for the study of biological interactions in environmental health (le Centre pour l'étude des interactions biologiques entre la santé et l'environnement). Her research is in occupational health and she is the author of numerous articles and of *Occupational Health and Safety Concerns of Canadian Women* (Ottawa: Labour Canada, 1991).

MARVELLOUS MHLOYI, Ph.D. is a demographer and lecturer in the Sociology Department of the University of Zimbabwe Medical School. Her research interests include population policy and fertility, infant and childhood mortality, and the sociocultural dimension of AIDS.

BAILA MILLER is Associate Professor at the Jane Addams College of Social Work, University of Illinois at Chicago. Her research interests include the impact of gender and race on caregiving of older persons, the relationship between informal and formal long-term care, and minority use of long-term care and health services.

RUTH DIXON-MUELLER is currently a research associate in the Graduate Group in Demography, University of California, Berkeley. She was formerly professor and chairperson of the Sociology Department at the University of California, Davis, and is also a past member of the Committee on Population of the National Research Council and of the Board of Directors of the Population Association of America. Dr. Dixon-Mueller is the author of numerous publications on women's employment and reproductive behavior in developing countries.

BETTY GARMAN ROBINSON is the Project Director of the HIV Epidemiologic Research Study (HERS) at the Johns Hopkins School of Hygiene and Public Health. HERS is a study of HIV/AIDS in women. Ms. Robinson has worked in the public health field for fifteen years in various capacities, as computer programmer, data analyst and research coordinator. Ms. Robinson has a Bachelor of Arts degree in Political Science and experience in occupational health and injury prevention.

RUTH SIMMONS, a political scientist, has a joint appointment with the Department of Public Health Policy and Administration, the Department of Population Planning and International Health, and the Residential College at University of Michigan. Her major area of interest is in the administration/ management of family planning and maternal and child health programs in the Third World. She emphasizes both principles of organization and the substantive content of programs. She has done major research on the Indian Family Planning Program, as well as family planning in the United States. In recent years she has been participating in a large field project in Bangladesh through the International Centre for Diarrhoeal Disease Research. The project uses organization development techniques to improve the management of public sector programs.

EVAN STARK is an Associate Professor in the Graduate Department of Public Administration and The School of Social Work, Rutgers University-Newark and Co-Director of the Domestic Violence Training Project in New Haven, Connecticut. A founder of one of the first shelters for battered women in the United States, he is called frequently as an expert in civil and criminal cases involving domestic violence. He was the 1993 recipient of the National Health Council's "Trend Setter" award for contributions to women's health.

PATRICIA E. STEVENS, R.N., Ph.D. is a Postdoctoral Fellow in the School of Nursing at University of California, San Francisco. She is supported by a National Research Service Award Individual Postdoctoral Fellowship from the National Institute of Nursing Research at the National Institutes of Health. Her current research studies are about women and HIV/AIDS, community-based HIV prevention, and marginalized women's access to health care. She has published widely on access to health care, lesbian health, women and HIV, and feminist research methodologies.

T. K. SUNDARI is a Research Associate at the Centre for Development Studies in Trivandrum, Kerala, India. She received a Ph.D. in applied economics from Jawaharlal Nehru University in Delhi, and teaches courses on health, population, and development at the Centre. She has been actively involved for the past ten years with a rural women's organization in South India engaged in organizing women around health issues.

ANDREA KIDD TAYLOR is an industrial hygienist and occupational health policy consultant for the International Union, United Automobile, Aerospace, and Agricultural Implement Workers of America (UAW). Ms. Taylor has been with UAW's Health and Safety staff since March 1989. Her responsibilities include conducting in-plant health and safety investigations, writing and reviewing health and safety contract language, editing the health and safety newsletter, writing UAW position papers and testifying at government hearings, and providing health and safety education to employees. Ms. Taylor has a Doctorate of Public Health degree in occupational health policy from the Johns Hopkins School of Hygiene and Public Health and a Master of Science degree in industrial hygiene from the University of Alabama.

RUTH E. ZAMBRANA, a sociologist, is currently Dean of the Graduate School of Psychology at Wright Institute Los Angeles. She received her doctoral degree from Boston University in 1977, and then completed a two-year post-doctoral training program in medical sociology at the City University of New York Graduate Center, Department of Sociology, and the Mount Sinai School of Medicine, Department of Community Medicine.

Index

Page numbers in italics denote figures; those followed by "t" denote tables.